The Israeli Peace Movement

This book describes the predicament of the Israeli peace movement, which paradoxically, following the launching of the Oslo peace process between Israel and the Palestinians in 1993, experienced a prolonged, fatal decline in membership, activity, political significance, and media visibility. After presenting the regional and national background to the launching of the peace process and a short history of Israeli peace activism, the book focuses on external and internal processes and interactions experienced by the peace movement, after some basic postulates of its agenda were actually, although never explicitly, embraced by the Rabin government. The analysis brings together insights from social movement theory and theories on public opinion and foreign and security policy making. The book's conclusion is that, despite its organizational decline and the total lack of credit given it by policy makers, in retrospect it appears that the movement contributed significantly to the integration of new ideas for possible solutions to the Middle East conflict in Israeli mainstream political discourse.

Tamar S. Hermann is a professor of political science and Dean of Academic Studies at the Open University (OU) of Israel. She also serves as a senior research Fellow at the Israel Democracy Institute and a co-director of the Peace Index project at Tel Aviv University. Her present research examines the growing estrangement of citizens in many representative democracies from politics and the politicians and is meant to assess the potential outcomes of this process in terms of democratic governability and stability.

The Israeli Peace Movement

A Shattered Dream

TAMAR S. HERMANN
The Open University of Israel
The Israel Democracy Institute

CAMBRIDGE
UNIVERSITY PRESS

CAMBRIDGE UNIVERSITY PRESS
Cambridge, New York, Melbourne, Madrid, Cape Town, Singapore,
São Paulo, Delhi, Dubai, Tokyo

Cambridge University Press
32 Avenue of the Americas, New York, NY 10013-2473, USA

www.cambridge.org
Information on this title: www.cambridge.org/9780521884099

First published 2009

Printed in the United States of America

A catalog record for this publication is available from the British Library.

Library of Congress Cataloging in Publication data

Hermann, Tamar.
The Israeli peace movement : a shattered dream / Tamar S. Hermann.
   p.   cm.
Includes bibliographical references and index.
ISBN 978-0-521-88409-9 (hardback)
1. Peace movements – Israel – History.   2. Arab-Israeli
conflict – History.   I. Title.
DS119.7.H394   2009
303.6'6095694 – dc22   2009028157

ISBN 978-0-521-88409-9 Hardback

Contents

Acknowledgments

This study was conducted with the generous support of the United States Institute of Peace (A SHATTERED DREAM: The Israeli Peace Movement and the Collapse of the Oslo Process USIP – 216 – 01F). The writing of the manuscript was facilitated by a residency grant at the Rockefeller Foundation's Bellagio Study and Conference Center, Italy (February–March 2003) and visiting scholar positions at the Center of International Studies, Princeton University, United States (April–August 2004); and at the Center for the Study of Ethnic Conflict, Queen's University, Belfast, Northern Ireland (Summer 2005). The data collection could not have been carried out without the skillful assistance of Mr. Yuval Lebel and Ms. Hila Zaban. The analysis presented here was enriched by the cooperation and tolerance of many peace activist friends and colleagues, mainly Prof. Galia Golan, who despite their personal dedication to peace making and human rights and prolonged involvement in the activities described here, were able to share their reflections not only on the stronger but also on the weaker sides of the peace movement's agenda and activities. The text gained much clarity from the professional editing of Gila Haimovic. The Open University of Israel, my academic home for many years, was always highly attentive to any need and request in relation to this research project, as was the Tami Steinmetz Center for Peace Research at Tel Aviv University, as well as Prof. Ephraim Yaar, with whom I have been conducting the Peace Index surveys project since 1994. Last but not least, I would like to thank my family for their patience with having an entire (even if not overly large) movement as an extra resident in our home, and particularly at the dinner table, for almost a decade.

I

Introduction

The intellectuals of the left[1] are writing a new chapter: blaming a democracy which is at last defending itself from the Oslo terror regime of mouth shutting for allegedly deteriorating into despotism.

– Amnon Lord (2002)

There is no real difference between the peace activists who are defending the murderers and the murderers themselves.

Owen (2003)

Facts seem to have no impact on the left.... This is a left that doesn't know when to stop and ask itself questions or to reflect whether perhaps what it said yesterday is no longer correct today.... A meeting with them leaves one with the impression that the same [faulty] diskette has been implanted in their brains.

– David Fogel (2003)

Contrary to what the leftists argue, the price of being one is actually nil. It is even beneficial. You show the entire world that you are not narrow-minded or self-centered.... The preaching and nonsense of the left can be found even in food columns in the newspapers.... Defeatist remarks appear in the transportation

---

[1] For those unfamiliar with the local political context, the immediate association between the left and the peace movement should be highlighted here. In the public discourse, these two notions are not only inseparable but also almost identical. In the European context, and to a lesser extent in the American one, the term *political left* pertains to a sociopolitical ideological stream that includes communists, socialists, and perhaps even social democrats, and *right* connotes capitalism or a neoconservative socioeconomic agenda. In Israel, however, the notions of left and right are perceived differently. Thus, *left* most often connotes a preference for a political, not military, solution to the conflict, and readiness to make extensive territorial and other concessions in return for a peace agreement with the Palestinians. *Right*, on the other hand, connotes a noncompromising territorial position based on security and on nationalist/religious grounds. The relevant equation in Israel is left = doves, who do not necessarily hold a socialist outlook, and right = hawks, who do not necessarily endorse a capitalist worldview (see, e.g., Yuchtman-Yaar and Peres 2000).

section, in by-the-way comments of sports journalists and, of course, much more openly in the lectures of many university professors. After all, that's today's bon ton.

– Uri Orbach (2004)

The only thing the left, insisting on staying within the parameters of militarism and Zionism and their historical narrative, can offer Palestinians, is peace "from a position of superiority," hoping all the while that "Gaza will sink into the sea," as its beloved martyr Rabin once put it.

– Tel Aviv Critical Mass against the Wall (2004)

No, there is no peace movement in Israel and unfortunately...until you end occupation...and the civil society developed in Israel is liberated from Zionist ideology, only then we have a chance for reconciliation.

– Ilan Pappe (2005)

These are only six quotations, yet they represent typical examples of the harsh words aimed at the Israeli peace movement and its activists in recent years. These criticisms come from almost all directions – the political right, the center, and the radical left – as well as from the media: Internet talk backs, newspaper articles, radio programs, public lectures, political speeches, and similar venues. One must work very hard to unearth more gratifying comments on the disposition of peace activists and the movement's achievements. Paradoxically, as the peace movement became smaller and less vocal in the late 1990s and early 2000s, domestic antagonism toward it became harsher and more open. Indeed, international public opinion was actually more benign, which in turn inflamed domestic resentment toward the movement for allegedly collaborating with outside – that is, critical of Israel – forces. An observer unfamiliar with the facts could have easily arrived at the conclusion that all of the nation's troubles – from the security threats that it faces, hostile international public opinion, and even the deepening internal sociopolitical cleavages – were the work of this "demonic," "omnipotent" peace movement. In fact, the movement is so small that a random representative sample of Israel's adult population might well miss it altogether. Such allegations are even more absurd because there is nothing farther from most peace activists' minds than turning their backs on the Israeli national collective. The fact of the matter is that their main desire is to find an acceptable, just, and nonviolent solution to the conflict in order to secure the nation and reduce the bloodshed that has made life in this region intolerable.

The main conundrum that this book addresses is, thus, how it is that such a small movement, with a benign cause, has been politically ostracized and has in fact come to be perceived by many Israelis as "the enemy of the people." Scapegoating is a well-known – and admittedly sometimes useful – technique for strengthening collective unity, particularly when national solidarity is eroded by external or internal pressures. The question to be considered here, however, is why so many Israelis (and, as we shall see, also many Palestinians) chose the peace movement and not any other political actor as their scapegoat. To put it differently, why do so many like to hate the peace movement or – even more destructive politically – to ignore it altogether. The question is particularly compelling because only a few would deny that a significant number of the peace groups' predictions and prognoses came true over the years. For example, consider the prestate activists' exposure of the connection between the creation of a Jewish majority in mandatory Palestine and the maturing of the Jewish-Arab conflict; the argument of post-1967 peace groups regarding the highly destructive implications of the expansion of the Jewish settlement project in the territories on the prospects of Israeli-Palestinian peace negotiations; or, in the mid-2000s, the warning that the unilateral disengagement from Gaza would contribute to the dangerous rise of Hamas. Furthermore, some of the peace movement's major recommendations and ideas, mainly the "two states for two peoples" formula, have, in practice, been adopted by various Israeli governments since 1993. These ideas also have been incorporated into the state's formal policy as well as into the prevailing public outlook on the conflict and the ways to manage and perhaps even resolve it.

Being widely vilified is indeed bad for a political actor; however, being sweepingly overlooked by relevant political individuals and bodies is no less problematic. Such disregard by the mainstream was the predicament of the Israeli peace movement, as exemplified in four recent books by people involved in the Oslo process that, although presenting different political readings of that process, have one common denominator: complete lack of interest in peace activism and the role played by the peace movement. The first book, *Oslo: A Formula for Peace*, was written by Yair Hirschfeld, an academic of the left and one of the two "architects" of this strategic move in the early 1990s (Hirschfeld 2000). Written in the late 1990s, the book was still fairly optimistic about the possibility of reaching a permanent Israeli-Palestinian peace agreement. The second book, *A Sad Story*, a collection of essays from the 1990s by right-wing Knesset member (MK) Ze'ev Benyamin Begin, was, as its name suggests, pessimistic. The book basically states that the entire Oslo process was doomed to fail because there has never been, nor will there ever be, a Palestinian partner for peace (Begin 2000). The third book, *Manual for a Wounded Dove*, was written by Yossi Beilin, then a Labour party politician and later leader of the left-of-center Meretz party, founding father of *Yozmat Geneva* (the Geneva Initiative), and one of the Israeli politicians most closely associated with the Oslo process and its predicament (Beilin 2001). Beilin focuses on the highly negative impact of the hard-line policies of Likud-led governments on the chances that the process will bear fruit. The fourth book, *Within Reach*, by Gilead Sher, a lawyer and close aide of Labour Prime Minister Ehud Barak in the late 1990s who accompanied Barak throughout the Camp David fiasco of July 2000, places most of the blame for the collapse of the negotiations on the Palestinians (Sher 2005). As mentioned previously, however, irrespective of their different interpretations of the reasons why Oslo did not lead to a permanent Israeli-Palestinian peace, a closer look at all these books (and many others that discuss the process)[2] reveals that none of them mentions the Israeli peace movement when telling its "Oslo story."[3] The movement that took as its banner peace with the Palestinians and strove for years to achieve this goal is not given a single line in all of these authoritative accounts of the process, as if the movement had never existed.

This disregard for Israeli peace activism is not confined to written histories. More important, this kind of exclusion was manifested by most Israeli decision makers prior to the signing of the Oslo Declaration of Principles (DOP), throughout the 1990s, and after the collapse of the process. Not one peace activist as such has ever been invited to join the many Israeli delegations to the peace talks. No representative of the movement participated in the signing ceremonies of the various agreements along the way, although several Israeli citizens representing groups relevant to peacemaking, including veteran soldiers, bereaved parents, and diplomats, were invited to join the formal Israeli entourage. Furthermore, none of Israel's prime ministers who were in office during the relevant era – Rabin, Peres, and Barak of the Labour party, or Netanyahu and Sharon of the Likud party – ever initiated contacts with the peace movement, let alone used the movement's open channels of communication to the Palestinian side to push the process forward. None of them publicly recognized the movement's activity or acknowledged any contribution that it might have made to the passage from armed conflict to peace negotiations.

The majority of the Jewish-Israeli public – most of whom have never been involved in peace activism of any kind[4] – by and large followed their leaders' dismissive view of the peace movement. At best, the movement is widely considered politically naïve and hence irrelevant, and at worst, peace activists' patriotism, motivation, and loyalty to the state are questioned. People with right-wing political views often openly accuse the peace activists of encouraging Palestinian violence and being responsible for their excessive demands (e.g., Nissan 1994, Zidon 1994). On the other hand, left-wing radicals (e.g., Ofir 2001, Pappe 2005) hold the movement accountable for tacitly collaborating with the mainstream political establishment's anti-peace policies and creating a façade of opposition while in practice, by adhering to the Zionist creed, serving as a fig leaf for the atrocities of the Israeli occupation.

---

[2] Other such examples are Peres 1995, Horovitz 1996, Makovsky 1996, Peleg 1997, Savir 1998, Rabinovich 1999, Rothstein, Ma'oz and Shikaki 2002, Enderlin 2003, Ben Ami 2004, Meital 2006, Ben-Porat 2006, Grinberg 2007, and Kurtzer and Lasensky 2008.

[3] Ben-Porat does mention *Shalom Achshav* (Peace Now); however, he says nothing about its activities but relates to its human and socioeconomic composition in the context of his discussion of the effects of globalization processes over Israeli society (Ben-Porat 2006, 157). In Kurtzer and Lasensky's (2008) book, "designed as a guidebook for future U.S. negotiators," not even one peace activist is included in their list of Israeli interviewees, apparently an indication of their assessment of the movement's minor political and diplomatic relevance (p. xvi).

[4] According to the Peace Index survey of April 2001, only 1.5% of the Israeli Jewish population was ever involved in any Israeli-Palestinian meetings. An even smaller number – 0.5% – is given in the Israel/Palestine Center for Research and Information (IPCRI) report on participation in people-to-people activities in the 1990s (Baskin and al Qaq 2002, 4).

For different reasons, which are discussed at length below, the Palestinians, who in theory should have been highly supportive of Israeli peace activism, have also been quite critical of the peace movement. Apparently, in the early 1990s, when the peace talks moved from the extraparliamentary level to the formal one, the limited political weight of the peace activists in Israeli society made them less attractive and too "easy to get" for the Palestinians. Since the mid-1990s, after Rabin's assassination and the electoral defeat of Peres, when no one close to the peace movement held any formal position in the government or in the high ranks of the civil service, the movement became politically redundant. This made it – from the Palestinian point of view – a much less rewarding target audience compared with the perhaps much resented and feared but more "valuable" and respected right-wing bodies and politicians. Thus, particularly after the collapse of the Oslo process in the late 1990s and the outbreak of the second Palestinian *Al-Aqsa intifada* in 2000, the Israeli peace movement was not only bashed by Israelis but also became a favorite target of the Palestinians, even those who had been its counterparts. The latter blamed the peace movement for not sufficiently protesting the Israeli government's rejectionist and uncompromising positions, and for not fiercely disputing, and perhaps thereby preventing, the reoccupation of Palestinian territories in the early 2000s. This Palestinian position was highly damaging because it both discouraged many Israeli peace activists and made the movement the target of sardonic reactions from its Israeli rivals.

If mainstream records and typical Israeli and Palestinian informants are the only sources of information available to those who, in the future, will try to understand the essence of the Oslo decade, then all of the peace movement's initiatives – hundreds of anti-occupation demonstrations, sit-ins, weekly protest vigils, numerous pro-peace petitions and flyers, joint dialogue groups, and secret and overt Israeli-Palestinian gatherings forbidden by written and unwritten law – are probably doomed to oblivion. This book is meant partly to compensate for this "collective amnesia" by describing and analyzing the movement's ideological, organizational, and operational points of strength and weaknesses.

In a classic first-rate thriller, the mystery is not solved until the very end. In this case, however, particularly against the background of the gloomy exposé described previously, it seems important to reveal at this early stage the bottom line of this investigation of the peace movement's long and, in many respects, unrewarding journey, to point the reader to the tiny light at the end of the tunnel and make it somewhat less frustrating to follow its protracted course. As is discussed in great detail in the concluding section, it seems that despite the peace movement's ongoing low visibility and political marginality and its undisputed failure to gain influence over the national decision-making processes, and without turning a blind eye to its acute structural, ideological, organizational, and strategic flaws, a close examination reveals a growing proximity between the "traditional" agenda of the peace movement and the prevailing attitudes toward the conflict and its resolution. In other words, although the peace movement usually failed to change the concrete policies at which it was aimed, it was more successful at changing the overall "climate of opinion" in the country and challenging some previously unchallenged national myths and narratives. This is true on both the elite and the general public levels in Israel today. However, most of the people whose views on these matters have changed over time would never admit to any connection between these changes and the ongoing but seemingly infertile peace activism.

Thus, as is explained in the methodology section, because of the informal and unofficial character of the subject of inquiry as a social movement, it is almost impossible to categorically establish causal linkage here. It is equally difficult, however, to empirically refute the argument made here, that the peace movement has contributed considerably to the change in the Jewish-Israeli climate of opinion about the conflict and the ways to manage, if not resolve, it. It is argued here that today's wide acceptance, on both the leadership and the grassroots levels, of the "two states for two peoples" formula, an idea that has been the main pillar of the peace movement agenda since the 1970s and that less than 20 years ago was accepted by only a tiny outcast minority of "disloyal" Israeli Jews, is but one example of this suggested effect. This is the solution preferred by an absolute majority of Jewish Israelis and is in fact a cornerstone of Israel's formal policy today. This even seems to be true for many groups whose dream used to be Greater Israel. Thus, in December 2001, one of the bloodiest low points of Israeli-Palestinian relations, a leading figure in the dovish orthodox party Meimad, when announcing that in his own view the Oslo process was dead and buried, also asserted: "Today, the majority of the orthodox public consider the option of Greater Israel as no longer plausible.... Furthermore, the basic assumption that resolution of the conflict should be based on the establishment of a Palestinian state as the basis for a permanent solution – if a suitable partner is found – is today shared by a majority in the country" (Brin 2001). Even the former secretary general of the right-wing Tzomet party acknowledged, "One of the false and strange myths that prevails in the political arena today is that the Israeli right defeated its rivals of the left, while in fact, nothing could be further from the truth. In the final test, the right has been trounced by the leftist camp.... Amazingly enough, instead of taking the repeated invalidation of the left's forecasts as evidence of its error... the leaders of the right have done the unbelievable and the incomprehensible:... they have adopted precisely this defective and detested policy and are dedicating themselves to its implementation" (Sherman 2001). In 2007, Moshe Arens, former minister of defense of the right-wing Likud party, when calling for the replacement of the "two states" paradigm with a new and more suitable one (which he actually did not specify), confirmed the influence of the peace movement without any qualifications: "This pattern for the resolution of the Israeli-Palestinian conflict, which was raised first by the extreme left, who adored and cherished Yassir Arafat, and by the supporters of *Shalom Achshav*, has inculcated into the cognition of most Israelis and was also adopted even by those who had formerly strongly opposed it, like Ariel Sharon" (Arens 2007).

One of Israel's leading journalists, however, posed an intriguing question that is also at the core of the discussion here: "How is it that when the basic solutions to the Israeli-Palestinian conflict offered by the left have become the property of a solid majority of Israelis, the left itself, as an entity, as a political culture . . . is still detested and denounced by such large segments of the public, including those who wholeheartedly agree with it?" (Dankner 2003). This apparent discrepancy between the prevalent disregard or disdain for the peace movement on one hand and assessments of its significant influence on Israeli politics and politicians on the other takes us beyond this specific case study. It raises the crucial question of the necessary conditions and relevant criteria for measuring the success or failure of social movements and civil initiatives, particularly those that concern national security policy–related issues. This question has major significance today with the mushrooming of citizen and grassroots activities relating to foreign policy matters, and the prevailing view that peace and war are no longer matters to be handled only by the formally authorized decision makers and generals (e.g., Bell and O'Rourke 2007). It is of extreme importance therefore to understand under which conditions citizens and grassroots organizations can or cannot influence the making of national foreign and security policies and public opinion, and what the relevant indicators are for measuring their success or failure.

The goal of this book is therefore two-fold: first, in the context of the Israeli case, it aims to introduce the peace movement into the picture of the events and processes of the Oslo process and its aftermath, based on the premise that the peace movement did make a political difference. It is argued here that, despite long being located on the political periphery, the movement has been a significant factor in influencing the climate of opinion in Israel by persistently putting forward some unconventional and much-contested alternative readings of the conflict, thereby cultivating the ground for the transformation from armed conflict to peace negotiations,[5] that is, for the strategic policy shift that the Oslo process embodied. Later, when this process collapsed and the Israeli-Palestinian dialogue became imbued with heavy layers of destruction and blood, it was apparently the only political body in Israel, perhaps in the region, that continued to keep the ashes of the hope for peace in the future warm.

The second aim of this book is of wider scope. Based on an analysis of this specific case study, the book endeavors to show the significant explanatory potential of combining two theoretical schools of thought that rarely converge: social movement theories and theories that involve public opinion and national policy making. As is shown here, these two bodies of knowledge are traditionally located in different disciplinary domains: the former in political sociology and social psychology, and the latter mainly in political science and international relations. Even a superficial examination of the references in the numerous books and articles of both schools shows that, probably owing to the prevailing tendency to safeguard academic disciplinary boundaries,

[5] For the potential influence of grassroots actors in this realm, see, e.g., Lederach 2003, 34–35.

students of social/peace movements and students of public opinion and its relevance to national policy making completely ignore each other's work. This is the case even when their subject matter is in many respects almost identical: peace movements are clearly part of the "public" and influenced by it, and there is little doubt that they promote a kind of "public opinion." Nevertheless, when discussing the public's input and interest in national security policy making, theories and empirical studies that originate in international relations almost always ignore peace activism – the most highly elaborated form of organized and distinctive public opinion in this realm. Instead, they portray the "public" as a faceless and shapeless collection of individual persons, putting forth poorly constructed, often inconsistent, and ill-informed "public opinion." Social movement students, conversely, because of their analytical framework, tend to focus on specific movements – their human composition, organizational structure, networking, resources, and relations with the authorities. They pay limited attention, if any, to their wider operational context – unorganized general public opinion, which is critical to the movement's ability to gain momentum and mobilize activists and supporters, a capability that actually determines such movements' political effectiveness.

The book is divided into five sections. The first section, "Exploring Peace Activism – a Roadmap," presents the theoretical framework of this study and the key concepts that are used to analyze the Israeli case. Special attention is paid to the concept of "political opportunity structure" (POS). This section also includes the reasons for suggesting a synthesis of the two theoretical bodies mentioned previously and describes the methodology employed in the study.

"Mapping the Israeli Sociopolitical Terrain" briefly discusses the historical-ideological legacies and the structure of sociopolitical cleavages against which background Israeli peace activism developed. This section also reviews the changes in the POS that Israeli grassroots activism in general faced between the formative era of the Israeli polity and the present.

"Paving the Road to Oslo – Israeli Peace Activism through 1992" outlines in brief the features of Israeli peace activism prior to 1993, when the Oslo process was launched, with special reference to the effects on the peace movement of the changes in the local POS during these years. The discussion in this section relates to the ideological, structural, and operational features of Israeli peace activism until the launching of the Oslo process and outlines the peace movement's internal and external networking.

"The Path Strewn with Obstacles (1993–2008)" is the core of the book. The focus here is on perhaps the most frustrating 15 years of Israeli peace activism, at the beginning of which peace seemed to be almost at hand, whereas now, at the end of this era, it is out of sight for most Israelis,[6] Palestinians, and external

---

[6] Not everyone, however, is utterly pessimistic. For example, Kurtzer and Lasensky (2008) claim that wiser U.S. diplomacy can still bring about a breakthrough: "Fortunately, this is not where the story ends. Despite the setbacks of recent years, Washington still has an enormous reservoir

observers. This part of the trail is divided into five subsections: The rest area zone – 1993 to late 1995; the bumpy zone – early 1996 to mid-1999; the check point zone – mid-1999 to summer 2000; the dark tunnel zone – summer 2000 to early 2003; and the dead-end point – early 2003 to mid-2008.

The first subsection discusses the ways in which the peace movement responded – ideologically, structurally, and operationally – to the dramatic change (paradoxically, mainly for the worse) in the POS created by the electoral victory of the Labour party in 1992 and then the signing of the Oslo DOP in 1993. Apparently, the very adoption by the government of certain pillars of its agenda cast some doubts on the movement's raison d'être.

The second subsection describes the various ideological, structural, and operational responses of the peace movement to the gradual shattering of the Oslo dream that occurred following Rabin's assassination, the first massive wave of terror shortly afterward, and the electoral triumph of the Likud party, led by Netanyahu, until Labour's short-lived comeback in 1999. During that period, it is maintained, the movement had to come to grips with not only the fact that the Oslo process had come to a halt and perhaps to an end but also with the grim reality that the peace camp, in its widest definition, was considered the party guilty of this allegedly defective strategic move.

The discussion in the third subsection focuses mainly on the unexpectedly malevolent POS created by Barak's Labour government, which – contrary to the expectations and hopes of many – failed to break the deadlock in the peace talks that culminated in the July 2000 fiasco of the Camp David summit, and gave life to the powerful and long-lasting "no partner" concept.

The fourth subsection attempts to assess the effect on the movement of the outbreak of the Palestinian *Al-Aqsa intifada* in fall 2000, with its extreme violence, and the Israeli reoccupation of the Palestinian territories. This deterioration led to the first (2001) and second (2003) electoral victories of Prime Minister Sharon, apparently based on what was considered by a majority of Israelis his potential and then seemingly proven skills in fighting Palestinian terrorism. For the same reason, the relevance of the peace movement in the public sphere declined, and its POS contracted dramatically. The movement reacted to that by structural reorganizing and agenda reformulating.

of influence with the parties. . . . The steep decline in relations between Israel and the Palestinians may be reversing. . . . The test will not be easy, however. Success will depend on heeding the lessons of the past . . . and will also require U.S. negotiators to have a clear sense of the changing context that surrounds Arab-Israeli peacemaking on the ground, across the region, and within the broader strategic environment" (Kurtzer and Lasensky, 6). Another example is Golan's assessment that "the two sides will opt for realism – leaving the issue of trust to a later stage – and adopt something quite close to the peace plans that have emerged" (Golan, 142). Last but not least, in their research report, the Aix group members state: "The current widespread pessimism seems to choke any initiative that dares to think about a permanent arrangement and to present an alternative to the continuation of the violent conflict. We should not surrender to the pessimists and should not accept their vision of 40 more years of death and suffering" (Arnon and Bamya, 20).

The fifth and last subsection opens with Ariel Sharon's second term, which started with acceleration in the construction of the separation barrier and all of the legal and other complications this entailed and culminated with the introduction and then implementation of his Disengagement from Gaza plan. The plan rested on the notion of unilateralism, the complete antithesis to the bilateral rationale that stood at the basis of the peace movement agenda, as well as that of the Oslo process. This strategic shift created another rift within the movement, between the supporters and the opponents of the plan. It also once again changed the POS in terms of the movement's position vis-à-vis the Israeli public and authorities, as, similar to the early days of Oslo, the moderate parts of the peace movement stood on one side of the fence with the government and the mainstream, whereas the radicals found themselves on the other side, with the right-wing opposition and the settlers. This internal rift, and the bitter disappointment with the political chaos and accelerating violence that followed Israel's disengagement from the Gaza Strip and later the electoral victory of Hamas in early 2006, led to a complete halt of peace activism in Israel. Not even the highly contested and militarily apparently rather unsuccessful Second Lebanon War in the summer of 2006 and the soldiers' protest in its aftermath, nor the Annapolis peace initiative of late 2007, were successful in revitalizing the movement, which is admittedly a historical remnant today and no longer a relevant political actuality.

Beyond telling the story of the movement and analyzing the ideological and organizational changes that it underwent in the relevant years, its various external relations are also explored: between the various peace groups that together make up the peace movement, and between the movement and the Israeli authorities – the government, the military, and the political parties. Special attention is devoted to the complicated and painful interactions between the movement and its activists on one hand and, on the other, the general Israeli public and other civil society actors, such as the media and other types of citizens' initiatives. Another set of contacts of interest to this analysis is that between the movement and non-Israeli bodies – the Palestinians, the Jewish Diaspora, international foundations and other donors, the international media, international public opinion, and foreign peace movements.

The conclusion, "A Path Finder – Getting Lost or Paving New Roads?," is an effort to assess the accomplishments of the Israeli peace movement in the years under investigation here. Only time will tell if the Oslo process was indeed a turning point in the protracted conflict between Israel and the Arabs or merely a mirage, a transient episode of hope that left no real mark on the bloody history of the Middle East. The answer to this riddle is critical from the point of view of the peace movement, in a rather complicated way. At the time of this writing, the Oslo process is widely considered to have been a monumental fiasco. If this is indeed the case, it is important to find a reliable answer to whether the Israeli peace movement was in any way responsible for this tragedy; that is, did it manage to influence the political decision-making process to the extent that its recommendations were actually adopted? If so, the current bleak state of affairs must, as many of its opponents argue, reflect a basically mistaken reading of the regional situation by the movement. Another possibility is that somewhere along the way, the politicians distorted the movement's agenda, in which case its "innocence" should be established. Last but not least, using the theoretical framework in the theoretical section (exploring peace activism), the final part of this section puts forward a theoretical suggestion on how social movements and public opinion scholarship together can produce an analytical tool for examining the top-down and bottom-up flows of influence as far as national security matters are concerned.

A "red flag" regarding the purpose of this book should be raised here, just before starting out: it by no means seeks to tell the formal story of the Oslo process. This has been done, quite skillfully, in many other books and articles and from many vantage points, by people on all sides who personally participated in the negotiations, who were close to the participants, or who examined the process from afar and analyzed it using various academic tools.[7] As the book concentrates on the extremely frustrating story of the Israeli peace movement in the Oslo decade, unlike most other books, it does not seek answers to questions that, although very important, are not highly relevant to this analysis. These include, "Was the Oslo process really doomed to failure from the start?" "Which side fulfilled – and which did not – its obligations through the years?" "To what extent did the developments depend on the personalities of the leaders involved?" Finally, it does not seek to answer the most frequently asked question – "What happened at Camp David in July 2000?" Instead, this book concentrates on possible contributions of the nongovernmental, grassroots peace camp to the transformation in Israel's official policy, and in turn on the possible effects this process had on Israeli peace activism.[8] At the same time, the book does not aim to function as a catalogue of all Israeli peace groups and organizations, or to detail every peace activity conducted over these dozen years. This book does, however, aspire to paint an overall picture of the movement during this period, including its main features, processes, and dynamics. These can help us to understand how, just when the promise of a solution was so close at hand, the peace movement did not turn into a pivotal political actor, and why, when conditions seemed best for it to grow and flourish, the movement was unable to retain its energy even when it became clear that the peace process had been derailed.

[7] The literature on the Oslo negotiations and agreements is immense. Beyond those mentioned in note 2, it is worthwhile looking at, e.g., Abbas 1995, Watson 2000, Said 2000, Ross 2004, Savir 2006, and Ben-Porat 2007.

[8] It is also important to keep in mind that this case study is neither unique nor sui generic. For example, many Western ecological movements faced similar experiences and dilemmas in terms of the movements-authorities relations, when, beginning in the 1980s, their green agenda was "hijacked" by governments that, in the eyes of many activists, sometimes distorted or even abused it for their own purposes.

2

Exploring Peace Activism – A Road Map

The story of the Israeli peace movement in the Oslo era is agonizing yet fascinating. After all, rarely does a small and poorly resourced social movement face a situation in which some of the main pillars of its agenda that were formerly widely rejected are suddenly integrated into formal national policy. However, this is exactly what occurred when the Rabin government, elected in 1992, presented its blueprint for peace and launched the Oslo process a year later. When this happened, the peace movement was presented with at least three dilemmas: first, it had to choose between the normal organizational (and human) tendency to claim "copyrights" – in this case for the political breakthrough that Oslo embodied – and the realization that the less it is associated with this strategic shift, the better the chances that the process would gain wide public support. Second, the government takeover of the peace agenda raised questions about the movement's raison d'être. The second dilemma therefore became, should the peace movement dissolve itself or search for a new set of aims? Third, once the decision was made to continue its activity, the movement had to redefine its relations with the political establishment and the mainstream, because for the first time in its history, it found itself in concert, in principle at least, with decision makers and large public sectors and not on the side of the opposition. This change called for a basic transformation of the movement's state of mind. Before the peace movement could consider these three problems, the situation dramatically changed once again, and it was faced with new predicaments.

With the assassination of Prime Minister Rabin in November 1995, the rise in the number of Palestinian terror attacks in early 1996, and the electoral defeat of the Labour party several months later, for many Israelis, particularly those not deeply committed to the Oslo agenda, the high hopes invested in the peace process were shattered. The peace movement then faced a second major reversal in its fortunes and the need for strategic re-evaluation: it had to adapt itself to increasingly unfavorable surroundings: the hostility of the newly elected right-wing government, the cold shoulder of the public, and its own members' growing frustration with the state of the negotiations, which seemed to have reached a dead end. On top of these attitudes, the peace movement also had to come to grips ideologically with the uncompromising positions put forth by the Palestinian leadership and the wide Palestinian public support for the use of violence against Israelis, including suicide bombings.[1] As if all of this were not enough, the movement had to deal with the drying up of much of its external financial support. Under the new circumstances, peace activism looked irrelevant, if not counterproductive, to certain major past donors. The formal collapse of the peace talks in July 2000 and the outbreak of the Al-Aqsa intifada in October of that year provided the movement's rivals with the, allegedly, ultimate proof that its agenda was fundamentally wrong. This was not an easy challenge for the movement: indeed more than a few former peace activists had some regrets of their own and quit, whereas others became more convinced than before that had their message not been distorted by the Israeli authorities peace could have prevailed. For them, the collapse of the formal talks and the increased violence indicated that without a radical transformation of the Israeli national ethos, peace was unattainable. The very short honeymoon between the peace movement and the Israeli mainstream thus ended in strong discord.

The story, presented briefly here, raises many empirical and conceptual questions. For example, what in the pre-Oslo era made hundreds, and at times even thousands, of peace activists, most from the more privileged strata of Israeli society, vigorously and publicly challenge some of the core values that the mainstream held, in particular, the reliance on territorial depth and military supremacy as the basic "insurance policy" for the state's survival? What drove these people to contest the leadership's frameworking of the conflict as zero sum and to develop the empirically still-unsubstantiated premise that peace could be attained if Israel acknowledged the national rights of the Palestinians and made extensive territorial compromises? On the organizational level, the Israeli peace movement's inability through the years to reach out to audiences beyond its traditional base of support – the Ashkenazi, educated, urban, secular, and economically better-off sector – calls for an explanation beyond merely repeating this well-known fact. Another puzzling but opposite phenomenon is the movement's ability to maintain some level of activity, both when the government seemed to have taken over the peace agenda and again when the peace process came to a dead end, when escalating violence supposedly contradicted its diagnosis and prognosis. One might also wonder why at such times, particularly after the outbreak of the Al-Aqsa intifada, the peace movement at large, with the demobilization of its moderate components, radicalized its peace advocacy and its criticism of the Israeli government rather than assuaging it, thereby consciously distancing itself from the national collective. On the national level, it is interesting to explore the paradoxical situation in which, in certain crucial

---

[1] See, e.g., the December 1996 CPRS survey, http://www.pcpsr.org/survey/cprspolls/96/poll25a .html, in which 39% of the Palestinians supported armed attacks against Israelis.

respects, the launching of the peace process changed the political opportunity structure (POS) for the worse and not for the better.

To answer these and other questions systematically, a theoretical framework is needed. Two distinct theoretical bodies seem relevant here – one that focuses on social movements as political actors and one that deals with public opinion and national security policy making. As is explained here, each neglects some important aspects, so there seems to be no single research body that can encompass both the movement's internal processes and its interface with its multilayered operational context. The picture can be seen in full only if the two "lenses" are used simultaneously. What is suggested here is synthesizing certain key concepts and insights from these two theoretical bodies when attempting to delineate the contextual conditions under which peace activism could become politically germane, as well as those under which it is expected to fail to transmit its message.

Theoretical and Historical Milestones

Social Movement Research

Tarrow defines a *social movement* as "collective challenges by people with common purposes and solidarity in sustained interaction with elites, opponents and authorities" (1994, 4). These four basic characteristic properties set social movements apart from other, unorganized, quick-to-perish, lacking self-identity, and amorphous types of collective behaviors, such as riots, or panic reactions. On the other hand, social movements differ from political parties, which are the more institutionalized format of public political participation. Unlike parties, social movements normally adopt a one-issue agenda, for example, nuclear freeze or prevention of war, although certain movements do adopt multiple aims once they reach a high level of institutionalization, which brings them close to a political party format, or when their original target either is achieved or proves to be unachievable (e.g., Hermann 1993b). In addition, unlike political parties, social movements do not take part in the electoral process, nor do they compete for policy-making positions. Moreover, whereas political parties usually demand exclusive membership (i.e., a person is not allowed to be a member of more than one party), individual social activists often are simultaneously concerned with issues dealt with by several social movements and become involved at the same time in the activities of more than one movement.

Whereas this characterization focuses on the movement's internal features, others emphasize the external aspect: the notion of conflict that lies at the heart of every social movement: "A social movement is a network of informal interactions between a plurality of individuals, groups and/or organizations, engaged in a political or cultural conflict, on the basis of a shared collective identity" (Diani 1992, 13). Similarly, it has been observed that social movements "are often engaged in conflict with power-holders and other status-quo representatives. As such, movements develop collective identities as part of their ongoing activities, as part of their complex self-definition processes as challenging groups, and even through their waging of conflict to bring about social change" (Coy 2001, viii).

Often, the social movement's demands that the state protect or augment through its policies certain rights or procedures encounter substantial resistance from a range of state agencies and private organizations that favor other policies and other distributive effects (Maney 2001, 106). It should be noted that, in general, social movements tend to enable individuals who take part in their activities to blame their grievances on a structural, rather than a personal cause, in order to develop a political conscience (Goldner 2001, 77).[2] Thus, these movements usually identify a faceless "system" as the cause of the trouble. It is not surprising, then, that social movements have traditionally been involved in confrontational or contentious politics. Successful confrontational campaigns by social movements usually involve several ingredients: the matter at stake is clearly defined; the campaigns aim at attainable goals; the campaigns are carried out with careful planning and discipline; and they are aimed at logical targets – people with the power to effect policy changes (Dorman 1974, 163–164).

The literature offers a variety of social movement formations: by size – ranging from very small to very large; by orientation – norm-oriented movements, which are usually more moderate, versus value-oriented movements, which tend to be more radical (Smelser 1963); by membership – inclusive versus exclusive movements (Zald and Ash 1966); and by aims – value-oriented movements, which strive to introduce new values; power-oriented ones, which are more interested in taking over power centers; and participation-oriented movements, which are mainly interested in wide mobilization (Turner and Killian 1957). When confrontational acts are carried out in the interest of unprecedented, far-reaching demands (compared with well-known and middle-of-the-road mainstream positions), and when the other side – usually the political establishment – is unable to grant concessions without appearing to surrender, activists are readily branded as frivolous and irrational: "Confrontation politics, the historical experience suggests, cannot be practiced on an ad-lib, catch-as-catch-can basis" (Dorman 1974, 163–164). Thus, another categorization refers to differences among movements based on their public image: among respectable, peculiar, or revolutionary movements. The first are widely considered acceptable by the public and the authorities even if their agenda is debatable; the second are perceived as irrelevant and suspect; the last are seen as threatening and therefore a legitimate target for repression (Turner and Killian 1972). This last categorization is theoretically highly influential and distinguishes between "old" and "new" social movements. Old social movements – like the Unionist or Labour movement – represent the usually materialist,

---

[2] In the case of the Israeli peace movement, 'occupation' is the system that it identifies as the source of the trouble.

concrete interests of a specific social cluster – for example, class, denomination, or gender. These movements generally emerge in earlier stages of the industrial-capitalist system and use only a limited set of protest techniques (e.g., protest marches and strikes). New movements, on the other hand, typically develop in the later stages of industrial-capitalist society, represent a wider range of mainly postmaterialistic interests, and employ a variety of actions and techniques to promote general public goods such as identity, human security, or environmentalism (Boggs 1986, Offe 1990).

The study of social movements can be very frustrating for political scientists and sociologists trained and working in mainstream academia. First, social movements are essentially different from all conventional political formations in terms of their quick-to-change structure, verified modes of operation, intricate internal dynamics, relatively short life span, and noninstitutionalized mobilization techniques. Second, the common denominators of all social movements, as indicated by the definitions given here, should not overshadow the structural and operational diversity that characterizes this category of political participation agencies. In fact, within the same movement, diversity in operational modes and even ideological nuances among various subgroups is fairly common. Third, social movements in most cases also "excel" at inconsistent record keeping and at formulating undocumented (sometimes unsubstantiated) mythologies about their early days and successful operations. Thus, to study a movement, a researcher must become deeply involved with the activists and the activities, often in real time, an imperative that can distort the objectivity of the research. Often accepting the postmodernist assumption regarding the essential unattainability of scholarly objectivity, some social movement students find the idea of *action research*, a combination of being active in the movement and doing research, quite appealing, whereas more "conservative" scholars find this method totally unacceptable, epistemologically and methodologically.

The complexity and volatility of the subject matter and the methodological debates have led to what Lofland (1993) referred to as the fashion of "theory bashing" in the study of social movements. Social movement scholars, he maintains, are inclined to partake in the intellectual ritual of bashing the theories for which they have not opted, for whichever reason, and none of the existing bodies of theory on social movements – sociopsychological theories, breakdown theories, resource mobilization theories, or political process theories – have escaped it. The joy of bashing competing social movement theories, he claims, has impeded scientific progress in explicating this phenomenon. Other scholars in the field disagree with this diagnosis, however, and refer to what Lofland calls "bashing" as a vivid intellectual discussion, which contributes positively to the construction of a multifaceted body of knowledge:

The "secret" of the success of social movement theory and research has, indeed, been its characteristic openness to criticism and new approaches, but only insofar as this has been accompanied by a readiness to put new ideas to empirical test. This, and the creative employment of a variety of research methods, has in our view turned the study of social movements into a real empirical science and successful enterprise (Klandermans and Staggenborg 2002, ix).

The first generation of contemporary grassroots action scholarship, the mass behavior theories, emerged in the 1950s and 1960s (e.g., Kornhauser 1959, Blumer 1960, Smelser 1963). Their reading of collective behavior was of accumulated irrational and emotional responses by alienated individuals. This reading dealt with the causes and formations of eruptions of citizen discontent as well as with the dangers of massive civil political participation, which, under the painful memories of the totalitarian – communist and fascist – experience, were viewed as a severe threat to the stability and proper functioning of democratic regimes. The basic hypothesis of these theories was that people would be politically irritated and would protest when deprived of the (mostly material) assets to which they thought they were entitled. In reality, however, we know that the man in the street often gets involved in political protest not only when hungry or disenfranchised but also, for example, when feeling relatively deprived compared with others in terms of recognition, identity, and the like (Gurr 1970). Furthermore, as the new social movements phenomenon suggests, participants in many such contemporary citizens' campaigns – human rights activists, environmentalists, or anti-globalists – do not have a more personal stake in the causes that they pursue than do other members of the same political collective. Self-interest alone therefore does not serve as a satisfying explanation for all sorts of grassroots participation.

The second-generation theories therefore addressed a different research agenda: what is needed for grassroots movements to gain momentum and achieve their goals? These theories, often referred to as the *resource mobilization school*, mainly proposed that the availability and allocation of human and material resources determine the campaign's mobilization capabilities and practical outcomes. This postulate diverted scholarly attention away from the reasons for the protest, to the social movement organization (SMO): its internal and external networking, decision-making routines, mobilization techniques, and life cycle (e.g., Zald and Ash 1966, McCarthy and Zald 1973, McAdam 1982, Zald and McCarthy 1987, Kriesi 1996). In addition to the SMO concept, two other central notions were developed by the second-generation theoreticians: (1) the social movement infrastructure (SMI), that is, all SMOs included under the umbrella of a given social movement; and (2) the social movement sector (SMS) – the infrastructures of all social movements in a given polity at a given point in time (Kriesi 1996, 153).[3]

---

[3] In our case, then, SMO refers to a specific Israeli peace group, SMI describes the peace movement in general, and SMS is the entire Israeli extraparliamentary/third sector. As we shall see, certain openings and obstacles are relevant to the same extent for the entire SMS, some are more relevant for a specific SMI, and others are pertinent to one SMO but not to others.

Several sets of parameters for analyzing the organizational development of a social movement were developed in the resource mobilization framework and are referred to in this case study:

1. Parameters that capture organizational growth and decline – mainly changes in SMI size or in the number of active SMOs and the changes in the amount of resources available to them;
2. Organizational structuration – the level of formalization of work routines, professionalization of staff, division of labor among the different SMOs, and the level of integration by horizontal coordinating mechanisms;
3. External structuration, that is, level of SMI integration in the overall organizational environment in terms of the movement's relations with its constituency, allies, opponents, and authorities;
4. Goal orientations and action, that is, the SMO's location on the moderation-radicalism continuum (Kriesi 1996, 154–156).

Perhaps the most notable contribution of the resource mobilization school is the notion of social movement networks[4] – interpersonal, intraorganizational, interorganizational, and political (Zurcher and Curtis 1973; Zald and McCarthy 1987). The network analysis that they introduced into social movement exploration probes the linkage between the nature and achievements of a social movement and its embedding in preexisting networks. Such analysis can reveal how the network locations of individual people shape their decisions to become politically active and how the network location of specific SMOs accounts for their influence, visibility, and mobilization capacities. It also helps to determine to what extent social and organizational networking between activists and their SMOs is helpful or harmful to pursuing their causes and attaining their goals, as well as to the subsequent development of protest activities or subcultures (Diani 2002, 173–174).

Social movement theory did not remain fixed in the resource mobilization phase, however. Another conceptual framework, the *political process* theoretical framework, emerged in the late 1970s and early 1980s (e.g., Tilly 1978; Tarrow 1983, 1994; Kleidman 1999; Coy 2001). The questions addressed here were why social movements emerge or decline when they do so, and why they take different trajectories. The basic answer was that "Changing opportunities help explain why movements emerge at one point in time rather than another, and differences in political opportunities help explain why movements are successful in some countries or regions and not in others" (Klandermans and Straggenbord 2002, xi). The new theories of political process, which developed mostly in Europe, while those of resource mobilization were often created and endorsed in the United States, were explicitly intended to counter the microtendency of resource mobilization theories by situating social movements in the

---

[4] A *network* can be defined as "a set of actors connected by a specific type of relations" (Knoke and Kuklinski 1982, 12).

tumultuous intersection between society and the state (Adir 2001, 149). For this purpose, the core notion of political opportunity structure (POS) – the set of environmental elements that catalyze movements, translating the potential for collective action into actual mobilization – was developed (e.g., Eisinger 1973, Tarrow 1994). The POS represents "consistent but not necessarily formal or permanent national dimensions of the political environment which either encourage or discourage people from using collective action" (Tarrow 1994, 18). A favorable POS, it was maintained, arises more sporadically than grievances and organizational resources, yet exerts a far more critical influence on a movement's prospects. In practice, it even determines the movement's resource mobilization abilities (e.g., Kitschelt 1986), structure (Tarrow 1994), behavior (della Porta 1995), and interpretative frameworks (Snow and Benford 1992).

A social movement's POS is composed of (1) the formal structure of the political system within which the movement operates; (2) the system's informal procedures; and (3) its prevailing strategies with regard to challengers and the power configuration (Kriesi, 1996). McAdam, McCarthy, and Zald list four dimensions of POS on which almost all studies within this analytical framework rest:

1. Level of openness of the institutionalized political system;
2. Level of stability of the elite alignments;
3. Existence of allies within the elite;
4. The state's capacity and propensity for repression (McAdam et al. 1996, 10).

The POS concept thus suggests that social movements emerge in response to specific circumstances and not necessarily to the level of frustration or the human and material resources available for the movement or its networking skills. In other words, according to the political process theoreticians, for a social movement, the *when* – when the POS is "ripe" – goes a long way toward explaining the *why* – why people get politically involved in this way. The POS concept also helps to understand when a social movement is able to gain access into the political system and how and when it is more likely to evaporate at a very early stage, leaving no traces behind. Taking this a step further, Tarrow presents an interesting categorization of two sets of POSs:

1. State-centered opportunity structure
2. Proximate opportunity structure

The *state-centered* opportunity structure is helpful in comparing state-movement relations in different nations, with the main independent variable being the specific context respective level of "statism." The *proximate* opportunity structure focuses on signals that groups receive from their immediate political environment or through changes in their resources or capacities. The latter category is in turn subdivided into (1) policy-specific opportunities, indicating how policy and the institutional environment channel collective action around particular issues and with what consequences; and (2) group-specific opportunities, reflecting the opportunity structure facing a specific group and the change in it over time (Tarrow 1996, 42–45).

Naturally, the POS changes with time, thereby changing the movement's mobilization potential, strategies, and potential and practical achievements. A change in the POS would be the result, for example, of the reshuffling of global or regional structures, electoral realignments, divisions among elites, or the emergence or disappearance of influential allies within the political establishment. Empirical studies point to the possibility of POS *expansion*, that is, making it more conducive to the movement's purposes (Goldner 2001), its *contraction* (Melucci 1995), and even the possibility of *simultaneous expansion and contraction* (Suh 2001). When the POS expands, the movement tends to open up, increases its mobilization efforts, and often moderates its message to attract new members. On the other hand, when the POS contracts, the movement is expected to respond by operating on a smaller scale and maintaining the "old guard" commitment rather than recruiting new participants (Goldner 2001, 72–73). To increase the chances for the movement's success, its activists need to explore thoroughly the specific POS within which they operate as "the structures of everyday life may ultimately be changed by collective action, but in the short run they are relatively fixed, and serve as the relational underpinning for most collective action" (McCarthy 1996, 147). Still, a movement is not completely passive as far as its POS is concerned. For example, it can expand its POS by expanding its tactical repertoire, in anticipation of catching the authorities unprepared (Tarrow 1996, 58).

Popular as they have become, POS theories seem to be facing growing criticism lately. The most common criticism concerns POS as an ex-post-facto analytical tool – success or failure are explained by it only in retrospect, as the result of an expanded or contracted POS. The critics of this notion argue that despite its popularity and attraction, it actually provides us with no theoretical tools to test the water in real time (e.g., Meyer and Minkoff 2004).

A second stream of criticism complained that POS theories paid very little attention to changes in technical facilities available to the movements. One clear example of such a change is the emergence of computer-mediated communication (CMC) – the Internet and e-mail – which was completely ignored in POS theories although it dramatically increased the operational abilities of social movements. In fact, CMC seems to represent an entirely new field of social activity, sustained by a community of activists with a special ethic and way of doing things:

[The WWW] is providing media substitution for self-censoring news services, censored either for reasons of the purse or for reasons of the state, or any mix thereof. [It also serves as] media substitution; creating interaction; enhancing interaction; breaking the censorship of silence; electronic perforation (closed societies can be opened up); bypassing hierarchy; crisis communication; linking the periphery; public service and developmental intervention; distributing knowledge; advocacy; renegotiation of social contracts (Walch 1999, 100, 145).

One might then safely expect this technology to operate as a powerful facilitator for social activism through "the maintenance of dispersed face-to-face networks" and the development of cultural and "socio-spatial 'enclaves'" (Calhoun 1998, 383, 384), and hence it represents a major facilitator of grass-roots activity. The defenders of classic POS definitions would argue that the contribution of CMC to the creation of new types of communities and the spread of new democratic practices is not yet clear; it might turn out to be no more critical than previous technical innovations, for example, radio, telephone, or television. They also claim that there is significant doubt as to the authenticity of the virtual community – participants in virtual communication often hide their identities, participate only occasionally, and most important, are not joined in any sort of committed relationship. It is argued that most virtual networks operate at their best when backed by actual social linkages in localized communities; their capacity to create new communities is uncertain. Finally, they say, the overall democratizing impact of CMC might be severely hampered by two types of resource constraints: its contribution to the operations of social control agencies, that is, the military, governments, and corporations; and the fact that access to CMC is, at least for the time being, still heavily correlated to class and wealth (Diani 2001, 126–127). However, as discussed in more detail in the following chapters, the case of the Israeli peace movement suggests that technical improvements are more critical to social activism than original POS theoreticians were ready to assume.

The third line of criticism argues that POS theoreticians have focused too much on the practical manifestations of protest (the sort of work advocated and performed, for example, by Koopmans and Rucht, 2002) while neglecting central issues such as ideology, culture, identity, and emotions (e.g., Goodwin and Jasper 1999, Aminzade and McAdam 2001). This sort of critique produced the notion of *framing* as another tool for analyzing social movement activity. Framing is commonly defined as "conscious strategic efforts by groups of people to fashion shared understandings of the world and of themselves that legitimate and motivate collective actions" (McAdam et al. 1996, 7, based on Snow and Benford 1988). The complementary notion to framing is *resonance* – the extent to which the way the movement frames the problem is accepted by its audience and sustains its mobilization efforts. The proponents of framing theories did not aspire to create a new school of thought on social movements but only to enrich the theory so that it includes more than the study of POS and strategies of resource mobilization. Framing is actually meant to amalgamate earlier social movement theories: "mediating between opportunity, organization and action, are the shared meanings and definitions that people bring to this situation" (McAdam et al. 1996, 5). However, as suggested by the theory bashing ritual discussed earlier, even this rather modest aspiration was not always welcomed by devoted adherents of POS theories who often opposed the idea of expanding "their" key notion to include the framing aspect. POS mainstreamers think that "this 'cultural turn' may herald a new direction for the field, but... unresolved methodological and measurement problems with regard to identity, emotions and culture may frustrate the development of this cultural perspective into a new paradigm" (Klandermans and Straggenbord 2002, xii). Two pivotal scholars in the field put forth their criticism of the critics of classic POS theories who introduced new notions, such as framing: "The concept of political opportunity structure is in trouble, in danger of becoming a sponge that soaks up virtually every aspect of the social movement environment – political institutions and culture, crises of various sorts, political alliances and policy shifts.... It threatens to become an all-encompassing fudge factor for all the conditions and circumstances that form the context for collective action. Used to explain so much, it may ultimately explain nothing at all" (Gamson and Meyer 1996, 275). Nevertheless, the classical POS notion is indeed highly complex and multifaceted: some scholars use this term as the independent variable to account for the emergence or demise of social movements. Others use it as an intervening factor when comparing movements in different countries, and still others, seeking to understand the long-term influences of a movement on policy, relate to the POS that movements can create as a dependent variable (op. cit., 276). They conclude, "Political opportunity structure can serve all these uses, but we need to be more clear about our purposes, what we mean by opportunity, and about the interaction between movements and opportunities" (ibid.).

These reservations about POS theory concisely indicate the rather unadventurous state of mind of mainstream social movement research. This was no secret, as suggested by the following diagnostic remark by Sidney Tarrow, one of the most prominent researchers in the field: "The current need of the field lies not in implementation but in the conceptual placement of social movements. We propose to advance towards this goal by... attempting to integrate or confront these new aspects and concepts with those that have shown their worth by stimulating empirical research or producing theoretical insights in social movement theory over the past two decades" (Tarrow 2001, 6).

Public Opinion Research

Social movement students almost unanimously adhere to the participatory democracy model and hence attribute great importance to grassroots political participation, postulating an articulated and rational citizen. However, almost all public opinion and national security policy scholars, regardless of their "generational" positioning, strictly adhere to the representative model of democracy, with a large part of them also undermining or at least doubting the political competence of the average citizen (e.g., Miller and Stokes 1963, Dahl 1971, Sobel 2001).[5] In other words, they see the elected decision makers and the authorized civil servants of the administration as the pivotal players in this central field of "high politics," whereas the citizenry is considered at most to be backbenchers.

---

[5] For the juxtaposition of these two models, see Haskell 2001.

This predisposition was set by early writings on the topic by the early generation, which is sometimes labeled "the Almond-Lippmann consensus" (e.g., Holsti 1992; Rosenau 1992).[6] All studies that come under this umbrella portray, with slight variation, an uninformed, panic-stricken, apathetic, and inactive public. Three main postulates stood at the heart of the "consensus": (1) public opinion is volatile and thus provides inadequate foundations for stable and effective policies; (2) it lacks coherence or structure,[7] but (3) in the final analysis, it has little if any impact on national policy. These theoreticians therefore viewed the elected representatives as the "guardians of the collective interest," allowing for only limited bottom-up influence on decision making so that political stability and continuity are maintained. To appease the democratic postulate regarding the people's sovereignty, they suggested making governmental processes somewhat more transparent to the public, although still recommending only very limited civil participation in politics beyond voting.

As the rationality (or, according to these theoreticians, irrationality) of the public was difficult to measure directly, classical students of public opinion focused on finding empirical evidence for the volatility of the public's views as well as for their internal incoherence. These were not too difficult to expose, perhaps, as later scholarship suggested, because these studies only rarely took into consideration external factors and processes that might have accounted for and explained the allegedly irrational attitudinal shifts indicated in their surveys, the central means of studying public opinion at the time. Furthermore, changes in public opinion were never compared in these studies with the strategic shifts made by the decision makers, when their reading of the circumstances changed. Such benefit of doubt was not given to the general public when significant transformations in attitudes were measured. Furthermore, as certain critics suggest, the classical students of public opinion often avoided in-depth exploration of the alleged perceptual inconsistencies that, as the later analyses suggest, might have been, at least in certain cases, the result of the interviewees' misunderstanding of the ill-formatted, too-complicated, or high-language questions. Neither was the possibility of the researchers' misunderstanding of the logic underlying the respondents' answers ever seriously considered (e.g., Bourdieu 1993).

Probably under the influence of the overall democratization of the public sphere and the growing empowerment of the citizenry, in the newer studies of public opinion, particularly on national security, both the portrait of the citizenry and the view of its rationality, cognitive stability, and even preferred political effectiveness have considerably changed for the better (e.g., Cohen 1973, Chittick and Billingsley 1989, Wittkopf 1990, Page and Shapiro 1992, Holsti 2004). Moving in parallel with developments in political psychology, theoretical and methodological advances led to an increasingly widely shared

---

[6] The "consensus" is named after Almond (1950) and Lippmann (1922).
[7] Philip Converse wrote about "nonattitudes" of the public (Converse 1864, 1970).

view that the public holds reasonably sensible and nuanced views, that these help to shape their political behaviors, and that these in turn help to shape and constrain national policy making (Aldrich, Gelpi, Feaver, Reifler, and Sharp 2006). Furthermore, the "right-wrong" criterion used in the past by certain scholars when analyzing and evaluating public attitudes has been replaced by less judgmental approaches, for instance, the *real-to-random continuum*, which examines to what extent attitudes are based on knowledge of relevant facts, and not whether they are stable, or "right" or "wrong" (see, e.g., Sinnott 2000). Thus, in his comprehensive study of American public opinion on foreign policy matters, Holsti concludes that although the American public is not well informed about many aspects of foreign affairs,[8] its opinions are usually stable and reasonable reactions to real-world events. They are also not lacking in structure and can often have an important impact on foreign policy (Holsti 2004).

The greater credit given today to public positions is accompanied by much more interest in its internal diversity. We therefore see intensive scholarly examination of the national consensus in various countries and particularly of the deep cleavages that developed in it in many countries in the West, and mainly in the United States after the end of the Cold War (e.g., Wittkopf 1990). All studies of the matter reveal that public opinion is not unified and that different public sectors hold distinctive national security preferences. The conclusion is that decision makers do not face *one* public opinion, but *several* public opinions to which they should try to be attentive if they wish the support of the electorate. The differences among the views, attitudes, and sentiments put forward by different public groups and sectors can be attributed to a variety of sociodemographic and sociopolitical determinants, such as place of residence, income, gender, generation, education, religion, and race, which have been closely studied in the United States and in other countries (e.g., Hermann and Yuchtman-Yaar 2002). The critical factors change from one national context to another, although some valid generalizations can be made in this regard. For example, higher education tends to go hand in hand with lower support for the use of military means in the international arena. Urban people are more interested in foreign affairs than the residents of remote agricultural communities, and, by and large, women seem to hold more "middle-of-the-road" views and are less self-assured when it comes to national security matters.

A very interesting and related question, which has been much studied in the literature, is how does the public shape its views on national security – what

---

[8] It appears that today, probably to a large extent because of the variety of media available to the average person, people all over the world have become more interested in international relations. Thus, the World Public Opinion survey of 2007, which polled over 21,000 people in 15 countries, found that in all countries, at least two-thirds of the interviewees said that they were somewhat or very interested in news about relations of their country with other countries (World Public Opinion, 6).

are the main sources of information used, who are the relevant social agents whose interpretations are regarded as relevant to the matter, and so forth. Because national policy matters are by nature remote for most citizens of democratic states (although much less so in countries like Israel, because of its ongoing involvement in a protracted conflict), most information about the events as well as the formal decisions made in this regard are brought to the public by "impersonal" information resources, such as the mass media (e.g., Margolis and Mauser 1990, Gamson 1992; Mutz 1998) and, today the Internet. Still, in almost every study, significant correlation is found between individuals belonging to, for example, specific churches and other reference groups such as ethnic groups or even professions, and the views of those individuals on national security matters. This is true too of the correlation between these views and the individual's gender and other sociopolitical characteristics. This in turn suggests that the impersonal information provided by the media does not remain impersonal, and that it is absorbed by the public after it goes through a variety of rather personal sociodemographic and socioeconomic "filters." This once again sustains the argument presented previously, that in reality there is more than one all-inclusive public *opinion*, but rather different public *opinions*.

This leads us to another fairly new source of concern, which indicates the greater importance attributed today to the public's views on national security matters: the gaps between the preferences of the leaders and those of the public. Empirical studies indicate that although some of these gaps can be explained by lower attention and less information available to the public compared with the political elites, other gaps are found to be the result of a different set of values and interests of each side. This implies that what motivates and appeals to the nation's leaders does not necessarily motivate and appeal to that nation's citizens (Page and Barabas 2000). This in turn casts some doubt on the adequacy of the pure representative model of democracy and sustains the logic of participatory democracy, because if the representatives do not consider the representation of their constituencies' values and interests as their ultimate duty, the people should have more voice and perhaps even easier access to the deliberations, if not directly to decision-making processes.

As the main source of information to the citizenry, the various media form a critical link between the decision makers and the public. Apparently, in today's world, to succeed in mobilizing enough support for their foreign policy, national leaders need to "sell" their versions or framings of political events to the news media and through them to the public. Since the end of the Cold War, however, with the unprecedented erosion in the moral authority of political elites, journalists have increasingly resisted the official framing, and in many cases offer their own interpretation on events. What then determines whether the media accept or reject the official perspective? What are the consequences that this new media environment might have for policy making and public opinion? Entman (2004) introduces a *cascading activation* model to explain news framing.[9] Whereas the classic *indexing* model holds that news reflects the dominant, homogeneous narrative of the political elites, according to the alternative cascading-activation model, political communication goes both ways: each elite (congressmen, ex-government officials, lobbyists, academic experts) is discretely guided and constrained by the news, just as news organizations tailor the news to public opinion, actual or anticipated.

The next question is what determines the influence of public opinion on the policy-making system? In the past, it was assumed that the major determinant was the issue at stake; for example, the common wisdom reflected in the Almond-Lippmann consensus was that national politics is almost immune to public influence. More recent empirical studies, however, suggest that the impact of public opinion is determined not so much by the specific issues involved or by the particular pattern of public attitudes as by the specific political establishment structure and the coalition-building processes among the elites (e.g., Risse-Kappen 1991). The government-opposition relations were also identified in the literature as a critical factor in the amount of influence over the decision making that nongovernmental actors can exert. It appears that the more in concert on a specific issue that the government and the opposition are, the less the leaders have to listen to the people. When the government and the opposition do not see eye to eye, however, they compete over the public's support and become more attentive to the electorate's preferences (Hagan 1993).

Even those contemporary studies, which still perceive public opinion as mainly a constraint rather than a legitimate source of influence on national security affairs (e.g., Sobel 2001, Burstein 2003), acknowledge decision makers' high levels of sensitivity to public opinion trends and therefore indirectly also the bottom-up flow of influence. It is no secret that office holders in almost all democratic (and also nondemocratic) countries use a wide range of means to test the waters on the grassroots level before making a strategic decision – no national leader in today's world is likely to embark on innovative foreign policy without working out the chances that the majority of the nation will eventually rally around the flag. In his study of the American public's influence on U.S. foreign policy since the Vietnam War, Sobel uses what he recognizes as "simple and powerful methodology" to support this statement about the leaders' attentiveness to public opinion by

... using their words, typically in public statements and memoirs, as prima facie evidence. If decision-makers refer to public opinion or polls, they show a sensitivity to public attitudes. If they discuss the need for public support or discuss the way their decisions are limited by public opinion, they admit an influence of public opinion. If they mention or intimate that they might have done more with higher support, they suggest constraints (Sobel 2001, 6).

---

[9] Entman defines framing similarly to the definition used by social movements scholars: "The process of selecting and enhancing some aspects of a perceived reality, and enhancing the salience of an interpretation and evaluation of that reality" (Entman 2004, 5).

It is therefore almost a truism to state today that

Relations between governments may dominate the news but public opinion plays a significant role in influencing the nature and direction of these relationships. While this influence is greater in some countries than in others, its presence can be found in all nations. Government leaders arise from the broader culture in which they live. Understanding this context better can provide insight into the behavior of governments (World Public Opinion 2007, 5).

The role of the public in national security matters is even formally acknowledged in various contemporary peace agreements that allocate a specific role to civil society in the transformation of the relationships between the former enemies (Bell and O'Rourke 2007). The specific clauses in these peace agreements allow civil society to take part in the "big bang" that peace agreements create in various ways: humanitarian relief, legitimizing peace agreements and resulting administrations, peace agreement monitoring, and the like (ibid.). Peace organizations are perhaps the civil society organizations most involved in first pushing toward the signing of peace agreements and afterward and in sustaining the authorities' efforts to translate these documents into a new reality. If this translation process does not occur, reality is not changed, and the peace accords turn into worthless paper.

Clearly, in all places and at all times, most citizens, even those who hold solid attitudes on one issue or another, will normally stay at home or, in the better case, observe the political "gladiators" fighting each other in the political arena. The interesting question that the theories thus need to answer is what are the relations between the general public (the audience) and the active groups, such as the peace movement? *The* public, as Warner explicates, "is a kind of social totality. Its most common sense is that of the people in general.... *the* public, as a people, is thought to include everyone within the field in question ... even though to speak of a national public implies that others exist ... whenever one is addressed as *the* public, the others are assumed not to matter" (Warner 2002, 49). According to Warner, *the* public is different from *a* public, which he defines as a space of discourse." A public, he maintains, is

...never just the sum of persons who happen to exist. It must first of all have some way of organizing itself as a body and of being addressed in discourse.... A public can only produce a sense of belonging and activity if it is self-organized through discourse rather through an external framework.... Belonging to a public seems to require at least minimal participation (op. cit., 50, 51, 52).

How do *a* public's sentiments and opinion, then, become politically operative? For members of a specific sociopolitical collective, these are shaped through their multiple social relations – with family members, neighbors, coworkers, friends, media reports, and others. Numerous studies have also confirmed that people are aware of their own attitudinal positioning vis-à-vis the mainstream, or *the* public, and this is, for example, how the "spiral of silence"[10] phenomenon comes to life (Noelle-Neumann 1993). Public opinion polls based on random national samples therefore are unlikely to pinpoint the preferences of small political minorities. Despite their numerical marginality, however, these minorities, each of which is *a* public in Warner's terms, are often more relevant to policy making than the majority – *the* public, because if they become organized, they are highly likely to overcome the paralyzing effect of the "spiral of silence" and are more prone to become politically active. Politicians pay attention to minorities because they embody the risk of massive and organized public protest for or against moves, and acquire "voice," whereas the majority often remains silent.

The relations between *a* public (e.g., a social movement) and *the* public often take an "oppositional" pattern, turning the former into a *counterpublic*. A counterpublic (in our case, the peace movement) is thus defined in relation to *the* public (general public opinion) – a premise on which the call here for the inclusion of general public opinion into the movement's POS is based. The conflict between the two

extends not just to ideas or policy questions, but to the speech genres and modes of address that constitute *the* public.... The discourse that constitutes it [the counterpublic – TH] is not merely a different or alternative idiom, but one that in other contexts would be regarded with hostility or with a sense of indecorousness.... Alternative or counterpublics are often cast as social movements, thereby acquiring agency in relation to the state (Warner, 86).

By now, it is hoped, the relevance of both social movements inquiry and public opinion scholarship has already been established. What is still lacking is the conceptual link between the two bodies of knowledge. Such a link, it is maintained here, is offered by the pluralist theory of democracy, according to which public opinion is expressed through the competition between several organized nongovernmental groups: "The only opinion, the only one which exists, is the opinion, the will, of special groups" (Everson 1982, 12). Public opinion is translated from a potentiality to a political reality when latent groups become active, often in the shape of a social movement:

Democracy is certainly not possible in the new millennium if it applies only to politicians elected to office through the work of campaigners who then withdraw and expect their candidates to intuit their will. While direct democracy...is impractical on a national or international stage, representative democracy does not work without the continued activism of many ordinary citizens.... Without citizens' commitments to put their own

---

[10] Because they fear social rejection, people will be unwilling to publicly express their opinion if they believe they are in the minority, although in fact they might hold a majority position without knowing it (pluralistic ignorance). Public opinion polls are a means of empirically establishing what the majority position is, thereby often changing the structure of opinion in a given society as people who remained silent based on their perception that theirs was a minority opinion, begin to express it and even become politically active once they realize that it is actually a majority position.

bodies on the line and their willingness to demonstrate in front of courthouses and congresses, there can be no democracy (Kaplan 1997, 188).

For years now, pluralist theory has been the target of extremely severe criticism because of its emphasis on the role of competing interest groups and lobbies, without taking much interest in noninstitutionalized groups nor in the gate-keeping forces that in practice exclude large public sectors from entering this competitive arena, although theoretically, it is open to everyone. The pluralist school is returning to center stage today, however, this time with the growing realization that there is in fact neither empirical nor normative justification for distinguishing between interest groups and other sociopolitical associations, including social movements and citizens' campaigns: "There exist simply organizations – interest organizations – trying to influence public policy" (Burstein 1999, 19). The new pluralist versions also put forward open recognition that the chances of the various players are by no means even. This intellectual "repentance," which allows for a wider variety of political actors to be considered relevant and yet recognizes that they do not enter the arena on equal footing, seems to make the pluralist approach quite a suitable option for framing the race in which the peace movements compete to make their voice heard by decision makers. It also contributes to the understanding of how the various competitors address the public so that unorganized individuals support their cause and do not stand behind other competitors who also aspire to influence the making of national security policy.

Peace Movements as Social Movements and National Security Agents

Peace movements manifest all the features of a social movement, including a common purpose, solidarity, and ongoing interaction with the general public and decision makers. Ironically, although their main goal is the reduction or elimination of warfare, the notion of conflict – taken as a core feature of such gatherings by Diani and others – is always at the heart of these movements' activities. This has two main reasons: first, although peace movements as such do not foster political realism, which is normally adhered to by national leaders, they do acknowledge the international reality of conflicts and look for means other than war to managing or even resolving them. Peace movements, much like everyone else around them, do not turn a blind eye to intergroup or international tensions and enmities, nor do they foresee a concrete world in which the wolf dwells peacefully with the lamb.

Second, almost by nature, peace movements often stand at the heart of heated political conflict because they are often widely perceived as politically problematic. Leaders' speeches, media reports, and public opinion surveys reveal that the accusation most frequently aimed at peace movements is that they are either politically naïve or, worse, they cater more to the needs and interests of the other side – the enemy – than they are concerned with the interests and well-being of their co-patriots and country. This stereotypical image engenders rather negative and sometimes even violent reactions in individuals and state agencies, which view themselves as the sole protectors of the nation's interests. Thus, the European pacifists of the 1930s and 1940s were accused of siding with the fascist regimes, the American anti-Vietnam war protesters of the late 1960s were charged of siding with Hanoi, and those who protested the installation of Pershing missiles in Europe in the late 1970s were accused of supporting and being supported by Moscow. As is discussed in detail hereafter, Israeli peace activists are widely considered "Arab lovers," and it was even occasionally suggested that they served as agents of the other side for money.

Like other social movements, peace movements are also highly wide-ranging ideologically and operationally. Hence, one retrospective observation of the anti-Vietnam war movement, which is also highly applicable to the Israeli case, maintains that in fact it was not one movement but a highly diversified combination of "mobilizations and moratoria, letter-writing campaigns, draft resistance, silent vigils, tax protests, picketing, teach-ins, court cases, electoral politics, petitions and newspaper advertisements, civil disobedience, and even self-immolation" (Small and Hoover 1992, xv). The peace groups are usually small, but even here their size can move between small cells and tiny groups to medium-sized movements, with some correlation between the size of the group and its ideology – the smaller groups are usually also the more radical ones and vice versa – the larger are the more moderate.

Following the typologies of movements presented earlier, as to their aims, none of the peace movements are power oriented, that is, striving to take over the nation's official decision-making positions. As to their ideational orientation, they do not necessarily share one core. They are often spread along a moderate-radical continuum, that is, varying from norm-oriented movements to value-oriented ones and are thus perceived differently by the general public and the political elites: the largest and moderate ones are usually seen as respectable, whereas others are perceived as weird (e.g., the extremely pacifist ones). Often, when small and radical, ideologically or operationally (e.g., those that use nonviolent resistance techniques such as chaining themselves to the fences of army camps or sitting on railroad tracks used by trains carrying nuclear weapons), peace groups might even be framed as revolutionary and therefore threatening.

Most contemporary peace movements, including the Israeli one, belong to the new social movement category. They focus on the nation's power relations: oppose war and other forms of military force as means of settling ethnonational and international conflicts. From their focus, then, they are concerned with a classic "public good": national security, a term they prefer to replace with the more universal one – human security ("freedom from fear and freedom from want," according to the 1994 UNDP definition). Such security is – theoretically at least – equally relevant to all segments and members of a given of society and not to a specific class or social sector. A closer look, however, reveals that today most peace activists (although not necessarily supporters) belong to the specific socioeconomic-political stratum often referred to in the literature as the *new middle class* (e.g., Eder 1993, 166–167). This human composition led their opponents occasionally to claim that the avoidance of armed conflict advocated by the peace movements is not completely class detached, because peace better serves the interests of certain societal groups than others. For example, it might have a positive effect on the more affluent groups in the society, which are involved directly or indirectly in international commerce, but harm less well-off people serving in the army or employed in the military-industrial complex. Apparently, if the peace movement's advice is followed, the army would let off many of its servicemen, and the conflict-related industries – many of their workers. Furthermore, if peace prevails, other industries could be relocated to former enemy territories, if labor were cheaper there. Therefore, it is not unusual for peace movements to be perceived by certain public sectors as their bitter rivals on the economic, although not necessarily on the purely ideological, level.

As mentioned above, social movements are often organizationally and ideologically heterogeneous. Thus, the peace movements' "red line" regarding the use of force, the topic at the heart of their agenda, is often not agreed on unanimously. Therefore, pacifist activists and movements (which in almost every country are a tiny minority even within the peace movement) oppose all use of force, some on universal moral grounds, others on religious grounds (most often Christianity, Hinduism, or Buddhism, since mainstream Islam and Judaism do not hold antiwar creeds). Political antiwar movements and activists, on the other hand, normally object to a particular military campaign because they consider the specific conflict to be resolvable by other means, but basically accept, or at least do not reject, the notion of a just war.[11] For example, they might define a war as "just" in the case of self-defense or when its aim is to come to the rescue of others who are being brutally victimized (e.g., peace-keeping operations). Some researchers use the term *pacificism* to describe the opposition to a war on political or practical grounds, in contrast to principled pacifism, which rejects war and militarism per se.[12] It should be stressed here, however, that in itself, opposition to the use of force as a means of attaining certain collective goals does not make a movement a peace movement. For example, national liberation movements that rely on nonviolent resistance because of strategic or tactical considerations are not automatically peace movements, because their main aim is not the prevention of war or reduction of conflict. They simply pragmatically believe that because of the large disparity in power existing between the two sides, a nonviolent struggle is more likely to achieve their goals (Sharp 1984).

The intermittent course of peace activism summarized here points to a major and universal feature of this sort of grassroots political participation: it appears, disappears, and then reappears, beautifully illustrated as a

---

[11] For a definition of the "just war" concept, see Walzer 1977.
[12] For a discussion of the term *pacificism*, see Hermann 1989 and 1993a.

"whale-swim" (Young 1986). This pattern has its pros and cons; from the organizational point of view, it is problematic because time after time, campaigns have to be built almost from scratch. Ideological continuity and member loyalty are difficult to maintain under such circumstances. On the other hand, the pattern enables peace activism to maintain its fresh and young image and to slow down the institutionalization and hence the degeneration of peace groups. Finally, recollections of success can fade with the whale's disappearance below the water's surface. However, this is also true for the much more common situation when peace activism fails to achieve its goals, in which case a new page can be a blessing.

Organized resistance to war dates back almost to the beginnings of war. Almost everyone is familiar with the women's sex strike that Lysistrata led in ancient Athens (5th century BC), as described in 411 BC by Aristophanes. Early Christianity also advocated pacifism, although as early as the fourth century, the church, which had become the church of the Roman state, adopted, instead of pacifism, just war as its official dogma. In fifteenth century Europe, the reformation movement challenged the established church by, among others, rejecting the 'just war' dogma and reopening the theological door to Christ's original pacifism. This shift served as fertile ground for the emergence of a variety of pacifist sects, some of which still exist today, such as the Brethrens, the Anabaptists, and the Mennonites. Persecuted by the early European states because of their absolute refusal to carry arms, large groups of these sects left the old continent for America, where they were welcomed by the Quakers, who also professed a pacifist creed (e.g., Brock 1972, Chatfield 1973). In America and in certain European countries at certain periods, members of pacifist churches were granted the legal status of conscientious objectors and were exempt from military service, a precedent on which later political war resisters rested their case.

The nineteenth and early twentieth centuries saw the emergence of a plethora of peace groups and movements in Europe, England, and the United States. These were based on various ideological grounds: isolationist sentiments in the United States, pacifism à la Tolstoy mostly in Europe, women's war resistance, and on both sides of the ocean, socialist movements that justified rejection of war on the basis of solidarity of the proletariat, an argument that collapsed under the pressure of swelling patriotism with the outbreak of WWI. Although there were manifestations of pacifism in the 1930s, notably in leading English universities where the appeasement policy was celebrated, pacifism gained little public support or influence on either side of the ocean because of the black-and-white nature of WWII – a modern crusade of good against evil.[13]

The Gandhian liberation struggle of the 1940s made the Hindu legacies of nonviolence globally known, but a few more years elapsed before these were incorporated into the strategic repertoire of peace movements in other parts of the world. Except for a few highly contested manifestations of

---

[13] For sharp criticism of the intellectual pacifism of the 1930s, see Benda 1941.

anti-nuclear activism in the early 1950s (mainly the Moscow-supported World Peace Movement, which organized the Stockholm Appeal signed by millions all over the world), it was almost 20 years after the defeat of Nazism and Fascism before a massive grassroots campaign could emerge in the West and gain legitimacy. With the dissipation of the trauma of these totalitarian regimes, which had used mass mobilization as their main political tool, the mid-1960s witnessed the blooming, in the United States but also in Europe (mainly Germany), of a massive, young, and vigorous antiwar movement in response to expanding U.S. military involvement in Southeast Asia. This campaign, which was in a sense the prototype of contemporary peace campaigns, has been the subject of numerous studies (e.g., Lake 1976, Small and Hoover 1992), because it epitomized the growing legitimization of citizens' involvement in the realm of foreign and security policy, as well as the rejection of Cold War logic. From this point on, the traditional taboo on civil involvement in the "high" politics of international relations, particularly "when the guns are firing," was shattered.

Furthermore, apparently the anti-Vietnam war campaign contributed to the development of the Vietnam syndrome, that is, awareness on the part of decision makers all over the world of the political costs of military actions – that such actions might produce intensive grassroots protest against an ongoing war. Although grassroots pressure in America seemed not to be the main reason for ending the war (Brown 1976), it clearly changed the prevailing views on the potential penalties that leaders who opt for highly unpopular foreign policies might have to pay. Indeed, legacies of the anti-Vietnam campaign, which often used techniques of nonviolent resistance, fuelled massive demonstrations in the Netherlands, England, and other European countries in the late 1970s against the installation of Pershing II missiles (e.g., Eichenberg 1989) as well as the activities of the Nuclear Freeze movement in the United States in the early 1980s (e.g., Meyer 1990).

The dramatic events of 1989 inspired a flow of explanations for the collapse of the Soviet bloc. Some academic analysts, using historical process-tracing research methods, went as far as to suggest that peace movements in the East, which were openly (or covertly) supported and assisted by their Western counterparts, significantly contributed to this strategic transformation by introducing critical alternatives to the security debate in both East and West in the late 1980s (Meyer 1999, 183–184). The peace campaigns promoted policy alternatives that slowly percolated into the public mind and heart (op. cit., 184). More mainstream analyses would question the assessment that the peace movements in the East contributed even minimally to the collapse of the Soviet bloc, but even they would often admit that human rights campaigns and activities of churches in the West might have had such an effect.

The next, and thus far, last wave of antiwar activism was apparently quite ineffective tactically, although not necessarily in strategic terms. On perhaps the widest scale ever, around the globe – from Australia and Japan, to Europe, to the Americas – multiparticipant global civil protest swelled in late 2002 and early 2003 in opposition to the planned American military campaign in

Iraq. Millions of people of all races, ages, religions, classes, education, and gender marched in the streets of Tokyo, Sydney, Tel Aviv, Rome, Paris, London, Madrid, Buenos Aires, and Rio de Janeiro calling for a nonmilitary resolution to the conflict. This was an unprecedented overseas antiwar campaign, which relied heavily on new communication technologies. Obviously, from the tactical point of view, it was a failure, because these protests failed to stop the war that began in March 2003. Despite the high visibility and extensive media coverage of the global antiwar campaign and its strong public voice, the war was launched by the Bush administration with the support of several European governments (and the opposition of others). This failure can be attributed to the fact that larger numbers of citizens in the United States and Europe supported the war, citizens who, according to the polls, approved of the campaign against Saddam Hussein. This fact is important, because when we focus on peace activism, we often tend to forget that in almost all cases we are discussing a minority, albeit vociferous, opinion that as such has poorer prospects of effecting national policies. As Burstein correctly observed, "elected officials are intensely concerned about reelection; they must respond, first and foremost, to the wishes of a majority of their constituents. When these wishes are clear and strongly felt, interest organizations cannot directly influence policy" (Burstein 1999, 19). Very few, however, would challenge the statement that this global antiwar protest suggests that the legitimization of the war as a means of conducting foreign and security policy has been diminishing in the last few decades and that the peace movements have gotten closer than they have ever been to the mainstream in this regard.

Apparently, because of certain strategic global developments today, the peace movements' chances of winning the public attention and hence that of the leaders are better than in the past. First, there are the achievements of semipeace campaigns, mainly the anti-mine movement, on which there seems to be a wide consensus. Although this movement was promoted by celebrities such as the late Princess Diana, it gained power and effect because of the persistence and dedication of numerous, less glamorous, local activists. As already mentioned, some scholars attribute the shattering of the Soviet bloc civil foundations at least in part to the chain of mostly nonviolent grassroots revolutions influenced by the example set by peace activism in the West in the 1970s and 1980s (e.g., Sedaitis and Butterfield 1991, Meyer 1999). Another apparent success is the emergence of the worldwide peace/anti-globalization movement. The combination of CMC and the movement's innovative message sharply increased the public visibility of grassroots activism, reduced the sense of isolation of small, local groups of activists, enabled the organization of campaigns on a global scale, and expanded the availability of financial resources and the ability to transfer them from one place to another. The fact that the meetings of G8 leaders take place today under the shadow of possible interruptions by activists has dramatically increased the sense that although perhaps difficult to measure, citizens' activism could well become politically effective. This model has encouraged local grassroots endeavors, including the Israeli peace movement. It has also left its mark on politicians' and analysts' perceptions of their potential efficacy.

Another, and perhaps even more conducive factor from the peace movements' point of view is the emergence in many democracies of "anti-politics" sentiment, that is, growing public skepticism with the political establishment and the political leaders' wisdom, sincerity, and dedication to the promotion of the public good (Schedler 1997, Boggs 2000, Hay 2007). Specifically, at present, it is much more difficult for the political and military elites to convince the public in the West of the necessity of military operations (Everts and Isernia 2001) and to justify their costs in human life and material resources. Apparently, never in the past would an anti-presidential, anti-administration documentary film such as Michael Moore's *Fahrenheit 9/11*, which openly cast doubt on the motivation of American leaders for launching their War on Terrorism, have been screened all over the world and been applauded by so many. Beyond the basic erosion in people's trust of their leaders, the close media coverage of the conduct of wars today, including the horrible damage inflicted on the other side, also seems to sustain the moral arguments made by peace movements, humanize the enemy, and bolster the legitimacy of the peace activists to become an agent in the public debate over national security matters.

Of note is the special situation of peace organizations against the background of growing global criticism of civil society organizations that unintentionally serve the neo-conservative goal of "liberating" the state of its responsibility to maintain the welfare, health, education, security, and other aspects of community life and reducing its investment in social services. Today it is often argued that by stepping into the lacunae created by the state's well-calculated withdrawal from these budget-consuming roles, service-providing civil society organizations actually operate as safety valves that prevent the accumulation of societal pressures that might otherwise erupt and shake the malfunctioning state apparatus. This is because the citizens to whom they cater do not have the urge (or the rage) to put pressure on the state to fulfill its duty to grant them these services. Whether correct or mistaken, this criticism does not apply to the peace organizations sector, as here the reverse is actually true – it is the citizens who need to force their way into a realm that governments would like to maintain as their sole patrimony and would prefer not to let anyone else enter. Peace organizations actually claim a voice and influence on matters of high politics that no government would willingly release, be the regime democratic, autocratic, totalitarian, capitalist, socialist, or communist. In other words, peace movements do not contribute to the "privatization" of the state's national security duties but rather try to interfere with the state's absolute control in this regard.

The study of the outcomes of social activism is one of the most interesting, yet perhaps not surprisingly, least investigated topics in social movement literature (e.g., Giugni 1998, 372). The reasons for this scholarly lacuna are both theoretical and methodological. To start with, no rigorous agreed-on criteria exist for assessing the outcome – success or failure – of collective behavior because, owing to its essentially uninstitutionalized nature, the aims of the action are not always put forward clearly. Having no clear-cut list of goals, different analysts often assess the achievements of the same movement differently, thus creating a critical problem of subjectivity. For example, Sam Brown, a central activist in the anti-Vietnam War movement, views it as a failure: "Although the antiwar movement had strategic goals . . . , it accomplished very little of what it set out to do" (Brown 1976, 121). Melvin Small, a student of this movement, presents the opposite view: "Although attracting attention did not result in any immediate policy changes, it did contribute to the overall official perception of growing dissatisfaction with the administration's programs" (Small and Hoover 1992, 196).

The relatively rare efficacy studies (e.g., Gamson 1990, Rochon and Mazmanian 1993, Giugni 1999) usually concentrate on two main inputs – external and internal:

a. Which strategies work or do not work for a social movement when dealing with the "outside" bodies, and under which circumstances? For example, when and to what extent are disruptive strategies (in particular, violence) effective?

b. What are the organizational features that determine the social movement's achievements?

Some classic assertions state, for example, that the use of disruptive tactics is positively associated with goal achievement, that single-issue groups are more successful than multiple-issue ones, that the use of selective incentives correlates positively with success in terms of mobilization, and that more bureaucratized, centralized, and unfactionalized groups are more likely to succeed than others (e.g., Gamson 1990). However, there is no consensus among scholars on these assertions and certain empirical studies indeed question them in terms of the movement's success in gaining long-lasting political impact (e.g., Kitschelt 1986, Burstein 1999; della Porta 1999). Other studies focused more on specific policy changes as they relate to the movements' demands (e.g., Piven and Cloward 1977). This approach has apparent disadvantages, however: even if one assumes that social movements make rational efforts that aim at a defined social change, the consequences of these efforts are often unintended and not always related to the demands, and vice versa – changes in the desired direction are not necessarily the outcome of their own activity (Giugni 1999).

This relates to what appears to be the greatest problem in assessing a social movement's efficacy: the difficulty in establishing *causality*. Valid efficacy assessment necessarily involves establishing causal relations between the decisions or actions taken by the movement and the observed political changes. When complex, multifaceted phenomena such as national decision-making processes are considered (particularly critical decisions such as launching war or making peace, which are the highest priorities for so many actors in the system), such causality is almost impossible to establish, let alone measure. Actually, it is the accumulation of the indistinguishable effects of numerous factors that usually gives rise to such political outcomes (Tilly 1999, 268–270). Students of political elites often prefer to overlook difficulties in determining causality and make do with establishing circumstantial linkages between decisions and results, based on the widespread assumption that the authorized decision makers' impact on critical political processes is both the greatest and the most self-evident. Only few would doubt, for example, that Yitzhak Rabin and Shimon Peres directly influenced the change in Israel's foreign policy, as expressed in the Oslo process. Such a laid-back approach, however, is not feasible when evaluating the efficacy of non-establishment political actors such as social movements or other nongovernmental political actors, including peace movements.

Indeed, the question of efficacy bothers peace activists in all countries, because whether they feel themselves to be winners or losers, their ability to claim credit and get it is quite limited. First, peace movements have no legal or other authority and are not part of the formal national political decision-making process, nor are they politically accountable. Thus the activities of peace organizations, particularly because they focus on matters of high politics, are often presented by leaders and perceived by the general public as impairing the basic representative principle that underpins the democratic system (thus far, direct democracy has not been adopted by any state on the national level). For obvious reasons, it is easier for peace movements and similar bodies to gain influence in political systems in which the notion of participatory democracy prevails. Even then, most politicians, wishing to manifest their tenacity and professionalism, tend to deny that such external actors have any political influence on their decisions. This is a global phenomenon, as observed in the following assessment of the American anti-Vietnam War movement:

Given the officials' proud tradition of refusing to admit that they might bow to the caprices of an uninformed public, those interested in the impact of dissenters on them must use a variety of sources and methods that may lead to what are, at best, educated guesses about the problem.... I generally backed off from the direct question of influence and satisfied myself with trying to discover what drew the decision-makers' attention – what impressed them among the welter of the dissenting activities of the period (Adams, in Small and Hoover 1992, 186).

Second, peace organizations touch on matters of national security that are – according to the pluralist model – of interest to numerous political, economic, religious, and other social, economic, and political actors. Through their efforts to influence national policy, these movements thus enter a race in competition with stronger, wealthier, and more experienced participants, some with agendas that fit that of the peace movement and some with contradicting ones. In such a crowded arena, even if the pluralist logic is adopted, the particular effect of the peace movement is very difficult, if not totally impossible, to isolate.

A third stumbling block in assessing the efficacy of peace movements is the structured tension that they experience between sticking to purist agendas and consolidating a wide support base. Purist agendas define principles by which the state should "behave" in the international arena. Thus, if the movement first puts forward such clear policy guidelines and afterward the national policy changes in this direction, efficacy is somewhat easier to establish. However, it will always be impossible to eliminate alternative explanations for this change; for example, for the movement to prove beyond doubt that no other factors also contributed to or determined this change. In terms of mobilizing extensive support, such a purist agenda is a nonstarter. On the other hand, the adoption of a broad, less strictly defined platform enables the movement to address wider audiences. Unfortunately, such an "airy" platform not only alienates hard-core activists who tend to be on the purist side but also makes it far more difficult for the movement to claim credit for bringing about specific political changes.

A fourth difficulty in assessing the efficacy of peace organizations is the high probability of unsound or biased evaluation. Because these groups exert influence over policy-making processes mainly through indirect channels, solid documentation of these interactions is practically nonexistent. In other words, even if peace organizations were indeed effective, retrospective studies would not be able to detect their influence through official records. Furthermore, mainstream historiographers tend to document and analyze political developments as they are viewed from the political center. They are therefore inclined to underestimate or even completely dismiss the influence exerted by extraparliamentary bodies such as peace movements, which are located on the political periphery. Who maintains records and which kinds of records? Normally, it is the movement's core members who keep some meeting protocols, brochures, lists of members, and so forth. However, this documentation is almost always incomplete, unorganized, often undated, and of course partial. For example, a peace activist is highly unlikely to keep records in which the movement is presented negatively. He or she will, however, keep records of events that indicate success, such as reports of large demonstrations. It is therefore very difficult to establish, by regular academic standards, valid cause-and-effect assessment, based on such partial records.[14]

A fifth impediment to developing a correct assessment of peace activism's achievements and failures has to do with its usually rough interface with the mainstream. Admittedly, the public-counterpublic conflict motif is very noticeable in the relations of peace movements and the general public in which they are embedded. Their universal or objective positions and activities are

---

[14] The lack of reliable records is particularly problematic when trying to get a proper sense of a social movement's cash flow and funding. The first, and lesser, impediment is practical: such organizations, in particular the smaller ones, often fail to keep orderly financial records and, as they come and go, the past documentation, even if once available, is often lost or thrown away. The lack of proper documentation can also be explained by the fact that administrative functions are often kept to a bare minimum and carried out by volunteers. Finally, in certain cases, social activists are quite conspicuously unwilling to discuss financial issues, although very interested in discussing ideological and other operational matters. Apparently, particularly the activists of the more radical groups are apprehensive that the disclosure of their donors' identities, even when legal, could lead to further negative stigmatization of the group.

often interpreted by the mainstream, politicians and ordinary citizens alike, as a threat to the national consensus, and sometimes even to national security, because peace activists often try to put themselves in the shoes of the "other side," the enemy, or judge their own nation's policies and activities from an external point of view. Such voluntary disassociation from the national collective poisons the movement's relations with *the* public, particularly in times of war or other forms of external conflict. At such times, *the* public's reactions to such self-positioning can be negative to the extent that the movement and its activists are ostracized or even physically harassed. Thus, even if eventually the peace movement's argument eventually does inculcate into the mainstream, its contribution is widely denied.

No wonder, then, that Kowalewski and Hoover ask, "What can movements do?" and soberly respond: "About the only thing they can do is *act*. Perhaps we call dissenters 'activists' for a good reason. Activity is one of the few components of the system they can control by shifting their responses" (Kowalewski and Hoover 1995, 121). This observation could explain the reality that peace organizations are usually not very target oriented, and that efficacy is not one of the major criteria they employ for self-assessment. Many activists continue to participate in peace activities regardless of their effectiveness, because they obtain some other benefits from doing so, such as solidarity, social support, an outlet for their personal frustration with the situation, or other rewards.

This does not mean that peace activists are not interested in improving their abilities and that they do not ask themselves what went wrong. A fine example of this self-reflection can be found in a recent internal discussion around the American anti-Iraq peace movement's achievements, or lack thereof (Wittner 2007):

One explanation for the weakness of the U.S. peace movement... is that demagogues spouting patriotic propaganda easily hoodwink people.... People can be convinced to rally 'round the flag', but not all the time and not indefinitely. Both the Vietnam War and the Iraq War provide illustrations of how popular sentiment can grow increasingly dovish as a war's consequences become clear.

Another explanation... is that the Democratic Party is a sort of reactionary vampire that schemes, successfully, to drain the blood of the peace movement.... But this explanation begs the issue. After all, if the peace movement were strong enough, would the Democratic Party dare to abandon it? Perhaps the peace constituency is actually one constituency among many that is wooed at election time, but is too disorganized and ephemeral to have more than marginal influence on public policy.

A third explanation for the peace movement's ineffectiveness is that corporate, communications, and political elites favor policies of militarism and imperialism.... But, even if [this explanation] is correct, what can the peace movement do about it?... [T]he movement will have to face the unpleasant reality that simply securing majority support for its programs will not be sufficient to secure victory....

There is another source of movement weakness, however, that the peace movement can control more readily – and that is its own structure and focus.... Indeed, it suffers from the great American disease of individualism, atomization, and sectarianism. What it needs is collective action and solidarity. And what it has is thousands of groups, mostly small, each pursuing its own projects and going its own way. Not surprisingly, then, the movement is not as powerful as it likes to claim, and politicians do not always take it very seriously.

To sum up, indeed, as social movements, the peace movements' political efficacy is basically more limited and more difficult to establish than that of other political agents. Furthermore, the content of their message often places them head on against the mainstream – both the political elite and the general public. There seem to be some strategies, however, by which these movements can increase their voice and perhaps even effect influence, particularly as today's *Zeitgeist* is much in concert with these movements' ideology and spirit.

Methodology

"The methodological repertoire employed by students of social movements is extremely rich: it includes both quantitative and qualitative studies, surveys and in-depth interviews, archival studies and participant observations, single-case studies and complex comparative designs, mathematical simulations and protest event analysis, ecological studies of multi-organizational fields and life-history interviews, discourse analysis and studies of narratives" (Klandermans and Staggenborg 2002, xii). The variety of research methods used – separately or in combination – is a direct outcome of the nature of the subject matter discussed before. First, as already mentioned, the available past information on the activities and efficacy of social movements is usually limited, unorganized, partial, and often one-sided. In many cases, the researchers have to dig their way through piles of relevant and irrelevant position papers, brochures, newspaper clippings, receipts for bus transportation to demonstrations and old electric and telephone bills from offices closed years ago, in dusty suitcases, pulled out for them, after endless telephone calls, from under the sofas of former activists. (Because today much of the activity is conducted via e-mail and the Internet, the fate of future researchers will be even grimmer, as it is highly likely that no physical records at all will be maintained.) In many cases, it is impossible to determine beyond a doubt the authenticity and representativeness of these documents, because no one knows which others have been dumped and for what reasons.

If the problem of defective record keeping is somehow solved, then the researcher is faced with another problem: social movements often lack a clear organizational structure, with the result that strategy-building and decision-making processes are very difficult to follow and analyze. In "authentic" social movements, the internal hierarchy and chain of authority, if such exist, are almost always informal, either because the movement has not gone through institutionalization processes or because any form of acknowledged leadership contradicts its egalitarian ethos. Thus too many, or alternatively, no leaders can be traced to get a gist of the way strategies were decided and tactical decisions were made. Clearly then, elite-oriented research methods are irrelevant here because of this informal leadership pattern and the unique selection processes, which differ greatly from the nomination or selection procedures used in conventional political bodies. In fact, the social movements' so-called leaders are often individuals identified as such, rightly or not, by the mass media or by those who present themselves as such, and are perhaps recognized by some but not necessarily all of the movement's members. Interviews with prominent persons can therefore be of interest but can rarely represent the movement in full.

Activities of social movements tend to be sporadic and spontaneous, and therefore, rules of conduct are not only unwritten but also often nonexistent. We have already mentioned the whale-swim pattern of peace movements' life cycles, which often forces researchers into questioning whether they are looking at a resurging group (i.e., one that disappeared some months, years, or even decades before) or at a completely new formation. The fact that the human composition of the two is similar can be very misleading if one does not take into account the fact that "old soldiers never die" – that people with a propensity for grassroots activism usually get involved in various, sometimes very different, campaigns, more than once in their lifetimes. Another fact to consider when studying a social movement is the overlapping membership between certain groups in the same "industry" (SMI). When the overlap is extensive, it can be difficult to differentiate one organization (SMO) from another.

This brings us to the membership problem: many social movements are unwilling to become overly bureaucratic and therefore dispose of the formal status of membership. Furthermore, membership is not conclusive in many social movements that opt for an inclusive, open mode of participation. When this is the case, the researcher can find it very difficult or even impossible to make a valid quantitative statement about the objective size of the movement or analyze the profile of its members. In such a case, the assessment cannot go much beyond an impressionistic account. The same goes for protest-event analysis, which is also almost impossible when record keeping is poor, because police records are often closed to academic enquiry. An effort to assess the intensity and scope of social movement activity through media reports is doomed to failure, because the media often ignore small, nonviolent, or repetitious activities.

The composite research tool employed in this study tries to overcome at least some of the difficulties mentioned previously. It combines four main techniques, three of them qualitative and the last one quantitative:

Participant observation – The author participated in numerous meetings and other kinds of activities of various peace groups, moderate and radical. In larger activities, such as mass rallies and large demonstrations, the observation did not necessitate the consent of the organizers and other participants. Such consent was necessary when the meetings were closed to the public or open but very small.[15] To attend closed or small meetings, some prearrangements were necessary, normally making contact through pre-meetings with prominent activists to present them with the research purposes and to ask them to make sure that the other participants in the meeting did not mind the presence of a researcher. In most cases, the answer was positive. In all cases, however, I was asked not to cite anything said by the participants or any decisions made there. In other cases, I was asked to bring references or recommendations from other people active in the peace movement who knew me academically or socially, before the permission to attend the meeting was granted. This personal linkage might have interfered somewhat with the objectivity of the following analysis (if objectivity is at all attainable in such studies). On the other hand, it proved to be of utmost importance in gaining access to specific groups and office holders within the movements and substantiated the observation already made by others that "being a participant can facilitate access to a movement and promote the trust and rapport necessary for collecting sound data" (Blee and Taylor 2002, 97). This personal positioning helped immensely in confidence building, which is so crucial in a semi-ethnographic study, particularly when the study touches on highly sensitive issues such as personal risk, personal and collective relations and sentiments, and above all, perceived gaps between aspirations and reality. It should also be noted here that the author has been involved in several research projects and took part in political-academic meetings that included face-to-face interactions with Israeli policy-makers of the Oslo era.[16] Once again, these personal contacts made access to the decision makers and their advisers considerably easier but also could have effected the overall assessment of the peace movement's achievements and efficacy.

Qualitative content analysis of both primary sources, that is, original texts of various Israeli peace groups and peace activists (e.g., minutes of meetings, articles, brochures, advertisements, petitions, Internet websites, and messages sent to e-mail lists) and secondary sources (e.g., academic analyses, newspaper articles and editorials by academics, analysts, journalists, and politicians). Beyond achieving factual accuracy regarding events, positions, and interactions, this juxtaposition of primary and secondary sources seeks to explore and explain discrepancies (or similarities) between the movement's narrative and its

---

[15] Indeed, much has been written about the effects of a researcher present at such closed meetings. In most cases, this effect seems to be minimal. In one case, however, when disagreement between Palestinian and Jewish women participating heated up, the chairwoman, who was of course well aware of my presence there and apparently did not want the group's internal disagreements laid bare, suddenly stopped the discussion, and in a tactical move that was apparently meant to cool down the argument, asked me if my presence there was because of my "academic interest" or because I shared the group's aims. The answer that it was my academic interest resulted in the group's stopping the argument and moving on to procedural matters.

[16] E.g., the oral history research project, "What Went Wrong in the Israeli-Palestinian Peace Process?" conducted by the Leonard Davis Institute for International Relations at the Hebrew University, Jerusalem, a summary of which can be found in Kacowicz 2004.

framing of the political scene and its role in it, and views of external observers on these issues.

Personal communications by key informants: peace movement activists, politicians, journalists, and experts on Israeli politics as well as peace activists outside Israel. This source of information has been found to be particularly useful in research on loosely organized or thinly documented social movements (Blee and Taylor 2002, 93). The personal communications, the content of which, in most cases, I was again asked not to include as attributed citations, were intended to go beyond the mere facts about events or processes, and to unearth the feelings and motivations of activists, of those watching them from the side, and of their adversaries. Particularly helpful here were two meetings with activists from various peace groups organized in May and June 2004, specifically for the purpose of this study. With no public or media people present, the activists talked with remarkable openness and sincerity about their personal feelings, organizational problems and interorganizational perceptions, and networking. These discussions, carried out in Hebrew, were recorded, transcribed, and translated into English (Hermann 2005).

Public opinion polls – This was the only quantitative tool used in this study, and it was not implemented in regard to the peace movement itself but to substantiate various statements regarding their operational context, and in particular to exemplify the gaps between the movement's views and those of the general Israeli Jewish public. The importance of the POS and in particular of general public opinion for observing the positioning and positions of the peace movement has already been mentioned. The findings of public opinion for the years covered in this study are mainly based on the findings of the Peace Index polling project, which has been conducted since 1994.[17] These figures are used to compare and juxtapose the positions of the peace organizations and the views of peace activists with those of the Israeli mainstream. Points of convergence and divergence at different points of time and on different issues are thereby highlighted.

This methodological combination, it is hoped, substantiates the expectation that "different methods contribute different types of evidence and theoretical insights that add to the collective enterprise; restricting ourselves to a limited methodology would necessarily make us fall short of the theoretical synthesis needed" (Klandermans and Staggerborg 2002, xv).

Although much attention is given herein to specific Israeli peace SMOs, the efficacy of Israeli peace activism is examined in this study mainly on the *aggregate* level. In other words, the unit of analysis is the peace movement as a whole, the SMI, and only rarely individual peace organizations (SMOs). This aggregative approach can be justified on the grounds that the process involved here is of such magnitude, importance, and complexity that no single peace organization, large and successful as it might be, can claim – or be given – individual credit for it. The primary questions to be answered when assessing

---

[17] The full set of data and its analysis for these years can be found at www.tau.ac.il/peace.

efficacy on this level are (1) did the peace movement as a whole contribute anything, directly or indirectly, to the launching of the Oslo peace process? And (2) if so, to what extent and in which ways? To assess the peace movement's efficacy, one must first identify its target audiences and then explore the ways in which it conveyed its message to these audiences.

It is suggested here that the aggregate efforts of the peace movement could be declared effective if some evidence were found to indicate that it has succeeded in achieving two different sorts of goals:

Concrete and immediate – that is, promoting a specific decision that contributed to the resolution of the conflict by nonviolent means (or forestalling decisions that were meant to impede nonviolent resolution of the conflict); convincing some powerful external actors to put pressure on the parties to the conflict to promote nonviolent conflict resolution.

Intangible and long term – that is, modifying public opinion and discourse about the feasibility and desirability of conflict resolution by nonviolent means; convincing significant actors and public sectors on the "other side" that there are people of public standing on "this side" who are ready to choose nonviolent means to resolve the conflict; and/or promoting an external image of the society involved as a pluralistic and nonmonolithic one, in which significant players adhere to the idea of nonviolence.

The data presented and analyzed in this study of the peace movement were gathered in three different projects. Peace activism between 1925 and 1985 was investigated in the author's doctoral dissertation (Hermann 1989), using a mostly historical-ideological orientation. The years 1967 to 1996 were examined from the organizational point of view in the context of an international study of conflict resolution/peace organizations sponsored by the Aspen Institute – Third Sector Division (the findings of this study were published in Hermann 2002). The third enquiry project focused on the years 1993 to 2005 and was conducted under a research grant from USIP. The focus here is on the peace movement's ideological and organizational responses, first to the launching and then to the collapse of the Oslo process, and on the assessment of its political effectiveness.

3

Mapping the Israeli Sociopolitical Terrain

The Israeli peace movement's course of development, characteristics, and fate were deeply influenced by three main features of the Israeli sociopolitical terrain through which it made its way: the legacies of the troublesome Jewish historical experience as reflected in the Zionist narrative and the Israeli national ethos; the sociopolitical cleavages across Israeli society, and the political opportunity structure (POS) facing grassroots activism in general. The first two features are touched on only briefly herein because they have already been thoroughly examined in numerous other studies of Israeli society and polity.[1] The less-investigated issue, that of the national repertoire of political modes of operation, is reviewed more closely in this section.

Historical-Ideological Legacies

The troublesome history of the Jewish people, culminating in the Holocaust, and its framing by the Zionist ideology, were basically not fertile ground for the emergence of vibrant peace activism and movements. This is mainly because both fostered a negative reading of the intentions of the other nations toward the Jewish people, a reading that to this day is a cornerstone of the Israeli Jewish cognitive and emotional frames of reference.

The highly influential "victim motif" of this historical experience and framing was strengthened and not lessened by the complex situation created by the violent Arab-Jewish struggle over Palestine/the land of Israel. One of the main aims of early Zionism was *normalization* of the Jewish people from what was perceived here as an unnatural exilic state of mind and existence, to a normal, "healthy," territorially based one. This idea of normalization changed focus

---

[1] For mainstream sociopolitical analyses of Israel, see, e.g., Eisenstadt 1967, Horowitz and Lissak 1978, 1988, Arian 1995, Dowty 1998, Yaar and Shavit 2001. For critical readings of Israeli polity, see, e.g., Lustick 1980, Smooha 1997, Peled and Shafir 1996, Yiftachel 1999, Kemp et al. 2004.

from occupational structure and mentality to the development of self-defense capabilities, with the realization that the designated land – in which Zionism aspired to gather all Jews of the world, and particularly those who had been victimized in their places of residence – was not empty but populated by the Palestinians (referred to in early Zionist writings as *Arabs*). Soon enough it became clear that the Palestinians looked unfavorably on the massive Jewish return to and resettlement of their historical motherland (immigration that some scholars of the post-Zionist school characterize as colonialist).[2] Mainstream Zionism in its turn did not acknowledge the Palestinians' "natural" right to national self-determination. This mutual antagonism led rather rapidly to an open clash between the two ethnonational communities. The normalization to which the Zionists aspired was therefore now widely interpreted as a matter of attaining a military force that would ensure the safety of the Jews residing in their homeland and later in their state. For obvious reasons, this early interpretation of the Zionist normalization project gained even greater strength after the Holocaust and the 1948–1949 War of Independence, which resulted in the establishment of the State of Israel (and the destruction of Palestinian society and institutions, or the *nakba*, the Palestinian term for this national catastrophe).

The logic of self-defense and hence of a just war (of defense) has remained one of the pillars of the Israeli national ethos ever since. In fact, the peace movement, except for its tiny pacifist factions, embraced this tenet as well. What the peace activists challenged were the political conclusions drawn by the Israeli mainstream. They pointed out that at a certain point, Israel and Israeli Jews, by relying too heavily on the argument and means of self-defense, changed from victims to victimizers. This reading of the reversal of the power relations was fiercely opposed by the mainstream, who maintained and fostered the traditional view that the Jews were those whose existence was in constant peril. It is not surprising, then, that in the eyes of the Israeli Jewish majority, peace activism under such circumstances seemed irrelevant and even dangerous – it made little sense for the sheep to preach peace to the wolves.

This historical legacy of persecution and victimhood, plus the extensive and prolonged national mobilization efforts of the Zionist endeavor needed for the realization of the dream of national renaissance (particularly against the background of the ongoing external struggle[3]), contributed significantly to the creation of a uniform collectivist mentality that left little room for nonconformism. The rapid institutional, demographic, and economic development of

---

[2] Lustick 1980, Yiftachel 1999.

[3] From its establishment to the time of this writing, Israel has been involved in six full-fledged wars (1948–1949, 1956, 1967, 1973, 1982, 2006), one war of attrition (1968–1970), several large-scale military operations, the latest being the Gaza Operation in December 2008, two low-intensity conflicts: the Palestinian *intifadas* of 1987–1991 and of 2000–2004, and the critical first Gulf War in 1991, in which Israel played only a passive role but was hit several times by Iraqi long-range missiles, an experience of vulnerability that dramatically changed the Israelis' perception of national security.

Jewish Israeli society, with the socialist ethos dominant in the formative years of the state, also encouraged the emergence of such a national mentality that was not typical of classical Jewish culture, which was famous for its internal diversity and heterogeneity. Thus, for many years, nonconformism and even more so individualism as a worldview and as a way of life were widely unacceptable to the Israeli Jewish mainstream, because they were interpreted as a manifestation of egotism, allegedly hazardous to the nation's ability to meet the external and internal challenges that it faced.[4] Because the peace movement always addressed the individual conscience and called on the individual to examine critically the collective views and beliefs regarding the conflict, it actually challenged a basic collective postulate about the proper hierarchy of personal versus collective preferences and therefore found itself located on the sociopolitical margins. This collectivist mentality was further strengthened by the statist orientation taken by the government in the first decade of independence, a state of mind that did not encourage the ideational and practical dissent that peace activism always represented.

As the ongoing friction between the peace activists and the mainstream will demonstrate, the universalism that characterized the former was looked down on by the latter because, by definition, nations in their state-building days are self-centered. This primary exclusivist mentality went hand in hand with the traditional Jewish perception of the "chosen people," which, it is argued here, contributed to the Israeli mainstream's lack of enthusiasm for all-encompassing notions and ideologies. Universalist concepts were always considered secondary to Jewish values, interests, and concerns. Because the peace movement always struggled against this particularist approach by inscribing on its banner universal values such as the right to self-determination and human rights, it was denounced as unpatriotic and therefore faced considerable hostility.

Sociopolitical Cleavage Structure

We see then, before even touching on the peace movement's specific political recommendations, how its unique epistemological position placed it on the political margins. Paradoxical as this might sound, however, on other no less important levels, its activists were always at the center of the Israeli Jewish sociopolitical arena. This "schizophrenic" situation invested the movement with structured tensions and critically impaired its mobilization capabilities, particularly regarding three considerably sizable constituencies: the non-Ashkenazi Jewish sector, the Jewish orthodox sector, and the Israeli-Arab sector.

Since 1948, the Jewish population of the state has grown from 600,000 to about 7 million, largely through successive waves of large-scale immigration.

---

4 For example, emigration was looked on as desertion, and individual Israelis who relocated to other countries were termed *yordim* – those who descended (metaphorically, from a higher level of existence to a lower one).

The newcomers, some ideologically motivated by the Zionist creed and others driven by the physical dangers or economic hardships in their countries of origin, created a rich sociocultural mosaic, in which certain "colors" remained strong while others faded with the geographical and cultural dislocation. Admittedly, although located in the Middle East, the Israeli state and society always looked to the Western sociopolitical model, while slighting and even suppressing non-Western political-cultural legacies held, for example, by non-Ashkenazi newcomers from Middle Eastern countries.[5] These legacies were not only perceived by the Zionist leaders as contradicting their modernized political conceptions but also were sometimes rejected as being too close to the values and cultural features of the Arab foe. Feeling stripped of their legacies and therefore their identities and self-respect, for both practical and ideological reasons, many among the newcomers from Arab countries renounced their traditional cultures and, at least superficially, opted for the Western sociopolitical model. Deep inside, however, they developed great frustration and anger with the Ashkenazi political and cultural dominance. The fact that the Western orientation was also strongly present in the ideology of most Israeli peace groups, and that most activists were themselves Ashkenazi, created an almost unbridgeable gap between the Mizrahi sector and the movement, which, as is discussed later, severely curtailed its mobilization efforts.[6] This gap was further widened by the fact that many of the Mizrahi immigrants reacted to the immigration crisis by openly adopting ultra-hostile attitudes toward the Arab world and culture. Many of them thus renounced the very idea of nonviolent solutions to the Israeli-Arab conflict promoted by the peace movement, based on the argument that their first-hand familiarity with the Arab-Muslim world suggested that Arabs "only understand force."[7] There were indeed a few who argued that owing to the Mizrahi acquaintance with the cultures and modes of operation of both sides, Jews of Middle Eastern origin could serve as a bridge between Israel and its Arab neighbors. These voices, however, were barely heard and certainly not politically effective.

The second sociopolitical cleavage that is of importance when analyzing Israeli peace activism is the secular-orthodox one. Whereas the traditional attachment of the Jewish people to the land was religious, the Zionist endeavor was secular, which in turn accounts for today's mainly secular self-definition of the Israeli Jewish population.[8] This incongruity nourished a major

---

[5] For an analysis of the expunging of the cultural legacies of the Mizrahi Jewish communities in the wake of immigration to Israel, see, e.g., Shenhav 2003.

[6] Indeed, *Gush Emunim*, the strongest grassroots movement of the right, was also in fact mostly Ashkenazi, particularly at its core, and yet it managed to avoid being stigmatized as such, whereas the peace movement failed to steer clear of this negative "ethnic" stigma.

[7] The prevalent hard-line attitudes among Israeli Mizrahi Jews have been a constant source of concern for left-wing Mizrahi activists (see, e.g., Chetrit 2001, 2004).

[8] Based on self-definition questions, public opinion surveys suggest that, at present, about 45%–50% of Israeli Jews define themselves as secular, about 30%–35% as traditional, 12%–13% as orthodox, and 8%–9% as ultra-orthodox.

sociopolitical cleavage within Israeli society, which is highly relevant to understanding the ordeal of the peace movement. To be sure, political alliances between secular and religious political actors were very common (Cohen and Susser 2000); however, the deep divergence between secular and orthodox Jews regarding the essence and purpose of the state of Israel is strongly reflected in the two sectors' conflicting views of mainly territorial compromises as a means of achieving a peace agreement. Although the secular majority, of which the peace movement is part, generally views such compromises as acceptable in principle, the orthodox sector generally places cherished religious values, mainly the wholeness of the land of Israel as promised and given by God to the children of Israel, higher on its scale of priorities than resolution of the Israeli-Arab conflict.[9] Empirical studies have indeed shown that in the Israeli context, a Jewish person's level of religious observance is the best predictor of his or her political attitudes, particularly those pertaining to the Israeli-Arab conflict and its resolution (see, e.g., Yuchtman-Yaar and Peres 2000, Hermann and Yuchtman-Yaar 2002). Secular Jewish Israelis are thus heavily and disproportionately represented in the political left, which advocates solutions to the Israeli-Palestinian conflict that entail significant territorial compromises. Orthodox and ultra-orthodox Jewish Israelis, on the other hand, are disproportionately represented in the right, which opposes such compromises. Owing to the much higher birth rate of the latter two groups,[10] their share in the population is expected to grow significantly, thereby increasing the political weight in the Jewish electorate of those holding attitudes regarding the Israeli-Palestinian conflict that are antithetical to those put forward by the peace movement.

The situation becomes even more complicated because of the overlap between the Ashkenazi-Mizrahi divide and the secular/orthodox one. Ashkenazis are more heavily represented in the secular camp, whereas Mizrahis are more strongly represented in the traditional-orthodox one. Together with the previously mentioned linkage between political views regarding the regional conflict and level of religiosity, a three-dimensional cleavage is created, with the Ashkenazi, secular, dovish amalgamation on one pole, and the Mizrahi, traditional-orthodox, hawkish amalgamation on the other. Although this is an "ecological" characterization, it is a pattern that essentially dominates the Israeli sociopolitical map and reduces the likelihood of the peace movement being able to reach large subsectors of the Jewish Israeli population.

The socioeconomic dimension complicates the situation even more. Israel's national economy, which at the beginning of the century was based primarily on agriculture and local commerce, has developed throughout the years into a modern, high-tech and light industry–based economy. Today, Israel is located

---

9 Yoram Peri (2005) has characterized this cleavage as between two Israeli subcultures as the *Metro* (secular, Ashkenazi, urban, left-wing) and the *Retro* (orthodox-traditional, Mizrahi, peripheral, right-wing).

10 Among the Jewish 10- to 18-year-old age group, the orthodox and ultra-orthodox sectors already number about 10%–12%.

quite high on the global national production scale, with a recent GNP per capita of about 18,000 USD. The average standard of living (of the Jewish population) matches that of citizens of European counties such as Italy or Spain, and the illiteracy rate is close to nil, with an average of 12.6 years of schooling (statistics for the Jewish population in 2003). The egalitarian nature (or myth?) of Jewish Israeli society has been severely eroded in recent years with the dissipation of its socialist orientation. Socioeconomic gaps within the Jewish sector have therefore grown wider (Gutwein 2002), with the correlation between poverty or wealth, and both ethnic origin (Mizrahi and Ashkenazi, respectively) and level of religiosity (ultra-orthodox and secular, respectively) also becoming stronger and more significant than in the past. As already mentioned, the majority of those taking part in peace activities in Israel are Ashkenazi and also often middle class and higher. The overlapping of these characteristics in peace movement activists narrows the movement's grassroots mobilization capabilities even further, as we shall see.

The third relevant sociopolitical cleavage, where again the peace movement was among the insiders and not the outsiders, is the Jewish-Arab one. Although Israel is self-defined and widely acknowledged as a Jewish (and democratic) state, one should keep in mind that today well over one million of its citizens are not Jewish, with the largest sector among these being Arabs (the majority of whom are Muslims, with Christian and Druze minorities).[11] Obviously, the fact that the Arab Israeli minority considers itself part of the Palestinian people and of the greater Arab nation makes its security concerns and political perceptions quite different from those of the Jewish majority, and it also creates some tensions between this minority and the Jewish majority that are difficult to resolve. The Arab citizens of Israel cannot identify with the Zionist creed, with the Jewish nature and symbols of the state, or with the sense of enmity with the Arab world. They certainly do not view the Israeli army (IDF) as their savior but rather as the tool with which Israel has inflicted numerous calamities on their nation.[12] All Arab Israelis above the age of 18 years are indeed eligible to vote and enjoy all *individual* civil rights; however, the state authorities have systematically and intentionally denied this sector's *collective* rights. The ability of the Arab Israeli minority to translate individual political rights into influence, for example, over the state's symbols or self-definition, and transform it into a state of all its citizens, as many of them would like, is

---

[11] There is also a large group of non-Jewish immigrants from the former Soviet Union and a group of thousands of non-Jewish foreign workers. The latter groups are not (yet?) politically organized or active; however, their very existence has to some degree blurred the binary Jewish-Arab nature of Israeli society. In other words, the fact that today thousands of people in the country do not belong to either sector in a sense changed what was once a black-and-white social fabric and could, in the future, produce sociopolitical alliances that seem unlikely today and that could prove relevant to matters covered by the peace movement.

[12] Israeli Arab citizens are exempt from military service, which is often used by the Jewish majority sector as an excuse for excluding them from the public discourse on national security matters and even for allocating them fewer state resources.

highly limited. Certain analysts therefore challenge the description of Israel as a liberal democracy and define it instead as an *ethnic democracy* (Smooha 1997), or worse – as an *ethno-democracy* (Yiftachel 1999). As mentioned, despite its critical view of Israel's security policies and its advocacy of the Palestinian national rights for self-determination, the peace movement is in critical respects quite close to the Jewish mainstream when it comes to the Western orientation, as well as to the recognition of the potential threat by the Arab world that calls for maintaining a strong Israeli army. On the tactical level, the movement could not openly associate itself with the claims of the Arab Israeli community because doing so would further undermine its already rather unstable foothold with the Jewish majority. This opens a wide conceptual and operational gap between the movement and the Arab minority and accounts for the otherwise difficult-to-understand paucity of Arab activists in the peace movement.

Israeli Grassroots Political Participation Landscape

Although much scholarly work has been devoted over the years to the Israeli polity, very little attention has been paid to the nongovernmental aspects of Israeli politics or to its extraparliamentary actors and activities. This scholarly inattention went hand in hand with the political marginalization of grassroots activism in Israel until the late 1960s. This is not at all trivial or self-evident, considering that in the thousands of years of Jewish historical experience, only very few and short periods were marked by political sovereignty, none of which occurred in the modern era. In other words, statism has never been an integral part of the nation's political culture, although communal, nongovernmental bodies and modes of operation certainly were. Furthermore, 50 years of communal existence (the *Yishuv* era,[13] see Horowitz and Lissak 1978) preceded the establishment of a fully independent nation-state in 1948. Therefore, the marginality of nongovernmental activism and organizations in Israeli politics calls for some explanation.

One explanation is historical-developmental: In the prestate *Yishuv* era, lacking sovereignty, all the political activity of the Jewish community in Palestine was legally defined as voluntary and hence extraparliamentary. In essence, however, this was not authentic grassroots activism, because it was conducted through highly institutionalized semiparliamentary modes of action. This casts a doubt over the definition of this communal mode of operation as voluntary, a critical feature of civil society organizations. Those who refused to function within this framework; for example, the ultra-orthodox community, were deprived of important communal rights and of services provided to others by *Yishuv* institutions. This basic institutionalization enabled the rapid transformation of the Jewish community in Mandatory Palestine into a stable and

---

[13] In the *Yishuv* era, the Jews in Mandatory Palestine created statelike institutions – assembly, elections, political parties. These were mostly modelled on eastern Europe, with the school system, trade unions, and health services in most cases attached to the political parties.

functioning political system immediately after the establishment of the State of
Israel. Rapid institutional, demographic, and economic development of Jewish
Israeli society, in conjunction with the socialist ethos dominant in the formative years of the state, encouraged, as mentioned previously, the emergence
of a collectivist national mentality. This collective mode of thinking strongly
contributed to the creation of a political climate in which grassroots political
activity, although never legally banned, was for many years unacceptable.

Indeed, the first two decades of statehood (from 1948 through the late
1960s) were heavily state centered and party oriented (e.g., Horowitz and
Lissak 1988). Political endeavors in the form of grassroots citizens' organizations were therefore discouraged and even de-legitimized. Particularly in the
1950s, while the newly established Israeli government was preoccupied with
creating, exercising, and demonstrating its political supremacy, any spontaneous, independent, and noninstitutionalized citizens' activities were looked
on as a threat to the political order. The statist orientation (*mamlachtiut*),
promoted with considerable zeal by Israel's first Prime Minister, David Ben-
Gurion, downgraded so-called parochial political interests and especially the
aspirations of smaller political bodies, labeling them petty and counterproductive with regard to general national interest. The political parties and the
elections were the only channels through which the public was expected to
transmit, bottom up, its political preferences and demands. Israel of that time
can be unequivocally defined as a typical party-state (Akzin 1955); therefore,
the few antigovernment demonstrations, not to speak of the fiercer disturbances
that spontaneously erupted in the *ma'abarot*,[14] or the workers' uprisings (e.g.,
Eshel 1994), were strongly denounced by senior officials, and sometimes even
suppressed by the police. Because the national radio broadcasting service at the
time was managed by the prime minister's office and most newspapers were
organs of the political parties, information about these occurrences was often
kept from the general public (Hermann 1995a).

The negative impact on the POS, which potential grassroots activities faced,
of the statist institutional orientation was reinforced by the ever-present reality of an external existential threat and frequent military confrontations with
neighboring Arab countries. The sense of danger facing the nation and the
desire for domestic order was indeed shared by the leaders of the country and
most of the general public. This combination is one of the reasons why when, in
the mid-1950s, a group of young activists (many of whom were academics and
university students who would later become prominent public and professional
figures) – *Shurat Hamitnadvim* (the Line of Volunteers) – tried to turn public
attention to corrupt norms that prevailed in certain branches of the new Israeli
political establishment, they were quickly and easily silenced by the political
center.[15]

---

[14] Transitional camps. Here Holocaust survivors and newcomers fleeing from Iraq, Morocco, and
other Arab states were placed by the government until they were given permanent housing.

[15] The group was taken to court by Ben Gurion's son, then the deputy chief of police, for libel
and found guilty. Following this verdict (1957), the group dissolved (see Kabalo 2007).

The economic crisis of the mid-1960s and the overall improvement in the standard of living and rising consumerism after the Six Day (1967) war, with general relief following Israel's remarkable military victory and the collective fatigue after years of extensive national mobilization, sustained the tendency at that time among a large majority of Jewish Israelis to concentrate on the private rather than the public sphere. Grassroots political activity was therefore sporadic and small scale in the late 1960s, not because it was still considered illegitimate but because relatively few had an interest in conducting it. Thus, for different reasons, the 1950s and most of the 1960s presented a fairly contracted POS as far as social activism was concerned.

Grassroots activism, a category of civil political participation that includes peace activism, became a normal, even if not very common, element of the Israeli repertoire of political modes of participation only in the late 1960s (Hermann 1996), or, as other observers argue, only in the early 1970s (Sprinzak 1986, Lehman-Wilzig 1990), when the overall POS gradually became more favorable. Several reasons for this change can be identified: first, the stability of the political system and the authority of decision makers had by then become well established. Therefore, the Israeli political elite was less defensive and hypersensitive toward grassroots activism. Second, the military victory of Israel in the 1967 war sharply curtailed the external security threat, greatly relieving the existential anxieties of the public and the elites. Several other changes also occurred at that time, making grassroots political activity a more acceptable option. The Israeli media reports on the American civil rights movement, the anti-Vietnam War campaign, and student uprisings in the West made the notion of direct, noninstitutionalized political participation by ordinary citizens more familiar and acceptable. Another factor was the generational change that took place in Israel from the late 1960s onward: young people who had been born and socialized in the Israeli milieu reached now the political age. These youngsters felt much more at home there than their usually immigrant parents; they knew the language and were familiar with both local political culture and the rules of the political game. No less important, their economic situation was, for the most part, better than that of their parents at the same age, so that they could afford the time to become engaged in grassroots political activism. Moreover, never having experienced collective traumas such as the Holocaust or the prolonged and bloody struggle for national independence, the basic sense of security and self-reliance of these young people was much stronger than that of their parents' generation, who had experienced life-threatening personal and national crises. The result of this demographic development was mounting noncompliance and a growing search for alternative paths of political self-expression. Such juvenile self-confidence became manifest in 1968 in the first of several "Letters from Seniors" (*Michtav haShministim*), sent to Prime Minister Golda Meir by a group of high school students, just before being drafted – by the general legal conscription obligation – into the IDF. In the letter, these seniors – all of whom were Israeli born, resided in the center of the country, and were from middle-class, secular families, all features similar to those of the average adult peace activist – wrote that they had doubts about the authentic desire of the Israeli government to make peace with the Arabs. This was something that made them question the rationale for their impending military service. Although the authorities and mainstream public opinion viewed such manifestations of nonconformism extremely negatively and expressed this openly and unequivocally, in effect, such actions were tolerated and therefore became more frequent.

These developments in the POS enabled the emergence of a few yet noticeable citizens' initiatives in the late 1960s (e.g., the Movement for Greater Israel and the Movement for Peace and Security, to be discussed in the next section), and in the early 1970s (e.g., the Israeli Black Panthers[16]). With a relatively underdeveloped third sector at the time, this first phase of significant grassroots activism mainly took the shape of protest activities – on national security matters in the first case and on domestic socioeconomic matters in the second.[17] The use of protest sharply increased in the aftermath of the 1973 war, in which Israel was caught by surprise and was not far from being defeated militarily. This war was a classic example of a change in the POS following a traumatic national event that shakes up the entire political system, creating cracks through which citizens' initiatives make their way from the political periphery to closer to the center in terms of making their voices heard (Eisinger 1973).

From late 1973 to early 1974, the massive postwar wave of soldier protests (Ashkenazi 2003, Hermann 2004) stirred an open debate on the competence of political and military decision makers. It contributed significantly to the legitimization of citizens' political participation and voice in the national security debate. In the early to mid-1970s, Israel witnessed far more manifestations of civil activism than ever in the past, often motivated by civil discontent with various aspects of the ruling national ethos, mainly the security ethos – from *Gush Emunim* (Bloc of the Faithful) on the right, to the left-center *haTnua leZionut Aheret* (Movement for a Different Zionism). The growing cracks in the homogeneity of the Labour movement ruling elite, which matured with the political upset in the 1977 elections (*hamahapach*) in which the right-wing Likud came to power for the first time, also facilitated the incorporation of grassroots activism into the national political repertoire. This happened because, as mentioned in the previous chapter, split elites present a better POS for civil participation in politics.

At that time, the general propensity of the State of Israel to restrict grassroots political protest by Jewish Israelis was low. This propensity for repression was

---

[16] For a chronological account of the Israeli Black Panthers movement, see http://www.kedma.co.il/Panterim/Chronika.htm.

[17] Another, atypical criticism of the government and its policies was put forward in 1970 in the theater, in the satirical revue *Malkat Ambatia* (Queen of Bath). The playwright (Hanoch Levin) criticized Israeli hubris after the 1967 victory and warned of its future dangerous outcomes. The revue had 21 parts, which included, for example the song "Beautiful Moments," which lamented the fact that because of the many wars, an Israeli man has no chance of dying of natural causes. The play was negatively viewed both by the censor and by the public and was therefore shortly closed down (it was, however, staged again in the early 2000s).

much greater, however, when the activities were organized and conducted by non-Jewish citizens, mainly Arabs, a reality that sustains the specific groups' proximate POS assumption discussed in the theoretical section presented earlier. This is a clear case in which different grassroots actors active at the same time face different conditions, based on whether they are defined by the mainstream as respectable (unthreatening) or revolutionary (threatening). This discriminative practice was exemplified by the Israeli state authorities' harsh reaction to the *Yom haAdama* (Day of the Land) protest (March 30, 1976), a visible and vigorous protest organized and conducted by the Arab Israeli community. The demonstrations protested discrimination against the Arab citizens of Israel in general and particularly against the vast appropriation of Arab-owned lands by the state for the purpose of "Judaisation" of the Galilee. The demonstrations included blocking roads, stoning passing cars, and even several cases of throwing Molotov cocktails. The authorities' response was exceedingly harsh – six Arab protestors were killed by security forces during the demonstrations.[18]

The tendency of the state to repress grassroots activism in the Arab sector has not been limited to this event. Constant interference from above, even in completely legal activities, was supported by the widespread notion among Jewish Israelis that Arab Israelis are disloyal citizens and should be treated strictly by the authorities when expressing their anger and concerns.[19] Security agencies have always very closely and openly followed all Arab grassroots initiatives, infiltrated them, and investigated their financial resources and transactions. They have occasionally detained prominent activists until they explained where they obtained the money, sometimes taking them to court for having received financial aid from "illegitimate" sources, mainly Arab states or organizations. Leaders of these initiatives were often harassed when leaving the country and/or on returning. They were systematically exposed to a variety of threats to defame them or their families or cause them to lose their jobs. This made the proximate POS for the Israeli Arab sector at any given time much narrower than for its Jewish counterpart.

As mentioned before, the state was usually fairly restrained regarding Jewish grassroots initiatives, although here again the approach varied, depending on the specific grouping. Surveillance was much lighter than in the Arab case (yet not unheard of). In fact, many Israeli political activists, even those with nonconflormist views, were employed by the civil service and served in IDF

---

[18] This event, which lasted about a day, is commemorated annually by large, usually nonviolent, demonstrations in major Israeli Arab cities and villages, which underscore the repressive actions of the state during the original protest. Few Jewish Israelis and Jewish grassroots organizations take part in these annual commemoration rallies, a rather symbolic fact that indicates the strength of nationalism in Israel, even on the extraparliamentary level of activity.

[19] In a survey conducted in 2003, 58% of the Jewish Israeli interviewees thought that if a Palestinian state were established, Arab Israeli citizens would be more loyal to it than to the State of Israel. Of these interviewees, 14% said that the Arab citizens' first loyalty would be to the State of Israel and 13.5% – equally to both states. The remainder had no clear opinion on this issue (Peace Index, December 2003).

reserve units. This restrained style was particularly apparent when it came to right-wing activists, even those suspected of contemplating and conducting vigilante, subversive, and clearly illegal actions (Sasson 1995). Unless found guilty by the courts, Jewish activists of the right were usually not punished. There was less tolerance of Jewish left-wing groups and activists than of the right, although of course much more than vis-à-vis Arab Israelis. They were usually not physically hurt, however, and, unlike their Arab counterparts, their freedom of movement within the Green Line (the border between Israel and the West Bank before 1967, when still under Jordanian rule) and their freedom to leave the country and return as often as they wished was never significantly curtailed.

Still, here and there some moves were taken by the authorities to remind Jewish activists that they were viewed with disfavor "from above." For example, in the 1950s, when foreign currency allowances for travel abroad had to be authorized, leaders of the Israeli chapter of the World Peace Council, *Vaad haShalom haYisraeli*, faced intentional delays in getting the necessary official permits to go abroad; for example, to the conference of nonaligned states in 1955 (Hermann 1989, 243). In several cases, police were sent in to calm angry demonstrations – mostly of frustrated newcomers from North Africa or traumatized Holocaust survivors – in the transit compounds where they were housed for years before being offered decent accommodation by the Housing Ministry. Particularly noticeable was the case of the Wadi Saliv riots in 1959, where the police used massive force to stop the disturbances. Also, the police used rather harsh means toward several protest activities of the Israeli Black Panthers. This unusual reaction nourished the argument that Mizrahis were treated and considered by the authorities to be more like Arab Israelis than like privileged Israeli Ashkenazi Jews. Still, this did not come close to the force used, for example, by the American police and National Guard during the 1968 Chicago convention, or, at about the same time, by French security forces against the students revolting in Paris. In the 1980s and 1990s, several activists complained about being checked in an offensive manner by security officers at the airport when they left or came home just "to make a point," and it is no secret that some activists' phones were tapped. In an unusual move, in 1988, Michael Warschawski, a radical left-wing activist and the director of the Alternative Information Center (AIC), was taken to court by the state for allegedly allowing Palestinian activists to carry out anti-Israeli activities in his organization's offices. After a long trial, during which the allegations were changed from "abetting" to "turning a blind eye" to these activities, he was sentenced to 9 months in jail. Other left-wing activists maintained that they were harassed by the authorities because of their views, and in certain cases even fired from their jobs (e.g., Bitterman 2003, 150). Although it might lessen their aura of martyrdom, by and large, the level of repression used by Israeli governments over the years against Jewish social activists has been quite limited and was certainly not enough to cause people to fear to continue their activities.

To return to our chronological account, the dominant position of the political establishment in the public sphere was severely challenged in the 1970s. Prevailing public opinion that the state apparatus had become too cumbersome and inefficient and incumbent policymakers too settled and therefore negligent of their duties gave rise to a wide variety of newly empowered sociopolitical agents. Feelings of political estrangement and antigovernment criticism became quite powerful at that time, particularly in the aftermath of the military debacle of 1973. These led to the downfall of the Labour party in the 1977 elections and the rise to power of the Likud. Labour's defeat led not only to a change of government but also shifted the center of gravity of the political system from left to right, as well as sharply increasing its level of competitiveness. Because since then electoral primacy has not been guaranteed to any party, politicians have become more and more aware of and courteous toward nonparty actors, including citizens' bodies, viewing them as potential political allies. In certain cases, alignments between a political party and a citizens' initiative became open and well consolidated, as was the case between the Mafdal (the National Religious Party) and *Gush Emunim*, and later between the left-wing Mapam party (and later on Meretz) and the extraparliamentary movement, *Shalom Achshav* (Peace Now).[20] In other cases, the link was also quite evident, as between the Shinui party and the campaign for a "Constitution for the State of Israel." Growing dissatisfaction of the citizenry with the government and mounting political competitiveness of the party system in the late 1970s clearly expanded the POS of Israeli social movements at the time.

The realization after the 1977 election that leaders who do not deliver can and will face electoral retribution considerably increased not only the leaders' attentiveness to grassroots pressures and demands but also augmented the Israeli public's sense of competence, and over the years, the bargaining positioning of grassroots organizations vis-à-vis the political establishment (Hermann 1995). Optional modes of political participation could no longer be restricted to political parties only because this was the channel favored by the politicians, left and right. Israeli citizens claimed their right not only to shift their preferences from one party to another on election day but also to decide on their preferred mode of political participation.

The 1980s thus saw a mushrooming of citizens' initiatives, protest groups, and nonprofit organizations in many spheres with a variety of agendas – from civil and human rights groups, through organizations for the protection of the environment, "pirate" radio stations and independent newspapers and magazines, to educational and medical service-giving private or semiprivate bodies (Lehman-Wilzig 1990). To a considerable extent, their emergence was the result of the gradual decline in the quality and quantity of state services. This suited the Likud's capitalist (later neo-conservative) economic agenda, which in retrospect proved quite detrimental in terms of retaining the party's wide

---

[20] Although these relationships were significantly stronger, in the public mind *Shalom Achshav* has always been closely associated with the Labour party.

working-class and lower-middle-class constituency. These voters in a sense were captives of the Likud and other right-of-center parties: they could not vote for left-of-center parties, mainly Labour, which fostered social-democratic agendas because they considered them historically responsible for their under-privileged socioeconomic and sociopolitical situation, as well as patronizing and insincere in their manifest concern for worse-off societal groups.

The Israeli social movement infrastructure (SMI) thus peaked between the mid-1970s and the mid-1980s. Thereafter, because of rapid institutionalization and the development of a sizable third sector, it gradually shifted its tactics from protest to service-giving and advocacy activities. Because of this shift, grassroots activism receded somewhat during this phase in terms of its public visibility and media coverage, although not in terms of its intensity, number of organizations, actions taken, size of budgets, and other important parameters, which all in fact rose in the 1980s. Indeed, the first Lebanon War (1982), widely perceived as a war of choice, again gave rise to a vast grassroots antiwar protest, and so did the first Palestinian *intifada* (1987–1990). These civil phenomena are discussed in detail in the context of the peace movement's history.

The two decades from the mid-1980s onward witnessed a noticeable decrease in the status and public image of the established political and state bodies in general,[21] which facilitated the stabilization of the civil society orga-nizations. The establishment tried to stop this process of confidence erosion, but with little success. Structural changes, such as the adoption of various primaries procedures by the larger political parties,[22] meant to increase their popular appeal, did not work as expected. On the contrary, the replacement of the old narrow bodies for candidate selection, with the deals done by many politicians desperate to ensure their nomination by the much larger party's central committees, only invested the parties with a darker image of growing corruption and decreased voter identification with all of them. Some of the efforts to forestall grassroots activism were more successful; for example, the authorities' absorption of the main right-wing extraparliamentary movement – *Gush Emunim* – which had undergone rapid institutionalization (Newman and Hermann 1992). This absorption actually turned this extraparliamentary movement into a part of a government agency, and its leading activists were offered – and they accepted – key positions in the state apparatuses concerning settlement-related issues.

[21] A survey conducted in 1997 indicated full trust in the IDF by 90% of the respondents, in the Supreme Court by 85%, in the Knesset by 41%, in the government by 40%, and in the political parties by 21% (Yuchtman-Yaar and Peres 1997). In 2005, however, the figures were significantly lower: IDF – only 74%, Supreme Court – 64%, Knesset – 9%, the government – 12%, and the political parties – 3% (Peace Index, February 2005).

[22] In fact, only Labour adopted a "real" primaries procedure in which all party members could take part in the selection of the party's electoral candidates, whereas the other parties opted for a less inclusive procedure in which only the members of their central committees had a say in this regard.

The stable doors were already open wide, however. The late 1980s and the 1990s witnessed several massive grassroots protest events. The largest grassroots campaign of the early 1990s was the "Constitution for the State of Israel" campaign in 1991, which brought hundreds of thousands of Israelis into the streets (Bechor 1996). The success of this campaign in terms of grassroots mobilization rested on the deepening dissatisfaction of the Israeli citizenry with malfunction and corruption in the political establishment. Despite its large size and momentum, however, this campaign failed, to bear fruit, that is, to force the establishment to formulate a constitution that could have helped to "clean the stables." This was mostly because of the ad-hoc alliance created in the early 1990s between the religious parties (which opposed the idea of a constitution as they viewed the *Torah* as the constitution of the Jewish people) and certain secular politicians and parties (who opposed a constitution because it might narrow their room for political maneuvering). The failure of this grassroots campaign significantly contributed to the inculcation of the public image of the political establishment as fraudulent and inattentive, and to the growing political estrangement of large public sectors.

Although the early 1990s were still quite vibrant in terms of civil activism, the effectiveness and popularity of protest decreased in the mid-1990s, not only because of the authorities' low attentiveness or strategy but also because often highly visible grassroots activities had become routine and ritualized, and hence were devoid of real zeal and content even if numerically impressive. A fine example of this is the annual rally in commemoration of the Rabin assassination, which took place for the first time in October 1996, one year after the tragic event. Whereas the immediate spontaneous post-assassination grassroots reactions were rather emotional and had a clear political orientation, the commemoration rallies in the ensuing years, rather than projecting a clear political message for peace with the Palestinians and against political violence, have become consensus-oriented gatherings with a very inconclusive message in which supporters of the peace camp find themselves next to people from the center and even of the "soft" right, giving tribute to some vague Rabin legacy (see Vinitzky, in Algazi 2003). This routinization and ritualization apparently eroded the impact of this and other originally defiant events, lowered public attendance, and decreased the media interest in them.

The fact that protest campaigns received little response from the Israeli authorities and the wider public encouraged tactical changes on the part of the social activists and organizations. Thus, in the 1990s, grassroots protest was increasingly replaced by legal means, such as by appealing to the courts against certain state agencies and policies. This was a tactic of *haKeshet haDemocratit haMizrahit* (The Democratic Mizrahi Rainbow) when challenging the state authorities regarding public housing (Karif 2005) and also often of *Adala*, the Arab Israeli civil rights organization, and other legally oriented organizations such as *haTnua leEychut haShilton* (The Movement for the Improvement of the Government). Other civil associations replaced demonstrations with watchdog tactics; for example, *Shalom Achshav* with its Settlement Watch project, and the major human rights organization, *b'Tselem*, with its watch teams and elaborate reports that followed human rights violations in the occupied territories.

This switch from protest to other modes of action was accompanied by the institutionalization of the grassroots SMI in Israel. To exert impact and find its niche in this crowded civil society arena, a specific grassroots initiative could no longer operate from living rooms and depend on amateur management. This change necessitated the acquisition of organizational skills that many activists lacked. Therefore, support organizations such as *Shatil*[23] were established to instruct new grassroots groupings on how to organize, mobilize, maintain a budget, handle the tax authorities, and perform similar activities. In addition to institutionalization, the SMI thus underwent a process of professionalization. To compete for attention and resources more effectively, grassroots organizations needed to rely heavily on professionals, with the former voluntary basis becoming much narrower.

The institutionalization-professionalization tendency unintentionally helped the authorities to manage the SMI through registration and tax exemption regulations. Israeli law defines four types of nonprofit organizations: Ottoman associations, nonprofit companies, public endowments, and *Amutot* (sing. *Amuta*) (Gidron and Katz 1998, 6–8).[24] The *Amutot* law, which is relevant to most Israeli grassroots organizations, was enacted in the late 1970s, in a sense as a damage control reaction by the state to the expansion of citizens' bodies and activities at the beginning of the decade. The law states that any two persons who wish to incorporate for any legal purpose other than profit seeking are free to do so; however, the state may intervene in certain internal affairs of such organizations. For example, the *Amutot* registrar may impose, without having to explain why, a financial investigation of a certain *Amuta* by an external auditor. The law requires *Amutot* to present, on registration, resolutions that specify the internal arrangements and management procedures of the organization. The law also dictates the organizational structure of the *Amuta*, its governing bodies, their respective powers, and the frequency of their meetings. Records must be regularly made available to members, and minutes of meetings and financial reports must be open to the public.

These stipulations seem very logical; however, as many peace organizations experienced firsthand, the authorities sometimes used them to disqualify or, more often, to harass citizens' organizations not to their liking. To be eligible for tax benefits, a nonprofit organization must first be incorporated as an *Amuta*. Nonprofit associations are exempt from income and corporate taxes if they adhere to the definition of a "public institution," use their income to cover direct expenses, serve a public purpose, and do not receive income from trade or business dealings. Because the last stipulation is somewhat ambiguous,

---

[23] See www.shatil.org.il

[24] Although a nonprofit organization can choose among all these forms, most peace organizations active at present belong to the fourth category.

many public institutions find themselves taxed, even though their expenses might exceed their income. The Knesset Finance Committee is the body that grants or annuls the status of "public institution." In other words, the political establishment has the right to decide which grassroots organizations receive this favorable status and which do not (clearly depending to a considerable extent on whether the organization is considered by the authorities "respectable," "strange," or "revolutionary," and not only legal or illegal).

To sum up, the POS that Israeli grassroots organizations and initiatives faced definitely expanded over the years. State practices and regulations allowed for extensive grassroots activity, and repression was rare. Extraparliamentary activism, which in the early years of statehood was considered illegitimate although not illegal, became a widely accepted mode of political participation. Although certain public sectors and issues were less welcomed by both the authorities and the public, after the 1980s, no real legal or other critical impediments were placed in the way of Israeli social activists, even if their agenda was looked on with disfavor. For tactical reasons, however, with the time and the change in the overall situation, most of the civil society organizations replaced protest with other means of challenging the authorities, such as legal appeals and watching-reporting techniques. They also became more institutionalized and more professionalized.

4

Paving the Road to Oslo – Israeli Peace
Activism through 1993

The Israeli Peace Movement: Basic Features

The Israeli peace movement clearly puts forward all the features of a social movement as defined previously. The movement challenges national perceptions and tries to bring about policy changes in a critical realm; its members have a sense of common purpose even if they sometimes disagree on the specific "formula" for peace; solidarity among activists and groups is marked by organizational and social interaction; and it has sustained interactions and activities that go back several decades. Clearly, as most definitions of a social movement stress, it is organized around a conflict; in fact, it focuses on two conflicts: the Israeli-Arab conflict, and, no less important, the conflict with its rivals on the Israeli right.

The detailed description and analysis of the various peace groups past and present below might create the mistaken impression of a massive political force – recall that the movement has always been numerically small. It ranged from several tens of activists in the 1920s and 1930s, to hundreds in the 1950s and late 1960s, to thousands and even a few tens of thousands in the late 1970s, the 1980s, and the early 1990s (most of them supporters), to a few thousand and even less in the late 1990s, and even fewer than that in the 2000s. Against this factual background, the assessment of the movement's tactical and strategic achievements should be measured and evaluated. This should be kept in mind, because too often, particularly in the heyday of peace activism, the intensive national and international media coverage of the various peace activities and peace organizations magnified the movement's actual size. Exaggerated expectations were created from it in terms of political effectiveness.

Although the conflict with the Arab world in general and the Palestinians in particular was at the core of Israel's cognition and practices both before and after the establishment of the State in 1948, until the late 1970s, manifestations of peace activism per se were few and politically negligible. Small groups such as *Brit Shalom* (Peace Covenant) and its offspring, *Ihud* (Union), indeed manifested some typical features of traditional, central-European-style peace activism between the 1920s and the 1940s, yet they never defined themselves as peace movements (e.g., Hermann 1989, Heller 2003). Even when peace activism began to gain voice and volume in the aftermath of the 1967 war, activists and other political actors rarely used the term *peace movement*. This term became part of the Israeli political vocabulary only later, under the impression of the mushrooming of peace SMOs in the United States and Europe and their growing public popularity. Not only was the designation then imported by Israeli peace groups but so were the highly visible European and American protest techniques. The key term *Israeli peace movement* is, admittedly, to a large extent an artifact – an analytical tool more than a concrete entity. Thus the following operative definition cannot be concisely inclusive (who is *in?*) or absolutely exclusive (who is *out?*).[1] For example, certain Israeli groups and SMOs that put forward a dovish agenda do not view themselves, nor do they wish to be considered by others and indeed are not recognized, as part of the peace movement. A fine example of this is *haMoatsa l'Shalom u'Bitachon* (The Council for Peace and Security), a voluntary body of high-ranking ex-military officers with a rather dovish agenda.[2] Other groups are widely perceived as an integral part of the peace movement, yet their formal mandate is not related directly to the peace-war issue. An example is *b'Tselem*, which is formally a human rights organization, not a peace group (although it is widely identified as such), or *Ir Amim* (City of Nations), an NGO that focuses on maintaining a feasible and just state of affairs in the metropolitan area of Jerusalem and the preclusion of any move or misdemeanor that might prevent future political agreement, mainly the Separation Barrier. The same goes for *Bitterlemons* – a widely read weekly Internet magazine that deals exclusively with various aspects of the conflict and posts opinions with a very strong commitment to promoting peace. Its Israeli co-editor – Yossi Alpher – declares, "With all due respect, we don't belong to any forums of Israeli and Palestinian peace organizations. We operate on a different, and for us, a more significant level."[3]

Similar to many of its equivalents abroad, the Israeli peace movement presented a variety of ideological programs and a wide range of functional and organizational formations and modes of operation. In many ways, it has never been committed to one narrative or strategy. It is best described as a decentralized aggregate of several SMOs of different sizes, types, and strategies, united by their persuasion that peace in the region is possible and can be achieved in the foreseeable future by nonviolent means. To be able to define the

[1] For a list of Israeli peace groups and their characterizations, see Appendix I.
[2] The reasons for this exclusion from the peace movement are discussed in some detail later.
[3] Peacemakers or Peace Industry? http://www.bitterlemons.org/previous/bl280507ed19.html.

universe of relevant SMOs to be examined in this study, the following operational definition for a peace organization was employed:

A peace organization is any voluntary/non-governmental body or group of people residing in Israel, which has: sought a non-violent resolution of the conflict on the political,
social and cultural levels; promoted mutual recognition of national self-determination as
a necessary but not sufficient condition for achieving peace between Israel and the Palestinians; and has been involved with protest, consciousness-raising, dialogue, advocacy
or provision of professional services directed to assuage the injustice and grievances
caused by this conflict in the political, social, economic, legal, religious and cultural
realms.[4]

When this operational definition is deconstructed into its elements, several
interesting points seem to warrant a more detailed explanation:

Voluntary Nongovernmental Body
All Israeli peace SMOs view and present themselves as voluntary. Nevertheless, today this prevalent characterization is only partly correct empirically.
Rank-and-file members and supporters of the groups and movements indeed
participate entirely voluntarily, but most peace groups involved in advocacy
or conscience-raising or service-giving activities considerably rely on paid staff
that varies in size and organizational influence. In the early 1990s, the larger
peace organizations underwent a significant process of professionalization and
institutionalization (somewhat later than other Israeli SMIs, which, as mentioned previously, already experienced such a transformation in the 1980s),
and replaced or added paid employees to their volunteer office staff. These
salaried staff members, who are responsible for the day-to-day operation of
the organization and for tactical decision making (strategic decisions are usually made by the organization's boards or councils, the members of which still
mostly act on a voluntary basis), are usually ideologically committed to the
causes of the organization that employs them (some are former volunteers).
Today, however, some of them are professional NGO executives and hence are
motivated differently from those participating in the organization's activities
on a voluntary basis, a situation that in certain cases has produced rather severe
internal tensions and heated disagreements. The reasons for this discrepancy
are clear; for example, unlike the volunteers, the paid staff is expected to show
results, whether in terms of changing public opinion on a certain peace-related
issue or, most commonly, in terms of fund-raising. The growing weight of the
paid staff reflects on the way these peace organizations operate and cooperate
with one another as well as with external actors. This was particularly true
in the golden age of peace activism in the late 1980s and early 1990s, when
peace activism almost took on the format of a peace "industry." Nevertheless,

---

4 A similar definition was used in the international study of peace/conflict resolution organizations
   in South Africa, North Ireland, and Israel/Palestine in the years 1996–1998, and sponsored by
   the Aspen Institute, Washington, DC. The findings of this project are summarized in Gidron,
   Katz, and Hasenfeld 2002. The Israel case is discussed there in Hermann 2002.

with the shrinking of peace activism and support for it in the second half of the 1990s, the decrease in external financial resources available to the larger and more moderate Israeli peace organizations (mainly *Shalom Achshav*) and the decline in public support across the board forced a return to heavier reliance on voluntary work, which in turn somewhat lessened the influence of the professionals in the peace SMOs.

Also regarding the institutionalization process, it has already been noted that the state often uses its registration authority to formally recognize or deny recognition from NGOs, depending on their platforms. Despite some intentional delays caused by the specific person in charge of the registration apparatus in the 1990s (whose political views were incompatible with the peace movement's agenda), eventually most peace organizations, radical or moderate, that applied for formal state recognition as public nonprofit institutions and took the necessary steps to be registered as *amutot*, were recognized by the authorities as such. Those that remained unincorporated often voluntarily maintained this status to prove their noninstitutionalized nature to their relevant audiences or for some technical reasons.

Achieving Peace between Israel and the Palestinians

This element might seem somewhat strange today, when the centrality of the Palestinian factor in the Israeli-Arab conflict is self-evident to every Israeli, but one should keep in mind that until the early 1980s, the Palestinians were not recognized even by most Israeli peace organizations as partners in the peace dialogue. Because of their subsidiary political position in the region, their economic and military weakness, and the lack of united and acknowledged leadership, Palestinians in the 1960s and 1970s were not considered essential to regional peace negotiations. Although the Israeli peace movement recognized from the beginning that the Palestinians were the side most harmed by the conflict, until the 1980s they were expected to wait patiently for Israel and the Arab states to reach a settlement. Even those Israeli peace activists who met with Palestinian leaders and advocated direct Israeli-Palestinian rapprochement usually considered Cairo, Amman, and Damascus the major partners to negotiating formal peace agreements. This changed dramatically during the 1980s and even more after the outbreak of the first Palestinian *intifada* in 1987. In the years covered by this study, however, the Israeli peace movement and the Israeli authorities and general public already recognized the Palestinians as the most important partners to the peace dialogue.[5]

Mutual Recognition of National Self-Determination

Although today many tend to forget this, until the mid- to late-1980s, most Zionist peace groups did not openly recognize the Palestinian right to

---

[5] Note here the paucity of joint Israeli-Palestinian peace organizations, with the more successful examples being the Alternative Information Center (AIC), which used to have Israeli and Palestinian branches, the Israeli-Palestinian Center for Research and Information (IPCRI), and the women's organization, The Jerusalem Link.

self-determination and an independent state, a right acknowledged at the time only by the Communist party and a few non-Zionist peace groups. Actually, acknowledging this right was a serious bone of contention within the peace movement at large as well as within specific organizations. For example, in 1988 *Shalom Achshav* (Peace Now) experienced significant external and internal disputes because of its formal recognition of Palestinian national rights and thus their claim to statehood. Today, all Israeli peace groups recognize the Palestinians' right to self-determination as the point of departure for negotiations, not its result, which most peace groups hope will be the establishment of an independent Palestinian state side by side with Israel – the "two states for two peoples" formula. The more radical groups, however, add to this primary recognition of the Palestinians' right to self-determination the right of Palestinian refugees to return to their original places of residence within Israel, or even replacing the two-state solution with a single binational, Jewish-Palestinian political entity.

Nonviolent Resolution of the Conflict

All Israeli peace organizations, without exception, advocate a political, rather than a military solution to the Israeli-Palestinian conflict. Nevertheless, very few of the peace groups espouse a pacifist worldview. Those that advocate absolute pacifism (e.g., the Israeli branch of the international pacifist organization, War Resisters International [WRI]) are not only tiny but also have always been located on the fringes of the peace movement, and far beyond the boundaries of the Israeli national consensus. In recent years, the voice of groups advocating conscientious objection on antimilitaristic grounds, such as *Profil Hadash* (New Profile), began to be heard as well. Most Israelis barely notice either of these principled antiservice agendas, however. The reason for the marginalization of pacifism within the Israeli peace movement was beautifully put by prominent Israeli author Amos Oz:

I wish I could tell you that they [the Holocaust survivors -TH] were liberated from Theresienstadt by peace demonstrators carrying placards saying, "make love not war." But the fact of the matter is that they were set free not by pacifist idealists but by combat soldiers wearing helmets and carrying machine guns. We Israeli peace activists have never forgotten this reality, even when we struggle against our country's attitude towards the Palestinians, even as we work for a viable, peaceful compromise between Israel and Palestine (Oz 2005).

Thus, most Israeli peace groups accept the notion of a just war and define as such at least some of the wars in which Israel was involved over the years (primarily, the 1948 War of Independence and, to a somewhat lesser extent, the 1967 and the 1973 wars). With few exceptions, members of the various peace groups served in the IDF and many of them still serve in the reserves when called. This participation in the national security effort was the basis for their claim to the right to take an active part in the national debate over security matters. In its turn, this participation accounted for public alarm at the emergence, in the early 1980s, of the first organized peace campaign advocating political conscientious objection, *Yesh Gvul* (There is a Limit), which first related to the Lebanon War and then to military service in the occupied territories. It also explains the negative reaction of many within the peace movement, and certainly among the general public, after the outbreak of the second Palestinian *intifada*, to the emergence of *Ometz l'Sarev* (Courage to Refuse), a group composed of former soldiers and officers, which also called for selective, namely, politically based, refusal.

Injustice and Grievances Caused by This Conflict in the Political, Social, Economic, Legal, Religious, and Cultural Realms

In the past, most Israeli peace organizations were scarcely interested in any other aspects of resolution of the conflict, apart from the military and the political ones. Only a few groups, mostly non-Zionist (usually those with certain Marxist or neo-Marxist orientations), also explained the conflict and the means for its resolution in economic and cultural terms. Several service-giving organizations, some of which are directly related to the Israeli-Palestinian conflict, such as *Rofim l'Zchuyot ha'Adam* (Physicians for Human Rights [PHR]), and others that are indirectly involved with it, such as *Kav l'Oved* (Workers' Hotline), focused on health-related problems or the impairing of workers' rights caused by prolonged Israeli occupation of the territories, but even these concerns were not in the context of a comprehensive socioeconomic analysis of the roots of the conflict or the ways out of it. In the first half of the 2000s, however, with the collapse of Israeli-Palestinian peace negotiations, the resulting economic recession in Israel, and the devastating crisis in the occupied territories, there appeared to be a growing emphasis within the peace movement at large on economic and cultural-religious aspects of the conflict and similarly oriented potential solutions to it. This corresponds with the growing post-Oslo realization among Israelis in general that a political agreement alone is little more than a piece of paper that cannot guarantee real reconciliation between the two peoples, and that unless social, cultural, economic, and other chasms are bridged, the chances of a stable peace prevailing are nil.

Beyond these shared postulates, however, the ideological and operational diversity within the Israeli peace movement is, as mentioned earlier, considerable. The major internal ideological cleavage is between the significantly larger Zionist element and the smaller non- or anti-Zionist one; the proportions between the two changed over time with the shrinking of the moderate component. All Zionist peace groups, regardless of their ideological disagreements with the mainstream, acknowledge and support the Jewish nature of the State of Israel and based their criticism of the occupation on the harm it causes, first and foremost to Israel's moral essence and to Israeli interests and international image (Warschawski 2005). They acknowledge all Jews in all places as a nation, not only a religious or ethnic entity, and view Israel as their motherland. Thus, for example, most of them strongly reject the demand often raised by non-Zionists to abolish the Law of Return or to make it universal; that is, applicable to Arabs and other non-Jewish newcomers as well.[6] Whereas the Zionist Peace activists believe in the possibility of making Israel a fully democratic Jewish state, the non-Zionist groups denounce this formula as hypocritical and demand that Israel be turned into "a state of all its citizens," rather than a Jewish state.

This ideological difference is reflected in the political alliances fashioned by the two elements of the Israeli peace movement. Whereas the Zionist peace groups normally maintain strong relations with Jewish communities and Zionist Jewish peace organizations in the Diaspora, the non-Zionist ones tend to establish links with foreign non-Jewish, progressive political bodies such as European Green parties or pacifist Christian churches, or with non-Zionist Jewish peace organizations, mainly on the U.S. west coast.

Another feature that sets the Zionist elements of the peace movement apart from the non-Zionist ones and derives in certain respects from the first is their position regarding the IDF. As mentioned before, much like the Israeli mainstream, Zionist peace activists and organizations acknowledge the importance of a strong Israeli army for defense purposes. Therefore, none of these groups advocates unconditional conscientious objection or fosters a pacifist creed. In fact, as mentioned, quite a few of the Zionist peace organizations base their demand to participate in the public debate on security matters on their members' military service and rank.[7] In addition to the example of the *haMoatsa l'Shalom u'Bitachon*, whose members' military background was mentioned previously, perhaps the most noticeable group to emphasize this trait is the largest peace organization, *Shalom Achshav* (Peace Now), which was virtually founded on the basis of an Officers' Letter (see later discussion). Even the less conformist *Yesh Gvul*, which calls on Israeli soldiers to refuse to serve in the IDF as soldiers on duty in the occupied territories, has never denied or challenged Israel's basic need for a strong armed forces. The non- or anti-Zionist peace groups, on the other hand, view the IDF as just another tool for the suppression of the Palestinians and for promoting the colonialist aims of the Zionist project, and although not professing pacifism per se, they therefore call on their activists to do whatever they can to avoid military service.

Naturally, the manifest loyalty of the moderate peace groups to the Zionist creed left the way open for a more fruitful dialogue with the mainstream and ensured greater success in their public mobilization efforts. At the same time, however, it was a liability insofar as their ability to create solid alliances with Israeli non-Zionist organizations, Palestinians, and sometimes also with peace movements in other countries. These bodies often accused the Zionist peace groups of actually serving only Israeli interests and of having no real interest

---

[6] The Law of Return automatically grants full Israeli citizenship to all Jewish immigrants on their arrival in Israel. Non-Jewish newcomers have to go through a slow and painful process to gain citizenship, with high chances of not getting it in the end.

[7] The somewhat incongruous slogan inscribed on the banner of *Ometz l'Sarev* is in fact: "We are Zionists, we are Officers, we are Refuseniks."

in a peaceful resolution of the conflict, and considered their expressions of sympathy with Palestinian suffering as lacking in sincerity. Furthermore, the non-Zionist groups, along with the Palestinians, argued that the Zionist peace organizations served, even if unintentionally, as a liberal fig leaf, under which the abuses of the Israeli occupation could freely continue. In fact, Palestinians who are involved in the peace dialogue with the Israeli peace organizations often expect and quite openly demand their Israeli counterparts to side with their national cause, a demand that for all practical purposes means denouncing the Zionist creed, because both causes are in certain crucial respects mutually exclusive (e.g., Nasser-Najjab 2005). The Zionist peace activists tried hard to prove that Zionism can be sane and just if the occupation is ended. Non-Zionist and anti-Zionist Israeli peace activists, on the other hand, partially accepted this Palestinian argument by admitting that the conflict is rooted in the "original sin" of the Zionist project that took root and flourished in the Land of Israel/Palestine at the expense of the Palestinian people. According to this historical narrative, which is naturally considered treasonous by the Jewish Israeli majority, the Palestinians were deprived of their national rights and of their land by the Zionists. The frequent Israeli-Arab wars are explained here as the direct outcome of one factor: the basic colonialist nature and expansionist policies of the Zionist movement and later the State of Israel. Clearly, regarding the two camps' relations with their Palestinian counterparts, relations between the moderates and the Palestinians were always considerably tenser because of their adherence to the Zionist creed. Another source of tension, however, is the Palestinians' overestimation of the political abilities of the Zionist peace camp, and their unrealistic expectations that it can impact the formal policies and decisions, with the recurring disappointments this brings in its wake.[8] As the Palestinians realize that the peace radicals are a tiny minority, they express solidarity but develop no unrealistic expectations and are therefore much less frustrated and disappointed with them.

As noted previously, the differences between the Zionist and non-Zionist peace organizations relate not only to the causes and development of the conflict but also to the solutions they currently propose: a "two states for two peoples" solution by the first, and a binational state by the latter. The argument for binationalism is based on the principled objection to nationalism (or postnationalism, as some prefer to term it), as well as on the line of reasoning that a Palestinian state established along the lines of the Oslo accords or separated from Israel along the 1967 borders would be too weak economically, militarily, and politically to be really independent, a situation that would

---

[8] A sober assessment of the Israeli peace camp's potential impact was recently put forward by Ghassan Khatib, the Palestinian co-editor of the Internet weekly *Bitterlemons*: "But these organizations were only ever meant to be supporting actors to the headline cast. At some point, however, the importance of this aspect of peacemaking became exaggerated to a point where some parties, whether on either side or from third countries, thought that maybe these auxiliary efforts could compensate the parties for the absence of substantial achievement in the actual process" (http://www.bitterlemons.org/previous/bl280507ed19.html).

only serve the colonialist aspirations of Zionism. Some anti-Zionists also maintain that separation between Israelis and Palestinians is meant to prepare the
ground for the ethnic cleansing of the latter. Only a joint Israeli-Palestinian
political-economic framework, they say, will grant the deprived Palestinian
side a commensurate degree of prosperity and thus prevent further bloodshed.

Another issue, related to that described earlier, is that of the *peace dividend*.
For many years, the Israeli peace movement largely refrained from developing
this idea, hardly touching on the economic consequences of the resolution of
the conflict. This strategy was apparently intended to prevent discussion of the
problematic question of who in Israeli society would most benefit economically
from a war-free, open-bordered Middle East and who would not. Many experts
contend that members of the Israeli middle and upper-middle classes would be
the first and perhaps the only ones to enjoy the fruits of peace, clearly not
a constructive argument for the peace movement because, were it put on the
table for discussion, it would expose the movement – given its middle-class
sociodemographic composition – to the accusation that its struggle for peace
was actually motivated by its members' economic interests.[9]

Others maintain that it would not be wise for the peace movement to over-
emphasize the peace dividends issue for another reason: it could take many
years before such dividends are realized, and unfulfilled expectations of immediate benefits might well pull the rug from under those promoting the cause of
peace. Still, the more radical peace groups tried to expose – with little success, it
must be admitted – the connection they saw between the protracted conflict in
the Middle East and the socioeconomic problems within Israeli society, as well
as the growing inequality in wealth between Israelis and Palestinians and most
Arabs in the region. They often argue that a major feature of the capitalistic
Israeli society is the oppression of the weaker groups within and around it: the
proletariat, newcomers, women, Arab-Israeli citizens, Jews of Mizrahi origin,
and the Palestinians. According to this interpretation, the growing oppression of these subgroups within the Zionist state and of the Palestinians both
emanate from the same origin. As an ethno-national entity, Ashkenazi-Zionist
Israel cannot come to terms with either its Jewish minorities or a Palestinian
state next to it. Thus, radical peace groups maintain that the establishment of
a Palestinian state in and of itself is no remedy for the conflict, which can be
resolved only by a basic cognitive change on the part of the Israeli elites and
equalizing the standards of living within and between Israeli and Palestinian
societies.

The operational diversity of the Israeli peace movement is even more evident than the ideological variation. Throughout the years, the various peace
groups and organizations developed their activity formats independently and
insisted on maintaining their operational autonomy. Whereas certain peace

---

[9] "States and their elites always made claim to the peace and its fruits, instead of utilizing the
peace and its fruits for the promotion of social justice and the reduction of socio-economic gaps"
(Savir 2007, 42).

organizations concentrated on organizing protests, others preferred lobbying, dialogue, and solidarity-enhancing activities, dissemination of relevant information not distributed by the mainstream media, or offering services and help to refuseniks and humanitarian assistance to Jews and Palestinians suffering from the various consequences of the prolonged occupation, and so forth. This operational variety, in a situation in which it might have been more cost-effective to pull together the scarce human and material resources available, can perhaps be criticized. Still, one should acknowledge that this was the immediate by-product of the peace activists' individualist mindset and their inherent difficulty in living with compromises. Factionalism was another obstacle to coordinating the different pace of actions, because much energy was wasted on bringing together the many splinter groups and on the apparently not highly successful effort to identify a consensual common denominator between them. Thus, certain peace groups were reluctant to cooperate with others that they did not consider "kosher" for a variety of reasons. For example, certain women's peace groups preferred not to allow men to take part in their vigils and not to align themselves with mixed-gender organizations, moderate peace groups refused to allow more radical groups that call for a binational state to participate officially in their demonstrations, and secular peace organizations systematically favored the option of media coverage of their rallies on the Saturday evening news over the participation of orthodox activists who could not attend these gatherings because they were scheduled too early after the end of the Sabbath. Hence, although Israeli right-wing SMOs could usually rely on the nationalist-collectivist orientation of their members to bring them together despite the ideological and operational internal nuances within this political camp, the liberal individualism and hyper-intellectualism of peace activists often stood in the way of a massive ongoing joint effort, allowing perhaps for only some large one-off protest events to take off. It is also true that by adhering to a decentralized operational pattern, the various peace SMOs remained fairly detached from one another and each tried to find a niche for itself that would compensate for or rectify the flaws that its activists identified in the functioning of the others. Nevertheless, as one might expect of rational political actors and as is shown in detail in the discussion of the contraction in the late 1990s of the POS facing Israeli peace activism, the level of operative cooperation between the various peace SMOs increased considerably, giving more concrete content to the abstract term *peace movement*.

Despite the internal ideological and operational variation, structural differences, and the high level of organizational autonomy that characterize the Israeli peace groups, the decision to consider them one analytical entity for the purpose of this study can be justified on two main grounds:

First, most of the bodies studied here view *themselves* as forming something of a particular political camp, especially when juxtaposed with the national camp, that is, the political parties and SMOs of the right. Second, the various Israeli peace groups, despite the differences among them, are perceived *by others* as a single political actor. In fact, most people from the outside fail – or do not bother – to notice the nuances that seem so critical to the peace activists themselves, and thus place them all in the same basket – old and new, small and large, radical and moderate, Zionist and non-Zionist, feminist and mixed-gender.

The Israeli peace movement as a whole shares some basic similarities with peace movements in the United States and Europe. The movement certainly shares a common aim – replacing military modes of managing interstate or interethnic conflicts with political, nonviolent ones. Their mode of operation is also basically comparable – mainly demonstrations and peace rallies, petition campaigns, sit-ins, and, more rarely, acts of civil nonviolent resistance. The whale-swim pattern of activity mentioned earlier is also noticeable in the history of Israeli peace activism and so is the great importance attributed to written materials – leaflets, brochures, newspaper advertisements, and currently the extensive use of the Internet as a means of communication and disseminating ideas. Peace activists in Israel and in the West are also comparable in terms of the sociodemographic profile of the average activist: of higher-than-average education, medium and above income, often female, and residents of urban areas.

At the same time, in other significant respects, the Israeli movement diverges from the classic contemporary peace activity model. For example, peace activism in other countries often reflects profound estrangement from the state and sometimes even from the national collective. The Israeli experience is unique in this sense because most Israeli peace activists view themselves as an integral part of the national collective despite their fierce criticism of their state's policies in the context of the Israeli-Palestinian conflict or of what they denounce as the militaristic nature of Israeli society. Another unique although related trait causes the Israeli peace movement to stand apart from most other peace movements and accounts for the low level of international cooperation: the prevalence of Israeli peace activists who serve in the IDF, before and after their involvement in the movement, is exceptional and highly off-putting in the eyes of many foreign peace activists. An important difference between European and American peace activism and the Israeli peace movement is the almost total lack of religious components in the ideology of the Israeli movement, as well as the paucity of religiously observant or clergy among the peace activists. The secularism that characterizes the average Israeli peace activist is not as strong an identifying feature in American and European peace movements, which are quite heavily populated with churchgoers and even with clergymen. One explanation for this is that unlike Christianity, mainstream Judaism does not have a pacifist legacy. Historically it is the religion of a people without a state, and a minority that was not considered qualified for army work; therefore, the question of launching wars or military service was not considered by Jewish religious authorities. Mainstream Judaism, however, has always adhered to the biblical concept of a just war and did not endorse pacifism.

The last feature of the Israeli peace movement to be discussed here, which also sets it apart from global peace activism, is the traditional avoidance of its major groups from taking part in global peace campaigns and/or from openly associating themselves with foreign peace movements. This is mainly because such external association and cooperation might cast severe doubts in the hearts of Israeli mainstreamers about the primary loyalties of peace activists and sustain the efforts of the movement's enemies to de-legitimize it and its agenda. The first, and one of the very few such associations, which indeed boomeranged in terms of the peace activists' public image at home, occurred in the very early 1950s with the establishment of the widely denounced, even persecuted from above, Israeli branch of the Moscow-sponsored World Peace Council. It was more than 40 years before another effort to join a global peace campaign was made, with the launching of the Israeli branch of the antiglobalization pro-peace Indymedia network, which again met with a harsh public response at home. Less ill-fated and also less visible cooperation existed between the originally Israeli *Nashim b'Shachor* (Women in Black) with Women in Black groups in many other countries, but the practical implications of this association were not identified as being dangerous to the public in any way and thus were not exposed by the media nor interfered with by the authorities.

A zero-tolerance position, however, was taken by both the authorities and the media toward associations that were considered less ineffectual. It is not surprising, then, that almost no Israeli anti-occupation peace initiative dared to cooperate openly even with the International Solidarity Movement (ISM), a pro-Palestinian group[10] that was very active in the West Bank and Gaza in the late 1990s and during the second Palestinian *intifada*. ISM activists – all citizens of the United States or European countries – openly support the Palestinian liberation struggle and come to the Palestinian territories under Israeli occupation to serve as human shields for the Palestinians from IDF fire and what they define as brutal treatment by the IDF.

As a result of this self-isolation, acts of solidarity with the Israeli movement by foreign peace movements have been quite rare. Indeed, Israeli peace activists who were willing to denounce Israel and Zionism publicly outside of the country were often warmly embraced by their European and American counterparts. This is understandable from the tactical point of view, because such collaboration could sustain the argument of these Israeli activists as well as the foreign peace movements that their criticism of Israel is not basically anti-Israeli or worse, anti-Semitic, an accusation often made by Israeli and Jewish organizations and leaders. This, however, did not reflect a parallel enthusiasm from both sides for organizational cooperation.

The distance keeping between the Israeli peace groups and the American and European peace SMOs, however, does not include Jewish peace organizations in other countries and twin organizations (most notably U.S. Peace Now with the Israeli *Shalom Achshav*) – with which the Israeli peace groups maintain very close relations, although not always without tension. Despite their close

---

[10] The only Israeli organization that openly cooperates with the ISM is *Anarchistim Neged haGader* (Anarchists Against the Wall).

relations, because of their different locations and operational contexts, the two sides' narratives and interests are not always identical. The association between Israeli peace groups and Jewish ones abroad is ideology related – usually Zionist groups with Zionist ones and non-Zionist or anti-Zionist Israeli groups with non-Zionist or anti-Zionist organizations. Beyond ideological and moral support, the Jewish groups help the Israeli ones in fundraising, although with the global decline in interest in peace activism after September 11th and with the growing frustration with the dead end that the Israeli-Palestinian dialogue has reached, some rivalry – mostly tacit – over donors and donations between the Israeli and Jewish peace organizations abroad has emerged.

Walking Down the Footpath – the Prestate and the Formative Phase (1925–1966)

From the outset, Israeli peace activism was conducted against the background of a protracted ethnonational conflict. Although the conflict had ups and downs in terms of the violence exerted and the sense of acuteness, its enduring presence has shaped the nation's priorities, cognition, and emotional condition (e.g., Arian 1995; Shamir and Shamir 2000). In this respect, Israeli peace activists are in the same boat with their right-wing adversaries and with all mainstream Israelis. This explains why the POS for the peace movement changed in one direction or another in accordance with variations in the conflict.

The first manifestations of proto-peace activism go back as far as Mandatory Palestine in the mid-1920s, when the realities of the Jewish-Arab conflict began to reveal themselves and the need to find an acceptable solution before it fully matured began to be felt in certain Jewish intellectual and political circles. The first organized group (or intellectual circle, according to its self-definition) to emerge was *Brit Shalom*, founded in Jerusalem in 1925. This small association sought to persuade the Zionist leadership and the British Mandatory authorities of the need to prevent the growing Jewish-Arab tensions from developing into a life-and-death struggle by fostering a binational model. According to their vision, the Jewish and the Arab communities would reside in one polity and enjoy equal political representation, regardless of their demographic size (Hermann 1989, 2005; Heller 2003). In the late 1920s, following a series of violent Arab attacks on Jewish neighborhoods, *Brit Shalom* took a very unpopular position by calling the Jewish community's attention to the fact that there was at least some Jewish responsibility for the deterioration in relations. According to the group's interpretation, the Arab attacks were fuelled by the constant influx of Jewish immigrants and the growing stabilization and prosperity of the Jewish community in Palestine, which threatened Arab domination there. Ignoring growing Arab fears and hostility, whether justified or not, was disastrous, they maintained, and hence they advocated relinquishing the Zionist movement's manifest desire to create a Jewish majority in Palestine.

The reactions of Zionist leaders and the Jewish public to this "heretical" reading of the situation, particularly because it was made when the Jewish victims of the Arab pogroms were being buried, were, as one can expect, extremely negative. *Brit Shalom* members were accused of siding with the Arab riots, of defeatism and cowardice, of being naïve, and of placing abstract, universalistic ideas, mainly pacifism,[11] above Jewish interests in their priorities, the same accusations that Israeli peace activists face to this day.

Brit Shalom numbered only few dozen registered members, all of whom were self-professed Zionists, although not all of the mainstream type. The group was highly homogeneous in its human composition – all of its members were Jewish and Ashkenzi, most immigrants from Central and Western Europe (mainly from Germany and the Austro-Hungarian Empire). The group was also highly elitist – almost all *Brit Shalom* members belonged to the upper crust of Jewish society in Palestine. Some of its leading members held prominent academic positions in the newly established Hebrew University (e.g., Prof. Gershom Scholem, Prof. Shmuel Hugo Bergman, and Prof. Ernst Akiva Simon[12]), whereas others had high administrative positions in the mandatory civil service or the Zionist establishment (e.g., Arthur Rupin). Its elitist membership facilitated the group's ability to gain access to community leaders and to the newspapers, yet on the other hand, clearly constituted an obstacle to the group's ability to 'sell' its message to the Jewish community in general, again a typical advantage/disadvantage of most Israeli peace groups ever since.

Brit Shalom also set the conflicting status pattern of peace activists who personally belong to the socioeconomic center but politically are located in the periphery. Efforts to create a fruitful dialogue with both the Zionist leaders and the Jewish community at large failed on two counts: the above-mentioned elitist-exclusive image of the group, and more critically – the disagreements regarding the Jewish majority issue. The limited interactions it conducted with the Sephardi community and with a few Arab intellectual and political figures of similar views failed miserably, apparently more because of cultural gaps and misunderstandings than political disagreements. Admittedly, *Brit Shalom*'s attempts at cooperating with Jewish socialist organizations, which were ready at the time to consider the binational or similar solutions to the conflict, such as *haShomer haTzair* (The Young Guard) – who, like their Socialist counterparts in Europe, had high but eventually unfulfilled hopes that proletarian awareness would serve as a bridge between Jewish and Arab workers – also ended in failure. Again, specific sociopolitical and sociodemographic factors played at least as important a role here as the ideological disagreements between the *Brit Shalom* and its potential partners.

Although it formally existed for about eight years (1925–1933), in practice *Brit Shalom* was active for no more than six, quite frustrating, years. During that time, several of its founding fathers (e.g., Dr. Hans Cohen) left it, doubting

---

[11] Although some members of *Brit Shalom* (e.g., Nathan Hofshi) were indeed pacifists, most did not adhere to a pacifist creed (Hermann 1989, 150–151).

[12] In the mid-1970s, Prof. Simon's son, Prof. Uriel Simon, was one of the founding fathers of the Orthodox Jewish peace group *Oz v'Shalom*.

the relevance of its recommendations in light of the deteriorating conflict, while the remaining members witnessed all of their recommendations rejected by the Jewish leadership and completely ignored by Arab leaders. Furthermore, the negative public image of *Brit Shalom* as defeatists has been projected onto Israeli peace activism ever since, although none of the peace groups in the years to come presented themselves as its successors or advocated a similar political agenda.[13]

The clash between *Brit Shalom* and the Zionist establishment produced a very negative and persistent public view of anything that even smacked of peace advocacy. The first victim of this stigma was the *Ihud* (Union) peace group, which some tend to view as a metamorphosis of *Brit Shalom* – the next appearance of the same whale above the water's surface. *Ihud* was established at the beginning of 1942, in the midst of World War II. Its leaders were two prominent men: the renowned and highly respected philosopher Martin Buber and the highly controversial Chancellor of the Hebrew University, Dr. Judah Magnes.[14] The composition of *Ihud* was very similar yet not identical to that of *Brit Shalom* and so was their binational focus, although *Ihud*'s orientation was characterized by a stronger moralistic, pacifist flavor than that of *Brit Shalom*.

Ihud's leaders made some highly unorthodox moves in their time, including testifying before international investigation committees and institutions (e.g., the Anglo-American Committee of Inquiry in 1946 and UNSCOP in 1947) which looked into the roots of the Palestine Jewish-Arab conflict and ways to handle it. They testified despite the formal position of the Zionist establishment that the Jewish community would have unified representation and no single group or organization was permitted to present its own view of the matter. *Ihud*'s leaders defied this instruction, because they were apparently more concerned with what they considered the fatal repercussions of the Zionist establishment's policies than with its ire or with the stains on their public image. At that time, the feeling was that the situation in Palestine had reached a climax and that therefore the nature of the policy to be agreed on was more critical than ever. Apparently, they were not concerned with provoking the anger of the Jewish mainstream, because some members of the group, and Magnes in particular, had already been branded political outcasts and therefore saw little point in trying to disguise their recommendations under the cloak of consensus.[15]

---

[13] Today's versions of binationalism advocated by radical peace activists are based on the principle of "one man one vote" and are therefore essentially different from what *Brit Shalom* advocated (Hermann 2005b).

[14] Both Buber and Magnes were associated in the eyes of many, then and even today, with *Brit Shalom*, although they had never been registered members of that group.

[15] Although completely anecdotal in terms of size, visibility, and impact, in 1947 the official Israeli branch of the pacifist organization, the International Fellowship of Reconciliation (IFOR), was established in Mandatory Palestine by a member of *Ihud*, Nathan Hofshi. This tiny pacifist organization, which over the years split more than once mainly because of personal rather than ideological rivalries, focused on supporting and advising Jewish-Israeli youngsters (numbering

The general rejection, including by international bodies, of the binational concept that *Ihud* advocated, the acceptance of the U.N. Partition Plan (1947) by the Zionist establishment, and finally the declaration of the independent (Jewish and democratic) State of Israel (1948) doomed *Ihud*. For a while, it hibernated (or dived into deep water). Nevertheless, during the 1950s, the remaining core activists decided to resume their activities, this time in an effort to promote the notion of antimilitarism that they presented as a traditional Jewish core value.[16] If steps were not taken, they warned, Israeli society, with its admiration of the IDF, could well develop into a Middle Eastern Sparta. Once again, in the context of a state-building effort and in light of the Zionist normalization ethos described earlier, their message had no chance of being heard. At that stage in the nation's life, when the newly established army had just proved itself by winning the war of independence, antimilitarism seemed extremely at odds with the overall climate of opinion.

After failing to communicate their message to the public at large, *Ihud*'s leaders (mainly Buber, Magnes having passed away in 1948) concentrated almost desperately on trying to transmit warnings to the country's policy makers against maltreating Israel's Arab citizens who were under military rule that severely curtailed their civil rights (Buber 1988, 204–209). Opposition to military rule over the Arab sector, which remained in force until the mid-1960s, was very slow to bear fruit.

Ihud was also the only Israeli group – with the exception of the tiny Public Committee for Nuclear Demilitarization of the early 1960s – that in the early 1960s openly challenged the wisdom of the Israeli government's decision to construct a nuclear plant and acquire nuclear capabilities (Hermann 1989, 211). Its reservations were, of course, pushed aside by the authorities, which never admitted to such capabilities, hiding behind the oblique official statement that "Israel will never be the first to introduce nuclear weapons into the Middle East." Because the issue was never open to public discussion, *Ihud*'s position never resonated in the public ear. The group slowly faded away in the early 1960s, leaving behind a strong sense of pessimism among its few – and elderly – supporters, and an even stronger negative public image of peace activism as being completely detached from reality.

As already explained, in the early days of the state, when the government was anxious to establish its authority, the proximate POS facing all grassroots endeavors, peace included, was worse than the favorable POS that faced such activism beforehand. This explains, at least in part, why the few manifestations

---

about 250–300 by the early 1990s), who refused to serve in the IDF because of their pacifist beliefs, on how to deal with the military authorities. The organization still exists, but its weight within the peace movement is barely discernible.

[16] This antimilitaristic Jewish sentiment was noted at approximately the same time by sociologists in the United States: "Jews of all ages on [college] campuses sought ways in which they could reconcile commitments to science and to their political beliefs [...] émigré scientists, especially Jews and young scientists had political experiences that made them suspicious of strong military-science ties (Moore 1999, 113).

of peace activism that took place in the 1950s were doomed to oblivion, even if their scale at the time was significant. For example, very few today remember *Vaad haShalom haYisraeli* (The Israeli Peace Committee) of the early 1950s. This *Vaad*, the Israeli branch of the antinuclear World Peace Council global campaign, succeeded for a short time in making itself heard in the Israeli political arena but left behind absolutely no political or other traces. In 1951, it collected over 400,000(!) signatures on the Israeli version of the second antinuclear Stockholm Appeal – almost one-third of Israel's adult population at the time (Hermann 1989, 235–237). In 1952, this group also organized a workers' strike in the Tel Aviv port, with the workers refusing to load a cargo of orange juice to be shipped to American soldiers in Korea, in protest of the Korean War. The fact that *Vaad haShalom* had the support of certain leaders of the socialist United Workers party (Mapam) and the Israeli Communist party (Maki) made it the target of vicious defamation by the Mapai government, including Prime Minister Ben-Gurion himself, and soon had to beat a retreat. *Vaad haShalom* was accused of being a front organization for the U.S.S.R., which in the 1950s was shifting its support to the Arab side, and there were indications from the authorities that many of the signatures on the Stockholm Appeal were bogus.

The explanation for this fierce attack on *Vaad haShalom* could rest with several sins that it allegedly committed. First, it violated the political taboo of the time on organizing wide-ranging citizens' activities outside of the political party framework. Second, it openly identified with a global, non-Jewish, non-Zionist campaign, and maintained close relations with the U.S.S.R. Finally, it was bashed from above in the context of sheer partisan rivalry: as mentioned, it was backed by certain leaders of Mapam, then a party sufficiently popular to be regarded as competition to the ruling Mapai party, and by Maki, which was both communist and non-Zionist and therefore beyond the boundaries of the national consensus. This final issue points to an existential dilemma that faced *Vaad haShalom* and every Israeli peace organization that followed it – if they associate themselves with legitimate allies within the Israeli political establishment, the alliance might pose a threat to the ruling party and will be condemned because of electoral competition. On the other hand, if it allies itself with extra-establishment or foreign bodies, it will be delegitimized because it opted for unpatriotic "bad company." With no allies – inside or outside – the chances of a single group's making a difference is practically nil.

For many years, the legacy of these repeated failures was a strong disincentive for other potential peace activists to test the water. Indeed, the second half of the 1950s saw no such attempts, not even when the security situation escalated in the mid-1950s and against the background of Israeli participation, together with Britain and France, in the 1956 Sinai Campaign against Egypt, a military partnership that fixed Israel's image as part of the imperialist-colonialist West.

Exploring the Country Road – from the 1967 War to the Aftermath of the 1973 War

Somewhat increased legitimacy for grassroots political participation (the reasons for which were explained above) as well as new and pressing issues on the national agenda – mainly what to do with the occupied territories – changed the state-centered as well as the proximate POS for peace activism following the 1967 war. The turning point occurred in early 1968, with the appearance of the first "mass" peace movement, *haTnua l'Shalom uBitachon* (The Movement for Peace and Security). It was created in response to the emergence of a popular and highly visible extraparliamentary movement, *haTnua l'maan Eretz Yisrael haShlema* (The Movement for a Greater Israel), which advocated the immediate and full annexation of the occupied territories, and was supported not only by classical right-wingers but also many high-ranking IDF reserve officers, well-known writers, and other mainstream public figures, including of the Labour movement.[17]

HaTnua l'Shalom uBitachon was fairly visible between 1968 and 1973 and gained the support of a number of prominent academics (many of them faculty members mainly of the Hebrew University and the Weitzman Institute), students, intellectuals, artists, and other public figures of the left. It also made a conscious effort to integrate itself into the general fabric of the Israeli mainstream so as not to be relegated to the periphery, like *Brit Shalom* or *Ihud* in the past.[18] Thus, it adopted an inclusive strategy by defining itself as a grassroots initiative rather than an intellectual circle or any other similar exclusive format. Meetings were publicized and open to the public. Ideological debates and pluralism were encouraged. Furthermore, its activists were not asked to take on any organizational commitments or adhere to a fixed ideological formula. They were also allowed to remain members of political parties.

HaTnua l'Shalom uBitachon numbered only several hundred active members but apparently enjoyed the support of a few thousand Israelis.[19] It was the first organized endeavor to publicly warn of the political, military, and social dangers inherent in the Israeli occupation of the Palestinians. The movement,

---

[17] For a comparison of the two movements, see Isaac 1976.

[18] The movement was supported by several elderly former members of *Ihud* (e.g., Hugo Bergman, Gabriel Stern, and Ernest Akiva Simon) and used the facilities of the defunct *Vaad haShalom haYisraeli*. These connections would no doubt be taken as highly suggestive by proponents of the resource mobilization approach to the study of social movement, because they indicate that even when there is no open affiliation between movements of the same sector, they are often strongly connected and rely on each other's networks.

[19] The movement never defined its formal membership status, and therefore these numbers are based on activists' reports and some remaining protocols of meetings given to the author by the late Prof. Yehoshua Arieli, who was one of the movement's core group). Prof. Arieli's son was in due course one of the founding members of *Shalom Achshav*, and his daughter, of a radical left group that also took a neo-Marxist approach to the Israeli-Palestinian conflict, *Derech haNitzotz*.

which was apparently – although not declaratively – ideologically and strategically influenced by the American anti-Vietnam War grassroots campaign,
recommended putting an end to holding the heavily populated Palestinian territories of the West Bank and Gaza before the occupation became rooted in
Israel's political and economic reality, and, more important, in the nation's
psychological mindset.[20] To achieve this aim, its speakers proposed to open
a direct dialogue with any Arab leader or group willing to talk peace. They
also attempted to convince Israeli decision makers and the general public that
significant territorial concessions were a necessary and reasonable price to pay
for peace with the Arabs. The movement also insisted that further Jewish settlement in the territories be prevented, so that the territories could remain free
for political bargaining once peace negotiations were launched.[21] Finally, the
movement warned that, should Israel administer the occupied territories too
harshly, a violent rebellion eventually would break out among the Palestinians.

Nonetheless, the huge military victory of 1967, interpreted by many euphoric
and not necessarily religious Israelis as divine intervention on behalf of the
Jewish people, made the dissemination of such ideas almost impossible. Mistrust of the Arabs was far too deeply rooted. Thus, when in March 1970,
Dr. Nahum Goldmann, president of the World Jewish Congress, was invited to
meet with President Nasser of Egypt, the Israeli government refused to approve
the meeting, which *haTnua l'Shalom uBitachon* interpreted as an indication of
its opposition to peace. A protest demonstration organized by the movement
was brutally blocked by the police. Several demonstrators were so seriously
beaten that they needed to be hospitalized. In July 1970, the movement called
on the Israeli government, in what it called "the Israel Khartoum declaration,"
to relinquish its demand for direct peace negotiations with the Arabs, a demand
that was at the time totally unacceptable to Arab leaders since direct negotiations implied de-facto recognition of Israel's right to exist as a Jewish state
in the Middle East. The movement-government controversy became even more
heated shortly afterward, when Israeli authorities tried every trick in the book
to delay the opening of talks with U.N. special envoy to the Middle East,
Dr. Gunnar Jarring, convincing most Israelis that this was nothing more than
a hot air balloon.

[20] In retrospect, some critics pointed to what they consider a hypocritical distinction by this
   movement and its successors between the territories occupied in 1967 and the areas occupied
   in 1948. These critics maintain that the distinction makes it easy for the Israeli peace camp to
   ignore the realities of the ongoing occupation within Israel and even to enjoy its benefits, without
   having to suffer moral pangs, clearing their conscience by denouncing only the consequences of
   the 1967 war while turning a blind eye to the "original sin" – the 1948 war and its consequences
   for the Palestinians (e.g., Shenhav 2001).
[21] The question to what extent this position was acceptable to the Israelis is still open. Certain
   public opinion surveys conducted in 1968 indicated that 70% (!) of Israeli Jews were ready then
   to give up the territories in return for reliable international guarantees ensuring the safety of
   Israel (Bar-On 1996, 28). Although it reflects growing public readiness to give up the territories,
   a longitudinal survey project indicates much lower public support for such a move at the time –
   fewer than 50%.

The end of the War of Attrition with Egypt in late 1970 was taken as a positive sign by peace activists, but their moment of optimism quickly disappeared when the Israeli government, headed by Golda Meir, ignored the positive responses of Egyptian President Saadat to Jarring's peace proposals and Saadat's own pro-peace proposals. With the failure of this peace mission in 1971, the movement concentrated mainly on domestic issues, principally discrimination against Arab-Israeli citizens, and protested the harsh measures taken by the IDF against Palestinian civilians in Gaza in the context of its anti-terror activities. It also protested land expropriation of the Bedouins of the Negev and supported the return to their lands of the inhabitants of two Arab villages – Ikrit and Biram – in the north of the country, who had been driven out of their homes during the War of Independence and had never been allowed back by Israeli authorities, allegedly for security reasons, although the authorities had officially promised that when the war ended they would be allowed to return to their homes. *HaTnua l'Shalom uBitachon* died out in the second half of 1973, after five quite intensive years of activity and, for a peace grassroots endeavor, unprecedented public visibility. Its demise was mainly due to the growing fatigue of its activists, but also because of the traumatic effect of the outbreak of the October 1973 Yom Kippur war.

There were several reasons for the movement's inability to mobilize more support and to influence state policy and public opinion. Its adversaries succeeded in exposing it as another ivory tower experiment,[22] and maintained that although its ideas might have been noble, they were unrealistic in the best case and dangerous in the worst. The strongest attacks came, as expected, from the right. Here, there were two types of critics: those who focused on the security aspect, claiming that if realized, the movement's program might critically jeopardize Israel's security because the territories gave Israel the strategic depth it needed to protect itself, and those who related to the holiness of the entire land of Israel that God had promised to the Jewish people. For this reason, the occupied territories should never be given up voluntarily, not even in return for a peace agreement.

No less harmful to the efforts of *haTnua l'Shalom uBitachon* to win public support were the caustic criticism and fierce attacks on its patriotism and political rationality by the upper echelons of Labour, still the dominant political party in Israel and the main pillar of the mainstream. If this were not enough, the movement was also attacked by leading figures in Mapam, a prominent member

---

[22] One of the movement's critics, a professor of politics at the Hebrew University, equated its activities with the fallacies of *Brit Shalom* and *Ihud*: "The Hebrew University sustains a long anti-establishment tradition, which goes back to the 30s and the 40s, when Magnes and Buber, Senator and Roth, Bergman and Scholem, Bentwich and Leon and Simon were widely acknowledged as the representatives of the university's climate of opinion. Indeed, it was a group of extraordinary people, each an expert in his field, but from the political point of view, only one thing can be said of them: if the *Yishuv* had taken them seriously and listened to them, the State of Israel would not have been established. Only poor remnants of the *Yishuv* would have survived, living under the mercy of the Arab rulers and masses" (Akzin 1970).

of the Labour-led coalition, the dovish socialist party of the kibbutz movement, which was the peace movement's strongest base of ideological and logistical support. This criticism was primarily fed by the restrained but fairly well-known support for the idea of Greater Israel on the part of Mapam's leader, Meir Yaari, and especially for the Jewish settlement project, which he conceived as the successor to the Zionist pioneering project, a comparison opposed by the movement (and also admittedly by a majority within the party). Ideology aside, Mapam's resentment was also heavily nourished by the fear of certain party functionaries that if the peace movement became institutionalized as a political party, it might well take a large share of their own party's votes.[23] *HaTnua l'Shalom uBitachon* was thus stigmatized and politically isolated "at home." When it faded away in 1973, it left behind a strong sense of frustration, because its political achievements had been very limited although its potential to gain a real voice seemed so promising at the beginning. In retrospect, however, it appears that it did lay the foundations for a new dovish Israeli discourse on the options of peace and war and their costs, on the dangers of the occupation, and on the settlement project, thereby paving the way for more successful peace activism toward the close of the decade.

The Israeli national security consensus was shattered following the shock caused by the 1973 October (Yom Kippur) War, which started with a massive strategic surprise attack by Egypt and Syria. From a purely military point of view, the Israeli army won the campaign, which had caught Israel unprepared and vulnerable. The well-coordinated, premeditated Arab surprise attack, which cost the lives of many Israeli soldiers, made many Israelis think again about the real meaning of national security and convinced significant numbers that military might alone could not guarantee Israel's safety in the long run. In addition to the intense disappointment and frustration with the functioning of the civilian and military elites, the shock of this war convinced a far larger number of Israeli Jews than in the past that a political solution to the conflict should be sought without delay. Others, in the political center and right of center, reached the opposite conclusion from that war: that maintaining the occupied territories was critical and that they should therefore be settled by Jews, a concept that led to the establishment, in February 1974, of the grassroots settlers' movement, *Gush Emunim*.

As mentioned, the shock of the war and the citizens' protest in its aftermath altered the POS for Israeli grassroots activism for the better. *Gush Emunim* was indeed the first to use the new opportunities most impressively, even in the eyes of its adversaries, by changing the physical and human landscape with

---

[23] In the 1969 elections, to the dismay of most of the movement's members, a faction of *haTnua l'Shalom uBitachon*, inspired by Uri Avneri, decided to register as a political party under the letters NES ("miracle" in Hebrew) and join the electoral race, with their main candidate for a seat being Dr. Gadi Yatziv, who later became a Mapam MK. The list received only 0.37% of the eligible votes, thereby failing to cross the 1% threshold, and therefore did not win entry into the Knesset.

the establishment of more and more Jewish settlements in the territories (e.g., Newman 1985). Either because the Labour-led government was too weak at the time to prevent this, or because deep down its leaders thought that it was the right thing to do, very little, if anything, was done to prevent this massive creation of a new reality, which in years to come proved to be an enormous factor in shaping regional realities. The peace camp was slower to react to this POS change, and when it did, its methods, mainly short-lived protest actions, made its moves ineffective (e.g., Newman and Hermann 1992, Feige 2002). Still, beginning in the mid-1970s, the number of new peace SMOs, of various sizes, aims, and composition, grew rapidly. Because many of these bodies were tiny and short-lived, the discussion here highlights only the more significant or larger peace groups.

In 1975, the first peace SMO to emerge after the war had a rather unexpected nature – the religious group *Oz v'Shalom* (Courage and Peace). Some of the founders of the group had been involved in the activities of *haTnua l'Shalom uBitachon* and one of its founding members (Prof. Uriel Simon) even had family connections to a central figure in *Brit Shalom* (his father, Prof. Ernest Akiva Simon). *Oz v'Shalom* aimed to provide a counterbalance to the rapidly expanding influence of *Gush Emunim* in the religious-Zionist sector. The group tried to convince their target audience that the Greater Israel ideology of *Gush Emunim* and the establishment of Jewish settlements in heavily populated Palestinian areas were in fact antithetical to the Jewish tradition of not provoking gentiles so as not to inflame hostility (Breuer 1978). Orthodox Jews in particular should know better than to take other people's lands physically, they argued, because they were more familiar than secular Jews with the relevant Rabbinical writings on how to make the Promised Land their own. They also claimed that use of force had never been the way of the Jewish people to safeguard their existence. On the contrary, for a small nation, reliance on force is extremely dangerous; it is better to develop political skills and put its faith in God. *Oz v'Shalom* also challenged the political argument of *Gush Emunim* that the Jewish State should be the only sovereign in the land of Israel, whereas the Palestinians had no claim over it. They never questioned, however, the basic Jewish theological claim over the entire land based on God's promise to Abraham (*Oz v'Shalom* 1975).

Despite its Orthodox orientation, *Oz v'Shalom* also spoke to the secular Jewish majority. First, it tried to convey the message that the Orthodox sector was not unified in its support of the messianic, expansionist Zionist approach of *Gush Emunim*. Second, they saw themselves as the spearhead of an overall national moral awakening and aimed to humanize the character of Israeli society at large, so that it matched Jewish morality as set down by the biblical prophets (ibid.).

Because of its elitist nature – many of the group's hard-core members were again affiliated with academia, Ashkenazi, middle-aged, and middle-class, and many were not Israeli born but had immigrated from Europe or the United States – and its small size (a few dozen activists and perhaps a few hundred supporters), *Oz v'Shalom* could not organize street demonstrations or even sig-nificant public petition-signing campaigns. Instead, it used traditional Ortho-dox means of communication, which also suited its audience – the dissemi-nation of large quantities of written materials – booklets, leaflets, brochures, and pamphlets – all full of biblical and Talmudic references. The circulation of these materials was indeed narrow, but the main reason for their limited voice was that they were highly sectarian in language and character. Opting for "pure" Orthodox discourse might have been more fruitful as far as the Orthodox audience was concerned, had the group not faced a major problem: the lack of a Rabbinical authority to back it. In a society in which the rabbi is the sole source of authority for individual and collective actions, the fact that not one major Orthodox leader was ready to side openly with *Oz v'Shalom*'s ideas against those of *Gush Emunim*, which was supported by several promi-nent Rabbis, proved detrimental to the group's mobilization capabilities.[24] In addition, except for one politician (Moshe Una), all the other members of the then still moderate Orthodox Zionist party Mafdal (NRP), fearing for their electoral appeal, refrained from associating themselves in any way with *Oz v'Shalom* group, and it was thus left with no political sponsorship.

Despite the very impressive intellectual skills of its leaders and members, in the mid-1970s, *Oz v'Shalom* failed to win significant grassroots support in either the Orthodox or the secular community. Furthermore, owing to its Orthodox orientation, the group was also unable to integrate into the new and popular secular peace movement, *Shalom Achshav* (Peace Now), which emerged shortly afterwards. First, because *Oz v'Shalom*'s rhetoric was too unique to be comprehensible to secular peace activists, and from the ideologi-cal point of view, many secular peace activists thought that relying on Jewish sources was too nationalistic and not sufficiently universal. Second, and seem-ingly – although not in fact – a more trivial impediment was the inability of Orthodox peace activists to take part in activities organized by the secular peace groups, because most of them, particularly the large demonstrations, were held before the Sabbath ended, so observant peace activists were unable to attend and no Orthodox peace group could possibly endorse them.[25] Also, probably because it concentrated on Jewish audiences and used Jewish discourse, *Oz v'Shalom*'s involvement in the peace dialogue with the Palestinian side was fairly limited.[26] On the other hand, its relations with certain liberal Orthodox

---

[24] This changed somewhat for the better in the early 1980s when the group united with another Orthodox peace SMO – *Netivot Shalom*, which was supported by two prominent Rabbis – Rav Yehuda Amital and Rav Aharon Liechtenstein.

[25] Indeed, in the beginning *Shalom Achshav* tried to enhance cooperation with the Orthodox peace activists, and buses from certain Orthodox communities were planned to leave for the mass demonstrations against the construction of settlements later than the regular buses (i.e., after sundown, when the Sabbath was already over). Because very few used this service, however, it was discontinued.

[26] Some of its members took part in such meetings individually when they were organized by other peace groups; for example, by the Jerusalem-based mixed, secular-Orthodox group,

Jewish congregations in the Diaspora, mainly in Europe and the United States, was quite intensive, which helped to bring these Jews a message different from that of the settlers and their supporters.

Thus, although it still exists, *Oz v'Shalom* did not achieve much visibility, voice, or political influence. Events that it organized, often on Jewish holidays, were not well attended by secular peace activists, who felt estranged from the Orthodox peace argumentation, particularly with the basic postulate that the entire Holy Land is basically a Jewish patrimony even if politically it is better off divided if this could achieve peace. When secular people did attend these events, it was more of an anthropological experience for them than an expression of real political alliance or solidarity. The experience of *Oz v'Shalom* in the 1970s reflects the theoretical assumption on which the proximate POS is based, that beyond the general set of facilitating and impeding factors, specific groups witness specific POSs. Thus, this Orthodox group had to handle problems that the secular peace groups were fortunate not to have to deal with at that time.

A secular peace organization that used, quite skillfully, the more favorable POS of the mid-1970s was *haMoatsa haYisraelit l'Shalom Yisrael-Falestin* (The Israeli Council for Israeli-Palestinian Peace). The *Moatsa*, which like *Brit Shalom* was more an intellectual circle and a discussion forum than a grassroots movement, was established in 1976. By nature a small organization with no aspirations for wide mobilization, it brought together people with high public profiles located close to the Israeli power center. These included Uri Avneri (a highly experienced peace activist, journalist, and parliamentarian), Dr. Yaakov Arnon (former Director General of the Ministry of Finance), Prof. Matti Peled (a retired high-ranking military officer in the IDF, specialist in Arab studies, and later also an MK representing the Arab-Jewish party, haReshima haMitkademet l'Shalom), Meir Pa'il (also a retired IDF officer and an MK of the left), and Arie (Lova) Eliav (a widely respected parliamentarian, author, and tireless social activist).

With the backing of the strong public and professional positioning of its members, the *Moatsa* was the first peace organization that dared to state publicly that Israel should negotiate directly with the PLO, then considered by almost all Israeli Jews solely as a terrorist organization, not at all a partner for any political dialogue. It also called for recognizing the PLO as the legitimate representative of the Palestinian people, a dissident position at a time when recognition of the right of the Palestinians to self-determination was completely beyond the national consensus. The *Moatsa* did more than talk; its members developed close relations with certain prominent PLO leaders (chiefly with Issam Sirtawi, who was later assassinated, apparently because of his pragmatic position regarding negotiating peace with Israelis) and discussed a variety of issues of mutual Israeli and Palestinian concern. The idea of two states for

---

Rapprochement. Others later became involved in the activities of the tiny, much more radical orthodox group, *Rabbanim Shomrei Mishpat* (Rabbis for Human Rights), which maintained very close relations with its Palestinian counterparts.

two peoples began to gain consideration in these closed circles, while on both the formal level and according to public opinion, it was still a total taboo. Face-to-face meetings with Palestinians often took place in European countries such as France or Italy (Avneri 1986). The meetings were described as private, because the Israeli participants of the *Moatsa* had no official authority to negotiate with their Palestinian counterparts, who were usually PLO officials. Nonetheless, the content of the meetings was often reported directly to the most prominent Israeli decision makers.[27] By accepting the reports and not taking any action to stop the meetings, decision makers, including then Prime Minister Yitzhak Rabin of Labour, implicitly acknowledged that there was some value in this channel of communication between Israel and the Palestinians. In a sense, these meetings, together with other informal track-two meetings in the 1980s between Israeli peace activists and Palestinians,[28] can be viewed as a precedent to the informal Oslo negotiations channel, which gave birth to the Oslo DOP in 1993.

In 1977, a completely new kind of peace activism was launched. A village, *Neve Shalom* (Oasis for Peace), was established, located between Tel Aviv and Jerusalem and adjacent to the Green Line. The socially engineered village – lands for which were allocated by state authorities, thereby signaling state consent – was meant to serve as a model for a voluntary, mixed Jewish-Arab community. Participants in this experiment, which developed into a viable community of several hundred inhabitants – Arabs and Jews, all Israeli citizens – were carefully selected based on their commitment to Jewish-Arab coexistence.[29] Most of them were families with young children, highly educated, bilingual, and highly politically aware. In a sense, *Neve Shalom* can be seen as the mirror image of the model established by *Gush Emunim* settlements. Like them, although politically totally antithetical, *Neve Shalom* was based on the premise that to translate ideology into reality, it is not enough to attend one, two, or a hundred peace rallies and demonstrations; one must live the ideology on a daily basis. Jews and Arabs living together in peace and equality under one roof, it was argued, would be the best proof that Jewish-Arab peace is not a dream, but an attainable goal. All the village children – Jews and Arabs – attended the same school and mastered both languages – Hebrew and Arabic. Both nations' holidays were jointly celebrated, and community office holders were elected in a way that ensured some balance between Jews and

---

[27] According to a personal communication from Avneri to the author.

[28] One such track-two channel was opened in 1980 by Prof. Herbert Kelman, an expert in conflict resolution from Syracuse University. Kelman brought to these meetings leading personae from the academia, media, and politics of both sides, with the aim of getting to know each other, because according to his paradigm, personal relations between opinion leaders create a fertile ground for future formal peace talks.

[29] The original selection standards were indeed very clear-cut; however, when the villagers themselves were later able to make the selection, certain undeclared criteria developed. For example, Jewish applicants who were considered "too Zionist" even if they were strongly pro-peace and anti-occupation, were sometimes disqualified and turned down.

Arabs. To spread the message beyond the village, a "School for Peace" was established. At the school, groups of people of different ages, but mainly young-sters, Jewish and Arab, Israelis and Palestinians from the occupied territories, met for peace education courses lasting from one day to several weeks.[30] The experiment received significant publicity in Israel and abroad, and to this day attracts many visitors, media people, researchers, and funding.

The question to what extent this was indeed a successful experiment remains open. To begin with, today, almost 30 years later, *Neve Shalom* is still unique: no other village or town that follows this model has been established. In other words, it did not serve as a role model, although it did expand in time. Second, it appears that it was mainly those who supported the coexistence idea in the first place who employed the services of the School for Peace. In fact, in times of trouble, when tensions between Israelis and Palestinians rose, for example, in the late 1990s and early 2000s, the demand for courses was severely curtailed. Finally, it appears that external tensions, as well as those that emerged after the October 2000 events, in which the Israeli police killed thirteen Israeli Arab citizens during a wave of protest, did not remain outside the village but rather poisoned relations between the Jewish and Arab settlers of *Neve Shalom*. Hence, power struggles with a strong national base developed there which, to a significant extent, eroded the blissful image of the village, turning the oasis into a rather troubled place. For example, when the Jews annually celebrate Independence Day, the Arab villagers, rather than participating, commemorate the 1948 Palestinian national catastrophe (*Nakba*).

An even more distressing manifestation of antagonism occurred in 1997 when the soldier son of one of the Jewish families in *Neve Shalom* was killed when a military helicopter crashed on its way to an operation in Lebanon. Whereas the Jewish members of the community expected everyone to sympa-thize with the bereaved family, at least some of their Arab neighbors thought that the public manifestations of bereavement offended their national feelings, because the soldiers on the helicopter were on combat mission in which Pales-tinian refugees who were living in Lebanon could have been injured or killed. As one of the Arab residents of the village put it:

I was shocked and felt betrayed. . . . I knew of course that he was serving in the army but I had no clue that he was in a combat role. When I heard what had happened I cried. After all, he was our neighbor, one of the village. But then I took hold of myself and said, "What's going on here, is this supposed to be the left?" And I said to them, "My aunt lives in Lebanon and he went there to kill her." . . . This was the worst time of my life – I was between a bereaved mother, bereaved parents and my ideology (Waffa Zrik-Srur 2003, 68).

---

[30] In recent years, the school has also published a magazine, *Pitchon Pe* (Speaking Out), which promotes its dialogue philosophy. The magazine's editor is an Israeli Arab, attorney Rabah Halabi; however, the publication's language is Hebrew, which certain observers view as a classic colonialist situation (e.g., http://www.mahsom.com/article.php?id=4616).

At the same time, optimists would argue that the village has not fallen apart despite the difficulties that it faced. Some find comfort in the fact that despite the external and internal pressures, its residents prefer to stay there rather than move out, and the educational work done there presents the youngsters with a different, egalitarian, and self-conscious model of Jewish-Arab partnership, very different from the typical antagonistic neighbor model that prevails in the country at large.

Hitting the Highway – from the Israeli-Egyptian Peace to the First Gulf War (1978–1991)

The golden age of Israeli peace activism began in early 1978, with the emergence of *Shalom Achshav*, the largest, most viable, and best-known Israeli peace movement. In fact, many people in Israel and abroad cannot tell *Shalom Achshav* from the Israeli peace movement at large and view them as interchangeable.[31] The movement emerged spontaneously, yet not by chance, less than a year after Labour's first-ever electoral defeat and the establishment of a Likud-led government, and against the background of difficulties in the peace negotiations with Egypt. These two developments, plus the post-1973 trauma in the background and the much more open SOP for grassroots activism that developed in its aftermath, pushed certain groups in Israeli society to a higher level of political awareness and involvement, which in turn gave life to *Shalom Achshav*.

It all began with the publication of the Officers' Letter, sent to Prime Minister Menachem Begin in March 1978. The letter was signed by 348 IDF reserve officers, all men with combat experience,[32] against the background of growing concern in certain Israeli circles that the right-wing Likud-led government had no genuine interest in concluding the peace talks with Egypt and achieving a real agreement. The letter read as follows:[33]

Dear Sir,
Citizens that also serve as soldiers and officers in the reserve forces are sending this letter to you. The following words are not written with a light heart. However at this time when new horizons of peace and cooperation are for the first time being proposed to the State of Israel, we feel obliged to call upon you to prevent taking any steps that could cause endless problems to our people and our state.

---

[31] *Shalom Achshav* is the subject of a number of academic and nonacademic books (and numerous chapters and articles). See, e.g., Palgi 1979, Reshef 1996, Bar On 1996, and Norel 2002.

[32] Twenty years later, Omri Padan, one of the founders of *Shalom Achshav*, referred to the use of military ranks in the Officers' Letter: "I had no hesitation whatsoever about using our military ranks, as the very idea was to get the signatures of combat soldiers, so that Begin couldn't stigmatize us as 'leftists', thereby pushing us aside. For the same reason, we refused to put women's signatures on the letter" (in Dayan 1998, 37).

[33] http://www.peacenow.org.il/site/en/peace.asp?pi=43&docid=62.

We are writing this with deep anxiety, as a government that prefers the existence of the State of Israel within the borders of "Greater Israel" to its existence in peace with good neighborliness, will be difficult for us to accept. A government that prefers existence of settlements beyond the Green Line to elimination of this historic conflict with creation of normalization of relationships in our region will evoke questions regarding our path we are taking. A government policy that will cause a continuation of control over million Arabs will hurt the Jewish-democratic character of the state, and will make it difficult for us to identify with the path of the State of Israel.

We are aware of the security needs of the State of Israel and the difficulties facing the path to peace. But we know that true security will only be reached with the arrival of peace. The power of the IDF is in the identification of its soldiers with the path of the State of Israel.

348 signatures   March, 1978

In many ways, this letter fully reflected the characteristics of *Shalom Achshav*, which brought it fame and support on one hand and criticism and antagonism on the other. The letter reflected its patriotism and adherence to mainstream Zionism, together with a strong conviction that the Zionist aspirations could not be fully realized if there were no peace with the neighboring Arab peoples. It denounced the idea of Greater Israel, but had no hesitation whatsoever regarding Israel's right to full sovereignty within the Green Line. The challenge it presented to the authorities was severe yet constrained: the signers suggested only indirectly that if the government did not pursue the cause of peace, they might not fulfill their citizens' duties, that is, serve in the army when called. Although the text is critical of the government's conduct, the criticism in no way de-legitimizes it, nor does it convey estrangement from the national collective at large.

The letter became the formative document of a rapidly growing SMO, which very shortly was able to bring thousands of people out into the streets. The founding fathers of the movement recall that they were very surprised by the huge number of people who contacted them following the publication of the letter by the media and expressed solidarity with its content. They were even more surprised and unprepared for the call from below to continue their protest beyond this letter. This success, in terms of public mobilization, was undoubtedly nourished not only by concerns that the peace talks would not result in an agreement because of the Israeli government's positions but also by the anti-Likud feelings of many on the political left and in certain societal circles. These people had found it extremely difficult to come to terms with Labour's defeat in the 1977 elections, because it caused them to lose their dominant political position. In this context, the peace protest of *Shalom Achshav* was widely welcomed as it converged with much deeper and wider political dissatisfaction with the political turnover, and in a way represented perhaps unconscious rejection of the results of the 1977 elections. It is not surprising, therefore, that there were many on the opposite side of the political map who interpreted this peace protest as manipulative.

Furthermore, those on the political right considered *Shalom Achshav*'s readiness to give away parts of the land of Israel in return for peace as basically contradictory to the essence of Zionism. The Promised Land, they argued, should be fought for if necessary to attain it and not given up because of soft heartedness or universalistic naiveté.[34] In his memoirs, Yitzhak Shamir, Israel's Foreign Minister and later Prime Minister of the Likud, summed up the right-wing criticism, as follows:

> In 1977, 300 army reserve officers had signed an appeal to Begin asking that Judea, Samaria and Gaza be returned for the sake of 'Peace Now' rather than adhering to the wholeness of the Land of Israel, although unfortunately in real life no such alternative existed. It was a slogan that, like most slogans, contained a shining if misleading promise: if Israelis only wanted it enough – despite the cabal of warmongers that was the Government, and if the territories were only given back – then peace would at once descend on this troubled land. The implication, of course, was that only these high-minded champions of peace really thirsted for it or knew – though they couldn't define it – the path which we should take in search for it (Shamir 1994, 152).

By the early 1980s, *Shalom Achshav* was already a large and politically noticeable grassroots movement, with two centers of gravity – one in Jerusalem and one in Tel Aviv. Originally a one-issue SMO, after the signing of the peace treaty with Egypt in 1979, *Shalom Achshav* had to make a decision: dissolve or look for a new and viable raison d'être. The not unexpected decision was to carry on. Some of its rivals now viewed it as a mere cover-up for antigovernment sentiments that, they argued, pushed it into joining forces with anti-Israeli bodies abroad:

> In many ways, Peace Now, born out of genuine pain and anxiety, had turned by 1984 into a typical fashionable rather self-righteous protest movement, seen by its followers and even the general public (on whom its impact was minor) as the diametric opposite of *Gush Emunim*. Not overtly political, it was nonetheless distinctly leftist, basked in the support of the Labour Alignment, especially the kibbutz movement which supplied many of its members, and found favor, automatically, in Israeli's academic and literary circles in which the loathing of the Likud was both traditional and endemic. Because these circles were closely connected to their counterparts abroad, Peace Now had also developed an overseas network of sorts, and its anti-Government message, however confused, was well received wherever anti-Israel groups congregated (Shamir 1994, 152–153).

Viewing with alarm the growing popularity in Israeli society of the nationalist, messianic version of Zionism advocated by the right wing in general and by

---

[34] Some observers view the peace movement as responsible for the growing nationalistic position within the Orthodox Jewish public: "It is highly likely that the 'hawkish' position amongst Orthodox Jews and the simplistic identification between 'Judaism' and 'force' in its violent and suppressing sense is the response to the 'defeatism' of the left which has been perceived as estranged to the Jewish tradition. In the eyes of many of the speakers of Orthodox Zionism the very readiness of Jews in Israel to make territorial compromises for the sake of peace is a clear indicator of their feeble Jewish identity" (Luz 2006, 263).

Gush Emunim in particular, *Shalom Achshav* now set as its overarching goal the promotion of a sane, humanist version of Zionism and more specifically the de-legitimization of taking over Palestinian lands in the territories. The movement also decided to expose and denounce harsh measures taken by the Israeli army against Palestinians in the occupied territories, a move that reflected a measure of strategic radicalization since in its first phase of activity, it had been very careful to target the Likud decision makers, and not national symbols like the IDF. *Shalom Achshav* claimed that such acts proved that the occupation was far from benign and that, contrary to formal Israeli propaganda (and public opinion), no occupation, by definition, could be truly enlightened.

Although careful not to associate itself openly with former peace SMOs,[35] *Shalom Achshav*, familiar with their fate, was well aware that its viability and popularity depended primarily on its ability to prove its allegiance to the nation's collective core values. Thus, for example, in the early 1980s, some of its leading figures still objected to touching on the sensitive issue that in ensuing years became a focal point of its activities – the settlements. Omri Padan, one of the initiators of the original Officers' Letter and today a successful businessman no longer associated with the movement, was one of those who opposed adopting such a nonconsensual agenda: "There were people in the movement who tried to pull us into dealing with settlements, the PLO, the West Bank and Palestinians, while I thought that we should run from these issues like from fire" (in Dayan 1998, 37). Although positions like those advocated by Padan did not come to dominate the scene in *Shalom Achshav*, in the early 1980s, the movement's basic policy of remaining close to the mainstream did not basically change.

The tension between its peace agenda and the desire to remain part of the mainstream became especially visible with Israel's launching of the controversial first Lebanon War in 1982.[36] Although on a smaller scale than the 1973 earthquake and the dramatic 1979 shift in external relations following the signing of the peace treaty with Egypt, the first Lebanon War also marked a noticeable change in the patterns of civil activism in Israel. For the first time in Israel's history, antiwar protest emerged in the very first days of the fighting, provoking a fierce debate not so much over the content of the protest but over the appropriate timing of such grassroots activism. The question under discussion was whether it was legitimate for citizens to intervene in the decision-making process only before a decision was reached or after it had been implemented (in which case accountability is the mechanism that democracies established to enable politicians to step forward, take responsibility, and receive the verdict

---

[35] The disassociation from former peace groups did not spare it from criticism in this direction by its adversaries, exemplified again by Yitzhak Shamir: "I couldn't help wondering once or twice what *Brit Shalom*'s small elite membership would have thought of Peace Now and of the comfort and strength our enemies were deriving from observing these Israelis demonstrate against their elected government" (Shamir 1994, 153).

[36] The second Lebanon War took place in summer 2006.

of the people), or, alternatively, whether it was legitimate to intervene during the implementation process; in this case, while the battle was still going on.

Although it aspired to be the spearhead of the peace camp, *Shalom Achshav*, hesitant about the legitimacy of antiwar protest while the guns are firing and concerned with the potential harm to its public image, remained silent for ten critical days before denouncing this "war of choice." Its first antiwar demonstration was organized well after several other much smaller and less well-organized peace groups had raised their voices against what they called a "war of deception" (of the Israeli public by its leaders). *Shalom Achshav*'s silence during these critical days was strongly censured by the more radical peace activists who publicly challenged its right to lead the Israeli peace movement. In retrospect, it seems that the damage to its status within the peace camp was never repaired, not even after it was credited with organizing the large public demonstrations against the war in June 1982 (about 120,000 participants) and June 1983 (100,000 demonstrators), and the largest public demonstration in Israel's history in 1984, known as the legendary 400,000 demonstration, which demanded the establishment of a formal inquiry commission to investigate Israel's responsibility for the massacre committed by its Lebanese allies in the Palestinian Sabra and Shatila refugee camps during the war.

The protest against the war, although larger and, by the public's standards, in a way more legitimate than ever before, also raised much public resentment. On February 13, 1983, this resentment culminated in the assassination of *Shalom Achshav* activist Emil Grunzweig (and the wounding of nine others) when a hand grenade was thrown during an antiwar demonstration. The act itself was carried out by Yona Avrushmi, a formerly unknown and not politically involved Jewish-Israeli. The shock of this extreme act of political violence was overwhelming, and it drew together Israelis of different political views. The assassin was sentenced to life imprisonment. There were those in the peace movement, however, who thought that although he was the real perpetrator, the right-wing leaders who spoke out so fiercely against peace activism and against peace activists were morally and, in a sense, even in actual fact, responsible for this tragedy, but they were never punished in any way. *Shalom Achshav*'s ability to restore its dominant position within the peace camp was further undermined by its insistence on maintaining its lawful character, hence denouncing the refusal to serve in the IDF under any circumstances. This cautiousness was sharply criticized by the more radical peace groups: "... it was part and parcel of the whole Israeli society which didn't pay any price for the occupation and believed that the status quo could go on forever" (Tikva Honig-Parnas in Rosenwasser 1992, 135). Still, in the early 1980s, *Shalom Achshav* refrained and continues to refrain from crossing the clear boundaries of the national consensus, which some of the more radical peace groups crossed. The most noticeable group that emerged against this background in 1982, and in certain respects took over *Shalom Achshav*'s leading position in the movement at that time, was *Yesh Gvul* (There Is a Limit). *Yesh Gvul* called on its members to refuse to serve in Lebanon and the occupied territories, advocating – for the first time in Israel's history – the option of (selective, political) conscientious objection. This call represented a face-to-face confrontation with the Israeli mainstream, in whose eyes military service had to be totally separate from soldiers' political views.

Yesh Gvul launched a petition against Israel's invasion of Lebanon and collected 3000 signatures by reserve soldiers against military service in Lebanon.[37] The group's support of conscientious objection never had any anarchist or pacifist connotations; on the contrary, it was described as the ultimate way to express one's concern with maintaining the high moral standards of the nation (Kidron 2004, 16–17). When the first refuseniks were jailed, *Yesh Gvul* openly supported them and even raised funds for their families when necessary. It also organized protest vigils outside of military prisons in solidarity with the refuseniks jailed there. *Yesh Gvul* challenged the taboo on service refusal even more by disseminating leaflets to soldiers in active service in the bus and rail stations, at public events, and in city squares. The fact that *Yesh Gvul* leaders and its members had all served in the army and that several of them had been awarded medals for outstanding service made their far-reaching criticism of this major institution in Israeli society both much more noticeable and much more controversial. The public's verdict was no less harsh because they were ready to pay the price of imprisonment for their refusal, because many in Israel, both leaders and ordinary citizens, interpreted their act as tantamount to treason.

Beyond the open advocacy of conscientious objection, the first Lebanon War brought another novelty to the Israeli repertoire of peace activities – parents' and women's peace activism, which became more prevalent in the 1990s. The "women who actively called for withdrawal from Lebanon were not motivated by feminism nor committed to women's solidarity. Their activism stemmed, rather, from a motherly fear for the lives of their sons serving in Lebanon" (Muhlbauer 2001, 291). The first such group was *Imahot Neged Shtika* (Mothers against Silence) which, when it later gained momentum, changed its name (and gender specification) to *Horim Neged Shtika* (Parents against Silence). The group opposed the ongoing presence of Israeli soldiers on Lebanese soil. The common denominator of its activists was that they were all mothers (later parents) of soldiers serving in Lebanon. Most had no former political experience or experience in grassroots activism. Moreover, the group had no political agenda beyond its demand for the withdrawal of Israeli forces from Lebanon (Zukerman-Bareli and Bensky 1989).

---

[37] In a way following the footsteps of the organizers of the Officers' Letter, the organizers of *Yesh Gvul's* petition also allowed only "active" servicemen (reservists) to sign it. The practical exclusion of women and other nonserving Israelis in a way reflected an acknowledgment of the mainstream's perception of who is allowed to participate in the security discourse and who is not.

The use, first of motherhood and then of parenthood, as a basis for peace activism was contradictory to the conventional role of parents in Israel in such situations: parents were expected to serve as social agents who transmit the value of military service to their children, because this was crucial to the nation's survival (Zerubavel 2004, 66).[38] Hence, they were expected to encourage and support their children during their military service and follow the consensual mourning patterns if they were killed (Lebel and Doron 2005). The nonpolitical organization of bereaved parents of soldiers killed while in the army (*Yad l'Banim*) had always been an integral part of the state's establishment and received substantial state financial support over the years. *Horim Neged Shtika* actually turned this socializing role upside down when they protested against the state (although not against military service per se, a phenomenon that would only develop much later). The reaction to this role reversal by the group that openly challenged the politicians' rationale and decisions was mixed. Some members of Knesset went as far as to use the pejorative "Cows (kine) of Bashan"[39] to deprecate these mothers. Others met with the groups' representatives (by then of mixed gender), thereby legitimizing parenthood as a basis for civil political participation in general and for peace activism in particular. The public reaction was also mixed; however, the criticism was mitigated by the supreme importance attributed in the collective mindset to the protective element of motherhood (less so parenthood), which was perceived as justifying interference in times of pressure. Because *Horim Neged Shtika* had no specific political agenda beyond its basic demand, once a significant withdrawal of Israeli forces from Lebanon was carried out in 1984, it indeed dissolved as it had promised to do from the start. The model took root in the peace movement's action repertoire, however, and was again put to use by *Arba Imahot* (Four Mothers) in the late 1990s.

The trauma of Lebanon also influenced the religious-Zionist sector, which suffered heavy loss of life of soldiers in the special religious *(Hesder)* units fighting on Lebanese soil.[40] This painful experience caused some in this sector to question their leaders' priorities, and the political and theological agenda of the dominant *Gush Emunim*. In December 1982, a new Orthodox peace group, *Netivot Shalom* (Paths for Peace), was formally established. Rav Yehuda Amital

---

[38] For an innovative study of parenthood as a motivation for antigovernment activism in Israel, see Hasson-Rochlin 2007).

[39] An expression taken from Chapter 4 of the Book of Amos, which refers to rich and spoiled oppressors of the needy that graze and bleed the field dry.

[40] Most ultra-Orthodox *(haredi)* men do not serve in the IDF because of a special legal-political arrangement dating back to the early 1950s. Most religious-Zionist men, however, do serve in the army in regular units and some in special units that combine studies in Yeshivas *(Yeshivot Hesder)* with shortened military service. Some of these special units were directly hit during the Lebanon War, resulting in a particularly high number of casualties from the religious-Zionist sector.

and Rav Aharon Leichtenstein, two highly regarded rabbinical authorities of the Alon-Shvut-Har Ezion yeshiva, headed the group. Their many student-followers were mostly Israeli born, considerably younger than members of the earlier Orthodox peace group *Oz v'Shalom*, and had religious, not academic, higher education. All of these characteristics, plus the rabbinical support that the group enjoyed, which made it more comparable and more of a potential competitor to *Gush Emunim*, expanded the new group's voice and mobilization capabilities among the religious-Zionist community.

Netivot Shalom openly professed a rigorous Zionist position and stressed its theological commitment to the entire land of Israel. At the same time, however, the group's platform (Netivot Shalom 1982) stressed the prime importance that they attributed to peace as a Jewish value for which they were ready to make significant territorial compromises, and their opposition to Jewish settlement in highly populated Palestinian areas. Finally, its leaders warned that as Israeli society at large (i.e., the secular majority) is not sufficiently strong spiritually, the burden of the prolonged conflict could well lead to an internal collapse and external defeat; therefore, peace should be pursued immediately (Amital 1983).

The tactics used by *Netivot Shalom* were similar to those of the secular peace organizations – demonstrations, petitions, and the like. At the beginning, it seemed to be making a real breakthrough, because all of the necessary preconditions seemed to be there: a trauma, capable leadership, a coherent platform, and a preexisting organizational basis (the new group relied heavily on the groundwork of *Oz v'Shalom*). This hope did not materialize, however; all of these were not enough to counter the very strong foothold of *Gush Emunim* in the religious Zionist community. The early momentum of *Netivot Shalom* dissipated in less than 3 years, and its few remaining fragments united with the veteran *Oz v'Shalom* in 1985.

To sum up, the increase in peace activities following the launching of the first Lebanon War had significant influence on the Israeli political agenda and on Israeli public opinion and changed what was considered the appropriate timing in terms of the peace activists' readiness to challenge the authorities. There are those who believed that this was the movement's greatest day and greatest achievement thus far: "During the past two decades, the peace movement's greatest impact probably came from its opposition to the Lebanon War in the early 1980s. It helped shift public opinion to see that Israel's wars were not always based on existential threats, and that governments could choose against wars. But the peace movement has provided only minimal opposition to a quarter century of occupation" (Newman 1997, 420).

To return to *Shalom Achshav*, in the post–Lebanon War era, it left behind many of its earlier reservations and self-constraint; it accelerated its criticism of the government and in particular of the settlements, which now became its primary target. The 1980s were also characterized by intensification of the movement's involvement in direct dialogue with the Palestinians, including with

PLO officials.[41] During that period, *Shalom Achshav* also invested energy in contemplating ways to reach out to wider public circles, an issue that was a huge stumbling block for it over the years. Although this was never systematically tested, the general perception is that the movement was established and initially managed and supported mainly by people of the middle and even upper-middle class, mainly Ashkenazi, secular, urban (although with a heavy presence of kib-butz members, who, unlike agrarian sectors in other countries, are considered an elite group in Israel), and highly educated (once again the high visibility of students and university professors in the later stages of its activity invested the movement with the ivory tower stigma that had haunted the Israeli peace movement since the early days of *Brit Shalom*). People of other backgrounds were naturally not officially excluded but apparently felt quite out of place at its events and forums. Yuli Tamir, later a university professor, an MK, and minister from the Labour party, admitted in a press interview years later that "*Shalom Achshav* succeeded because it correctly identified the real source of distress of the elite. An entire political stratum was in need of *Shalom Achshav*. That is why it didn't want Arabs; that is why it failed to reach out to Mizrahi Jews and to the new immigrant community (Tamir, in Dayan 1998, 38).

Because of its central position within the peace movement, a word should be said here about the way in which ideological and practical decisions were made by *Shalom Achshav* over the years. With no formal membership status (it also never registered with the state's registrar under its own name), formal organs, or institutionalized procedures for selecting (or electing) its leaders, the decision-making processes of the movement remained both unstructured on one hand and highly centralized on the other. The movement therefore was often criticized for being undemocratic: managed by a small core group the members of which rarely changed and who had never been authorized by anyone to make decisions and were therefore not accountable to anyone. In the early 1980s, when the ideological and organizational competition between the senior Jerusalem branch and the younger Tel Aviv branch was quite heated, this issue was often and widely referred to. Tzali Reshef (of Jerusalem), the person perhaps most closely associated with the notion of the position of the movement's leader (although again he was never selected as such), related to this issue in retrospect at a recent press interview. In answer to the interviewer's question regarding the democratic – or actually undemocratic – nature of the movement, he said

Your case is not entirely baseless. Indeed, *Shalom Achshav* does not have any elected institutions; in fact, it does not even exist as a legal entity. You may correctly argue that we should have had an assembly, which elects a central committee, which in turn

---

[41] This marked a significant change in the movement's strategy because, for example, in October 1980, two of its most prominent activists, Yuli Tamir and Dedi Zuker, left it following the severe criticism that they received from others in the movement because they had met face to face with PLO officer Issam Sirtawi, although meetings with PLO members were not yet legally forbidden.

elects the chairperson. But the way I see it, it was really only a small group that led *Shalom Achshav* and "cooked" everything. Were it really detached from its public, it would have found itself totally abandoned.... I believe that in many cases we operated much like the ancient Athenian democracy. It was very important for us to attain internal consensus. In many ways, the small, inner circle of *Shalom Achshav* is in fact an assembly of delegates (Reshef, in Shavit 2002).

Admittedly, the specific ethnic base of support and the ongoing under-representation of non-Ashkenazi sectors were not unique to *Shalom Achshav*, although because of its high visibility, it was the main target of critical comments in this regard. Almost all attempts by various peace groups over the years to change that reality failed miserably. It seems that Israeli Jews of Mizrahi origin who hold political views that match those of the peace movement do not feel at home there (see, e.g., Karpel 1999, Penkar 2003). The strong association between peace activism and Ashkenazi descent might also have pushed them away from existing peace groups, unwilling to be – or to be considered – collaborators. In 1983, the first and so far the only exclusively Mizrahi peace group – *haMizrach el haShalom* (East for Peace) – was established. This small group, composed mainly of young Mizrahi intellectuals, was led by an older person of Moroccan origin, Shlomo Elbaz, an educator employed for many years by the Jewish Agency (a Zionist mainstream, mainly Ashkenazi-led, organization). In its agenda, *haMizrach el haShalom* exposed the connection it perceived between discrimination against non-Ashkenazi Jews and the occupation of the Palestinians. They therefore called for far-reaching social, economic, and political reforms within Israel that would improve the situation of Mizrahi Jews, and reaching out to the Arab neighbors in general and the Palestinians in particular. *HaMizrach el haShalom* emphasized the central role that Mizrahi Jews could play in an Israeli-Arab rapprochement because of their first-hand familiarity with the Arab culture and state of mind. To build this bridge, they took the more radical path and challenged the national consensus by meeting publicly with PLO officials. The group was too small and lacking in resources to take off, however. Even more frustrating was the fact that, in a way like the Orthodox peace groups, all of its efforts to disseminate its message among groups outside of the usual audience for the peace movement's messages, in this case the Mizrahi sector, did not bear fruit. Whether because their political agenda was unacceptable to this sector or because the group was unable to shed the snobby peacenik stigma, *haMizrach el haShalom* never took off in terms of publicity, voice, and mobilizing public support, and dissolved after a few years of frustrating activity.

In the mid-1980s, authorities could no longer ignore the growing number of public and private meetings between peace activists from the various movements and Palestinian officials and intellectuals identified with the PLO. The more moderate peace organizations were torn by controversy over to what extent such meetings were legitimate while the PLO had not relinquished its strategy of armed struggle and refused to recognize Israel's right to exist, but the

general tendency was to talk to Palestinians who were willing to do so, wherever and whenever possible. Not surprisingly, the Israeli political establishment
was disturbed by these mushrooming contacts, which clearly contradicted the
official policy of no negotiations with the PLO. In 1986, therefore, the Knesset
took a classic retaliatory step against the peace movement: it enacted a law
that prohibited meetings between Israeli citizens and PLO officials. Although
some peace activists were indeed sentenced to short prison terms for disobey-
ing it, the law proved unsuccessful in halting such meetings and was formally
abolished in 1993.

The late 1980s were the pinnacle of Israeli peace activism in terms of intensity and the number of the functioning organizations and people involved, as
well as in terms of donations arriving from external resources. National and
international media coverage of the peace activities was wide and usually fairly
positive. The overall – both state-centered and proximate – POSs were undoubtedly more open than ever before. The authorities were busy dealing with the first
Palestinian *intifada*, which had broken out in December 1987, and the public
ear was more attentive than ever to the peace movement's alternative reading
of the situation. Weekly and sometimes even daily peace demonstrations and
sit-ins protesting the iron-fist methods used by Israeli authorities against the
Palestinians were organized by the various peace groups. Indeed, this does not
mean that the whole nation was mobilized and participated in peace activities
or even endorsed them from afar, in fact, far from it. Peace protests became
a customary phenomenon on the national political scene of this era, however.
Actually, these acts of protest became so common at the time that their public
visibility gradually declined, leading certain peace activists to consider the use
of other means, such as the publication of a weekly magazine, or alternatively,
holding some dramatic street performances to regain visibility and maintain the
public's attention. Jewish-Palestinian dialogue groups became extremely popular and hundreds of them were organized, some by existing peace organizations
and others by new groups that drew together for the purpose of conducting
such face-to-face discussions. A veteran participant in one of these groups
(Rapprochement) explained her preference for this type of peace activism:

To me, the long-term dialogue groups are the important ones because there you really
have a chance to grow, to develop, to change.... Now that I've gotten to know Palestinian people, it seems to me impossible and undesirable to have to try to separate our
fates.... A lot of it is simply personal. We feel that these people have become very close
friends, so the idea that we won't see each other anymore if there is peace is really
unthinkable (Veronica Cohen, in Rosenwasser 1992, 24–25).

This sincere concern regarding possible "negative" outcomes of a circumstantial change in which peace is attained by these authentic grassroots activists
materialized at least in part, however, not because peace prevailed but because
of the intensification of the conflict in the late 1980s. Indeed, many dialogue
processes that developed in the mid-1980s failed to survive the negative effects

of the outbreak of the *intifada*. On both sides, people who had voluntarily participated in such activities, indicating that they had a basic propensity for peaceful conflict resolution, now thought that it was not the right time to get together with counterparts who belonged either to the occupying side (Israel) or to the insurgents (Palestinians). It was particularly the moderate peace groups and organizations that found it very difficult to deal effectively, ideologically, and practically with the upsurge of Palestinian violence and other anti-occupation activities that involved the targeting of many Israeli citizens in the territories as well as within the Green Line. The forceful steps taken by Israel to stop the *intifada* had a similar effect on the Palestinians participating in these meetings. Ten years later, one of *Shalom Achshav*'s leaders reflected on the dilemma that these groups faced: "The *intifada* put forward a difficult dilemma: between patriotism and political logic.... This was a real trial by fire and *Shalom Achshav* was not really able to get through it unharmed" (Dedi Zuker, in Dayan 1998, 38).

This difficulty notwithstanding, the unequivocal and uncompromising demand to end the occupation was fostered with even stronger zeal by many pro-peace/anti-occupation groups in the second half of the 1980s. One unique group, *haShana haEsrim v'Achat* (The 21st Year) emerged in 1988, its name referring to the 21 years that had passed since the 1967 war and the occupation of the Palestinian territories. Unlike most other peace organizations of the time, the main purpose of this group was not protest or advocacy; it aimed to produce a philosophical-political analysis of the roots and implications of the ongoing occupation, and the ways to deal with it. Its diagnosis was grim:

The occupation has become an integral part of Israel's regime. Israel is losing its democratic character. Maintaining a parliamentary government within the Green Line serves as a fig leaf to cover the control relations between the occupying Israelis and the occupied Palestinians. The occupation is not another political event, but the political and cognitive state of mind of Israeli society.

The occupation is here, within us, and its destructive influence is felt in each and every sphere of our life. The army and the national security concept are subdued to the occupation missions. The Israeli economy benefits from the shameful abuse of the Palestinian worker and has developed a perverted colonialist character (HaShana haEsrim v'Achat 1988).

The group's highly elaborate – but also extremely sophisticated – basic document details the ways in which Israelis who refuse, even indirectly, to take part in the occupation should expand their refusal beyond military service to civil spheres of activity; for example, not buying the products of factories that pay their Palestinian workers poorly or boycotting products made in Jewish settlements in what were – according to international law – occupied territories. On the more abstract level, it called for avoiding the use of the "new speech" developed under the cognitive state of mind of the occupation and using transparent language that reflected the harsh realities of the occupation (ibid.).

The group's analysis of the situation was indeed intellectually and morally very impressive, but very few then (and now) could follow the high language and the complicated argumentation of the core activists, mostly astute academics. Their high intellectual skills were in fact an obstacle to disseminating their message because this highly sophisticated document alienated most audiences. The elitist nature of the group was not limited to their insensitivity to the wider public's discourse skills; it was also highly problematic in terms of relations among its members. The 21st Year was mixed gendered; however, apparently the female members, who also were academics of solid standing, were not getting the same "space" or status as the men. According to certain former members, the group actually replicated the gender power relations prevailing in Israeli society. In later years, some of these women activists, in academic articles and monographs, exposed the extent to which, despite its highly egalitarian rhetoric, the group was actually dominated by the men, although women represented the majority of the activists. These analyses also laid bare the practices by which the women were practically forced into doing the clerical and other "inferior" jobs, their intellectual and political skills ignored (Sasson-Levi 1995; Mazali 2003, 24; Golan-Agnon 2005, 34).

A most significant and related development of the late 1980s was the growing number of women's peace groups and organizations in Israel at the time (Sharoni 1995, Kaminer 1996). This noticeable shift from mixed-gender peace activism to women's peace activism had several interrelated motivations: first, the growing feminist awareness among female peace activists that women could be more successful in reaching out to the women of the other side, based on their shared experiences and feelings as mothers, wives, and daughters, and as women operating in patriarchal societies. In other words, women's peace activism rested on the assumption that whereas the life experiences of Israeli and Palestinian men undermined their ability to sympathize and understand each other, women were better able to do so:

Women are very interested in the prevention of wars: they constitute the majority amongst refugees, they are susceptible to sexual harassment, they are responsible for the daily routines in times of peace and are expected to carry on somehow even in times of war. . . . In general, women see themselves as life givers and protectors. This is also the role allocated to them by society, and from there, they are able to criticize belligerent policies and express their compassion for human beings (Isachar 2003, 13).

Second, beyond the feminist awareness that linked womanhood and peace, as shown earlier, Israeli women who had participated in the activities of mixed-gender peace organizations were pushed into creating their own groups because they thought that not only had they been kept away from leadership positions in the mixed organizations but also that their voices there were not heard and even silenced. This is how a woman activist analyzed the situation, when relating to the question of why *Shalom Achshav* did not take part in the large Women for Peace conference in 1989: "*Shalom Achshav* is such a large movement, and I think they have their own concept of what such a movement should look like.

They lack any female consciousness... even though there are feminists there, including some of the leaders (Chaya Shalom in Rosenwasser 1992, 65).[42]

At that time, women activists began to develop their distinctive political peace identity, which highlighted similarities and the intricate connection between the occupation of the Palestinians and discrimination against women in Israeli society, including in the peace movement. This is how one activist explained the connection between feminism and peace activism:

The more you fight against occupation, the more you alienate women from the Israeli government; the more they are alienated from the Zionist regime, the more they can come forward with *their* values and not feel subdued by and inferior to the values of militarism, of the security of the state, and so forth. And the more feminist you are, the more capability you have for real solidarity with the oppressed (Tikva Honig Parnas, in Rosenwasser 1992, 141).

Finally, the first *intifada*, a basically civilian uprising in which Palestinian women took an active role, presented a new type of security threat that was more relevant to women as citizens than past wars had been. In this sort of fighting, there were no clear front lines, and the participants were not only, and not even mainly, soldiers. The military experts, all male, could not come out with better advice on how to handle the new development than anyone else in Israel, including women, who had been excluded from the security debate on the grounds that they lacked military experience. In other words, the new type of warfare adopted by the Palestinians actually changed the proximate POS for Israeli women peace activists, opening the door somewhat wider for them to enter the public debate on the best ways to increase national security. Many women opted for the peace agenda as the only solution to the problem and joined the new peace groups because

Grassroots generally implies being widespread and common, in the sense of being universal. The term also suggests being outside the control of any state, church, union or political party. To the women claiming its provenance, being from the grassroots generally means being free from any constraining political affiliations and being responsible to no authority except their own group. Though such women generally recognize their seeming powerlessness against corporate and governmental opponents, they also assert their moral superiority, their right to be responsible citizens, not according to official laws, but on their terms (Kaplan 1997, 1–2).

The sisterhood concept, based on the assumption of the universality of the life experience of women, their nationality, ethnic origin, or class notwithstanding, inspired several joint Israeli-Palestinian activities. For example, the (first)

---

[42] Other women peace activists were aware of the inherent weakness of women and women's organizations in a male-dominated society such as the Israeli one and therefore preferred mixed-gender organizations: "With us, much like with the Palestinians, the 'real things' are not being done in women's groups. Decisions are not made by women's groups so if you want to be part of circles that are relatively more significant and exert more influence within the peace movement, you cannot stay in a women-only group" (Harel 2003, 36).

Women's Peace Coalition, established in December 1987, brought together Israeli Arab and Jewish women peace activists and maintained close connections with Palestinian peace activists throughout the *intifada* years. As explained by an Arab Israeli woman peace activist:

Paradoxically, the first years of the *intifada* were years of hope, of hopeful activity. The occupation started in 1967, but the *intifada* marked its end. If you are suppressed but say nothing, no one learns about your oppression. This is also true about the oppression of women: if you do not cry out – no one will notice.... The first *intifada* and the joint work of Jews and Palestinians in Israel has had a positive influence on the feminist movement in the country in general. The feminists became more political and the Palestinians became more feminist (Espanyoli 2003, 29).

It must be admitted, however, that regarding the Ashkenazi-Mizrahi divide within the peace movement, the sisterhood concept did not prove very helpful. Most women's peace groups were Ashkenazi, like the mixed-gender peace organizations, and their ability to reach out to Mizrahi women proved quite limited. Few, however, were as candid as these two activists, who openly admitted to the situation:

I could not pretend to be of the working classes because am not working class, the same way I cannot pretend to be Mizrahi or Palestinian, because I am an Ashkenazi who belongs to the hegemonic group. I don't live their life, I don't speak their language and many opportunities which are open to me are not open to them. Still, I can translate my empathy into action and use the political means I have acquired in order to translate this sympathy into deeds. There are plenty of subjects that bring us together and enable us to work in concert (Lerman 2003, 76).

Wow! What a wonderful sisterhood! Unfortunately this sisterhood is a very Ashkenazi one, and because of our blindness – a blindness from which all privileged groups suffer – we did not notice that we imposed our discourse everywhere (Shadmi 2003, 132).

The failure to bring a significant number of non-Ashkenazi women to the peace movement was indeed partly the outcome of class and cultural discrepancies, but it was caused no less by the fact that Israeli non-Ashkenazi women, like non-Ashkenazi men, are by and large more traditionalist, even orthodox, and this sociodemographic trait, as mentioned before, is closely related to being hawkish in the context of the Israeli-Arab conflict.

Most of the new – and ideologically highly articulate – women's peace groups were small and often had a non-institutionalized, non-hierarchical character, but they managed to become highly visible. Perhaps the most visible was the least institutionalized of them all, *Nashim b'Shachor* (Women in Black).[43] Between 1988 and 1991, this women-only, authentically grassroots movement held much-noticed, Friday-noon vigils in central squares and at

---

[43] This effective, although spontaneous, color gimmick was used by other groups as well. For example, another group, Women and Mothers for Peace, chose a white outfit, while Women in Green, a radical right-wing women's movement, opted for green.

crossroads throughout the country, demanding that the Israeli government end the occupation. The location – central crossroads – and the recurring nature of the vigils made this a classic example of a successful contentious grassroots activity:

Contentious events often arise out of spatial routines that bring large numbers of people together in particular places. . . . Spaces are gendered, raced, and classed. . . . Protesters typically attempt to mount demonstrations or rallies in places with political salient meanings. . . . But while insurgent movements make use of the preexisting meaning of places, they can also – either intentionally or unintentionally – transform the significance of protest locations (Sewell 2001, 62–64).

Nashim b'Shachor's ritualistic protest delivered a clear message and gained wide attention. This can be attributed to its members' human assets – most were middle class, many were professionals, often with academic education, and even when lacking political experience, they had high political awareness or developed it during their participation in the vigils. The group managed to build close connections with Israeli and international mass media. All these brought *Nashim b'Shachor* considerable local and international public attention, although not necessarily public approval. The effectiveness of *Nashim b'Shachor* also lay in the ability to make do with a very simple basic statement: end the occupation. Ways to end the occupation were nowhere specified. This strategic choice enabled the group to be open to women of different political views – from the more moderates and Zionists to radical anti-Zionists. It also enabled the vigils to continue for years under the same banner, until they were halted during the first Gulf War in 1991 (the vigils were renewed in the early 2000s with the collapse of the Oslo process, although on a smaller scale).

Their success in marking women's opposition to oppression and war spread beyond the country's borders – Women in Black as a concept was "imported" into many other states where local groups using the same protest technique and outfit were established. The movement won international peace prizes and was even mentioned as a potential candidate for the Nobel Peace Prize several years ago. Nonetheless, the actual political impact of *Nashim b'Shachor*, if any, was small, because clearly the occupation did not end or even ease up. On the level of conscience raising, besides the problems shared by all peace groups in disseminating their message to the wider Israeli public, the fact that *Nashim b'Shachor* was an all-female protest group made it even harder. By standing and protesting on the sides of the roads and in the crossroads, they broke the unwritten rules of women's political participation. Indeed, women participating in these vigils endured severe negative public reactions – from comments with offensive sexual innuendos to violent physical assaults by passing drivers and pedestrians who accused them of being "Arab lovers" and traitors (e.g., Helman and Rapoport 1997). Actually, in the eyes of many in Israel, mainly men, these women peace activists embodied the threatening type of an overliberated, overintellectual, overcosmopolitan woman who, on both the personal and the collective level, had turned her back on the traditional loyalty and devotion to her family and nation expected of a "decent" woman.

"Collective actors, most often adopt mobilization structural forms that are known to them from direct experience and better avoid tactics which lie outside of the experience of their own people" (Alinsky 1972, 127). Nevertheless, perhaps because of their unwillingness to expose themselves to the aggressive public reactions experienced by *Nashim b'Shachor*, and perhaps because of their will to go beyond sheer protest, other tactics were also adopted by the women's peace organizations in the late 1980s. For example, *Nashim l'maan Asirot Politiot* (Women for Political Prisoners), established in 1988, dedicated itself to the physical and moral support of Palestinian women who had been arrested for various political offences – from membership in illegal organizations to participation in violent actions against Israelis. The group catered to the material and other needs of these female Palestinian prisoners, who were often either abandoned by their families and compatriots or prevented from maintaining any contacts with them and thereby left defenseless in the face of harsh treatment by security authorities. These women were often arrested under special security regulations that prevented them from getting proper legal advice. The Israeli (mostly) Jewish women activists of *Nashim l'maan Asirot Politiot* did not question the nature of the offense committed but acted based only on what they considered basic human rights. As one might expect, particularly against the background of the accelerating *intifada*, this nonjudgmental approach was not well received by most Israeli Jews, and when support for the women Palestinian prisoners was reported by the media, public reaction was very negative.

Another service-granting organization, *Rofim l'Zchuyot ha'Adam* (Association of Israeli and Palestinian[44] Physicians for Human Rights), was established in 1988 and is still active today. The idea of establishing a new peace/anti-occupation Israeli group that would openly support the Palestinian liberation struggle arose spontaneously at a social gathering in a private home at the beginning of 1988. Most of those who attended were experienced yet frustrated peace activists, disillusioned with the practical impact of existing peace groups and particularly unhappy with the impact of their protest orientation. Large demonstrations had not only become difficult to organize after the outbreak of the *intifada*, owing to the unfavorable public mood in Israel but also had proved futile in changing government policy. Petitions in the newspapers were prohibitively expensive and also seemed ineffective in the Israeli context of the time. The question of what could be done, after all, to help the Palestinians and to prevent further escalation of violence brought forth a variety of possible solutions.

---

[44] For legal reasons, after the establishment of the Palestinian Authority in 1994, the organization omitted the word *Palestinian* from its name and remained a purely Israeli organization, called *Rofim l'Zchuyot ha'Adam* (Physicians for Human Rights).

It was then suggested that professionally homogeneous Israeli-Palestinian groups could be more effective than mixed ones, first because of the participants' common language and experience, and second, because of their professional credentials, which under certain conditions could be translated into political influence. The decision was to address the medical community. An emotional shock of some kind was required to drive people to action; thus, with the help of a prominent Palestinian leader, Dr. Haider Abd el-Shafi, a visit to Shifa General Hospital in Gaza was organized, with twelve Israeli physicians participating. This specific destination was chosen to enable the group to encounter directly the appalling medical conditions in Palestinian areas. The visit had the desired emotional effect. Several weeks after the visit, a meeting was organized at which a decision was taken to launch a professional endeavor aimed at protecting Palestinian human rights, particularly the right to adequate medical treatment. Teams of Israeli physicians were recruited to go, as mobile clinics, to villages and towns in the occupied territories to diagnose and provide whatever treatment was needed.[45] Some Israeli physicians and medical staff were also very helpful in getting Palestinian patients admitted to Israeli hospitals. Throughout the almost 20 years of the activity of this group, thousands of Palestinian patients benefited from the high professional skills of the volunteer Israeli medical teams, whose members were driven mostly by their sense of professional commitment, although in certain cases without sharing the radical peace agenda of the organization's founders and staff members.

The visibility of such activities was considerably less than that of demonstrations and vigils; however, the more radical Israeli peace activists thought that visibility did not necessarily best serve them under the circumstances of the late 1980s. This was first because it only raised Israeli public opinion against them and second because they believed that the Palestinians expected more of their Israeli colleagues than words and weekly vigils:

People are not moved by slogans.... The very bitter and long argument within the peace camp became, "Does the protest movement have to be an educational group?" to which I and my friends objected. "Or shall we leave it open and only concentrate on objecting to the occupation accompanied by activities of solidarity? This last approach has proved to be right, because you can now see that more and more groups are working in solidarity [with the Palestinians – TH] (Tikva Honig-Parnas in Rosenwasser 1992, 132).

Similar criticism of the modes of operation of the large and more moderate peace organizations, and in particular of *Shalom Achshav*, was put forward by Palestinians and by Arab Israeli citizens as well. Arab Israelis were clearly

---

[45] Paradoxically, after the establishment of the Palestinian Authority, with responsibility for health services transferred to the Palestinian Health Ministry, the legal situation became more complicated. Indeed after 1993, the organization's activities in Palestinian-controlled areas decreased, although they increased again when Israel took over the territories during the second *intifada* in 2000 and the entire service system of the Palestinian Authority collapsed.

disappointed with these organizations' refusal, for both ideological and practical reasons, to take a more forceful stand against the Israeli government and its policies after the *intifada* broke out and to identify openly with the Palestinian liberation struggle: "A big part of it [the peace movement – TH] is trying to conduct activities just to justify their continuing to be here. I don't think that a lot of them are doing it because they are willing to pay for such a change. I'm speaking about big movements like Peace Now" (Nabila Espanioli in Rosenwasser 1992, 150).

Some Jewish peace activists with radical agendas were so appalled by the way Israel was dealing with the *intifada* that they went so far as to call for external pressure to be put on Jerusalem to end the occupation or at least to mitigate the harsh measures taken against the Palestinians: "I really believe that the main thing is calling upon the American public to stop aid to Israel. It's the only thing, the only pressure that can make any impact on this society. I mean not only the government but on the Israeli public" (Tikva Honig-Parnas op. cit., 137). Such ideas, which in certain cases were accompanied by letters and appeals sent to international institutions and public figures, brought no results in terms of changing Israel's policies; however, among many Israeli Jews, they sustained and even deepened the unpatriotic image of the peace movement at large.

The public image of peace activism further deteriorated because even if they are engaged primarily with protest, with service giving, or with advocacy, even the most devoted peace activists could not put forward any functional equivalent to the example set by the right-wing movement's activists. The latter "put their money where their mouths were" and went to live in the occupied territories, thereby going beyond merely declaring their commitment to Greater Israel. The common impression was that the peace activists were not sufficiently committed to their cause, beyond showing up for demonstrations or signing petitions published in the daily newspapers. This reality undoubtedly also contributed to the growing frustration of some of the more committed activists, some of whom were honest enough to admit that they were not ready to go beyond a certain point in terms of personal sacrifice:

I know we need radical measures to take us out of our paralysis, our feeling of hopelessness and failure; steps that we – middle-class, parents, people who still live too comfortably – will be able to adopt.... A total refusal is the only morally and politically sound form of participation in Israeli society during the occupation. It is something we can write or say, not something we can, or we are ready right now, to do (Dafna Golan, in Hurwitz 1992, 102, 105).

Despite the difficulties involved in gaining information on funding, it can reliably be stated that the financial resources available to the Israeli peace groups significantly increased in the late 1980s (and even more so immediately following the signing of the Oslo DOP in 1993). From a constantly underfinanced SMI, it developed into a fairly well-nourished one financially. The influx of money at that time was due to growing international interest in activities taking place in Israel against the occupation. Much of the money that went to the more radical groups was donated by various Christian peace churches, left-wing political bodies such as the German Green Party, and radical peace groups in Europe. The more moderate Israeli groups benefited mainly from liberal and affluent Jews, primarily in the United States, who wanted to strengthen the Israeli political actors close to their own political views, whom they expected would challenge the right-wing Likud government. It should be mentioned that in the late 1980s, the larger Israeli peace organizations established friends' associations in the United States, Canada, and western European countries. These associations were involved in intensive fund-raising campaigns for the Israeli groups, mainly addressing the Jewish communities in these places.[46]

Israeli peace activism experienced a severe blow with the outbreak of the first Gulf War in 1991. During the war, Israeli cities were hit by Iraqi missiles, considerably eroding the sense of personal security of the Israeli public. On top of this, the Palestinians expressed open support for Saddam Hussein (by dancing on the roofs, as reported in the media). Many, including some leading figures of the peace camp, found refuge – at least for a while – in the warmth of the national consensus, and even publicly repented for their former "soft line" attitudes.[47] Almost all peace activities stopped, and very few were resumed when the war ended. Only the very solid peace organizations or the very small yet ideologically sound ones survived this traumatic period, but they also kept a very low profile and lost a considerable share of their respective constituencies.

In less than 2 years, however, it looked as though the knocked-out peace movement had finally made it, and that it could and would change from a peripheral political actor into a pillar of mainstream politics with the growing optimism regarding the possibility of reaching an Israeli-Arab peace agreement (e.g., Lewis and Stein 1991). The regional as well as the domestic situation seemed to have profoundly changed with the convening of the Madrid Conference in 1991, in the context of the Bush administration's effort to establish a new global order, in which violent regional conflicts no longer had a place. The Madrid conference marked the beginning of multichannel peace

---

[46] This ongoing reliance on foreign resources was a clear liability in terms of the peace movement's public image, because rivals took every opportunity to use this to "expose" its far-off loyalties. Specifically Shalom Achshav, as the movement's epitome, was thus publicly accused by some speakers (e.g., MK of Likud, Michael Kliener in 1982) of taking money from bodies with distinct interests, such as the CIA, and even from clearly unfriendly ones such as Saudi Arabia. Although no evidence for such cash flow was ever presented, such accusations took roots in the wider public's cognition. In 2003, a new Israeli NGO – the NGO Monitor – was officially established to "generate and distribute critical analysis and reports on the output of the international NGO community" (http://www.ngo-monitor.org/articles.php?type=about). What it actually does, however, is report regularly – in a highly critical manner – on the financial support given by foreign bodies to Israeli peace and human rights NGOs.

[47] Perhaps the most famous such expression was the one made by Yossi Sarid, then a leading MK of Meretz party and a veteran peace activist who, when learning about the Palestinians' dancing on the roofs, said in a dismissive and angry way: "now they can start looking for me" [but will never find me again – TH].

negotiations, which, in less than 2 years, generated the Oslo process, even if indirectly (Bentsur 1997). One should not forget, however, that Israel's participation in the 1991 conference was not viewed by many, including the peace movement, as very significant. The Likud government, then headed by Yitzhak Shamir, agreed to participate in the conference only because of tremendous pressure by the American administration, and therefore doing so did not signal an authentic Israeli intention to change its formal national security outlook. Furthermore, the Palestinians, who were not represented in Madrid by their own delegation, formally attended under the umbrella of the Jordanian delegation. This was, of course, totally at odds with the position already held then by all groups in the Israeli peace movement, moderate and radical alike, which recognized the Palestinians and not the Jordanians as the partners for peace negotiations. From the point of view of the Israeli mainstream at the time, however, the fact that the Palestinians did not get their own separate delegation was highly welcome, because at that time the prevalent understanding in Israel was still that the key to the solution lay – if at all – with the Arab states, not the Palestinians (Hirschfeld 2000, 77). The conference ended with a document (*Terms of Reference*) and a decision to continue the peace negotiations in two channels of between Israel and the Arabs: bilateral and multilateral. There was little progress in talks in both channels, but despite this, the right-wing parties were very alarmed and left the coalition, which in turn led to the collapse of the Likud-led government and to new elections.

A Curve in the Road – 1992–1993

Labour's victory in the June 1992 elections, although by only a small margin, marked a turning point in Israel's domestic politics, if only because it indicated a renewed increase in the level of electoral competition, a situation that usually boosts the impact of public opinion and opens up the POS, enabling the public, and of course social movements, to be better listened to and heard (Hagan 1993). The 1992 change in government was immediately followed by a change in the formal policy regarding the peace talks, which at the time seemed to be leading nowhere (Hirschfeld 2000, 84). The new government, headed by Yitzhak Rabin, made the achievement of a political solution to the Israeli-Arab conflict in general, and to Israeli-Palestinian strife in particular, its main goal. At the same time, it should be recalled that Rabin's electoral victory was to a large extent based on his reputation as "Mr. Security." He was a former IDF Chief of Staff and Minister of Defense during the first Palestinian *intifada*, whose well-known concern for Israel's security topped all his other priorities. In other words, although the Israeli voters authorized Rabin to go ahead with the bilateral and multilateral talks according to the Madrid framework, they also expected him to guard Israel's security interests carefully.

Although the moderate peace groups were thrilled with the political developments, the more radical peace activists did not like this facet of Rabin's personal and political agenda. Already in late 1992, a new peace organization, *Gush Shalom* (the Peace Bloc), was established, with the aim of challenging the policies of his newly elected government. The new group, which never developed into a mass movement but made itself highly visible mainly through its regular bulletins, active Internet presence, and presence at all peace demonstrations,[48] was led by Uri Avneri, a veteran peace activist who was also one of the main figures in *haMoatsa haYisraelit l'Shalom Yisrael-Falestin*, discussed earlier. Avneri, who was well connected to the Palestinian side, including personal friendship with PLO leader Yassir Arafat, always knew how to challenge the mainstream without actually crossing the thin line that would have made him an outcast. Avneri and his followers were critical of what they considered Rabin's overly cautious muddling through the peace negotiations and his overly harsh policies in the occupied territories:

Gush Shalom was set up essentially as a protest, first and foremost, against Rabin. I don't know if people here remember the first T-shirts we wore, which said, "Rabin, go for peace," with a double meaning – either "Go and make peace" or "Start acting peacefully." And we stood facing the Press House just a short time after the insane expulsion of 415 Palestinians to Marj al-Zuhur in Lebanon, which was carried out by the same government that [later on –TH] signed on Oslo, the Rabin government (Teddy Katz, in Hermann 2005, 20).

Rabin was indeed extremely cautious when moving ahead with the formal peace talks taking place in Washington. This was probably why Shimon Peres and Yossi Beilin, both Labour party ministers in his cabinet, did not fully report to him on the informal negotiation channel, which was gaining momentum in Oslo under their guidance and encouragement. The Oslo talks were conducted in parallel to the formal but futile talks in Washington, until a breakthrough was achieved in Norway and the negotiations were taken over by authorized office holders. The Oslo architects hoped that a signed document would provide the sides with the framework and mechanism to begin a process of normalization, mutual recognition, and mutual confidence building, and therefore lead to future negotiations. This document – *The Declaration of Principles* (DOP) – listed the main issues that had to be resolved within the final or permanent status negotiations between the two sides. It also discussed the procedural issues in the long term. In the short term, the document (as well as a second one signed in 1995, shortly before Rabin was assassinated) only considered interim or temporary status issues, leaving the core issues of the conflict for later stages. In retrospect, Oslo critics considered this strategy to be one of the main sources of the failure of the process. The major issues of the conflict: borders, Palestinian sovereignty or statehood, Jerusalem, Israeli settlements, and Palestinian refugees were not included in the negotiations (Baskin 2002).

By adopting the Oslo framework in September 1993, the Israeli government publicly acknowledged – to the dismay of the right-wing parties and groups,

---

[48] Although *Gush Shalom*'s presence at peace demonstrations never numbered more than several dozen demonstrators, always headed by Avneri, its visibility was increased by their walking and standing in an orderly line and raising banners topped with their logo – a combination of the Palestinian and the Israeli flags.

which were still devastated by their electoral defeat and now deeply shocked by the strategic move of Oslo – that the territorial and other compromises that a political solution entailed, painful as they might be, were justified. In return, the Palestinians acknowledged Israel's right to exist safely as a Jewish State in the Middle East and viewed the conflict as resolvable.

5

The Path Strewn with Obstacles (1993–2008)

Road Signs

As of this writing in summer 2008, we still lack the historical perspective needed to make conclusive statements regarding the nature and outcomes of the Oslo process. This process, which ended in escalating violence on both sides, could prove in retrospect to be the beginning of a slow but comprehensive peacemaking process. The opposite is no less likely, however; the Oslo process could prove to be merely an inconsequential interlude in the protracted violent conflict between Israel and the Arab world. Despite the lack of historical perspective, however, we can already discern six main segments of the Oslo road, each with its own topography, ups and downs, and with its specific opportunities structure as far as the peace movement was concerned:

- The rest area zone – fall 1993–late 1995
- The bumpy zone – early 1996–mid 1999
- The checkpoint zone – mid-1999–summer 2000
- The dark tunnel zone – fall 2000–early 2003
- The dead-end point – early 2003–summer 2008

In part, as everyone familiar with Israeli electoral history can see, this periodization corresponds with the government of the various prime ministers of the time – Rabin, Peres, Netanyahu, Barak, and Sharon. The correlation is not perfect, however, because the multifaceted situation facing the peace movement is influenced by more than only the top person or the party in power.

Clearly, any periodization of this sort is oversimplistic, because structural conditions, political phenomena, and societal interactions do not simply appear and disappear on a specific date. Furthermore, different analysts, holding different ontological and epistemological precepts, might point to different cutoff points. Therefore, the criterion for acceptance or dismissal of any such chronological account is less to what extent it is objectively correct and more to what extent it is helpful in explaining otherwise incomprehensible trends of continuity and change regarding the specific phenomena under investigation.

From the point of view of the peace movement, the Oslo road was characterized by progressive debility, particularly compared with the remarkable period of the late 1980s, when its energy, visibility, and size reached what is at least thus far its historical pinnacle. Still, even within the dozen years covered here, a negative correlation between the diplomatic process and the fortune of the peace movement can be seen. When the process peaked, peace activism declined, and vice versa – when the process slowed, the peace movement showed more vibrant signs of life, a rather suggestive relationship in terms of POS theory. This negative correlation has much to do – as we shall see – with the interface between the political establishment and the movement, as well as between general public opinion on peace-related issues and the peace movement agenda in this regard.

The first years, between the signing of the Oslo DOP in August 1993 and the signing of the Oslo Accords in September of that year and fall 1995, are widely perceived as the more sunny and hopeful years,[1] despite devastating terror attacks, severe difficulties in negotiations, and on top of everything, the assassination of Rabin because of his peace policies. However, this prevailing myth of euphoria in Israel in the postsigning era seems fairly inaccurate from the empirical point of view if public opinion is taken as the standard measure. The Peace Index findings presented in Appendix 2 (measuring support for the Oslo process) suggest that even in those years, there was no comprehensive national consensus that the process was the right way for Israel to go.

The Israeli Jewish public, who had not been prepared at all by the leadership for the strategic departure of 1993, was not well equipped with the emotional and cognitive tools needed to deal with this "change for the better" in the eyes of the pro-Oslo people. Memories of the first Palestinian *intifada* were still fresh, along with images of the Gulf War and Palestinians dancing on the roofs in support of Saddam Hussein. Participation at the Madrid Conference in late 1991 was widely viewed by the public as bowing to American pressure, and the ensuing bilateral and multilateral talks did not look promising either. Then, one fine morning, Israelis were informed that a declaration of principles was about to be signed with the Palestinians, "cooked up" by admittedly unauthorized persons, whom many in Israel did not know or did not trust.

---

[1] This is how a young peace activist, who now holds a very critical approach to the Oslo process and was in high school in 1993, recalls the overall climate of opinion at the time from the point of view of a teenager: "I'm ashamed to say that I actually remember the Oslo years as years of euphoria. As a teenager, I too had the feeling, which a lot of people had then, that it was a privilege to be living in this historical period. In terms of activity, this euphoria was of course very incapacitating. How great that one no longer had to hold demonstrations and hector Rabin, since he'd already been persuaded" (Uri Ayalon, in Hermann 2005, 43). Even in retrospect, certain analysts still referred to the early days of Oslo (i.e., late 1993 and 1994), as "the right moment" – although a missed one – for peace making (see, e.g., Bercovitch and Kadayifci 2002).

Not only was the public highly skeptical; in fact, at the signing ceremony on the White House lawn, the body language of "Mr. Security," Yitzhak Rabin, signaled that he was not signing the agreement whole-heartedly, because he did not trust Arafat, who represented the other side – the Palestinians.[2] Not only were most challengers of the process unconvinced of its chances of success, but even its most dedicated supporters were not thoroughly convinced.

These hesitations percolated to the public immediately and created a steady gap between support and belief in the Oslo process (as the graph in Appendix 2 clearly indicates). Actually, according to the peace index measurements in the Rabin-Peres era, the average level of public support was only approximately 50%, with a minimum of 41% in January 1995 (apparently resulting from the traumatic impression of several deadly Palestinian terror actions conducted at that time) and a maximum of about 59% in November 1995 (immediately after the assassination, probably as an immediate, short-term result of the shock). Levels of belief in the process were significantly lower,[3] with a minimum of 40% in August 1994 and a maximum of 56%, again in November 1995. Furthermore, in August 1994, only 14% (!) of the Jewish respondents thought that the Palestinians were fulfilling their commitments according to the Oslo agreement, whereas 84% thought that Israel was (Peace Index: August 1994). In October of that year, the same percentages were found (Peace Index: October 1994). The number of respondents who thought that the Palestinians would keep their word dropped to fewer than 10% a year later (Peace Index: October 1995).

Beyond their fatal physical impact, the deadly terrorist attacks by Palestinians against Israeli civilians conducted in parallel to the peace talks were psychologically devastating, because they made it difficult, if not impossible, for Israeli Jews to develop a more positive view of the other side's intentions. For example, in fall 1994, 65% of Jewish Israelis agreed that the Palestinians would destroy Israel if only they could (Peace Index: November 1994), and 68% thought so a year later, with 56% maintaining that the Palestinian leadership made no effort to fight terrorism against Israelis (Peace Index: November 1995).[4]

In the context of the ongoing debate over the construction of the separation barrier between Israel and the Palestinian territories, of interest is that already during this first, allegedly optimistic, phase of the Oslo process, the prevailing

---

[2] A few hours before the event, Arafat came up with the demand – which was very difficult for Israel to accept – that the PLO be mentioned in the agreement as a partner and hence as the functional equivalent to the Israeli government (Hirschfeld 2000, 150).

[3] The level of support was always higher than the level of belief in the prospects of the process. This implies that people who supported the process did not necessarily believe in its potential, which could in turn explain the rather rapid dissipation of public support for the process when it began to face difficulties.

[4] This figure remained high throughout the Oslo decade, irrespective of vicissitudes in the negotiations, meaning that a fair share of those expressing support for the Oslo process did so despite the fact that they considered the Palestinians utterly hostile toward Israel.

view among Israeli Jews was pro-separation. In fall 1994, 64% said that fences should be built between Israel and the Palestinian territories to reduce terror (Peace Index, October 1994) and by early 1996, 73% (!) of the Jewish respondents agreed that there should be a clear and closed border between Israel and the Palestinian territories so that strict separation between the two peoples was maintained (Peace Index, January 1996. And yet, views regarding the establishment of an independent Palestinian state seem to move in the direction of peace making – in late 1994, 47% thought that Israel could live with a Palestinian state, with 69% believing that the chances were high that the process was leading there in any case (Peace Index, December 1994). In early 1996, the figures were 46% and 76%, respectively (Peace Index, January 1996). In fall 1994, 52% said that to promote peace, cooperation in various realms with the Palestinians should be promoted (Peace Index, 1994). Therefore, as is discussed in detail later, from the peace movement's perspective, these first years of the Oslo process were in certain respects a rest area zone, because despite the mistrust of the Palestinians, there were indications of some goodwill on the side of the Israeli general public.

As for the interface with the authorities, this phase was mixed; it opened with a sigh of relief by most activists and high hopes for the rapid transformation of regional relations from conflict to coexistence. Conversely, motivated at least partly by frustration at not having received credit for cultivating the ground for the Oslo breakthrough and at being pushed out of the Rabin government's decision-making circles, the understandable and expected reaction of the movement was one of visible withdrawal and demobilization. These reactions were accompanied by accelerated institutionalization and professionalization. Peace activities now focused on Israeli-Palestinian dialogues, which for the first time did not stand in sharp contradiction to the general public climate of opinion or to the government's policy. When it shortly turned out that the diplomatic progress was significantly slower than expected, and that the Israeli government's negotiation strategy under Rabin and Peres was less soft line and compromising than the peace activists would have wished, they opted for a very mild response. This was first because the energy, resources, and people to launch massive protests were no longer available but also because they feared that by responding harshly they might strengthen the right-wing opposition to the Labour government.

The period between late 1995, after Rabin's assassination, and the May 1996 elections was a sort of a limbo from the movement's point of view. The shock of the tragedy pushed many Israelis off the fence and made their support of the process less latent. The right was licking its wounds, because it was widely held responsible for the prime minister's murder. In addition, the incumbent Prime Minister Peres was more of a "peace person" than Rabin. The slowdown in the negotiations and the increase in Palestinian terrorism against Israel, however, presented the peace movement with some stumbling blocks that were difficult to overcome. The fear that Likud, headed now by

Netanyahu, was about to make a comeback soon also had something of a paralyzing effect on the movement.

The second phase, the "bumpy zone," which began with the mid-1996 elections, indeed marked a political reversal of fortunes from the peace-making point of view. It was characterized by clear antagonism on the part of the newly elected Netanyahu government toward the Oslo agenda and of course toward the peace movement. Nevertheless, rather than abolishing the accords, the legal validity of the Oslo agreements was confirmed by the prime minister, and channels of communication with the Palestinian side were not yet closed. There was even some progress in those years, with the implementation of the Hebron agreement in January 1997 (supported by 67% of the Israeli Jewish public: Peace Index, January 1997) and the signing of the Wye River memorandum in late 1998 (supported by 63% of the Jewish public: Peace Index, October 1998). As indicated by the graph in Appendix 2, somewhat surprisingly, the average level of public support for the Oslo process during Netanyahu's term was higher than in both the Rabin-Peres period and during Barak's term in office after Netanyahu, with a minimum of 50% in July 1997 and a maximum of around 61% in December 1998. On the other hand, it is significant that the gap between the support and belief indicators widened during this era: whereas the former rose, the latter (with a maximum of 54% in May 1996 right before the elections and a minimum of 39% in August 1997) declined, at least in relative terms. The prevalent public impression was that the Palestinians benefited much more than did the Israelis from the launching of the Oslo process. In early 1997, for example, 56% estimated that the Palestinians had gained more from the process, 28% that both sides had gained about the same, and only 8% believed that Israel had gained more from it (Peace Index, February 1997). This unbalanced distribution of opinion suggested that many supporters of Oslo and voters for parties on the left considered the Palestinians to be the ones who had gotten the better deal. A year later, 75% estimated that the peace process had in practice completely stopped. Of interest is that, at this stage, responsibility was not placed solely on the Palestinians – about 25% of the Jewish public put it solely or mostly on them, with exactly the same proportion putting it solely or mainly on Israel and 45% blaming the two sides equally (Peace Index, February 1999).[5]

From the point of view of the peace movement, the period between May 1996, when Netanyahu was elected, to just before his government fell in mid-1999 was characterized by a more contracted POS than the former phase,

---

[5] Of note, the propensity of the public to accept a critical reading of Israel's history and conduct was quite noticeable at that time. In the Peace Index survey of April 1998, conducted just before Israel's 50th independence day, the public was asked to which extent Israel had reached the stage of development when critical debates on the various wars and painful issues such the absorption of immigrants from Arab countries in the late 1940s and early 1950s, could and should be conducted. The majority (70%!) favored such discourse.

particularly in terms of the peace movement's relations with the government, but also in its relations with mainstream Israeli public opinion. To these one should add the peace activists' frustration with the Palestinian refusal to relinquish the armed struggle and with the decreasing interest of others in cooperating with Israeli peace activists. To their great disappointment, the Palestinians at the time seemed more interested in connections with people on the right, who, they believed, could deliver more than the peace movement.

In other respects, however, the POS expanded. The antagonism of some external bodies toward Netanyahu's agenda rehabilitated the goodwill of certain donors who had reduced their support for peace activism in the previous phase, on the assumption that it was no longer needed. Also, the change in government relocated the peace movement to its "normal" positioning as the opposition and to a certain extent invigorated it. Apparently, the clarification of movement-government antagonistic relations brought several veteran activists back and pushed some new ones into action. Tactical innovation is also noticeable in this phase. The inability of peace SMOs to return to their old modes of action owing to the shrinking of their support base pushed them to search for new operative options that would conform to the new realities. The extensive and unprecedented reliance on the web was one such tactical innovation, and so was the creation of issue-focused coalitions of several peace groups, tactics that are analyzed in detail later in this chapter.

Barak's election in mid-1999, the opening of the third – "checkpoint" – time zone of the Oslo decade, signaled that despite the disappointments, the country was still somewhat hopeful that peace was basically attainable. After all, the majority opted for a candidate who had declared his commitment to achieving a breakthrough and a permanent status agreement. Like Rabin, Barak was also a former IDF Chief of Staff – representing the distinctive Israeli blend of security mentality and peace policy. This made his election seem like déjà vu. The removal of Netanyahu through Barak's impressive victory was motivated more by dissatisfaction with Netanyahu's personal conduct than by disappointment or disagreement with his policies vis-à-vis the Palestinians. In no way did this vote indicate restored Israeli trust in the Palestinians or their leaders, in particular, in Yassir Arafat, whom 45% of the respondents to the Peace Index poll of July 1998 characterized as a terrorist, compared with only 26% who defined him as a statesman (the rest had no clear view in this regard).

As indicated in the Peace Index graph, however, it was only a very few months into Barak's term that public support and belief in the Oslo process began to sink. From 55% of respondents supporting the process immediately after Election Day (Peace Index, June 1999), it dropped to fewer than 43% in summer 2000, and around 40% in the fall of that year. The belief indicators showed a greater decline – from 47% (in June 1999) to a low of 40% in April 2000 and of 34% in October of that year. Moreover, suspicion of Arab intentions became stronger. In the summer of 1999, when it seemed that Barak's peace initiative was taking off and that Israeli relations with the Arab world perhaps were improving, about 50% (!) thought that the warm welcome that Barak had received in Arab capitals was only a trick to gain wider concessions, whereas fewer than 40% considered this an indication of an authentic Arab desire for peace (Peace Index, July 1999). In early 2000, 69% agreed that the Arabs would destroy Israel if they had the opportunity (Peace Index – February 2000). Now much more responsibility for the dead end in the peace process was placed by the Jewish Israeli public on the Palestinian side; in the same survey, 55% pointed to the Palestinians as the guilty party, with only 17% blaming Israel, and 28% considering both sides equally responsible for the stalemate in negotiations. The public therefore welcomed the Barak-led iron-fist policy in the territories, including the many checkpoints and closures, whereas the peace movement naturally opposed this.

Like the general public, the peace movement's activists reacted to Labour's electoral comeback by developing some renewed hopes that the Barak-led government would deliver in the direction that they favored. They expected this government to opt for more lenient treatment of Palestinians and to show greater flexibility in negotiations. Specifically, they expected the government to lend a more attentive ear to the peace movement's arguments than Netanyahu's government had. Most of these hopes proved groundless, however, with the acceleration of Jewish settlement activity (with the blessing of Barak's government) and the extensive use of a heavy hand in the territories in response to the Palestinian Authority's noncooperation in terms of disarming the armed militias and keeping perpetrators of violent attacks against Israelis under lock and key. This made the life of the Palestinian population at large unbearable; for example, checkpoints were set up throughout the territories, making free movement within the West Bank practically impossible.

As mentioned previously, however, because of the frequent terrorist attacks on Israelis and the ongoing frustration with the apparently growingly non-compromising positions presented by Palestinian negotiators, these practices raised no sympathy among most of the Israeli Jewish public. At the same time, much like in the Rabin era, the mobilization and fund-raising options of the peace movement were severely curtailed by having a seemingly peace-seeking government. In addition, the almost daily drop in membership, together with a contracted POS because of the government's cold shoulder and unfavorable public opinion, again forced the movement to solve the dilemma of how to function as an effective opposition to the government without strengthening the opposition of the right. The different responses of the various peace groups created deep chasms in the movement and increased internal rivalries, wasting sparse energy. The failure of the Camp David summit in July 2000, and even more, the "no Palestinian partner" spin by Barak's team[6] were highly detrimental to the movement. This and the outbreak of the Palestinian *Al-Aqsa intifada* in the fall of that year doomed the peace movement to the political periphery, facing an impossible POS in every possible sense.

[6] For a thorough discussion of this spin, see Rachamim 2005.

This ordeal was further accelerated by Ariel Sharon's landslide victory in early 2001 and again by his reelection in 2003. Irrespective of his later steps, mainly the disengagement from Gaza, Sharon's public image at the time of his first and second election was of a determined and experienced fighter against Palestinian terrorism, as well as a devoted supporter of the Greater Israel agenda and the settlement project. At that time, about 80% of the Israeli Jews supported Sharon's position that negotiations with the Palestinians should be halted until they stopped using violence against Israelis, and more than 70% were supportive of the use of harsher military means against them (Peace Index, March 2001). In fall 2001, 77% of the Jewish respondents expressed support for targeted killings of Palestinians, and 67% wanted to see the IDF take over Palestinians cities (Peace Index: October 2001). Not surprisingly, support for the Oslo process decreased between early 2001 – Sharon's first electoral victory – and early 2003, his reelection, to somewhere between 30% and 40%, and belief in it fell to a low of 20%–30% (these figures remain almost the same at the time of this writing). Nonetheless, 55% thought that Sharon was better qualified than Barak to negotiate peace with the Arabs on behalf of Israel while guarding its interests, a figure that indicates that the idea of resuming the talks was not considered completely irrelevant even in those dark days (Peace Index, March 2001). In April 2001, when it was already clear that the *intifada* was not a sporadic eruption of violence, 57% of the Israeli respondents to the Peace Index survey still supported the idea of direct, face-to-face meetings between Palestinians and Israelis. Only 38% opposed such meetings, not attributing any benefit to them. Moreover, on the eve of the 2003 elections, after two years of bloody confrontations, more than 60% (!) of Jewish Israelis supported the idea of conducting peace negotiations with the Palestinian Authority (Peace Index, December 2003).

In other words, despite the fact that the Oslo dream faded away, apparently peace had not been completely erased from the national agenda. Like the period that preceded it, however, for the Israeli peace movement, the 2 years between February 2001 and January 2003 were a dark tunnel with no light at its end. This phase seemed to present the peace movement with the worst state-centered and proximate POS. From late 2000 until the 2003 elections, the peace movement returned to the situation of the early 1980s in terms of alienated relations with the authorities and with the general public. Perhaps this phase was even worse, because in the pre-Oslo period, there was at least some hope that once peace negotiations were launched, some agreement would eventually be worked out. After the failure of the Oslo process and the ensuing violence, however, no such hope remained.

Owing to severe internal arguments and disagreements, the movement's level of internal coherence, not very high in the first place, further declined, with few organizations capable of maintaining some momentum and the newcomers to the movement creating their own, usually tiny and radical, organizations. Email lists now replaced the city squares as the public space for peace protest and anti-occupation discourse. Having almost no more public support to lose, some groups openly supported the Palestinian struggle or called for an externally enforced solution or for economic boycotting of Israeli goods by the European and American public and the like. As one would expect, this in turn led to massive de-legitimization of peace activism.

The mid-2000s saw two major developments that placed the peace movement in a dead-end point in terms of its conduct vis-à-vis the authorities and mainstream public opinion: the construction of the separation barrier (or *Wall*, the term used by peace activists) and the unilateral disengagement from Gaza, both representing a large tombstone on the grave of the Oslo process. The barrier, although ideationally disliked by all peace groups, was challenged seriously only by few radical organizations. Even this protest was not realistically aimed at stopping the construction, however, but was more a sort of conscience-washing act or an act of solidarity with the Palestinians. Even the most dedicated campaigners realized that with the enormous support of the general public and the tacit agreement of the moderate peace organizations that were reluctant to openly challenge the barrier, which was widely perceived as a highly effective means of preventing terror, the chances that the formal policy in this regard would be reconsidered, let alone changed under the pressure of a few dozen protestors, were nil.

As for the disengagement, here most of the peace activists found themselves in an unimaginable situation in which they actually supported – along with most Jewish Israelis – this unilateral move by Sharon, which actually meant that the Palestinians were redundant and that a major decision about their future could be made without their involvement. Indeed, as is discussed later, some fringe groups in the peace camp fiercely opposed the disengagement; however, most were captivated with the fact that Jewish settlements in the territories would actually be removed, and when they became convinced that Sharon was determined to do so, the critical voice of the movement was no longer heard. Certain radical peace activists took this as a clear indication of its passing away: "There is no Israeli peace camp," they declared (e.g., Pappe, 2005).

The hopes that the disengagement would invest the Israeli-Palestinian negotiations with new momentum did not materialize.[7] On the contrary, with Israel out, the Gaza Strip entered a bloody phase of civil strife between the various Palestinian factions, while the Palestinian authority failed to take control of the situation. The expectation that Gaza would serve as a small-scale role model for an independent Palestinian state and thus refute the "no partner" spin, faded away. The majority of the Israeli Jewish public attributed the failure to the immanent political incompetence of the Palestinians – 67% maintained that Israel could not influence the developments in Gaza in any way because it is all up to the Palestinians (Peace Index December 2005), while the moderate peace groups remained silent. The radical ones, however went head on

---

[7] In the Peace Index survey of September 2005, 57% of the respondents believed that the disengagement would advance the peace process.

with the mainstream and the government, arguing that the Gaza chaos was the direct result of Israel's siege of the area, not the Palestinian's fault whatsoever. Their view was totally dismissed. With the deterioration of the situation caused by the rocketing of Israeli southern towns and villages by various militias in Gaza, the gap between the government's positions and public opinion and the attitudes of the radical peace groups grew larger. In fact, each side developed its own narrative of the situation in total isolation. This schism widened further with the launching of the Second Lebanon War in July 2006, which the absolute majority – over 80% – of the public strongly supported (Peace Index polls, July-August 2006), and the radical peace groups strongly denounced. Yet, these groups were now so small and located so far in the political periphery that no real dispute actually developed. The fact that, neither during the war nor afterwards, the peace activists did not, or could not launch a significant protest campaign is perhaps the best indication of the political irrelevance of the peace movement.

We shall now move on to a detailed description and analysis of these five phases.

The Rest Area Zone

The rest area zone of the Oslo road, from summer 1993 to October 1995, and some would say to May 1996, included some critical diplomatic landmarks: the signing of the DOP, immediately followed by the signing of the formal accord in Washington; the peace treaty with Jordan signed in 1994; and the second interim Oslo agreement, signed in September 1995.[8] In certain respects, this first phase was the most confusing one for the peace movement, because it entailed, concomitantly, the best and the worst POS elements that can face an SMO as a political actor with a specific ideology and organizational interests. At least on the face of it, conditions on the ground at the time of the signing of the Oslo accord marked a tremendous change for the better in terms of the POS facing the Israeli peace movement. First, the incumbent government, although not particularly friendly toward the movement, was by no means hostile, and its agenda was clearly in many respects more in line with that of the movement than that of any previous Israeli government. Second, the political party closest to the peace movement – Meretz – was a senior partner in the governing coalition, holding very important portfolios, including the Ministry of Education. Third, the Labour government was not sufficiently

---

[8] Although almost the entire peace movement celebrated the signing of the Oslo DOP and the first accords, the two later events received no special attention from it. The peace treaty with Jordan was apparently not celebrated because it was somewhat irrelevant from the point of view of the movement, which concentrated on relations with the Palestinians (just as the movement related only rarely and with not much zeal to the Syrian issue). By the time the second (interim) Oslo agreement was signed, the movement already had growing doubts about the way that the government was negotiating with the Palestinians, and perceived the interim agreement as an unnecessary delay in the way of getting to the final status agreement.

self-confident or well based to turn a cold shoulder on its constituency, to which most peace activists belonged. Fourth, as already indicated, in the early 1990s, grassroots politics was already an integral and acceptable part of the national repertoire of modes of political participation. Fifth, in terms of the volume of activity, the number of organizations, and funding (although not in terms of the number of activists), this period was still part of the golden era that began in the mid-1980s. The significant volume of activity gave peace activists a sense of belonging to a politically relevant and even prosperous political camp. Donations from the outside were also quite generous (providing that the peace organization supported the Oslo formula):

Throughout the 1990s, the easiest way of getting cash between the Mediterranean Sea and Jordan River was to get a Palestinian and an Israeli together to establish a center / institute / organization / group / or committee for Palestinian / Israeli / religious / Middle East or Arab dialogue / democracy / non-violence / cooperation / research / peace / or reconciliation and the money would roll in. It mattered not what these make-work programs produced for they often produced nothing but stale reports written for even staler donors sitting behind stale desks in western capitals (or in Tokyo). What mattered was that the governments of Europe and North America could croon on and on to their constituents about promoting peace in this god-forsaken region (Baker 2007).

Finally, in the early 1990s, it seemed that significant sectors of the general public, not only the decision makers, had begun to move slowly in the direction advocated by the peace movement for many years, thereby somewhat bridging the gap between the peace movement and the mainstream. Empirical studies conducted just before the signing of the Oslo DOP showed that although Israeli public opinion was still indeed generally hawkish in reference to the conflict, in fact about one half of it had gradually become more dovish when it came to the idea of territorial compromise. People showed greater willingness to exchange territories for peace and to accept conciliatory solutions as the status quo became less and less valued, particularly after the launching of the first *intifada* (Shamir and Shamir 1993). It seemed that the public was rationally reacting to changing circumstances, understood the constraints set by domestic, regional, and international environments, and changed its policy preferences accordingly. Thus, the value of Greater Israel lessened, although that of Israel as a Jewish state remained intact (ibid.).

All of these seemingly positive conditions notwithstanding, soon after the signing of the DOP, the peace movement found itself facing a fairly problematic POS. This unexpected quandary was primarily, although not solely, the outcome of factors exogenous to the movement and even to the Israeli political system at large, that is, the same political, perceptual, and cultural obstacles, which in 1994 and even more so since 1995, had impeded official efforts to achieve a breakthrough in peace negotiations with the Palestinians. These difficulties reflected on all the political actors that were involved or supported the peace process, parliamentary and extraparliamentary, including the peace movement. A fact not widely remembered is that the peace rally of November 4,

1995, at the end of which Prime Minister Rabin was assassinated, was organized to encourage the declining number of those who still supported the Oslo agenda. This included the decision makers – mainly Rabin himself – who thought that they were unsuccessful in achieving a breakthrough in negotiations with the Palestinians and also losing public support.

Partly, however, the peace movement's uncomfortable situation was indeed the result of endogenous factors, that is, those inherent in the movement's particular ideological and structural ways of handling the unfolding reality as well as its specific relations with other actors on the political scene. The first difficult issue that the peace movement had to face was the widespread perception of its role in getting to Oslo. Three different narratives developed in this regard: the Labour narrative, the narrative of the right-wing parties and organizations, and the narrative of the peace movement itself. Before the differences among these narratives are delineated, note that they have several structural common denominators. They all acknowledge that – for better or for worse – the Oslo process marked a sharp departure from the traditional Israeli-Arab relationship. Each of the narratives was therefore constructed to provide a compelling answer to these major questions: what – if anything – had changed to justify replacing the long held zero-sum definition of these relations with a new, win-win interpretation? Had the zero-sum interpretation gradually become dysfunctional or was it perhaps wrong from the start? Was the transformation inevitable owing to sociodemographic and sociocultural changes that lowered Israeli society's willingness and ability to fight wars? Was it perhaps that the global environment had changed so much in the early 1990s that a fundamental revision of some of Israel's basic political premises was unavoidable? Had perhaps the intentions of the Arabs essentially changed, and if so, why? In addition to the search for the sources of change marked by the signing of the Oslo DOP, each narrative presented a scenario of the future that depended to a large extent on the answers given to the questions listed here. All three narratives tried to answer the question of whether the Oslo process would serve as a step toward national and regional prosperity and security or, alternatively, as a step toward the escalation of violence and the erosion of Israel's ability to defend itself. Finally, and most important for our discussion, all three narratives tried to identify the initiators of the Oslo process, either to praise or to blame them for its potential and actual consequences.

The Labour Party's Oslo Narrative

Labour's narrative developed when the party was in power; that is, at the political center. It therefore basically differed in content and function from the narratives of the right-wing opposition and of the peace movement, which developed on the political periphery. First, as the narrative of the party in power, it was essential that the Labour narrative be "central"; that is, acceptable to the widest possible public. Furthermore, because the process had been fostered by Labour leaders, their narrative had to be supportive of the transformation that the Oslo process represented while underplaying the risks it entailed.[9] This had to be done with great care and subtlety, because Labour had for years rejected the ideas on which the Oslo process was based when these were raised by the peace movement and other political actors of the left. Among these were recognition of the Palestinian people (whose existence Labour Prime Minster Golda Meir, for example, had openly denied), of the right to self-determination and of the PLO as the sole representative of the Palestinian people; defining Israeli-Palestinian relations as win-win and not as zero-sum; viewing a political solution rather than military supremacy as the best guarantee of Israel's long-term security; and acknowledging that, in return for full peace, territorial compromises in the territories were both acceptable and worthwhile. Labour's narrative therefore was meant to rationalize the Oslo transformation without allowing that the party had made any mistakes in this regard in the past. Finally, the Labour narrative had to ensure that, if the process were successful, the party received full and sole credit for it, to be realized next election day. In particular, Labour could not afford to let the peace movement be credited with originating or leading to the Oslo process. Because of the unpatriotic stigma that marked the peace movement, such recognition could easily de-legitimize the entire process, and with it the government in the public eye. Thus, one of Labour's primary needs when it returned to power in 1992, after 15 long years in the opposition, was to confront the claim by the right that the government was a tool in the hands of leftist interest groups. Labour had to disassociate itself from the peace movement. Labour party politicians, who in fact had been well connected with the peace movement both before and after the Oslo process was launched, also publicly distanced themselves from it. For example, Yossi Beilin, one of the Oslo architects, took part in several leadership meetings of the movement. In a book in which he describes the unfolding of the events that led to the Oslo process, however, the peace movement is mentioned only once, and even then in a rather detached, faultfinding manner:

Shortly after the [1992] elections, I met with Peace Now leaders while in the US. Apparently, they felt then that they had already reached their destination, that a peace-oriented government had taken over and that things would take care of themselves. When they realized that I didn't share their euphoria, they wondered why. I told them that nothing would happen by itself. Four years could be either a short or a long period of time. It would be possible to change the world in these years but it would also be possible to more or less go on along the already paved and familiar road leading nowhere (Beilin 1997, 15).[10]

---

[9] Admittedly, the Labour party itself was not unanimous in its support for the Oslo process; however, those Labour politicians who were skeptical about the justification for the strategic shift the process implied did not develop organized internal opposition to the government's policy nor did they put forward a discernible alternative narrative about the process.

[10] Admittedly, Ron Pundak, one of Beilin's two informal delegates to the Oslo talks, was more appreciative at the time of the contribution of people-to-people negotiations: "I am one of the Israelis that has had – and am not alone in this but part of a small group of Israelis – the largest number of encounters with the widest range of Palestinians, from pupils and students and above. In those years (the early 1990s) we did not make do with discussing the political agreement but

Furthermore, sharing credit might also have electorally strengthened the Meretz party, which was close to the peace movement but also next in line to Labour in the center-left political camp.[11] These considerations were similar to those that, as mentioned earlier, accounted for the government's crackdown on the Israeli Peace Committee, supported by its main rival, Mapam, in the early 1950s, and the Labour Alignment government hostility toward the Movement for Peace and Security in the late 1960s.

The shift inherent in the Oslo process was evidently more difficult for certain Labour leaders than for others to accept and in particular, more difficult for Rabin than for Peres.[12] Thus, whereas Rabin often rationalized the shift by emphasizing the pressing need to reduce Israel's military burden and lessen the number of Israelis killed and injured,[13] Peres emphasized the far-reaching economic benefits of the Oslo process, as well as the potential of promoting the cultural integration of Israel into the region – his famous "New Middle East vision."[14] Thus whereas Peres seemed to be almost euphoric in the years 1994–1995 concerning the positive outcomes of the Oslo process,[15] Rabin was clearly seriously concerned with the possible dangers that might stem from the course of action that his government was undertaking. Despite the cognitive differences between them, however, the two Labour party leaders joined forces in outlining a narrative that rationalized the Oslo process and endowed it with its raison d'être.

were engaged extensively in what is referred to as civil society cooperation, which in my view is extremely critical in order to reach an agreement. If you ask me, an agreement should be based on a political agreement, an economic agreement, a security agreement and civil society cooperation." Interview with Ron Pundak, 18.2.2002, in the context of the Leonard Davis Institute "What Went Wrong in the Israeli-Palestinian Peace Process?" oral history project.

[11] This might explain, for example, why Rabin was said to have been much annoyed by a sticker that appeared in Fall 1995 bearing the clever play on words: "Peace is the work of Meretz" (work = labor in Hebrew). Always disaffected by the peace movement, Rabin was also upset by the large number of its placards prominently displayed at the peace rallies at which he spoke, including the one on November 4, 1995, at the conclusion of which he was assassinated.

[12] In the pre-Oslo days, Rabin was basically much more in favor of working toward a peace agreement with Syria, whereas Peres placed the Palestinians first in line.

[13] According to Eitan Haber, Rabin's close aide, Rabin said to him once, "If we had 5 million more Jews; were we to number, say, 10 million Jews in Israel, I would never give up one inch of Judea and Samaria" (Haber, personal communication, 24.3.2002, at the Leonard Davis Institute, "What Went Wrong in the Israeli-Palestinian Peace Process?" oral history project).

[14] Although differences in their respective preferences on the peace-making front can be easily identified, the disagreements and tensions between Rabin and Peres in this realm could not have been completely divorced from their personal tense relations and personal rivalry, which were quite open and a widely known for many years before the launching of the Oslo process.

[15] In retrospect, some analysts define Peres's New Middle East vision (as well as that of people around him who encouraged Rabin to pursue the Oslo course) as "messianic." They characterized it as the intentional elimination of the gloomy past, portraying the Oslo process as a genesis – the new beginning of a new, much better world, the desire to see a rapid and total transformation, and the conviction that the process is the only logical path to take (see Lahat 2004).

The narrative described the decision to begin the process as very difficult in light of the Arabs' hostility toward Israel since and even before 1948, and concomitantly, as the only rational choice based on a reading of the global, regional, and domestic political map of the early 1990s. It was this current reading, Labour's narrative argued, in addition to the high price that Israel was paying for the protracted conflict, that led to the realization that negotiating peace with the Palestinians was now a timely solution. Ending the bloodshed was a central theme in this narrative.[16] When he informed the Knesset of the agreement that Israel had signed with the Palestinians, Rabin related to this theme at length (showing, it is worth noting, no sympathy whatsoever for the Palestinians):

Our lives in this tormented land have been accompanied by rocket fire, mines, and hand grenades. We planted, and they [the Palestinians – TH] uprooted; we built, and they destroyed; we defended, and they attacked. Almost daily, we buried our dead. 100 years of war and terror hurt us but did not impair our dream. For 100 years, we have dreamed of peace.... This Government has decided to try to put an end to hatred, in order that our children and grandchildren will not experience the painful price of wars, terrorism and violence. This Government has decided to safeguard their lives and security, to ease the sorrow and the painful memories, to pray and hope for peace (Rabin 1993, available at http://www.mfa.gov.il).

This pragmatism was not Rabin's alone. Shimon Peres, the more visionary of the two leaders, also emphasized the matter-of-fact nature of the Labour government's decision to pursue the Oslo process and negotiate with the formerly ostracized PLO:

There was no point in waiting any longer. The Likud government had run its course and the political freeze – the product of its ideological beliefs – is over. Terrorism continued, and the demographics were changing fast. If Israel were not careful, it would lose its lead in population growth between the sea and the Jordan River, and thereby invite a tragedy – the same sort of ethnic conflict that destabilized Yugoslavia (Peres 1993, 16).

Moshe Shahal, then Minister of Police and Energy, in his keynote address at the opening session of a conference on "Political and Structural Arrangements in the New Era of Israeli-Palestinian Relations" (December 1993), openly expressed a pragmatic, almost deterministic, view on why the Oslo process had been launched: "Neither side has an alternative. This is not a peace that comes from better options" (Shahal 1993, 12). One of the most relevant changes in the objective situation, which – according to this narrative – caused and justified the strategic change of course, was the Palestinians' professed – and unprecedented – readiness to come to terms with the existence of Israel: "Some indications of change taking place in the PLO have been noticeable recently;

[16] Later on, as terror continued even with the peace process under way, the notion of "victims of peace" (Israelis who paid with their lives for the sake of peace) was added to the narrative to explain why the negotiations that were meant to end the bloodshed failed to do so.

they can no longer lean on their covenant that called for the annihilation of Israel; they are no longer sure of themselves or that terror is the most appropriate strategy to serve their national interest" (Peres 1993, 25).

As mentioned previously, reading the situation as one that had only then changed provided reasons for explaining why the launching of the peace process in the early 1990s did not imply that the party's leaders had made mistakes in the past. On the contrary, it actually sustained the validity of the party's earlier definition of the situation as zero-sum. It also served Labour's effort to pull the rug out from under the argument often made by the right, that Rabin's government had betrayed not only the Zionist mission but even traditional Labour party policy, thereby misleading its voters. Finally, presenting the situation as a very recent change allowed Labour to refute the peace movement's argument that the new policy could have or should have been adopted years earlier.

The Oslo Narrative of the Right

Israeli right-wing parties and groups all strongly opposed the Oslo process from its inception. This position had two major explanations: the first was their automatic response, as the major opposition body, to all Labour government policies, irrespective of their contents.[17] The second, and more substantial one, had to do with their authentic perception of Israeli-Arab relations as inevitably antagonistic, and therefore the Oslo formula as illusive (see, e.g., Ben Meir 2005). The Oslo process ran against the right's fundamental view that maintaining the territories in Israeli hands was a sine qua non as far as state security was concerned. The anti-withdrawal policy was also based on several equally important and cherished religio-nationalist values, the first of which was the precept that the territory claimed by the Palestinians was and always had been part of the God-given and thus immutable patrimony of the Jewish people. Therefore, it should never be negotiated or given to anyone else (e.g., Netanyahu 1993, 48–50). Furthermore, from the perspective of the right, the peace negotiations jeopardized the future of Jewish settlements in the West Bank and on the Golan Heights. These settlements were not only ideologically important to the right but also populated by right-leaning voters. Their removal, an unavoidable step in the context of the Oslo framework, therefore would clearly be contrary to a critical interest of right-wing parties.[18]

The Oslo process, and the rationale given by the incumbent Labour government, pointed ipso facto to the failure of the right-wing governments that

---

[17] It is not surprising, then, that in 1993 someone – apparently from the right – scribbled graffiti over a highway near Tel Aviv that said, "Once the whole world was against us. Now the [Israeli] government is as well" (Orr, 49).

[18] Indeed, the evacuation of the Gaza settlements in the context of Ariel Sharon's 2005 unilateral withdrawal plan created a severe ideological and political crisis, following which the Likud was divided, with the Prime Minister and his followers establishing the new centrist Kadima party.

preceded it to control the Palestinian uprising and to mitigate the severe impact it had on the collective Israeli psyche. In other words, the Israeli public's growing war fatigue, which clearly served as a major catalyst in Labour's decision to try another way of managing the conflict, could be viewed as evidence of the right's failure to strengthen the nation's sense of security. Finally, the international community as well as many Israelis considered the Oslo process a tremendous political achievement by the Labour party and its leaders, Rabin and Peres, who had defeated the Likud in the 1992 elections. It was therefore logical for the right to try to expose the Oslo fallacies and to undermine the achievement it implied.

The Oslo narrative adopted by the right reflected a wide range of reservations about the process: the unreasonable security risk, impairment of the Zionist endeavor, religious transgression, and Labour's lack of political judgment. The narrative also maintained that although peace per se was a desirable aim, the peace that the Oslo process would bring about was only a mirage. How then to explain why so many Israelis were taken in by it in the early 1990s? Shortly after the signing of the DOP, Dr. Dore Gold, then a political analyst of the right and later political adviser to Prime Minister Netanyahu and Israel's ambassador to the U.N., explained this phenomenon: "For a society that has sustained conflict for so many years, when the taste of peace is put on the table, the immediate reaction is that we have reached the days of the Messiah, and that perhaps explains the euphoria that initially accompanied the signing of the September 13th arrangements" (Gold 1993, 55).

Had it been possible, the narrative of the right would have placed most of the blame for the ill-conceived Oslo step on Labour party decision makers. Because the Israeli public knew most of them and Rabin in particular for their many years of experience in handling Israel's national security matters, accusing them of neglecting or underrating the important issue of security did not make much political sense, however. Therefore, the right wing's narrative had to present another villain as responsible for the misguided strategic change that the process entailed. Placing the blame on the left as a whole, and on the peace movement in particular, made perfect tactical sense. Paradoxically, considering the prolonged antagonism between these two political camps, the narrative developed by the right, much like that of the peace movement itself (which is discussed later), maintained that the Labour government's decision to begin negotiations and to agree to far-reaching territorial and other concessions had been strongly influenced by this movement. Obviously, unlike the peace movement's narrative, the right considered this influence entirely negative, and used the impact of the movement on the process to de-legitimize it altogether.

Politicians, publicists, and other speakers on the right-wing's behalf portrayed peace activists as obsessed with abstract moralistic ideals, as unpatriotic, and as lacking a sense of solidarity with the history and destiny of the Jewish people. Moreover, in the eyes of many supporters of the right and particularly the religious sectors, the peace movement was viewed as both the source and the embodiment of the many weaknesses of modern Israeli society. Thus, it was often argued that the secularism, excessive individualism, skepticism, and pampering of the younger generation that the peace movement promoted had eroded the survival instincts and capabilities of all of Israeli society. To support this claim, the right cited the peace movement's demand to pull out of Lebanon in the early 1980s and later out of the West Bank, so that soldiers would no longer have to perform oppressive duties related to the occupation. This implied that Israelis, and in particular the secular sector, were now unwilling to make the individual sacrifices necessary to achieve the nation's major collective goals (e.g., Nissan 1994, 10).[19]

The narrative of the right defined some of the peace movement's "tainted" ideas that had "contaminated" Labour, which had once been the spearhead of the Zionist enterprise. Yoash Zidon, MK of the right-wing Tzomet party, analyzed the destructive impact of the peace movement as follows:

The term 'peace now' is being translated today into the language of policy as 'territories for peace'. The aim of those who demand 'peace now' is to disengage themselves from the control over (part of) another people, as soon as possible, even if the cost includes certain Zionist values, national assets, and a significant deterioration of the state's security and economic potential, . . . It is two years since the 'peace now' policy was adopted by the Israeli government. It has brought in its wake the total collapse of the Labour party's foreign and domestic program on one hand and, on the other, far-reaching security and political sacrifices to restitute the PLO. . . . It is time to pause and identify the genuine bases for peace in the Middle East as it really is, and not as we would like it to be (Zidon 1994, 22).

Some proponents of the right were even more scornful than Zidon. In January 1996, shortly after Rabin was assassinated by Yigal Amir of the radical right, an article in a right-wing journal described the late Prime Minister's way of making decisions concerning the Oslo process as conducted under the negative influence of the peace camp, thereby insinuating that Rabin was no innocent victim but a politician who neglected his democratic duty: "Rabin put himself in the front line of a political camp located outside the national consensus. Furthermore, with the help of a parliamentary minority, he tried to impose a radical political move unacceptable to the majority of the Israeli public. . . . From a Zionist activist, he became a messenger of leftist demagoguery" (Stav 1996, 6, 7).

Others on the right, when telling the Oslo story, also openly stated that the peace movement had manipulated Rabin, who was unaware of their scheme. When already well into the process and realizing that the general public did not back his decision to follow the peace movement's plot, this narrative

---

[19] A similar argument regarding the weakness of secular liberal circles was emphasized by Rav Yehuda Amital of the orthodox *Netivot Shalom* peace group, in his peace advocacy.

maintained, Rabin merely discarded the democratic code, replacing it with various dictatorial means of government:

The Oslo agreements were made in secret, hidden from the nation, by two personal representatives of Yossi Beilin, two openly declared Peace Now-niks,[20] who negotiated with the PLO without the government's awareness.[21] Peres and Rabin came in when it was already a fait accompli, to find a table set for them by two young leftists who disappeared from the political scene immediately after their role as PLO agents was completed.... The Jewish people never gave up parts of its land, but Peres and Rabin did just that, with no public discussion of the matter, as required by the democratic code.... This arbitrary policy, the wholesale trade-off of the Land of Israel and of Zionist values was, and still is, being performed by typical dictatorial methods (Papo 1996, 26).

The Labour leaders' manifest aversion to the peace movement – the main reason why it could not claim to have had direct influence on their decisions – was also the reason why the narrative of the right had to find a convincing explanation for how the peace movement had actually pushed Rabin and Peres into launching the process. The missing link identified by their narrative was the Meretz party:

Meretz, the umbrella movement of Peace Now and its descendants *b'Tselem*, Women in Black, and the like, views itself as a "post-Zionist" stream.... What Uri Avneri put forth some decades ago has become the current political program of Shulamit Aloni and Yossi Sarid.... In the first week of June 1993, the representative of the [Labour affiliated – TH] United Kibbutz Movement, MK Hagai Marom, divulged the great secret: seven ministers in the Labour government supported the idea of negotiating with Yassir Arafat. In other words, the [difference] between the Labour party and Meretz has completely ceased to exist (Shiloah 1994, 26).

[20] The reference here is to Dr. Yair Hirschfeld and Dr. Ron Pundak, neither of whom was ever affiliated with Peace Now. It should be noted that not everyone in the peace movement was pleased with the way the Oslo process had been carried out. Some were dissatisfied with the unauthorized and hence undemocratic way the DOP had been adopted: "I definitely had a problem in that period because a large part of the preparations for the Oslo process were made – and by the left – in secrecy and stealth, behind people's backs. Yes, it was the right that invented the method of acting in secret and behind people's backs, but we were those who would climb up on the roof and blow the whistle against these acts. Let me remind you all about the peace process with Egypt, which Dayan began, officially, but behind everyone's back, and only when it was all worked out did he bring the wrapped 'package' to Begin who only had to cut the ribbon. The Oslo process was quite similar – Yossi Beilin and Shimon Peres worked everything out in advance, and only then brought it to Rabin to persuade him of it" (Mulik Bar, in Hermann 2005, 20).

[21] The sense that Rabin was forced into the Oslo Process is shared by people who definitely do not belong to the right wing in Israel. To the question of how Rabin had gotten involved in the Oslo process, Gen. (ret.) Ami Ayalon said, "I am telling you that Rabin was framed, he was actually 'raped'.... and he also lied to all the people who voted for him" (27/6/2002, in the Leonard Davis Institute, "What Went Wrong in the Israeli-Palestinian Peace Process?" oral history project).

The narrative developed by the right thus de-legitimized the Oslo process by describing it as the handiwork of the unpatriotic, post-Zionist, and marginal peace movement that, by various means, had succeeded in manipulating the Labour government. This narrative was meant to expose the government as spineless and undemocratic, thereby substantiating the right's opposition to the Oslo process without taking the risk of being denounced for warmongering.

The Peace Movement's Narrative of Oslo

This is how Tzali Reshef of *Shalom Achshav* described his feelings and thoughts when, with other Israeli and Palestinian peace activists, he watched the White House lawn ceremony at which the first Israeli-Palestinian agreement was signed:

For us, September 13, 1993 was the day when the goals to which we had aspired for so many years finally materialized.... The fact that we chose to be there together, Israeli and Palestinian activists, reflected our success in establishing relations of mutual confidence, as well as the end of a complicated process through which we learned to identify our common interests. This process had its ups and downs, its exciting peaks, and more than a few crises. But all these together – at least that was how I felt that day – made our bond one of our greatest achievements, giving us the full right to be very proud (Reshef 1996, 10).

The occasion undoubtedly brought much pride and satisfaction to most peace movement members, who for many years had called on Israel to embark on a direct dialogue with the Palestinians. Having failed to change not only official Israeli policy but also public opinion prior to 1993, they now justified their years of seemingly futile grassroots activity by arguing that the exchange of ideas and ongoing joint activities that they had conducted with the Palestinians since the mid-1970s had prepared the ground for the future official negotiations. Because the peace activists had established some degree of mutual confidence with prominent Palestinian personae, official Israeli representatives found it easier to sit together at the negotiation table when the time came. Thus, not only did the peace movement openly and strongly support the launching of the Oslo process but also perceived it as a victory of its own making, as explained – in retrospect – by a pivotal *Shalom Achshav* female activist who in 1993 was too young to take part in the celebration:

As for Oslo, if I understand correctly, if I read correctly what the mythology says, there really was a sense that the process we had led was now complete, essentially decided.... The movement not only argued for legitimizing contacts with the Palestinians, but its leaders actually met with all the top Palestinian leaders of the time. That was basically what Peace Now contributed to the discourse, to politics, to Israeli public life, and it was basically this that Shimon Peres and Beilin took and made peace from (Moria Shlomot, in Hermann 2005, 16–17).

To refute the right's allegation of deviation from the Zionist endeavor, the mainstream peace movement's narrative at that time (although not that of the radical groups who have always considered Zionism the source of the trouble[22]) linked the Oslo process to the original, mainstream Zionist creed and its advocacy of peace. This explains the claim by Haim Oron, a Meretz MK and a long-time supporter of *Shalom Achshav* (although never one of its leaders) during the Knesset discussion of the Oslo DOP in the summer of 1993:

These days we are returning to the true Zionist path from which we have drifted away for the last 26 years or so because of the total eclipse of the sun [i.e., since the 1967 war]. For the true Zionist way led to a real compromise with the Arab people. . . . What is happening now, and the breakthrough we are discussing here, actually means the end of the detour that brought us nowhere except to one confrontation after another (Oron 1993).

People close to the peace movement also pointed out that Rabin and Peres had been hesitant before taking the necessary decisive steps towards reconciliation. They were often described as apprehensive about the price demanded by the process. It was the peace movement that, according to this narrative, furnished the indispensable grassroots pressure that encouraged – and sometimes even forced – the Labour government to make the necessary, although painful, concessions that it otherwise might not have had the courage to make.[23] These revelations can be attributed not only to the impatience of the peace activists with the slow pace of the process and with the overly cautious positions of the government but also to their difficulty in coming to terms with the fact that the government had now appropriated the dialogue with the Palestinian side, leaving the peace movement virtually bereft of its raison d'être.

Some of the criticism of the Oslo agreement and process by the radical peace groups and some activists within the more moderate groups stemmed from their skepticism regarding the true intentions of Labour, the party that they considered the originator of the Israeli zero-sum security ethos. Ironically, they were also afraid that the integrity of the peace movement would be harmed because of its association with Labour decision makers:

From the moment the Rabin government won the elections in May 1992, and following the talks in Madrid – which are remembered, but not favorably – held in the fall of that year, the movement changed in nature. . . . The Rabin government did not replace Elyakim Rubinstein, head of the delegation appointed at the time of Shamir, whose only desire was to create delays and not get anywhere. Israel also obstinately kept on insisting on talking only with representatives of the Palestinians in the territories and not with the PLO abroad, even though they knew the PLO was giving instructions to the Palestinian

---

22 "Let me stress that I am concerned here with Zionist ideology rather than with the practice of the Zionist project. That the latter is an absolute obstacle to resolution of the conflict is self-evident: it is a colonizatory project, an implantation of settlers, which was – necessarily – implemented at the expense of the mass of indigenous people and by denial of their national rights. Indeed, the Zionist project is the root cause of the conflict" (Machover 2005).

23 The often heard slogan "*Yumratz Rabin*" ("Rabin should be energized") in the context of the Oslo process, which for all Hebrew speakers clearly alluded to name of the pro-peace Meretz party, was but one example of the peace movement's image and self-perception as the mainstay of the process.

delegation. Some of us concluded that we needed to state openly that these talks were not leading anywhere and Israel had to speak directly with PLO-Tunis.... It was clear that the leadership of the movement was defending the position of the government. Only then did I began to understand, though I couldn't yet say it out loud, that basically Peace Now had become an extra-parliamentary arm of the government. Pure and simple (Judith Harel, in Hermann 2005, 33).

Other skeptical peace activists maintained that the agreements signed by Rabin and Arafat virtually deprived the Palestinians of their natural right to a really independent state, leaving them with a Bantustan-type semistate:

The controversial negotiations over deployment in 9 percent or 3 percent or 50 percent of the territories, in this settlement or that – this is not the kind of peace I dream of. This map, composed of different-colored patches – areas A, B, C, reminds me too much of the Bantustans and not enough of opportunities for peace. Here too, just like in South Africa in the 1980s, there are white belts around orange areas on the map.... In South Africa the plan to build small enclaves and call them independent 'homelands' did not work – why should it work here? (Golan-Agnon 2005, 102).

Moreover, according to this interpretation, the agreements did not ensure a full Israeli withdrawal from all of the territories occupied in the 1967 war, without which the noxious occupation could not be abolished (e.g., Orr 1994, 160–170). In an open letter to *Shalom Achshav*'s leaders, Michael Warschawski (Mikado), a key figure in the non-Zionist peace camp and founder of the Alternative Information Center (AIC), exposed the reason why, in his view, this largest yet moderate peace movement rejoiced in the signing of the failing DOP when it was obvious to him and to people of similar political views from the very beginning that the chances that it would lead to peace were minimal. Still, at this early stage he did not completely despair of the possibility that the Oslo agreement would make things better:

You danced in the squares because you were happy about this peace. Not just plain peace, but a blend of peace, security, Palestinian chest-beating over sins committed (renunciation of terrorism), and far-reaching concessions by the other side.... To you the Israeli-Palestinian connection was always a zero-sum game: anything we give them means less for us.... If you were really capable of thinking in terms of peace, you would understand how far wrong you are; the more rights the Palestinians receive...the more we too profit.... Nevertheless, the two of us are now committed to the same campaign to bring about the full implementation of the Oslo agreement, in hopes that the new arrangements will prepare the ground for a true peace between Israel and the Palestinians. "In hopes," I say, because unlike you I do not rely on "historical necessity," nor on Yitzhak Rabin and his government (originally sent in 1994 and cited in Warschawski 2001).

By and large, however, the narrative adopted by the peace movement in the early 1990s emphasized the positive sides of the process, as well as its own role in setting in motion this highly desirable change in the regional political reality. To counter Labour's narrative, it maintained that it was the movement's members' early meetings and ice-breaking discussions with their Palestinian counterparts that facilitated (if not made possible) Israeli and Palestinian delegates' sitting together at the negotiation table in Oslo and afterwards. Still, as mentioned before, the movement could not claim to have had direct influence on the strategic Oslo shift, because it was widely known that its access to national decision-making circles had always been very limited and that public opinion was not very supportive of their cause, not necessarily on principle but because of the movement's negative public image. While rejoicing, then, certain peace activists were also truly troubled by the question of how important the role they played had really been: "What was our contribution to this historical occurrence? Would Israeli public opinion have been ready to accept the agreement without the untiring activities of the groups that had maintained that this was the only possible solution? What would have happened had we not joined forces to nourish the flames of the demand for peace negotiations?" (Reshef 1996, 12).

With this uncertainty in mind, the movement's narrative portrayed the historical development as follows: The peace activists were a small vanguard of realists with foresight (and not naive idealists as their rivals often claimed), who understood, well before anyone else in Israel, that the protracted regional conflict could be successfully and finally resolved by political means only and never by military force. They were also the first to see the moral and practical justification for the Palestinians' demand for self-determination and to realize that it would eventually gain worldwide recognition.[24] Neither the public nor the national leaders accepted the logic of this analysis until the early 1990s, when the Labour Party and its followers, formerly convinced of the exclusive validity of the zero-sum view of the Israeli-Arab relationship, began to realize that there was some truth to the peace movement's ideas. The party's leaders and those who voted for them in the 1992 elections sensed that critical structural and cognitive changes in the global, regional, and domestic environments necessitated changes in the earlier definition of the situation and in the practical inferences of its now outdated and dysfunctional program. Nonetheless, captives of their long-held confrontational argumentation, Labour leaders and supporters found it very difficult to admit to the obsolescence of their interpretation.

The peace movement's narrative also openly called for some broad public recognition for having opened the communication channels to the Palestinian

---

[24] The non-Zionist left claims the credit for this accurate forecasting: "Recognition of the Palestinians as a political entity was also a victory for the anti-Zionist left in Israel, which had fought for this recognition since 1948. This left, which was attacked in hysterical tones by the entire Israeli media, proved not only its moral integrity but also the validity of its political analysis. All the 'Arab specialists' of the Israeli establishment, all its 'think tanks' and 'brain trusts' failed to foresee what a handful of Israeli anti-Zionists had predicted for years – the re-emergence of the Palestinians as a political factor and the slow but inevitable decline of Zionist policies" (Orr 1994, 127).

side. Indeed, some did not feel the need to be openly credited for their contribution to this path-breaking move:

I was a Peace Now activist through all the years of the [first] *intifada*. When Oslo 'broke out', I personally didn't feel that they weren't giving me the credit that was due me. That is, I took it for granted that I had worked for peace all those years and if it arrived – that would be the compensation. I didn't expect any other credit. I don't think any of the members of the leadership of Peace Now openly expressed any sort of frustration in this regard" (Judith Harel, in Hermann 2005, 14).

Other peace activists, however, were disappointed that the leaders did not recognize their contribution to achieving the breakthrough:

It stood out very starkly that no one gave credit, not only to Women in Black but actually to any of the peace organizations, the Twenty-First Year, Peace Now, and the other organizations that were active and visible in the field. It was impossible to believe that Shimon Peres or Beilin or others didn't know and didn't see. These were organizations with great visibility in the field, in the media, and so on. And this gave a sense of leaders who were really generals in a way, some of them actually were generals, who wanted to take the credit for themselves and were not prepared to recognize the few people in the field who really prepared the ground for the step that was taken. I, in any case, and several people I spoke with, had the feeling that the leaders' ignoring this key element could eventually be to the detriment of the process (Diana Dolev, in Hermann 2005, 27).

With the government committing itself to the peace process, both those peace activists who celebrated the signing of the Oslo agreement and those who criticized it had to make a strategic choice of where to go from there, because, at least on the face of it, their historical mission had been fulfilled:

Immediately afterward, we started to think about what should be Peace Now's role in the new period. I remember that a meeting was held in Jerusalem that could be called a founding event. Some of the people there even bewailed the fact that Peace Now had reached the end of its path.... People felt that it was time to close the book and go home, and they regretted it.... Three clear voices could be heard: those who thought Peace Now had completed its mission; those who strongly warned that we needed to be the watchdog of the process, that problems were likely and we needed to keep our 'finger on the pulse'; and a third group, to which I belonged – naively.... With all its might, this group pushed the issue of 'peace-building' and of building peace ties through dialogue (Judith Harel, in Hermann 2005, 17).

Where to Now?

These hesitations and disagreements on what to do next were not unique to members of the peace movement; many in Israel, both among the political elite and in the public in general, now viewed them as passé. After all, in a representative democracy, it is the elected leaders who are in charge of shaping and implementing national policy, not grassroots organizations, which in the best case put new ideas on the table and try to convince the others of their value.[25] Once the authorized bodies adopt these ideas, the organizations have done their part and should either dissolve or seek other goals. Furthermore, if there is peace, who needs a peace movement? These qualms were accompanied – and sustained – by more personal factors, mainly the immense weariness of many peace activists after their intensive activity in the 1980s and early 1990s. Many of them were mentally burned out, and with the prevalent sense that it was the government that was now in charge of peace making, they found it morally acceptable and justified to withdraw and concern themselves with private matters – studies, families, and careers. The level of voluntary participation in various types of peace activism decreased considerably in 1993–1994, perhaps with the exception of the dialogue channel, which flourished for a bit longer.

The high hopes of many Israelis and many peace activists, when watching the historical signing of the agreement by Rabin and Arafat on the White House lawn on September 13, 1993 – that the signing of a full, permanent peace agreement with the Palestinians was just a matter of time – were not, as is well known, sustained by ensuing developments. Negotiations moved ahead very slowly, with both sides, each for their own reasons, adopting hard-line bargaining positions. Indeed, until early 1995, the larger parts of the peace movement remained hopeful that eventually things would improve, despite the minimal progress achieved in the negotiations, and the slow yet ongoing erosion of the public's belief that peace was indeed around the corner.

In their desire to see the process continue and realizing that close association with it might actually damage or even destroy the chance that the process would gain wider public support, in 1993 and 1994, the leaders of the moderate peace groups who supported the government abstained from organizing massive pro-peace rallies. They also suppressed their criticism of the process even when they realized that Rabin and his government were reluctant to go all the way to a Palestinian state and that the government's iron-fist policy towards West Bank Palestinians did not soften significantly after the signing of the agreement. In a symposium on the pros and cons of the Oslo process and the tactics that the peace movement should adopt under the circumstances, Yael Dayan, a Labour Party MK and activist of the women's peace movement exhorted: "Much as we refrained from openly assisting the government in other matters connected to the process, we should now avoid criticizing it, as such criticism may eventually adjoin the criticism of the right.... I only ask for what is attainable, providing that this government stay in power at all" (The Alternative Information Center 1996, 6).

It should be noted that this "rational choice" of the peace movement at large not to associate itself overtly with the Oslo process nor to criticize it openly was almost unavoidable, taking into consideration the cold shoulder that the movement had received from Rabin, with his high popularity inside and outside

---

[25] Such a view was put forward, for example, by MK Meli Polishuk-Bloch in a round table discussion dedicated to the role of citizen diplomacy in conflict resolution (in Shamir 2005, 79).

Israel (e.g., among wide Jewish circles in the Diaspora, the donations of which were critical for the peace movement). This tolerant treatment of the Labour government had a very high price tag attached to it: the streets were left to right-wing protesters while the pro-peace Israelis stayed at home, a situation that gave the anti-Oslo camp a clear strategic advantage. Moreover, the peace movement lost much of its credibility as a sincere political and moral political actor. Its lenient position also created a crisis of confidence among its Palestinian counterparts and worsened relations between Jewish Israeli activists and Arab Israelis, as indicated in the following reaction by Amir Machul, an Arab Israeli peace activist, to Dayan's warning above: "The left today is a captive of the Labour party. The peace movements have also been taken captive, and no longer present an alternative. By and large, our dream has been shattered" (The Alternative Information Center 1996, 7).

It must be admitted, however, that even when the more moderate peace groups did try to make the public aware of errors in the government's conduct, mainly the continuation of settlement activity, which clearly contradicted the Oslo spirit, the public's readiness to listen was very limited. For example, in the mid-1990s *Shalom Achshav* invited new immigrants from the former Soviet Union to participate in educational day trips to the West Bank and visit settlements there. Because it was well known at the time that the Russian immigrants often held hawkish views and usually voted for right-wing parties, the idea was to show the newcomers who joined the trip how and why the settlements were a major impediment to peace by exposing them directly to the problematic realities of the territories. Although the organizers claimed that their message was quite well taken, other observers were far more skeptical and maintained that the opposite of the desired result was actually achieved: not only were the participants not convinced of the organizers' anti-settlement message, but after these tours they became more interested in relocating to cheap housing available in West Bank settlements.

The more radical groups and activists were less affected than the moderate peace organizations by the launching of the process, which as mentioned previously was not their cup of tea from the beginning, and they therefore kept a distance from it:

What was the Oslo agreement if not just re-colonization of the Palestinians and of the Middle East? I never believed in Oslo.... Indeed, the agreements were important because of the establishment of the Palestinian Authority, and because they marked the beginning of a dialogue between Israel and the Palestinians. But the Oslo agreements were in fact no more than an effort by Shimon Peres to build a 'New Middle East', i.e., to establish Western-style Israeli control through the power of the market instead of by force. They meant that Israel would economically control the Palestinian Authority, and that the Authority would do the policing in the service of the Israeli regime.... It took me a while to understand these connections, but when Peres started to talk about the 'New Middle East', I felt that something was wrong there (Shadmi, 134).

The radical Jewish activists were also highly critical of the ill-conceived rapprochement of their moderate colleagues with the political establishment: "We have to re-educate the people about the sources of the conflict. It didn't start between two national movements – it started between a colonialist movement which dispossessed Palestinians, and we don't come as equals" (Tikva Honig-Parnas, in Rosenwasser 1992, 139). Less sensitive to their own image, which was in a shambles anyway and at odds with government interests, they maintained some ongoing small-scale protest during these years, more to make people think than in the hope of changing formal policies. Their argument, which contradicted the prevalent public view of matters as presented previously, was that the Israeli government and not the Palestinians was not meeting its Oslo commitments, problematic as this agreement might have been in their eyes:

In 1993, *Gush Shalom* also declared that upholding the Oslo agreement meant, first and foremost, honoring the cardinal Israeli commitment, which was to stop building settlements. This commitment was not upheld, since even in the Rabin period, they continued building settlements without letup. The Rabin government also did not fulfill the clear commitment to release everyone who had been arrested prior to Oslo.... I don't see 1993–1995 as a good period at all. Quite the opposite. It was a very bad period, a period in which we proved, to whoever still needed proof, that there is almost no connection between what sane and nice Israel signs and what it does. And after that, of course, there was no end to accusations against the other side (Teddy Katz, in Hermann 2005, 20).

The fact that the Israeli government under Rabin was not fully implementing its obligations vis-à-vis the Palestinians was not clear to most Israelis at the time. It was apparently much clearer to IDF soldiers – from the high commanders to the soldier in the field – because they were witnessing it in the territories. In due course, this awareness drove some of these soldiers to join the peace camp. The speaker of the refuseniks movement, *Ometz l'Sarev*, recalls his personal experience as a young office serving in the territories in those years:

In the media they talked about the peace process, there were joint patrols and all sorts of signs that the Palestinian security systems and the IDF and GSS [General Security Service – TH] were learning how to get along. But in the field the lie was blatant, and we went along with it: I remember how we guarded Joseph's Tomb in Nablus in civilian clothes instead of uniforms. You understand – IDF soldiers were guarding not in uniform but in civilian clothes, so that if someone asked who we were, they would have said – those are settlers, not soldiers, because the IDF isn't supposed to be at Joseph's Tomb. And that's not the only example. There were all sorts of other little lies that really exploded in our faces more than once. Everyone knew it wasn't supposed to be that way, but we fooled ourselves that we're on the way out, and so actually we stayed there. And since then, in fact, we are supposedly on the way out (Arik Diamant, in Hermann 2005, 44).

Despite these ideological and operative problems, the early 1990s saw the establishment of several new peace organizations, mainly feminist ones, which combined peace activism with activities empowering women. The notion of social justice was often also introduced, apparently to respond to the often-heard criticism of the peace movement as representing the interests of the better-off social segments in Israel. The most notable new organization was perhaps *Bat Shalom* (Daughter of Peace), which developed into one of the most active peace organizations in Israel in the 1990s. Still functioning to this day, it exemplified some of the basic characteristics and problems of peace activism in this era.

Based on the preexisting organizational substructure of *Reshet Nashim l'Shalom* (Women's Network for Peace) developed in the late 1980s, and after a prolonged dialogue between Israeli and Palestinian women activists that had begun in Brussels in 1989, the organization was formally established in 1994 as the Jewish side of the Palestinian-Jewish Jerusalem Link umbrella organization. From the start, financial support came mainly from European donors, who were active in shaping its constitution and modes of operation so that they would fit the Oslo spirit. Thus, by its constitution, *Bat Shalom*, with offices in West Jerusalem, is one of the few Israeli peace organizations that has a twin Palestinian organization – The Jerusalem Center for Women, located in East Jerusalem. In this capacity, it was meant to institutionalize ongoing dialogue between Israeli and Palestinian women with the aim of ending the occupation and improving the status of women in both societies. Over the years, this cooperation produced some path-breaking and very visible activities such as the 1997 "Sharing Jerusalem – Two Capitals for the Two States" conference, perhaps the first public gathering of such magnitude with the participation of an Israeli peace organization that openly called for making East Jerusalem the capital of the future independent Palestinian state. Considering the fierce opposition of the lion's share of Israeli Jewish public to sharing Jerusalem,[26] this was a very groundbreaking political move, which caused – as expected – severe criticism of *Bat Shalom* on the Israeli side.

However, the Israeli-Palestinian cooperation in this organizational framework, which was in a way laid down by the donors, was by no means smooth. Indeed, on the individual level, strong friendly relations between Palestinian and Israeli-Jewish women activists emerged and were maintained over the years, but the group meetings between Israelis and the Palestinians were often rather tense (e.g., Golan-Agnon 2005, 120–121). Israeli activists' explanation for these tensions focused on the different priorities of Israeli and Palestinian women: the Palestinians considered their struggle for national liberation more important than the feminist struggle. The Israeli women, while strongly opposing the occupation (although, as part of the dominating side, they were not overly affected by it), were equally interested in promoting the feminist agenda (op. cit., 109).[27] This, however, reflects only part of the picture. Whereas the

---

[26] For example, in the July 1997 Peace Index survey, 62% of the Jewish respondents objected to giving East Jerusalem to the Palestinians even if this were the last obstacle on the way to signing a permanent peace agreement.

[27] The combination of feminism and peace activism is well reflected in the organization's credo: "Bat Shalom is a feminist organization composed of Jewish and Palestinian women, citizens of Israel, working to end the occupation and for a just and lasting peace with the Palestinian people... Ending the occupation and establishing peace are essential for creating a just society in Israel. In line with its principles of equality, Bat Shalom is committed to the continuation of

Palestinian women held strong nationalist positions and unreservedly supported the Palestinian leadership, thereby remaining part of the mainstream
nationalist movement despite their peace activism, the Israeli partners of the
Jerusalem Link, because of their blunt criticism of Israel's policies and leaders
and manifesting solidarity with their Palestinian colleagues' causes (e.g., sharing Jerusalem), were clearly positioned outside the boundaries of their side's
national consensus. At joint meetings, they were constantly apologizing to their
Palestinian counterparts for the Israeli government's harsh policies, to which
they of course objected. In a sense, they were viewed by the Palestinians as
responsible for them because of belonging to the occupying society.

The straightforward demand by the Palestinian women peace activists that
the Jewish ones openly denounce their own collective and sympathize with
the Palestinian liberation struggle while refusing to reciprocate, for example,
by denouncing terrorist attacks on Israeli civilians, created a real dilemma
for *Bat Shalom* activists, who also had to deal with their home constituency.
Bat Shalom's feminist agenda included reaching out to women of a variety of
political views, including those who were more "patriotic." The organization's
activists were thus caught between the anvil and the hammer. They had to
choose between pleasing their Palestinian counterparts and perhaps thereby
being loyal to their own beliefs, but losing their chances of reaching out to
wider women's circles in Israel, or to be less openly sympathetic to the Palestinian struggle and less critical of Israel and its policies and perhaps gain a
stronger foothold and some support on the Israeli side, but lose the confidence
of their Palestinian colleagues.[28] The dilemma was never openly put this way
for discussion, and hence no decision was ever made. The natural dynamics
over the years and the ensuing developments pushed the organization away
from the mainstream Jewish public. For this reason, women peace activists
holding more moderate or more patriotic sentiments, including some of its
founding members, left it; however, the move away from the center did not
ease *Bat Shalom*'s relations with its Palestinian counterparts.

The social justice aspect of *Bat Shalom*'s agenda also proved very difficult
to implement, again because of the wide discrepancy between the activists
and those whom they were supposed to reach. The latter – women of the
socioeconomically underprivileged strata, often holding the right-wing views
typical of their socioeconomic reference groups – sensed that the support the
organization offered them was often a fig leaf to cover up its real intentions – to
convert them to the peace camp, a feeling that was not completely baseless. The
Bat Shalom Social Justice and Peace outreach project was launched in 1995, and
aimed at introducing the organization's ideas on peace, feminism, and social
justice to Jewish Mizrahi women from poorly educated, low-income sectors,

its struggle against all forms of social discrimination and exclusion and for the achievement of
equal rights between Jewish and Palestinian citizens in Israel" (http://www.batshalom.org).
[28] This dilemma recently emerged once again in the Israeli branch of the International Women's
Commission and tore apart the Israeli delegation between those who strongly denounced the
Gaza War and those who were reluctant to do so (Eldar 2009).

living in development towns and inner-city neighborhoods. Several women's clubs were established in the next few years, mainly in Jerusalem and a few in Tel Aviv, which held weekly small-group meetings organized by *Bat Shalom*'s community workers. At these meetings, the participants discussed issues such as domestic violence, women's health, parenthood, and other topics of special interest to women. Still, the organizers' clear, although not necessarily explicit, agenda was that the women who participated regularly in these seemingly nonpolitical activities would in due course become local opinion leaders, who would mobilize wider circles of women residing in their neighborhoods to take part in *Bat Shalom* peace activities. Although the long-term effectiveness of these social activities still cannot be assessed, *Bat Shalom*'s leaders and activists gradually became pessimistic about the prospect of this project's bearing fruit. Apparently, most of the women who participated in these activities in 1995 and 1996 voted, in the ensuing elections, for either religious or right-wing parties, both of which rejected the peace movement's agenda.

Bat Shalom (like the other large, yet already defunct, peace organization, *Dor Shalom*, which is discussed later and which was also established in the mid-1990s) manifested another facet of peace activism in the 1990s touched on only briefly thus far: the higher level of institutionalization compared with the past and with that of more veteran organizations. *Bat Shalom* exemplified a growing propensity in the peace movement for heavily relying on a professional organizational framework, in the expectation that this would prove an effective vehicle for extensive, long-term, and well-planned campaigns. Personal networks and networking, although still of considerable importance, seemed at this stage to be less crucial than proper organization. Whereas it took 10 years after its establishment for *Shalom Achshav* to hire its first part-time paid staff member in 1989, and 2 years for the *Rofim l'Zchuyot ha'Adam* to do so, *Bat Shalom* (and *Dor Shalom*) had paid staff members from day one. This was partly because the new organizations were supplied with funds for specific kinds of operations, but it also reflected a different view on how peace activism should look in the Oslo era. With more funds and a less favorable POS than in the late 1980s, greater difficulty in mobilizing the masses, and the apparent need to design innovative activities to catch the eye of the growingly indifferent media, and hence of the public and the decision makers, the need for professional organizational skills seemed much greater than before.

In the formerly fully voluntary peace organizations (which often turned semiprofessional in the years under discussion here), as well as in the new ones that professed a high level of institutionalism and professionalism, interactions between the professional staff and the volunteers were not always smooth. Because they were responsible for the daily running of the organization and often also for fund-raising, the influence of the professionals increased, sometimes reversing the traditional internal balance of power in which high-profile unpaid activists were considered those who set the tone. Conflicts over the "ownership" of the organization, and in particular over the right to shape its agenda, developed in certain organizations, occasionally leading to open power struggles.[29] The professionals were annoyed with the volunteers who they thought were interfering with the proper running of the organization without being involved enough in it on a daily basis or being accountable for the results, whereas the volunteers thought that the organization had been hijacked by "technocrats" who distorted its original aims or character.

The institutionalization of peace activism in that period was also expressed in the transition from protest to well-organized dialogue/people-to-people activities. Involving in many cases pupils and youngsters, these activities were now organized not only by peace groups but also by schools, with the blessing of Israel's Ministry of Education. In fact, the "People-to-People" agenda was officially embraced by the Israeli authorities in the context of the Euro-Mediterranean Conference of Ministers of Foreign Affairs, held in Barcelona on November 27–28, 1995.[30] Still, many of these basically highly positive activities were somewhat flawed.[31]

Whereas the more or less successful dialogue activities by peace groups in the late 1980s signaled an authentic wish by the participants to learn how things looked from the vantage point of the other and aimed to pierce the cognitive curtain between the Israeli and the Palestinian collectives, many of the post-Oslo dialogue establishment–encouraged encounters were rather superficial and unauthentic. In fact, often to lessen the resistance of the participating students' parents, to avoid the security risks involved in conducting the meetings in the territories, and to soften the cultural shock, the other side to these dialogues were in many cases Arab Israeli citizens rather than Palestinians from the territories. Even here, the hot issues were not up for discussion. This is how one peace activist critically recalls her personal experience at such a meeting:

From my standpoint, one of the major problems of these meetings was that they lacked an educational process – the desire or the awareness, mainly from the Israeli side, to talk about history. In other words, the meetings centered on food, cooking, and soccer. Everything always revolved around the refreshments – we prepared lots of goodies, and so did they. Maybe on [the Jewish holiday of] Tu b'Shvat they also planted trees, but they didn't talk about the things that needed to be talked about if we really meant to achieve reconciliation – they didn't talk, and they didn't look each other in the eye. This, despite the fact that children in junior high are already starting to develop awareness and thoughts, and certainly their teachers already have political awareness (Adina Aviram, in Hermann 2005, 29).

---

[29] *Rofim l'Zchuyot ha'Adam* was one of the organizations that suffered most from this process. A crisis that exploded in 2005 left behind a traumatized organization and certainly strained personal relations.

[30] For more details on the Barcelona Process and the Barcelona declaration, see http://ec.europa.eu/comm/external_relations/euromed/.

[31] It is estimated that in the period under discussion here, a total of $20 to $30 million was donated for such activities by numerous governmental actors, foundations, and private persons (see Herzog and Hai 2006, 15).

Another peace activist took this criticism even further:

I could see that the teachers, the educators, even those who led the program and received more in-depth and extended training, did not feel comfortable with the contact with the Arabs. It was clear that the Arabs aroused in them, if not actual fear, then at least repulsion. So it was all totally artificial. And not only that, they would bring Arab children to *Neve Shalom* and force them into the sort of workshops where everyone bares his soul, which is completely foreign to Arab culture. Whoever forces these children into such situations doesn't understand a thing about Arab culture (Judith Harel, op. cit., 31).

Indeed, many of the dialogue activities of the early post-Oslo period lacked authenticity and therefore were hardly of significance in terms of making a real change or drawing attention. One noticeable exception to this was the unique forum of bereaved Israeli and Palestinian parents, which was established in 1994 by Yitzhak Frankenthal, following the abduction and murder of his 19-year-old son, Arik, by Hamas. Frankenthal, a well-to-do Orthodox businessman, founded the *Hug Horim Shakulim* (Parents' Circle), an organization of Israeli and Palestinian parents who had lost their children in events related to the conflict. The organization is still active today, bringing together over 500 bereaved families from both sides.[32] The basic function of this new SMO – a sort of joint support group – was to enable parents on both sides to share their grief in the understanding that both sides are victims of the raging violence. The second manifest aim of the *Hug Horim Shakulim* was no less important: to promote peace and coexistence through educating to tolerance and compromise by showing everyone that even parents who lost those dearest to them could reach out to the other side, based on their understanding that this was the only way to prevent further bloodshed. By promoting the Jewish moral and religious obligation to preserve and value human life above all, the group organized a variety of activities with the participation of families from both sides, explaining the human toll paid in the name of Greater Israel on one hand and the equally detrimental maximalist ideologies on the Palestinian side. The group was very successful in raising funds, thanks in large part to Frankenthal's exceptional managerial skills. It therefore organized several very original peace-promoting activities – from educational programs, artistic political displays, and innovative Israeli-Palestinian interactive endeavors, such as connecting on the telephone, at no charge, Israelis and Palestinians of similar sociodemographic characteristics so that they could talk about the conflict, their feelings in this context and their preferred solutions.

As mentioned in regard to *Horim Neged Shtika* of the early 1980s, and as is discussed concerning the *Arba Imahot* (Four Mothers) movement of the late 1990s, the utilization of parenthood as a basis for peace advocacy became

---

[32] In 2004, Frankenthal himself left the organization that he had established and run almost single-handedly, due to severe disagreements with other activists on both ideological and operational matters. Later, he established another peace organization: The Arik Institute (www.arikpeace. org).

quite widespread and acceptable in Israel in the last two decades. Still, the fact that in the *Hug Horim Shakulim*, parents whose children were killed by the other side were together preaching forgiveness and reconciliation, was met with mixed feelings. On one hand, it was taken as a sign of extremely high morality and humanism; on the other hand, however, many in the general public as well as in other bereaved families considered this unnatural in the best case and abnormal, even sick, in the worst. Somewhat "in-your-face" articles and speeches, like the one cited below by the group's founder, strengthened the latter feeling:

My son Arik was born into a democracy with a chance for a decent, settled life. Arik's killer was born into appalling occupation, into an ethical chaos. . . . Let all the self-righteous who speak of ruthless Palestinian murderers take a hard look in the mirror and ask themselves what they would have done were they living under occupation. For myself I can say that I, Yitzhak Frankenthal, would have undoubtedly become a freedom fighter and would have killed as many on the other side as I possibly could. It is this depraved hypocrisy that pushes the Palestinians to fight us relentlessly. Our double standard allows us to boast of our highest military ethics, while this army is slaying innocent children. This lack of ethics is bound to corrupt us (Frankenthal 2002).

Moreover, at least in its early years, the message of the *Hug* was heavily religious in its content and discourse. It has already been noted in the discussions of *Oz v'Shalom* and *Netivot Shalom* that the secular public, including the peace activists, found it difficult to relate to Orthodox discourse, whereas most of the Orthodox public familiar with it was politically opposed to the peace movement's agenda. The group's chances of expanding its audience and therefore its political influence were further undermined by its religious rhetoric.[33]

The assassination of Prime Minister Rabin by an Orthodox, extremist right-wing Jew on November 4, 1995, shortly after the signing of the interim Oslo agreement in September of that year, was a national shock. The event clearly indicated that even if embraced in one form or another by the authorities, the peace-making rationale advocated by the peace movement was far from acceptable to the entire Jewish-Israeli public (Peri 2005). Although the assassin was not part of a larger subversive group, there were many on the right side of the political map and particularly in the settlers' community, who, even when denouncing the act itself (sincerely or not), were now hopeful that it would lead to the termination or reversal of the Oslo move. The massive hate campaign against Rabin and the Oslo process that took place in the year before the assassination, with the participation of a number of Likud leaders, including future Prime Ministers Netanyahu and Sharon, indicated that opposition to the strategic shift that Oslo entailed was extensive and vicious, even if usually legal.

---

[33] Since 2004, with the personnel change mentioned before, the group's discourse has significantly changed and no longer has religious connotations.

Without going into the question of to what extent this campaign of the right was successful in changing public attitudes or whether it was the grim reality of violence and unbridgeable disagreements that pulled the rug from under the feet of all peace-making efforts, it was already clear (as shown in the graph in Appendix 2) that in the period before the assassination, Jewish public opinion in Israel was shifting away from the peace process. In the September 1995 Peace Index survey, 51% said that they were disappointed or very disappointed with the Oslo process, whereas only 25% said that they were satisfied with it (the rest had no opinion). Either because of a tendency toward social desirability or because they finally saw the light after the assassination, 65% thought that the assassination would make more people supportive of the peace process (Peace Index, November 1995).

Ironically, although traumatic to everyone, from the POS point of view of peace activism, the assassination was a useful crossroads, because this horrifying event supplied the almost dormant post-Oslo peace movement with a new thrust, a new raison d'être, and a much-needed (and most probably contrary to his wishes) martyr. After resting since 1993, facing great difficulties in working out a suitable new agenda and new modes of operation that would fit the new political reality, the grassroots struggle for peace seemed relevant once again, because of the murder of the nation's leader, which occurred because of his peace policy. Paradoxically, then, although all saw the assassination as a death blow to the Oslo process, from the point of view of the peace movement, it marked a significant even if temporary expansion of its POS.

Following Rabin's assassination, many of the peace activists who had gone home in 1993 and 1994, with scores of Israelis who had not been politically involved before, felt the urge to become active, as if to compensate for their inactivity while Rabin was still alive. This urge was fed by the claim, made by people close to the late prime minister, that while his adversaries on the right chased him from one place to another, protested against his policies, and even threatened him personally, the pro-peace camp did virtually nothing to counterbalance this hate parade. This complaint, expressed mainly by Rabin's widow and friends, went on to say that hardly any pro-Rabin vigils had taken place when they were badly needed, thereby increasing his sense of being alone. This accusation was only partly justified, considering Rabin's open dislike for the peace movement and peace activists. Furthermore, as mentioned, public support for him and his policies by the peace camp might have served as a weapon in the hands of Rabin's rivals, proof of his betrayal of the mainstream Zionist cause and of associating with an unpatriotic body – the peace movement.

Paradoxically, yet perhaps not surprisingly, the strongest motif in Jewish Israeli discourse after November 4 was not peace and peacemaking with the Palestinians or with Syria, with whom Rabin was seriously negotiating a settlement, but domestic peace, that is, national unity. The call to strengthen the bond between the different political camps in Jewish Israeli society was the call of the day. The peace movement could not side with this tendency, and therefore the activities that it conducted concentrated not on the domestic scene but on the external one (Rabin's legacy of making peace with the Palestinians). Naturally, at the time, this message was not widely encouraged or welcomed, because it was considered divisive. In other words, the post-assassination period exemplified the theoretical argument regarding the possibility of SOP to expand and contract simultaneously: thus in terms of regaining its traditional support base, the POS in those days improved and became more beneficial and open in terms of the revival of the willingness of peace process supporters to be active again. It was also positive in terms of the reemergence of its raison d'être – the almost self-evident post-assassination need to put forward a counter-balance to the right camp's anti-peace agenda. On the other hand, the POS facing the peace movement was contracted in terms of the ability and desire to come forward with an alternative agenda focusing outward, while the climate of opinion pointed inward.

In addition to the somewhat higher level of activity in the veteran peace SMOs such as *Shalom Achshav*, two new peace groups emerged immediately after the assassination: the low-key yet viable *Mishmarot haShalom* (Guards of Peace) and the much larger yet ephemeral, *Dor Shalom* (Peace Generation). *Mishmarot haShalom*, which started its activity immediately after – and as a result of – Rabin's assassination, is a perfect example of a "tame" peace organization. Despite its self-definition as a protest group (Chen 2000, n118), even if an apolitical and nonpartisan one (although its participants' identification with the Labour party was almost self-evident), not much in this group's prolonged activism was in any way challenging or contentious. It always opted for very soft means of protest, which made it uninteresting and almost unknown. In fact, this group served mainly as an outlet for its members' grief over the dead leader whom they adored. If anything, one can argue that it reflected nostalgia for the early days of the state, when control over the shaping of the country's political and societal agenda was in the hands of the sector to which this group's members belonged – Ashkenazi, secular, mainstream Zionist.

The group's original rather abstract aim was to challenge the peace "spoilers" – those who opposed the peace process. It was not clear who they were or how this was to be done, however. Protecting Israeli democracy was the second theme inscribed on this group's banner, but this faded away when it became clear that, traumatic as it was, the assassination had not shaken the foundations Israel's democratic regime. *Mishmarot haShalom*, which continued their weekly meetings until the early 2000s, never had any formal organization, defined membership status, or political platform. The group's activity was unidimensional and steady – it held vigils every Friday afternoon near the spot where Rabin was assassinated. Attendance at these vigils ranged from a few hundred in the group's golden age immediately after the assassination to dozens in later years. At the beginning, participants were somewhat sociodemographically diverse, particularly in terms of age and place of residence. The percentage of women, which at the beginning was only a bit more than half, increased in time, and the number of younger participants visibly dropped. The program of each vigil included a short guest presentation on current political matters relevant to the peace process and then an hour or so of singing Israeli folk songs, which was considered by the participants as an act of defiance. In reality, however, their activity lacked any defiant character – the songs were without exception highly mainstream and popular, even patriotic, and most were quite old, so that they hardly appealed to younger age cohorts. *Mishmarot haShalom*'s mainstream agenda never clashed strongly enough with anyone or anything to create enough heat to make it visible. Thus, its original aim, to bring together thousands of Israelis who supported Rabin's peace policy and thus create a real political force to prevent the derailing of the peace process, did not materialize. This left a wide space for the much wealthier and more energetic *Dor Shalom* movement, which proved significantly more successful in addressing the very same audience.

Dor Shalem Rotze Shalom (literally, "an entire generation wants peace"), or as it was widely called, *Dor Shalom* (Peace Generation), was established in November 1995 by a group of young people in their twenties and thirties, many of them still students or young professionals. Under the traumatic impression of the assassination, it seemed to have the right timing, the best lineup, unprecedented public readiness to listen to its message, wonderful media coverage, and above all – in contrast to all former peace groups – enough money not only to carry out extensive public activities but also to hire first-rate staff, from media officers to PR specialists and financial and legal experts. Indeed, *Dor Shalom* proved very attractive to the general public, and the number of its registered, tax-paying members reached almost 17,000 (!) in 1996 and 25,000 in 1998 (Dolev 1998). Its financial support came mainly from members of the Israeli industrialist milieu, who had been close to Rabin and were interested in a peaceful Middle East, because peace, aside from its own merits, is also good for business. With all this, however, *Dor Shalom* was perhaps the biggest disappointment in the history of Israeli peace activism, because for a brief moment it gave birth to the illusion that the dark spell that had overshadowed the peace movement for so many years had lifted. *Dor Shalom* of those years was self-defined as the largest peace organization in Israel's history to date. The movement thus had all the chances to succeed but failed colossally. Some 10 years down the road, it is clear that its contribution to peace was nil, and if anything, it left only negative spots on the Israeli political scene.

From the very beginning, *Dor Shalom*'s leaders identified the problems involved in the outcast positioning of all other peace groups as outcasts. Therefore, they openly expressed their wish to be located at the center of the ideological map – not even the moderate left, where *Shalom Achshav*, for example, was located, and certainly not on the radical left, where some other groups were. In this respect, the movement exemplifies better perhaps than any other the problem of outlining the exact scope of the peace movement. It was also the first in a chain of smaller and larger groups in the years to come that indeed aimed for peace but because of marketing considerations disassociated themselves from the peace movement (e.g., *haMifkad haLeumi*). *Dor Shalom* inscribed on its banner the preservation of Rabin's legacy, a rather abstract notion that was never defined in so many words but to the Jewish Israeli audience carried connotations of a blend of mainstream Zionism, a security orientation, and acceptance of the Oslo agenda.[34] *Dor Shalom*'s openly middle-of-the-road platform and self-positioning gained it wide publicity and invested it with unprecedented public appeal. This is how one young Israeli author and cultural studies expert explained his support for the movement that repeatedly expressed its willingness to join forces with "all" segments of Israeli society to strengthen national unity:

The peace camp has convinced the general public in Israel for years that peace is made with enemies, not with friends. It should, however, convince itself now that one does not make coalitions only with those who say exactly the same thing. Also, the aim of demonstrations is not to pat oneself on the back and quiet one's conscience, but to gain real political influence. If *Dor Shalom* is indeed able to bring out to the street all the people scared of potential deterioration to war, and that's apparently what it is doing, with much common sense – this could develop into a real power. It is easy to ridicule the demonstrations of the center. However, the center is exactly what it takes to change things; it is impossible to win wars of which the center, the majority, disapproves (Taub 1996).

Surveys commissioned by *Dor Shalom* reaffirmed the political wisdom of pursuing a consensual agenda. This entailed further efforts to set itself apart from the peace movement (O. Galili 1997).[35] Fleeing from being identified with the left and with politics at some point changed from a means to an end to the end in itself, as recollected years later by one of *Dor Shalom*'s core members:

I recall repeated disappointments which we inflicted on other movements of the [peace] camp when refusing again and again to take part in their rallies or to pay for advertisements on political matters.... The paralyzing fear of making a commitment to concrete positions critically dulled the political sting of the movement and its ability to change anything beyond the micro-level.... Even in those rare cases when the movement was kind enough to remind itself of its old association with the peace movement, it was done in a populist way and by flattering some imaginary mob.... Why did I keep my mouth shut at the time like many of my fellow activists? Probably because I felt it was worth biting my tongue for the sake of the great goal on the horizon. And what was that? For me at least, and I suppose I wasn't the only one, it was contributing in any possible way and in any possibly framework to the defeat of Netanyahu and to a return to sanity (Misgav 2001, 52).

---

[34] The bonding of *Dor Shalom* with the beloved assassinated leader was sealed when Rabin's son, Yuval, became the movement's icon leader, right after the defeat of Labour in the 1996 elections.

[35] The anti-peace movement sentiment was exemplified in an interview given by Yuval Rabin in which he reacted to the resignation from *Dor Shalom* of some activists who opposed this disassociation and wanted to put forward a solid peace agenda: "Enough is enough with this leftist crap. Those people who resigned from *Dor Shalom* are exactly the same people who maltreated my father, embittered his life, never understanding, not for a minute even, what he was trying to do. We are not talking only about peace here but about peace that sometimes needs to be fought over. Not about some do-gooders slogan" (in Dolev 1998).

The tactics that *Dor Shalom*'s leaders used to separate themselves from the peace movement were to underplay the peace issue and emphasize socioeconomic issues, thereby gaining a foothold in the less-well-to-do social sectors and in the poor neighborhoods. This was done in the hope of reducing the impact there of the Mizrahi, Orthodox Shas party, which, despite its prevalent dovish image, in fact acted rather like a hawk on the parliamentary level, and its voters comprised one of the most right-wing segments of Israeli society (Yuchtman-Yaar and Hermann 2000). This effort was pathetic already then, and much more so in retrospect, as correctly observed at the time by one of the Shas party leaders:

Dor Shalom as a secular alternative to Shas? Don't make me laugh. Those who think this is a feasible option don't know what they're talking about. Shas has a comprehensive orthodox agenda – what does *Dor Shalom* have to offer? The Labour religion?[36] . . . We are marketing tradition to traditional people. Giving them a home. What can *Dor Shalom* sell them? The peace agreements again? Rabin's assassination once more? People have had enough of all this peace and war, after all, who are they – Tolstoy? All they want is a good life (Benizri, in Dolev 1998).

Not surprisingly, the real peace movement considered *Dor Shalom* not only competition in terms of public mobilization but also bogus and hypocritical. Particularly unacceptable and annoying for the peace movement were the efforts made by *Dor Shalom* to reach out to the settlers, as part of its national healing campaign. The level of interaction between the two sides was therefore too resentful to enable the creation of a peace camp large enough to become a significant political factor. Despite the enormous efforts it made not to be stigmatized as part of the left-wing peace movement, however, *Dor Shalom* could not avoid its fate. Like *Shalom Achshav* and *Bat Shalom*, it failed to gain a foothold in poor neighborhoods, where contempt for peace activism was strongly class motivated, precisely because its activists were immediately identified as the same as traditional peace activists. Much worse than that, their so-called apolitical peace message was perceived by these audiences as a plot, a way of marketing the peace movement's ideas in a different, misleading packaging. Less than a year after it was established, the movement had to deal with its raison d'être:

The founders of *Dor Shalom* are asking themselves a number of questions: Is the movement they created artificial? Was it only a response to urgent needs that emerged immediately following Rabin's assassination yet rapidly became irrelevant? Could it stay alive without turning into a center party, a move highly advocated by all recent surveys, and where is it located on the extra-parliamentary map? . . . The founders of the movement are also aware of the fact that in the eyes of the Israeli public *Dor Shalom* connotes 'yuppishness' and non-committing messages of reconciliation and unity. If this

---

[36] Benizri relates here to a creed known as *Dat haAvoda* (the religion of work or labor), developed by A. D. Gordon and fostered by certain factions of the socialist Zionist movement including the earlier formations of today's Labour party in the early 1900s, which highlighted the major value of work.

is true, its leaders asked themselves . . . can the movement be at all successful in breaking the historic stalemate in the next elections? . . . Other major questions were also raised: Should the movement construct its messages in the way the public wants, or the other way around, crystallize its message first and then think how to sell it to the public? (O. Galili 1997).

The Bumpy Road Zone

As maintained in the previous section, Rabin's assassination indeed presented the peace movement with a somewhat better POS. The election of Netanyahu less than one year later, in mid-1996, however, seems to have been a critical turning point for the worse in this respect, because both on the leadership level and that of the general public this electoral outcome marked the beginning of the end of the Oslo process. Admittedly, Shimon Peres, who replaced Rabin as prime minister in November 1995, was more sympathetic to the peace movement than his predecessor, even if his policies were not exactly in line with the movement's agenda. His dedication to peace making was beyond doubt, however. Therefore, his electoral defeat in May 1996 and the coming to power of the Likud and Netanyahu came as a blow to the movement.[37] The 1996 election results proved that the larger part of the Israeli public was located to the right of the political center in terms of their views on the policies and positions that Israel should adopt regarding the Palestinians, even if the majority had not yet forsaken the abstract possibility of peace. According to the Peace Index survey of June 1996, 71% of the Jewish respondents favored a tougher position by Israeli decision makers when negotiating with the Palestinians. At the same time, 53% preferred peace agreements with the Arab world to Greater Israel (favored by only 29%). The question that the peace movement faced in the post-election era was thus how to lessen the damage and use the change of government as leverage for its own rehabilitation.

One rather futile tactic was adopted by *Dor Shalom*'s leaders: they made the decision to go one step farther in their intentional disassociation with the peacenik image and changed their movement's name into *Dor Shalem* (An Entire Generation), leaving the word *Shalom* (peace) out of it. Some activists viewed this decision with disfavor: "Replacing the name *Dor Shalom* with *Dor Shalem* epitomized its natural tendency to blur its political views," recalls one of these disappointed activists in retrospect (Misgav 2001, 52.) Abandoning the extraparliamentary nature of the movement was also considered (as had been considered more than once by other peace organizations, such as *haTnua*

---

[37] It should be noted, however, that certain radicals of the peace movement (one example is Prof. Tanya Reinhart, who taught linguistics at Tel Aviv University and was a disciple of left-wing American intellectual Noam Chomsky) were so disappointed with Peres' policies that they called on their colleagues on the left to put a blank ballot in the voting envelope, even if this led to Netanyahu's victory. This is because from their point of view, there was no real difference between the two candidates.

l'Shalom uBitachon in 1969, and by *Shalom Achshav*[38] on several occasions). In the late 1990s, *Dor Shalem*'s leaders debated whether to plunge into the stormy electoral waters and run in the 1999 elections. The decision not to do so was motivated, at least in part, by negative reactions on the left, based on the assessment that this would not earn them more votes but only split the vote further, reducing the prospects for defeating Netanyahu (Dolev 1998).[39]

Against the background of the rightward-moving Israeli electorate, another tactic used was to focus on contexts other than national politics. Thus *Dor Shalem*'s activists took part in the student union elections in the universities and even won some of them (e.g., in Tel Aviv University). Also in 1998, they participated in municipal elections, mainly raising an education banner, with impressive results. Their list got enough votes to take over several rather significant positions in the Tel Aviv municipality. In the end, all these moves proved futile, and *Dor Shalem* faded away, probably mainly for the reason that a former activist cited in its eulogy: "Rabin was assassinated for his bravery. *Dor Shalem* disappeared because of its cowardice and hypocrisy" (Misgav 2001, 51).

Another strategy was used by Peres and people close to him to deal with the 1996 election results and Labour's being out of office: the creation of a hybrid, formally extraparliamentary organization, which was meant to serve as a safe haven for them under the new political circumstances so that they could continue to pursue the peace process. Finding himself in the opposition, Shimon Peres decided to continue his peace efforts through a nongovernmental channel, and *Merkaz Peres l'Shalom* (The Peres Center for Peace) was established in late 1996.[40] Relying on his reputation as a peace maker and on his Nobel Peace Prize, Peres used his solid connections with the global upper crust to raise the money and international support needed for the establishment of the Center. For this effort, he also recruited a highly professional team of Israelis who had been in the civil service or involved in the Oslo negotiations and who now, with the change in government, had to leave their jobs. The declared mission of the Peres Center was

---

[38] As a movement, *Shalom Achshav* never opted for parliamentary elections. However, some of its main figures joined existing parties – Dedi Zuker and Yuli Tamir joined Meretz in 1981, and Tamir and Tzali Reshef joined Labour in the mid-1990s). All three served for varying periods as MKs, and Tamir also held several ministerial portfolios.

[39] Certain central figures in *Dor Shalem* joined Ehud Barak's advisory team in the 1999 election campaign. One of them, the highly visible former secretary general of the movement, Tal Zillberstein, was involved in some dubious fundraising for Barak and later indicted, a scandal that unavoidably reflected on *Dor Shalem*'s public image.

[40] The decision to discuss the Peres Center here, while leaving out other similar NGOs related to peace-making activities such as the Economic Cooperation Foundation (ECF) established by Dr. Yossi Beilin and Dr. Yair Hirschfeld in late 1990 with the support of the European Community, was based on the fact that whereas the ECF and other similar small think tanks were never perceived by grassroots peace organizations as either belonging to their sector or as being a threat to it, the Peres Center was considered an intruder and indeed, as is shown later, stepped on the toes of several peace groups.

...realizing [Peres'] vision of a "New Middle East", in which people of the region work together to build peace through socio-economic cooperation and people-to-people relations.... We believe that the only solution to this conflict is through a negotiated agreement, which respects the national identities of both peoples.... The Peres Center projects aim to break through the boundaries of misconception and suspicion to arrive at authentic cooperation (http://www.peres-center.org).

The problem of an active politician's[41] operating in the extraparliamentary arena in a representative democracy is obvious. This cast doubt on the true nature and purpose of the new organization and the political ethics of the people involved in this venture, as it suggested that by establishing the Center, Peres was actually trying to circumvent the election results, in which the majority of the Israeli public rejected him and his New Middle East vision.[42] These troubling matters had to be addressed at the outset, and indeed, the new Center's mission statement explains

Our strategy remains constant and focused, although our tools and methodologies adapt to reflect the dynamic realities of the Middle East. As a non-partisan, non-governmental organization, The Peres Center for Peace works in parallel to, but independently from, the political process towards peace. It is this unique mandate that allows us to continue with our cooperative activities between Israel and her Arab neighbors despite the breakdown of political negotiations and upsurge of violence (http://www.peres-center.org).

Not everyone, however, was convinced by this argument, as is apparent in the following comment by one of the most proficient and original Israeli analysts of the Middle East:

Even when Peres was still Prime Minister and preached his "New Middle East" vision, which he is recycling in his new center, there was a gap – to put it mildly – between this vision and its implementation.... One makes peace through a grey and hard daily struggle to improve the miserable standard of living of millions of human beings, the causes of which are political and institutional, and not only economic. The Peres Center is a nice thing, but it would be very bad if it succeeded in creating the illusion of peacemaking (Benvenisti 1998).

Peres and his team were certainly not inclined toward street protest or any other grey, hard, daily struggle for peace in the streets. They opted for a much less sweaty venture. Despite the reservations put forth in earlier years by the (many) adversaries of the New Middle East vision on the Palestinian, Arab, and the Israeli sides, for its econo-colonialist nature, they considered a long list of joint economic projects to be conducted in the years to come, promising that

Our projects are based on a genuine identification of common Arab and Israeli economic and social interests, which are formed into peacebuilding projects through our

---

[41] Peres remained a Labour MK after the 1996 elections.
[42] In the Peace Index survey of November 1997, 72% of the Jewish respondents stated that the New Middle East vision was only a remote possibility or not at all possible.

partnerships with regional and international players. A key facet of our peacebuilding projects is the people-to-people aspect, in order that the wider publics may come to know "the other" and understand the reality of their intertwined history and future (http://www.peres-center.org).

The new *Merkaz Peres l'Shalom* – on whose Board of Governors one could find a variety of international dignitaries, from ex-presidents to financial tycoons, prominent clergymen, to well-known authors, intellectuals, and artists[43] – attracted much attention, admittedly more from abroad than from Israel; however, it was the international arena that was expected to provide the funds. Indeed, to make the planned large-scale projects possible, the Center's teams traveled the world to raise the necessary funding. Beyond the public doubts about the democratic awareness of the entire left following Peres's decision to opt (temporarily?) for the extraparliamentary arena after being defeated in the elections, the fund-raising realm is precisely where the clash of interests between *Merkaz Peres* and the other peace SMOs began to gain momentum. In light of the low visibility of peace activism in the mid-1990s, together with the glamorous nature of the new Center, it is not surprising that many donors who had previously supported various smaller-scale Israeli peace groups and activities now preferred to redirect their money to the new venture. In fact, in 1996–1997, many Israeli peace organizations were almost dried up and had to cut down on activities even further, when much of the external funding went to *Merkaz Peres*.

Mounting criticism of the new Center came from relatively expected directions. Obviously, the right opposed it from the beginning because they attributed to it – rightly or wrongly – subversive intentions. The peace organizations, on the other hand, were apparently more concerned with the new and clearly highly skilled competitor in the field:

Is there any need for a new center for peace? . . . The number of those involved in the "peace industry" is already large and the number of projects that could be conceived is infinite. . . . What then is the relative advantage of the new center over the older ones? After all, they are all busy seeking funding and researchers and mixing with potential entrepreneurs and with official political and economic bodies. Everyone is taking some 'overhead' for their center's administration and its expenses. If the number of institutes and peace centers were multiplied by their overheads, the total could provide for the needs of an entire Palestinian refugee camp (Benvenisti 1998).

Radical peace activists were more concerned about the Center's econo-colonial agenda:

. . . most of the members of the board of governors of the Peres Peace Center are representatives of Israeli and international big business or politicians affiliated with such. This indicates that the kind of peace Peres and his Peace Center have in mind is a peace for advancing neo-colonialist aims of the big corporations by the U.S. and Israel – strategic and economic partners in the Arab world. It is not a peace for the

---

[43] For the full list of the Center's international Board of Governors, see http://www.peres-center. org/fulllist.html.

people they have in mind, but a peace for big capital to exploit the cheap labor force in the Arab world. . . . Whether these designs will succeed and bring about peace in our region is to be seen yet. It will be the task of the people involved, and especially the working masses in Israel and the Arab world, to fight to turn this neo-colonial peace of the corporations into a real peace for the people (Lebrecht 1999).

In addition to these strategic and ideological reservations, in the late 1990s – both in Israel and on the Palestinian side – rumors raged that although the Center was doing an excellent job of advertising its projects, in reality most of them failed to go beyond the ceremonial inauguration phase, and too often the money did not reach those who could actually translate the vision into practice. The fact that Carmi Gilon, former head of the *Shabak*, the Israeli General Security Agency (at the time of the Rabin assassination), was named the first Director General of the Center, was also – for obvious reasons – a thorn in the side of many in the peace movement. To divest itself of this criticism, in the early 2000s the Center opted for much lower-key activities and focused on cultural-educational matters. The new Director General of the Peres Center was no other than Ron Pundak, one of the architects of the Oslo DOP, who was candid enough to state openly: "To the Peres Center, named after him, Peres is more of a stumbling block than an asset. For peace people – Palestinians, Europeans and even Americans – the brand name "Peres" has changed from an advantage to a disadvantage. . . . Peres indeed established the center five years ago, but today he makes no decisions there, not even in an advisory capacity" (Rappaport 2002).

Another interesting phenomenon in the realm of peace activism in the second half of the 1990s, the shape of which was strongly influenced by the domestically unfavorable POS of that period, was the establishment of *Yozmat Kopenhagen* (the International Alliance for Arab-Israeli Peace – or the Copenhagen Initiative). *Yozmat Kopenhagen* was an unofficial, semidiplomatic but rather high-profile peace initiative. Either because of the people involved (retired senior diplomats, intellectuals, prominent media people, and so forth) or because of their reading of the circumstances on the ground, the organizers of this initiative from the start decided against massive mobilization for protest, although they aimed to bring about a substantial change in public attitudes throughout the region, and thereby a change in the official policies of Middle Eastern governments. The organizers' difficulty in opting for the regular modes of action employed by other peace groups is revealed in the following quote by one of the initiative's founding fathers, formerly a senior officer of the Mossad and the Director-General of the Israeli Ministry for Foreign Affairs:

Have you ever stood in a busy intersection, holding up a large placard, demonstrating against your Prime Minister? I did that, back in May 1998, when Binyamin Netanyahu brought the peace process to its knees. I felt very foolish and embarrassed at first until I grew accustomed to the stares, the catcalls, the cars honking and also – fortunately – the well-wishers. . . . I believe that the fact that some prominent professors and a former Director-General of the Foreign Ministry [the speaker himself – TH] were willing to spend a week on an inhospitable Jerusalem sidewalk had an effect on some people. A hundred, nay, a thousand such acts would have had a considerably greater effect. And this, in a nutshell, is the dilemma of the peace movements in Israel – how to make an impact that can affect public opinion (Kimche 2003).

It all started in 1995 and 1996, with a group of influential Israeli and Egyptian intellectuals, politicians, and writers who were invited to closed meetings at the Louisiana Museum of Modern Art in Copenhagen. The participants attended the first and the ensuing meetings in their personal capacities, although most of them were connected to decision makers and the decision-making process in their home countries. The meetings of this forum were organized by Herbert Pundik,[44] former chief editor of *Politiken*, the Danish daily newspaper; Knud Jensen, founder of the museum; and by the Danish Ministry of Foreign Affairs. The initial aim of the venture was to warm up the cold peace between Israel and Egypt, yet fairly soon the organizers and participants understood that this would be impossible unless the Israeli-Palestinian conflict was brought to an end. This aim seemed unattainable with the original team; therefore, participation was extended to include key Jordanian and Palestinian figures.

Even if in the beginning some participants still entertained the idea of eventually establishing a popular regional peace movement, the evolving high profile of the core group in due course indicated that the initiative's prospects of being conducted on the grassroots level and sweeping the masses were limited. In January 1997 the participants in *Yozmat Kopenhagen* met for the inaugural conference. The coordinators of the gathering were Dr. David Kimche, former Director-General of the Israeli Ministry for Foreign Affairs; Dr. Lutfi El Huli, a leading Egyptian intellectual; the Jordanian former Chief of Air Staff, General Ahsan Shudrom; and, on the Palestinian side, Prof. Sari Nusseibeh, President of Al Quds University in East Jerusalem. The Danish Minister for Foreign Affairs and the Minister for Development Cooperation, in the presence of several international personalities, officially opened the conference. Each national delegation from the Middle East included about ten members. In contrast to almost all other dialogue forums, the Palestinian delegation included a representative of the Islamic organization Hamas and of the Popular Front and the Democratic front, left-wing organizations referred to as the "refusal front" because of their opposition to the Oslo process. The Israeli delegation to the meeting included several parliamentarians from various parties, including Labour, Likud, and others, whose presence made it if not actually official, then at least semiofficial. At the end of the conference, the participants issued a joint declaration that stated

Peace is too important to be left only to governments. People-to-people contacts are vital to the success of the peace efforts in the region. As long as the popular base

---

[44] Pundik had written in the past for the Israeli newspaper *Davar* (the organ of the Labour party) and is also the father of Ron Pundak, who was one of the two architects of the Oslo initiative and today the director of the Peres Center for Peace.

remains weak, the peace process may falter. We are gathering in Copenhagen to contribute to a comprehensive and lasting resolution to the Arab-Israeli conflict before the end of this century.... We plan to hold public meetings, lobby governments, monitor progress and setbacks in the peace-process as well as discrimination, collective punishment, abuse of human rights and violence. We will mobilize public opinion behind the peace effort.... We aim at the achievement of lasting and comprehensive peace based on the formula of land for peace, the implementation of UN Security Council resolutions 242 and 338 in all their aspects.... We, the International Alliance for Peace, call on all concerned governments to act vigorously and speed up the full implementation of the Israeli-Palestinian agreements in letter and spirit, faithfully and honestly, and particularly to restore full normality to and improvement of the lives of the Palestinians.... The final agreement between Israel and the PLO must allow the Palestinian people to exercise their right to self-determination, including statehood.... To create an atmosphere of amity for negotiations, no resort to violence or terrorism in any form should be accepted or condoned. To allay Palestinian fears, no new settlements should be built and no Palestinian land, state or private, will be expropriated.... [T]he founders of the Alliance invite regional and international groups and individuals concerned with the future of the region to support our declaration, join our movement and support actively its causes and goals (The Copenhagen Declaration, January 30, 1997, http://www.pforp.net/Declaration3.asp).[45]

Yozmat Kopenhagen was and still is little known in Israel, because the media mostly ignored it,[46] and thus far its political impact has been rather limited. In the Arab world, however, the initiative aroused some strong reactions – most of them negative. This is because it implied normalization of relations between the Arab world and Israel, and particularly because participants on both sides were not regular peace activists, but people with a foothold in the corridors of government:[47] "The problem with other attempts by intellectuals on both sides to influence Netanyahu's policies, for instance, as in the case of the Copenhagen group, is that they take place too close to governments who have a much narrower, much shorter view of things" (Said 2000, 275).

Still, following the first meeting of the group in Copenhagen, the Egyptian peace movement was established. In an interview to the *Bulletin of Regional Cooperation in the Middle East*, Abdel Monem Said Aly, director of the Al-Aharam Center for Political and Strategic Studies in Cairo, described the influence of the International Alliance as follows: "The movement is now part of the political life and people treat it as such. The issue now is to build the organization into an NGO and make it effective.... The impediments to launching activities like the Alliance were overblown. It was just that, in the past, people obeyed those who were against such efforts" (http://www.sfcg.org). Ihsan

---

45 A second declaration was issued in May 2003, saying among other things: "The International Alliance for Arab-Israeli Peace calls for a stop to the vicious cycle of violence between Palestinians and Israelis. Enough is enough" (http://www.pforp.net/Declaration1.asp).

46 An exception to this is the report in *Ha'aretz* by Danny Rubinstein, who was sent by his newspaper to the Copenhagen Conference; see Rubinstein 1997.

47 See Al Mahdi, Amin, 2001.

Shurdom responded to a question on the effect of the International Alliance from a Jordanian standpoint:

The Alliance initially caused a great controversy in the Arab world . . . The [Copenhagen] Declaration threatened those people who have built their political power base on the hatred of Israel and the Jews so they went on the offensive. . . . Had we spoken of war instead of peace, those same critics would have hailed us as national heroes. . . . The difficulties in the peace process have had a very adverse effect on our programs because people naturally became reluctant to take part in our joint activities. Nevertheless, the mission of promoting peace went ahead (ibid.).

As noted previously, this initiative went mostly unnoticed in Israel, and with the enmity that its participants faced in most Arab countries as well as among the Palestinians, it was unable to create the hoped-for regional wave of pro-peace public opinion that might have led to a change in the official policies of the participating governments.

To return to the Israeli peace movement at large, the presence of a hostile government indeed contracted its POS but at the same time also somewhat enhanced its recruitment efforts, as the theoretical literature on conditions under which grassroots movements flourish suggests (e.g., Gelb and Hart 1999, 176). The "bumpy zone" was thus characterized by open enmity on the part of decision makers toward the peace movement,[48] which in turn encouraged the partial return of peace activists who had taken a break during the Rabin-Peres era. This partial awakening was also nourished by the personal resentment toward the new Prime Minister that prevailed in certain sociopolitical groups. The peace movement remained much smaller and weaker than the right wing with its two main "battalions": the settlers and the religious/ultra-Orthodox sector. Contempt for the peace movement in wider circles, particularly among the Orthodox, was incredibly high considering its low public exposure in those years. Paradoxically, once again it was blamed for all negative developments, including the Palestinian violence that erupted in what was termed the "Wailing Wall tunnel disturbances" in September 1996, when eleven Israeli soldiers and sixty-nine Palestinians were killed in a series of armed clashes between IDF troops and Palestinian police. This is how a rabbi whose congregation is

---

[48] Netanyahu's spiteful attitude toward the peace camp was revealed at a ceremony in a synagogue in Jerusalem in 1997. Netanyahu was caught on camera whispering to Rav Yitzhak Kaduri, an elderly Cabalist with much spiritual authority, "The people on the left completely forgot what being Jewish really means. They think that we should leave our security to the Arabs and believe that the Arabs will take care of us" (reported in *Ha'aretz*, October 22, 1997). The preferential attitude of the authorities toward right-wing grassroots organizations revealed itself clearly in 1998. Several peace SMOs realized that they were being discriminated against, compared with the movements of the right, in the allocation of state funds for organizing the State's jubilee events. The peace movement planned to organize a mass event to mark the Fiftieth Independence Day and applied for financial aid. Their request was refused, whereas settlers in Hebron got NIS 300,000 (about $60,000) for the organization of an event marking 30 years of Jewish settlement in the city (Reinfeld 1998). Legal steps taken to change the government's decision failed.

located in the heart of Tel Aviv, the city which epitomizes Israeli secularism, and who is generally known for his open, welcoming approach toward his synagogue's secular neighbors, described his view of the negative role that *Shalom Achshav* played in the creation of a fertile ground for Palestinian violence: "I am not a politician, but what I understand is that as the biblical aphorism goes, 'Thy destroyers and they that made thee waste shall go forth from thee'. The demonstrations of Peace Now have given them [the Palestinians – TH] the legitimization to do what they did in the *intifada*. If there had been no Peace Now, there would have been no *intifada* and we would not be stuck in the situation in which we are stuck today (in Peleg 1996).

Thus, in terms of mass events, the peace movement was actually in hibernation through most of the second half of the 1990s, awakening only sporadically. Now and then, it managed to bring several thousand people to city squares in protest of acts taken by the Netanyahu government; however, these one-off events did not signify any real reawakening of the peace camp, nor did they present a significant political challenge to the government. A prominent Israeli journalist attributed this to what he considered as the two major disadvantages – one organizational and the other mental – of the political camp of the left. From the organizational point of view, its traditional vehicles, such as the labor unions, the kibbutz movements, and the youth movements, were critically weakened, thus making it more difficult for them to get the masses out into the streets. Mentally, the left was pampered, skeptical, passive, and basically not radical, and unlike the supporters of the right, did not automatically show up when called to a demonstration or a vigil. Furthermore, unlike the right, the peace camp was incapable or unwilling to conduct extreme protest activities, such as blocking roads, setting tires on fire, or clashing with the police. The conclusion of this analysis was that the mode of protest that the left was able and willing to carry out in the mid-1990s was ineffective. As the same critic realistically admitted, however, preaching to the pro-peace camp that it should change its ways was doomed to fail, because it could not change its nature. Instead, the mode of protest chosen should be tailored to better fit its participants. The means that he advocated were civil, nonviolent resistance and refusal to serve in the territories, which could, in his view, undermine the legitimacy of Netanyahu's government and would also "look great on the pages of the New York Times" (Asheri 1996).

Realizing that the chances for massive public mobilization and for vigorous protest were minimal under the POS of the late 1990s, some in the peace movement opted for the deterministic option: they argued that peace was inevitable and that therefore sooner or later an agreement would be finalized, the government's preferences notwithstanding. The signing and implementation of the Hebron Agreement by Netanyahu in 1997 was interpreted in this framework as decisive evidence of this inevitability:

After Oslo, the completion of the peace process began to seem inevitable.... The Hebron agreement's implementation only intensified the sense of inevitability amongst the Israeli

Left. Too much had changed for the grand picture to be reversed, even if the process was slowed. But the events of March-April 1997 questioned this assumption – yet demonstrations against Netanyahu's policies still did not occur. By emphasizing the renewed Palestinian terrorism within Israel... the government successfully diffused the peace movement's ability to generate opposition against its new hard-line policies.... They organized some impressive demonstrations to commemorate the anniversary of Rabin's assassination. But otherwise they have been ineffectual.... Even after Israel decided to construct a new Jewish neighborhood in East Jerusalem, and even after renewal of the Palestinian street violence in March 1997, the "save the peace" demonstration in Tel Aviv's main square... was poorly attended (Newman 1997, 420–421).[49]

Some people within the peace movement itself confirmed the existence of this sense of inevitability and that it caused a decline in the level of activity at the time, as shown in the following quotation by one of *Shalom Achshav's* leading intellectuals:

Much of the indifference of the left to what is happening is rooted in the prevalent feeling that the issue of the Palestinian state has already taken root, and as to the borders issue, there is the feeling that it's all about a couple of percentage points. Either way, the role of the left no longer seems interesting.... Strangely enough, it is the weakness of this government that contributes to this passivity, as it projects the sense that it will collapse by itself.... It is difficult to mobilize people when the question at stake is not clear and the life-expectancy of the government is perceived as very short anyway (Avishai Margalit, in Galili 1997c).

It should be emphasized that this reading of the situation – that in 1997 the Netanyahu government was stumbling in terms of public expectations – was not confirmed by the public opinion surveys of the time. Israelis were clearly worried about the stalemate in the negotiations,[50] as well as the internal disputes and the ongoing Palestinian terrorist attacks. The data did not reflect a sense of political instability or a prevalent wish to see the Netanyahu government collapse, however, as the peace movement's reading of the situation indicated at that time. Actually, the Netanyahu years, managed under the slogan "if they [the Palestinians] give [security], they'll get [concessions]; if they don't give, they won't get," were easier for the public to accept, because they demonstrated a tough and reserved approach, to the extent that even the Hebron agreement was endured relatively smoothly. This specific misreading is important, because it was typical of the peace movement's ongoing tendency

[49] The majority – 53% – of the Israeli Jewish sector supported the building of this neighborhood but a significant minority (41%) opposed it (Peace Index, May 1997). This finding highlights the peace movement's difficulties in mobilizing the pubic to its activities because, as indicated by the above figures, the sense of dissatisfaction with the government's policies was heavily present.

[50] In January 1998, for example, 83% said that they were worried or greatly worried about the situation of the peace process (Peace Index, January 1998). In the same survey, 60% said that Israel's greatest concern was its internal divisions (mainly the orthodox-secular division), whereas only 29% pointed to the conflict with the Palestinians.

in this period, as well as when Sharon was in power, to interpret various normal manifestations of public dissatisfaction with the government as signs of an upcoming wave of anti-government feeling and indications that the public was turning away from its right-wing positions. The same goes for eruptions of violence. Whenever these occurred, the expectation of many in the movement was that the public would soon realize that the use of force was not the right way to handle conflict, whereas in fact, after every such event, most Israeli public opinion turned against those who were preaching moderation and compromise. This wishful thinking is understandable, because it helped the peace activists to continue their activities against all odds. Such predictions, and the peace movement's repeated forecast of a national catastrophe if the government did not change its policies and conduct, were refuted again and again (Netanyahu's government lasted for 3 years, i.e., above average for Israeli governments). These prophecies both undermined the political realism of the peace movement in the eyes of those outside it (the "cry wolf" effect), and created much frustration within it.

The slow-moving, low-key activity of moderate segments of the peace movement during the "bumpy zone" era attracted criticism from the more radical elements. A journalist for the daily *Ha'aretz*, known for his militant dovish views and most of whose weekly columns covered the unbearable living conditions of the Palestinians in the territories, directly targeted *Shalom Achshav* members for their bourgeois lifestyles and state of mind that led to this decline in activities:

Shalom Achshav looks different in recent years. Those who used to wear T-shirts, blue jeans and sandals have gradually been replaced by those who mainly wear the fancy outfits they bought during their last sabbatical in the US. Today, most activists of the movement are university faculty members, much older than the founders and much less enraged. If *Shalom Achshav* was a protest movement at the outset, it certainly isn't anymore. Its latest protest action, against the construction work in Har Homa, which in the past could have brought out large masses, was a total failure (Levy 1997, 16).

If this were not harsh enough, another journalist went even further in his criticism:

A bad smell of defeat can be felt these days in the Gush Dan area[51] and its suburbs. Bad, sour and angry. The defeat mainly has a hold on the members of the mainstream of the left, on all the liberals, do-gooders and those who pursue the highest standard of living. This may reflect the beginning of the collective comprehension of the true meaning of the 1996 elections. However, it may also only be a life style. The left has always loved to moan. The defeat was signed and sealed last night – when only very few bothered to mark the fourth anniversary of the signing of the Oslo Agreements (Tzror 1997, 39).

---

[51] Gush Dan is the central region of the Tel Aviv metropolitan area, which, for the Israeli reader, connotes secularism, urbanism, a Western lifestyle, and dovish political positions.

Admittedly, this and other merciless expressions of disapproval of the peace movement from all sides completely ignored the huge obstacles or the contracted facets of the POS that the movement faced. For example, these critics seem to have been completely oblivious to the fact that the public refused to conduct a constructive dialogue with the peace activists: "Peace Now is busy talking now. They talk with Meretz, they talk amongst themselves, they say that the city squares should be filled again, that billboards should be put up along the main roads, the stickers should get back on the cars... All they do is talk and wail" (Kim 1997). The data regarding the public state's of mind presented previously, and plenty of other available data from that period,[52] suggest that the recruitment potential of the movement in the late 1990s was so limited that talking to itself and groups around it was perhaps the only possible means of self-expression open to a peace organization.

The Palestinians also grew highly critical of the Israeli peace movement. In particular, they became impatient with what they considered to be the patronizing approach of Israeli activists, which, with their apparent inability to exert influence on the Israeli government and the shrinking of the peace camp, turned them into a "dead horse" from the Palestinian point of view. This impatience was evident in a symposium organized in 1997 by *Shalom Achshav* at A-Najah University in Nablus. It began on the wrong foot – the Palestinian chairman opened the event by stating that Palestinian peace activists felt helpless and highly frustrated because they were losing influence in their community because they could not point to any successes. However, he expressed no sympathy for the Israeli peace activists' similar experience. In fact, he told his Israeli counterparts that most people in Nablus thought that meeting Israelis – even if they were peace activists – was a waste of time. He also warned that if the Oslo peace process crashed, no future Palestinian leadership would be able to sign another peace agreement (Levy 1997, 16). On their part, the Israeli participants insisted on discussing the details of a future agreement that would be more agreeable than the Oslo documents, as if they were negotiating the permanent status agreement. For an entire day, they amiably discussed Jerusalem, security, settlements, and terror, clearly in contrast to the gut feelings of their Palestinian counterparts, who expected them to pronounce some fierce expressions of mea culpa and dismay with Israeli conduct. Eventually, the false harmony was shattered when the Palestinian refugee issue was touched on: the Israeli participants insisted that recognizing the Palestinian right of return was the red line that they would not cross, and the Palestinians argued that not only the recognition but also the realization of this right was a sine qua non for real peace (Levy 1997, 14). The symposium ended with both sides feeling deeply disappointed in the other.

This event presents a classic antithesis to what Habermas defines as an *ideal discourse situation*, in which all participants have an equal right to put forth

[52] For example, in the annual surveys on public opinion and national security for the years 1996–1998, conducted by Asher Arian for the Jaffee Center for Strategic Studies, Tel Aviv University.

the best arguments they can find and convince their partners to the dialogue of the validity of their position – its authenticity, justification, and so forth.[53] In an ideal discourse situation, the discussion should be conducted on the basis of agreed-on rules that can be changed only with the consent of all participants; the "best" argument wins only thanks to its inherent superiority. Such a dialogue is totally rational; participants are free of all stereotypes and consider all arguments on the basis of their respective merits. The situation in the symposium described here certainly did not meet these requirements:

Even here, it is the Israelis who made the final decision on each and every matter. . . . As expected, it was only the Israeli side who set up the agenda; the committee reports were all presented by Israeli chairpersons. . . . All that was left for the stunned Palestinian activists to do was to wish their Israeli guests – who were rushing home – Shabbat Shalom, in keeping with the well-known Palestinian good manners (Levy 1997, 14).

The POS of the "bumpy zone" was also contracted in terms of the movement's ability to disseminate its message through the media. In the second half of the 1990s, the media became less and less interested in the relatively small and mostly ineffective peace activities and organizations. A generous explanation would argue that these activities and organizations were just not eye-catching enough from the media point of view. Another, much less benevolent, explanation, in terms of Israeli society's tolerance for off-mainstreamers, was offered by an Israeli local weekly magazine, which over the years had adopted a rather pro-peace editorial line:

Something happened this month that you haven't read about in any newspaper, and certainly not seen on TV: Women in Black, a protest movement which emerged in the first weeks of the *intifada* just marked ten years of activity. Ten years of standing in the crossroads every Friday at noon, of being targeted with bad-mouthing, spitting and sometimes even worse, of an ongoing effort to introduce a new, non-violent, not vociferous, almost non-Israeli protest mode into Israel.[54] This says something sad about Israeli society in general and about its media in particular; the media only seem leftist but, in fact, try very hard to keep as far as possible from everything that "smells" of leftist radicalism and of real alternative thinking (*Ha'ir*, 27/3/98).[55]

---

53 For an elaborate discussion of the difficulties inherent in creating an ideal discourse situation in the context of Israeli-Palestinian relations, see Ofir 2001.

54 This low public awareness about peace activities (even those that, when confronted, aroused very angry public reactions because of limited media coverage) was well exemplified in the Peace Index survey of August 1996. When asked to which extent specific groups were or were not interested in maintaining Israel's security, the percentage who were not aware of the very existence of *Nashim b'Shachor* (Women in Black) was as high as 34%. Of those who were familiar with it, 29% said that it cared or cared a great deal for the state's security, whereas 37% said that it did not.

55 In his book on the functioning of the media in the early days of the second *intifada*, Daniel Dor (2001) clearly shows how Israeli media, despite its leftist image, by and large conformed to the government's right-wing line. Gadi Wolfsfeld defines the media-government relations in such situations as "competitive symbiosis" (Wolfsfeld 2003, 87).

The various peace groups had to find ways to circumvent the negative effects of the dissipating interest of the media and the decreasing level of grassroots participation in protest activities. Addressing exactly the sort of audience that had both the access and the will to use new communication technologies, they opted for mounting use of the Internet.[56] Many Internet peace lists and sites were created, with their numbers and the intensity of communication skyrocketing in the late 1990s and the early 2000s. One can actually point to a correlation between the disappearance of the actual peace activities and the swelling of virtual interactions. The accelerating use of the Internet as a substitute for on-the-ground activities or as a means to organize them, marked a turning point in the peace movement's mode of operation. This transformation has its pros and cons. On the positive side, the Internet is a relatively cheap and highly accessible medium. Particularly for small and/or geographically dispersed sectors, it enables the creation of a sense of community, even if imagined. Not much technical knowledge is needed to establish an email list or to moderate a virtual forum, particularly for people of higher education and exposure to technology, which are, as noted, two typical features of most Israeli peace activists. Information transfer is quick and is not easy to censor by the authorities. Virtual communication can be carried out from home and can reach people all over the world, political and other boundaries notwithstanding. Therefore, when and where the media did not cover the peace movement's views and news, Israelis and others, including Palestinians, could learn about them through the Internet.

There are, however, also some negative sides to such communication: it is easily monitored (as opposed to censored) by the authorities; it enables – and in fact attracts – the intentional introduction of false and defamatory contents; and despite all of the safeguards, it is still highly vulnerable to penetration by computer experts working for the movement's adversaries. In addition, the flood of written material tends to result in large amounts of "garbage" that often buries the really important items. Perhaps the most problematic aspect of heavy reliance on the Internet, however, is that although it brings together certain groups of people, it alienates and excludes others. With the change in the center of gravity from actual operations to virtual efforts, peace activists who, for whichever reasons, did not use computers or the Internet were now left out: "snail mail" was out, and advertisements in the newspapers were far beyond the financial capacity of most peace groups. In other words, the perimeter of the peace movement mobilization and maintenance of activists changed in the late 1990s and became limited mostly to those who had access to computerized communication. In addition, Israelis outside the movement who had been exposed in the past, even if against their will, to its message – through billboards, newspapers, printed flyers, and stickers – now, if they chose not to log in to the peace movement's sites or did not register for one of its

---

[56] For a comparative study of Internet use by Israeli and Japanese peace organizations, see Hara and Shachaf (2008).

mailing lists, could avoid hearing it altogether. Thus, the use of the Internet has contributed (although, of course, unintentionally) to the further isolation of the peace movement; it provided it with a relatively protected bubble while considerably reducing its public voice. Finally, living in this bubble created a false sense of competence and power. The intense flow of communication obscured the actual minimal effect and peripheral positioning of the peace movement from both peace activists and external observers.

The contracted POS of the time also encouraged a greater degree of specialization or more elaborate division of labor within the movement, relinquishing the hope to change, at least for the time being, government policies or the wider public's attitudes. An example of an outcome of this development was the establishment of *haVaad haYisraeli Neged Harisat Batim* (the Israeli Committee Against House Demolition [ICAHD]), in 1998. ICAHD, a one-purpose coalition of several peace SMOs, concentrates on one issue only: fighting – using various tactics – the Israeli authorities' systematic policy of demolishing Palestinian homes in the territories.[57] This is how Jeff Halper, ICAHD's coordinator, explained the extreme negative political and moral impact of demolishing houses:

House demolition is the epitome of the occupation: the humiliation, the trauma and the cruelty. It may be likened to rape, where the very essence of people's humanity is violated. It is above and beyond the political aspects of it. The influence of this act is enormous, on the families and the villages around. However, it is spreading more and more. And what does that mean for the Palestinians, what does it mean that the occupier can come in and do that? That it has the power to force it on you. It is not only rape – it is serial rape (Halper, in Golan-Agnon 2005, 116).

ICAHD functions through two parallel tracks: legal – appealing to the courts, thereby forcing the state to explain why the demolition is unavoidable, and nonviolent resistance. It petitions the Supreme Court, which more than once accepted the appeals and made the state reverse the demolition decision. The judges, however, never challenged the demolition policy itself, which is of course the direction in which ICAHD would have liked the Court to go. As to civil resistance, ICAHD's activists go where the demolition is about to be carried out and, with the Palestinian residents, try to prevent it by employing techniques of passive resistance. Admittedly, these acts of civil resistance were only rarely successful in preventing demolition, and some activists were even prosecuted for interfering in a legal process. Still, the moral problems that the act of demolition entails gradually inculcated themselves into Israeli public discourse, particularly in the print media, which often reported on such house demolition events.

---

57 House demolition is carried out by the Israeli authorities under the legal claim that the houses were built without formal permits. Although legally valid, morally this argument does not hold, because Palestinians are never granted such permits. For a comprehensive analysis of house demolition practices, particularly in East Jerusalem, see Braverman 2006.

In most cases, grassroots endeavors have no direct access to the decision-making process or to decision makers. They therefore need the media and public support to resonate their agenda, and for this to happen, their activities must be eye-catching.[58] When the media – and hence the public – are not there for them, social movements, and in particular protest movements, lose their main leverage. This situation faced the Israeli peace SMOs that still opted for the classic legal and large attendance-based means of protest in the period discussed here: "Today, the life of the organizers of demonstrations is very difficult.... Maybe not enough people will show up, maybe the entire genre of street demonstrations has become obsolete.... The protest movement organizes one demonstration and then takes a rest. When it gets up, it looks around with great concern, and gives birth, after great labor pains, to another demonstration" (Samet 1997). Worse, if one demonstration is poorly attended, the chances are that attendance at the next one will be even lower. Numbers are extremely important here, because demonstrations are measured by their supporters and particularly by their opponents according to their volume – assessment of the success or failure of such actions depends almost entirely on the number of people in the street or the square where they took place. Very few would feel comfortable at a poorly attended demonstration that was meant to be a large one. Even fewer would be ready to repeat the experience. This is what happened to several peace activists in the late 1990s.

The causes of mobilization failures are normally identified by those who came as being on one of two levels – either they place the blame on their colleagues, who organized the event badly, or they criticize those who did not come, calling them ideologically weak, indifferent, or simply blind to the urgency of the situation. They hardly ever, however, reflect on the justification of their own agenda or wonder if perhaps their inadequate reading of the situation was the reason they were not joined by many others:

While waiting for the demonstration to start, the protestors discussed among themselves the reasons why the masses don't come out into the streets. Some put the blame on the movement itself for failing to strongly enough boost the general awareness of the threat hanging over the process. Others looked for answers in the deeper layers of Israeli existence. This was an intimate conversation among a closed circle, made up of people who had known each other for many years. No more than a handful of demonstrators in their thirties were present. "Those in the 20–35 age group are the least involved politically," says Mossi Raz, Secretary-General of Peace Now. "This sense of desperation is prevalent in the wider circle of my acquaintances; people feel that they cannot make any difference. I personally know people who used to attend demonstrations regularly for four or even ten years, and who have now withdrawn from all of that" (Galili 1997b).

Indeed, by 1998, *Shalom Achshav* had shown some serious warning signs of an approaching downfall. The sense of despair is strongly felt in the

---

[58] This need to gain attention makes certain activists opt for dramatic means that provide them with wide exposure, which Weimann referred to as the "terror theatre" effect (Weimann 1985).

following reflections of one of the movement's founders: "Peace Now suffered two tremendous blows. First, we failed to prevent the Lebanon War [in 1982 – TH] although we knew it was coming in advance. Second, we were not able to break the stalemate in Israeli society, not even after Oslo. We changed attitudes within the dovish half [of the Israeli population – TH] but failed to reach out to the other half" (Abu Vilan, in Dayan 1998, 38). The holders of some key positions in the movement, including the Secretary-General, quit their jobs largely because of mounting ideological disagreements between the old guard and the younger members on how the movement should best be managed, with the latter being more prone to shifting *Shalom Achshav*'s attention to social and educational matters. The veteran activists – who eventually proved the stronger party to this encounter – were more inclined to favor the movement's traditional mode of operation, that is, demonstrations and other protest activities directly related to peace. This was not because they devalued social matters, but because they were perhaps more aware of past failures in pursuing this course of action. This is how Janet Aviad, a key figure in *Shalom Achshav* for years, explained this approach: "What jeopardizes peace most is hopelessness.... Peace Now should focus these days on political activity, including demonstrations and the Settlements Watch. Youth education is important, of course, but today it seems possible to get people out of their homes for classic political activities, and this is what we should be doing" (Weitz 1998).

Evidently, Aviad was not alone in her hope that something could be done on the grassroots level to save the peace process; actually, despite the many disappointments that they had experienced, members of the old guard seemed more optimistic in this regard than the younger members. Some even claimed credit for bringing about a profound attitude change in Israeli cognition: "The biggest achievement of Peace Now is that it managed to erode the legitimization of continued occupation of the territories. Thanks to Peace Now, today, in every age group, more than 50% are not ready to come to terms with the occupation (Dedi Zuker, in Dayan 1998, 38). This reading is somewhat wishful thinking because, although territorial compromises have indeed become much more acceptable to the wider public throughout the years, the negative connotation of the notion of occupation has not become deeply inculcated, nor, to this very date, are most Jewish Israelis deeply upset with the expanding of the settlement project.

Against the background of decreased activity of the veteran mixed-gender peace organizations, the late 1990s also saw again the emergence of several new women's peace initiatives. In an article on Israeli women's peace activism published by the Israeli English-language daily newspaper, *The Jerusalem Post*,[59]

---

59 *The Jerusalem Post* was founded in 1932 and until 1950 appeared under the name of *The Palestine Post*. In the past, it presented a dovish editorial line, much like its Hebrew counterpart, the daily *Ha'aretz*. In 1989, the paper was sold and under the new editorial board adopted a significantly more hawkish line on the Israeli-Palestinian conflict and Middle East politics in general.

Prof. Naomi Chazan,[60] explained her optimistic assessment of why these new groups would be more effective than their predecessors:

The only new voices that have emerged with clarity and conviction in the past year have been those of women. Immediately after the Hebron Agreement was signed, a group of women – mothers of combat soldiers – came together to create a new movement, Women Against War. Twelve months ago, in the wake of the helicopter crash that killed 73 soldiers, another new initiative – The Four Mothers – spearheaded the call for withdrawal from Lebanon. This past summer, a group of orthodox women founded Women for the Sanctity of Life. Mizrahi women have organized peace activities in development towns and low-income neighborhoods. . . . The new generation of the women's peace movement is particularly varied and heterogeneous. More importantly, the initiators of these groups are primarily newcomers to peace activity. Most have been propelled into the political arena by motives quite different from those of their male counterparts; they have mobilized themselves and others to protest against unnecessary risks and dangers, to prevent avoidable disaster, and – by extension – to refocus attention and energy on the value of human life and the need to bring an end to conflict. . . . While the mainstream peace camp maintains a low profile when the threat seems to have disappeared, and has become frustrated when it comes not to see the light at the end of the tunnel, women peace activists just refuse to give up (cited in http://www.batshalom/nif.org, March 29, 1998).

One of the most visible and some would argue the most successful women's organizations of the second half of the 1990s was indeed *Arba Imahot* (Four Mothers),[61] which is often brought as an example of the political competence that civil society organizations can attain. Many attribute Israel's withdrawal from South Lebanon in May 2000 to this group:[62]

Sometimes it is soldiers who determine the outcome of a battle; sometimes it is the commanders who shape the course the campaign takes, sometimes certain leaders change the future of their nation, but it seems that there are not many historical examples of a small group of people who are not fighters, commanders, or national leaders, who so clearly and decisively influence the realities of the state and even the region. (A letter sent to *Arba Imahot* by Ofer Gavish, a member of Kibbutz Yiftach, http://www. youngknesset.org.il).

Israeli troops had been present in Lebanon since 1982, and little protest was organized around the issue of withdrawal. This changed when a succession of accidents in south Lebanon cost many soldiers their lives. The most serious of these was the 1997 collision of two helicopters in which 73 soldiers were killed.

---

[60] Prof. Chazan is a political scientist with a long record of peace activity, including taking part in the establishment of *Bat Shalom*, and, at the time that this article was published, she was an MK of Meretz and Deputy Speaker of the Knesset.

[61] The term *Four Mothers* has symbolic meaning in Jewish tradition because it represents the four biblical mothers of the nation (Lemish and Barzel 2000, 148).

[62] In the Peace Index survey of May 2000, 36% believed that *Arba Imahot* had significant influence over the decision to pull out, and 22% even labeled its influence on decision makers as very strong. Only 19% thought that it had only some limited influence, and 16% thought that it had no influence at all.

There was also the threatening presence of Hezbollah, whose leaders stated that northern Israeli towns and villages would be targeted by their rockets as long as even one Israeli solider was present on Lebanese soil. These served *Arba Imahot* as the immediate reasons for raising their voices in the late 1990s.

Following, to a great extent, in the footsteps of *Imahot Neged Shtika* of the early 1980s, the founding group of *Arba Imahot* used their maternal status (their sons were all serving in the IDF at the time) as their major political asset. The use of the maternal motif was quite helpful, because apparently it is less threatening to men, retaining the traditional view of women's having emotional rather than (challenging, male) rational arguments. The logic of the mothers' protest was explained by Vered Shomron, at that time an activist in a smaller group, Women and Mothers for Peace, and later in *Profil Hadash* (New Profile), that also applies to the case of *Arba Imahot*:

What is happening today in Lebanon is indeed a clear case of sacrificing our sons, a shameful waste of human lives. And we – we don't have spare children for unnecessary wars. This sacrifice is unreasonable. It has no logic to it. Lebanon is our Vietnam. It was just too late before America realized that Vietnam was a terrible mistake, much too late after thousands of soldiers had already been sacrificed. We shall not let it happen here as well; we shall revolt and will not stop until there is peace. The aggressive policy of the government is bound to change. We shall not compromise on anything less than that (in Mehulal 1998, 44).

In addition, all founding mothers of the group lived in the northern part of Israel, near the Lebanese border. This meant that they had clear personal interests in the matter at the center of their activity, a fact that made their protest look very sincere and authentic. Much less confrontational and more conformist than *Nashim b'Shachor* or even *Bat Shalom*, *Arba Imahot's* perceived achievements were apparently the result of working within "the 'rules of the game' rather than going against them. In their nonthreatening, legitimized, and accepted roles as concerned mothers, life-bearers, and caregivers, the public was willing to lend an ear to their message and was able to sympathize with their call" (Lemish and Barzel 2000, 167). Their success in becoming the most salient of the peace groups in the late 1990s stemmed from the widely acknowledged and highly respected natural desire of women to protect their offspring. To enjoy the benefits of the universal – and of course national – empathy with motherly love, *Arba Imahot* tried hard to clarify that their protest was not ideologically motivated. They also tried hard to avoid the feminist stigma:

The concern of mothers for their sons is a human, not a feminist issue. . . . Presenting the mothers' struggle for a solution to this problem [Israel's ongoing military presence in Lebanon – TH] as a feminist one is cynical and short sighted, or a scheme to divert public attention away from the real aim – withdrawal from Lebanon – to a marginal one. . . . The Lebanon problem should concern the public in general, not only mothers and women. Unfortunately, this is not the case. . . . The fact that the protestors are mothers of soldiers serving on the front lines who are expressing their personal worries, does not weaken their principal argument against Israel's presence in Lebanon nor rule out their right to protest and demonstrate (Ben Benyamin 1997).

Evidently, the more politicized women peace activists did not like the essentialist, allegedly apolitical, approach of *Arba Imahot* and in a sense viewed them as perhaps having the right cause but a false consciousness. This "back to basics" consciousness could prove disruptive to their own efforts to introduce alternative thinking about security and harm ideological peace activism that challenged the common wisdom on such matters:

Arba Imahot succeeded because they talked about motherhood. This is always acceptable. This remains within the consensus. However, we [*Nashim b'Shachor*] refuse to speak in the name of motherhood. We speak out as citizens, and this is why we have remained outside the mainstream. In Israel, not belonging – this way or that – to the blood covenant, not being part of the community of bereaved parents, deprives you of the right to take part in the political-security discourse (Traubman in Isachar 2003, 58).

Although on the face of it there was nothing more natural than strong cooperation between the well-established women's peace organizations and *Arba Imahot*, the difference in their respective self-image and audiences made such cooperation practically impossible: "One Friday we tried to join the *Arba Imahot* protest vigil . . . however, we were greeted with extreme hostility. They were reaching out to the right-wingers and the Orthodox and therefore rejected us. They did not see that all protest movements in this country are leftist" (Vered Shomron, in Mehulal 1998, 46).

Exactly as in the case of *Imahot Neged Shtika*, at a certain point when *Arba Imahot* gained volume and voice, a number of men joined it. In a short while, this gender mixing created internal tensions as the men were moved – or pushed their way – to the highest power positions. As one of the women activists put it: "As I was in the midst of my feminist empowerment process, I suffered a great deal from the fact that a man, and even worse, an ex-general, was put above me, a professional general who of course took control of the group just like that. I was told that this was the only way because these are the rules of the game in Israel and 'when in Rome, do as the Romans do'" (Lavnin-Dgani, in Isachar 2003, 143).

Even more than motherhood/parenthood, however, the now mixed-gender movement was able to take off, gain wide media coverage and access to prominent politicians, and mobilize the support of many Israelis because they did not involve themselves in the highly controversial Palestinian issue. The demand that they focused on – pull the IDF forces out of Lebanon – was shared by many in the mainstream.[63] Avoiding divisive issues such as the Palestinian

---

[63] In December 1994, the Peace Index survey found that only 11% of Jewish respondents thought that, against the background of the Hezbollah attacks, Israel should pull its forces out of south Lebanon (48% favored a large-scale military operation, and 23% preferred only local military responses, with the remainder having no clear preference). By November 1998, the survey found that 41% (versus 48%) thought that Israel should pull out.

question made the public attitude toward *Arba Imahot* much more positive than toward most other peace groups. For example, Israeli journalist Yoav Yitzchak noted that the European Union (EU), in the context of its aid to pro-Palestinian groups within Israel, allocated €250,000 to *Arba Imahot*. Whereas other peace organizations were harassed for taking EU money, *Arba Imahot* was not widely denounced for "serving external agendas."[64]

The successful combination of the maternal, nonideological nature of *Arba Imahot* and the massive public support that it received made it impossible for politicians to ignore them in the way that they had ignored other grassroots peace endeavors. Hence, representatives of *Arba Imahot* managed fairly easily to meet with the Defense Minister in Netanyahu's government, Prof. Moshe Arens, and another politician and ex-general, Itzhak Mordechai (reluctantly it should be pointed out), also met with them as did a few tens of Knesset members, foreign ambassadors and certain dignitaries when they visited Israel. The politicians of the left were much more sympathetic to their cause than the grassroots peace activists: Yossi Beilin, for example, openly identified with their campaign and helped the movement in many ways (some even argued that the movement was of his making). Whether they liked them or not, and despite the reservations of many on the left and certainly on the right, no one dared to refer to the protesting mothers of 1997 in the same dismissive and rude way that certain politicians had treated *Imahot Neged Shtika* in 1982 and 1983. This change was the result of the gradual improvement in the status of women in Israel in general but also at least in part due to the expansion of grassroots activities, including peace- and security-related activism and women's activism in particular:

The political establishment is hardly ever moved by extra-parliamentary groups and in particular doesn't fear women's ones. Therefore, the sole threat is in their steadfastness: past experience has taught us that women hesitate more than men when it comes to extra-parliamentary activity, but once they cross that bridge, they are much more conscientious than men. This may be related to women's difficulty in gaining entry into the political establishment and perhaps also to their unique cognitive mechanisms. Be it this or some other explanation, at the margins of Grand Politics, a significant extra-parliamentary phenomenon is taking place these days and is not likely to disappear in the foreseeable future (Galili 1997a).

Nothing is more successful than success itself – anyone in Israel who favored Israeli withdrawal from Lebanon at the time was identified, rightly or wrongly, as a supporter of *Arba Imahot*. The fact of the matter was, however, that quite rapidly the movement – like so many peace groups before and since – became bitterly divided. On one side were the four original founding mothers and their supporters from the north of the country; on the other was a group from the center and the south. The disagreement stemmed from two issues. First was

---

[64] Yitzchak admitted that in the end the money was not transferred to the movement because Israel had already pulled out of Lebanon, following which *Arba Imahot* was dissolved (Yitzchak 2001).

the way that the movement was managed – in an undemocratic way according to the latter group, who thought that they were systematically being marginalized, and even tried, although to no avail, to establish their own movement that would raise the same banner. The second issue the "rebels" raised was the dilettante way that *Arba Imahot* operated: like a kindergarten, according to these disappointed members who were unable to come to terms with the emotional discourse of the founding group: "It is impossible for an entire movement to operate on the basis of emotions alone.... It should operate rationally, and challenge the decision-makers using one argument after another.... We are also outraged by the fact that we have been turned into a group of professional national mourners.... We should move on and take the struggle off the street and into the offices of the decision-makers" (Sinai 1998).

The splintering tendency of the peace movement was manifested once again in February 1999, with the creation of a new organization called *Kav Adom* (Red Line) by former members of *Arba Imahot*. *Kav Adom* organized its own demonstration for a withdrawal from Lebanon in front of the Ministry of Defense office in Tel Aviv. This demonstration was less courteous than those of the mothers' movement; participants blocked the crowded street and even set tires on fire. The new organization's (male) speaker severely attacked the latter's soft tactics: "Soldiers are being killed, the army is 'drawing some lessons' and the mothers only mourn. I left that movement and slammed the door behind me because it is toothless, it doesn't bark and it doesn't bite" (in Fried 1999). He promised that his new organization would not refrain from using any effective means to achieve their aim: "If we have to, we shall employ violence, including harassment of politicians, banging on the doors of those who are responsible for the Lebanon fiasco, blocking traffic, and disrupting life all over the country and the daily routine of the decision-makers" (op. cit.). Another activist of the same splinter group, which quickly disappeared, also criticized *Arba Imahot*: "Their line is too soft, they give out flowers, plant trees, but stop nothing in Lebanon. We shall not let anyone shake hands with VIPs and say 'thank you' anymore" (ibid.).

Obviously, the more successful the movement seemed to be, the less liked it was from the point of view of the political right. A substantial criticism coming from this direction argued that

Arba Imahot used words and took a position that did not represent all mothers: the mothers in Kiryat Shmona, who also care for their children, were under a constant barrage of rockets from Lebanon. Instead, they used dichotomous, emotional language, declaring only one option as acceptable.... *Arba Imahot* presented one of two halves as the whole. They acted like the proxy of Peace Now, whose name alone is enough to eliminate the option of conducting a meaningful debate on contesting options.... Using the "Now" as the dominant term, as the sole goal, means rejecting the dialectic idea of development through dialogue between antithetical oppositions, a dialogue that is not limited to two contending options but accepts the existence of many more that together create a composite totality.... The term "Now" has destructive and anti-democratic power... it lowers the debate to the level of immediate satisfaction (Pinchas-Cohen 2001).

In May 2000, Israel withdrew its forces from Lebanon. It has never been officially stated that the decision was in any way affected by grassroots activity, but this time many unofficial accounts did give the movement credit. Besides its specific achievement, *Arba Imahot* and its supporters managed to leave behind a legacy of success, which was so necessary for peace activism to continue. This is how the former Secretary General of *Shalom Achshav* describes the role played by the peace movement in pulling the IDF out of south Lebanon:

An example of success is the withdrawal from Lebanon, not in the 1980s, but in the Barak period. What happened is that the peace movements kept saying for years that we had to get out of Lebanon; *Arba Imahot* definitely added a lot of momentum. That is, it's not dirty, it's not sick, it's not unnatural if somewhere in the corridors of power, you can find an ear to listen to the voice of protest. Yossi Beilin was the first who basically adopted that approach from the extra-parliamentary movements. The pressure was very strong and effective, until finally Barak had no choice and was forced to retreat from Southern Lebanon (Moria Shlomot, in Hermann 2005, 38).

If *Arba Imahot* represented a conventional interpretation of political motherhood in Israel of the late 1990s, then its antithetical group was *Profil Hadash* (New Profile), a new women-based (yet not exclusively female) organization established in 1998. *Profil Hadash* inscribed on its banner a motto that in the Israeli context, even to the moderate peace groups, was highly controversial: demilitarizing Israeli society. According to this group's interpretation, Israeli society has been controlled by militaristically minded men for too long to enable the emergence of a proper civil society in which women and people who do not share the militaristic ethos or experience can make their voices heard.[65] The focal proactive element in the group's activity was its support for individual choice about whether to join the army, without going into the question of which grounds for refusal are justified and which are not:

We support refusal to go to the army, avoidance of going to the army, as a major contribution to democracy, and maybe that's why – unlike some of the other groups – we don't "rank" the refusers. We support whoever avoids going to the army, and it doesn't matter how he does it or what his motives are.... We see ourselves as providing a service to the public because we reveal the truth about army service, since the state doesn't tell the truth about it. The state creates a situation where it's legitimate to give high school students false information about service, and so on. That is our agenda – to understand and learn how militarism motivates everyone, from the extreme right to the extreme left, and all the shadings in between, and to explain that until we change this, it will be impossible to progress in the direction of resolving the conflict and strengthening real democracy (Ronit Maryan, in Hermann 2005, 61).

[65] At a certain point in 1998, *Profil Hadash* tried to join forces with *Arba Imahot*, but because of their highly different perceptions of Israeli society, including the issue of the necessity of military service, the leaders of *Arba Imahot* refused to cooperate (Firestone, in Isachar 2003, 123).

While *Profil Hadash* defined itself as a feminist organization (and not as a peace SMO), it also opened its doors to men who shared this anti-militaristic-feminist ideology. Its relevance to our discussion is their statement that peace cannot be achieved until Israeli society undergoes a deep cognitive transformation – becomes civilian. Such a shift is not easy, they acknowledged, particularly under the stressful and threatening conditions of the Middle East. It is a chicken-and-egg dilemma, because according to this framing, no change in the conditions is possible as long as the militaristic state of mind controls Israel.

The first actions of *Profil Hadash* took the shape of reading groups, which discussed the status of Israeli women, the army, and militarism. The participants, almost all women, read academic materials but also placed emphasis on their personal experiences. Some of the women who participated in *Profil Hadash* activities had no former political experience whatsoever. Others, however, had been involved in such activities in the past and were well connected to the various peace networks. Most of them came because they were mothers[66] and felt the need to protect their sons and daughters from harm that might be caused to them in the course of military service, which most of the participating women considered unnecessary, or simply by living in a militaristic society (Mazali 2003, 25). The personal aspect was therefore salient in this group from the beginning as well: "*Profil Hadash* was set up, in my opinion, as a sort of support group for women who were troubled by these matters or interested in them. They met because of terrible distress and out of a feeling that something must be done, with the feminist outlook as a guide" (Ronit Maryan, in Hermann 2005, 60, 63).

In summer 1998, *Profil Hadash* organized a symposium, which turned out to be its launching event, under the highly provocative (from the point of view of the general Israeli public) title, "Aspects of being drafted and avoiding being drafted into the IDF." This agenda was in dramatic contrast to the prevailing positive Israeli public opinion regarding military service, which had not dramatically changed despite the slow erosion in the enormous prestige of the IDF and the declining percentage of those of relevant age who were actually being drafted (e.g., Peri 2002).[67] Because military service was a cherished value, the very organization of and participation in such a meeting marked a significant change for the better in the POS facing nonconformist peace advocacy in Israel of the late 1990s. This was not so much in terms of legal permission to do

---

[66] The fact that the participants had a clear vested interest in the matter they were dealing with cast some doubt on their sincerity. They were viewed in the same way that the industrialists who supported Peres's New Middle East vision had been accused of only seeking revenues and being oblivious to the nation's real interest, and in the way peace activists in general were accused of wanting peace just to promote the economic and other interests of their class.

[67] The ideal of universal conscription is more a myth than a reality – in 1980, 12% of men of military age were exempt from military service; in 1994, 17.7%; in 2001, 21.8%; in 2003, 23%; with 25% as the figure expected for 2006 (Harel 2004).

so, since this would have been granted before as well, but in terms of the public providing attitudinal and cognitive space to hold such a discussion in the open.[68] Indeed, attendance at the event was considerably beyond what was expected, and negative reactions were relatively minor.

The founders of *Profil Hadash* decided not only on an unusual agenda but also on an unusual way of running their group. Their rule of thumb was teamwork combined with individual responsibility. The treasurer was the only position formally set, to avoid the creation of an organizational hierarchy (and oligarchy), which, according to the organizers, could lead only to power struggles of the sort some of them had experienced – and disliked – in other peace organizations. Apparently, this worked quite well, because the good atmosphere that had characterized the early meetings of *Profil Hadash* was repeatedly mentioned in participants' accounts. One (male) participant recollected his impressions of the first meeting he attended: "This movement has a very strong basis of good social relations which hold the organization together, and this is of course thanks to the intentional effort to create very few reasons for internal politics or for power struggles to evolve. . . . It was love at first sight, and since then I have not missed a single meeting" (Sergei Sandler, in Isachar 2003, 130).

Despite its ideological radicalism in terms of challenging a major institution in Israeli society, and although *Profil Hadash* always considered itself part of the peace movement, throughout the years it avoided putting forward a political blueprint for their favored solution to the conflict. Instead, *Profil Hadash*

> . . . aimed more at the roots of our problem, not so much – basically not at all – at the questions of what Arafat or Barak had contributed to the failure of the Oslo process. *Profil Hadash* was meant to be a mirror, to help us look at ourselves as a society from a feminist standpoint. We identify militarism as the root of all evil, as something that underlies the motives or considerations that give birth to Israel's problematic policy (Diana Dolev, in Hermann 2005, 59–60).

To sum up this period – compared with the cognitive and operational confusion that characterized the peace movement's conduct following the unexpected POS that developed after the signing of the first Oslo agreement, which caused it to retreat; after the Rabin assassination and even more so after the 1996 elections, the peace movement seemed to have partly awakened. In more ways than one, the movement tried to adapt itself ideologically and operationally to the new realities. The presence of a clearly hostile government served the movement well in terms of making it regain its oppositional character. Still, in terms of its public appeal and political influence, the movement failed to take off for more than an occasional episode. This failure can be attributed to the

---

[68] The change was not drastic or all encompassing, however. Thus, the organizers had to find a new location for this gathering, because the proprietor of the original meeting place, on realizing the nature of the meeting, refused at the last moment to let the group hold it on the premises.

many obstacles that stood in its way at that time. First, because according to the movement's debatable strategic analysis, there was still some hope that the Oslo process would come back to life even under Netanyahu, the movement at large was careful not to damage this – even if minimal – prospect by blatantly attacking the foundations of the process, the way in which it did in the next phase of its activity. Second, the gap between public opinion and the agenda of the peace movement was widening, which incapacitated its mobilization potential. The frequent Palestinian terrorist attacks on one hand and the cold shoulder that Palestinian peace activists showed their Israeli counterparts on the other, also served as major deterrents to joining or even continuing peace activism in the late 1990s. Third, donors' interest in grassroots peace activities was considerably reduced, and if they contributed at all, it was mainly to more institutionalized and elitist pro-peace organizations that did not necessarily cooperate with the peace SMOs. Finally, internal ideological and tactical disputes between moderate and radical peace activists also did not contribute to the recovery process.

The Checkpoint Zone

Dating the opening of the third phase, "the checkpoint zone," with Netanyahu's electoral defeat and the establishment of the Barak government in May 1999 is almost self-evident and needs little explanation. Less obvious, however, is the cutoff point. Some would point to the failure of the Camp David summit in July 2000 and the ensuing outbreak of the second, *Al-Aqsa*, Palestinian *intifada* in October, although others would identify the downfall of Barak and the ascendance of Sharon in the 2001 elections as the division point between the third and the fourth parts of the Oslo years discussed here. Selecting the first cutoff point emphasizes the cognitive aspects of the proximate POS that faced the peace movement, that is, the shock of the collapse of the negotiations and the sharp increase in violence, both with devastating effects on the belief of the Israeli leaders and public in the Palestinians' interest in peace and therefore on their readiness to make any concessions to reach an agreement. The preferred option here is the second cutoff point, the electoral defeat of Barak and the rise to power of Ariel Sharon, at that time the epitome of evil in the eyes of the peace activists. This implies a greater emphasis on the state-centered POS, that is, the political room for maneuvering with which the movement was left, against the background of the unfavorable postelection political alignment and the deep alienation between it and the general public.

The 1999 electoral downfall of Netanyahu and his Likud-led government, and the comeback of the Labour party under the new leadership of Ehud Barak, seemed at the time to be a blessing for the peace movement. In many respects, Barak indeed seemed the perfect leader to pursue the Oslo course, which Rabin had launched and Netanyahu brought to a halt. Barak's commitment to renew negotiations with the Palestinians, combined with his indisputable military expertise, made him seem highly qualified for the enormous task of putting the process back on track.[69] Furthermore, from the peace movement's point of view, Barak's sociodemographic features – having grown up on a kibbutz of the Labour movement, being secular and Ashkenazi – all made him the classic prototype of a potential supporter. It is not surprising then that the more moderate elements of the movement were especially thrilled when Barak managed to take over leadership of the Labour party in 1997, declared his intention to challenge Netanyahu in the next election, and then actually succeeded to do so.

In retrospect, however, one can point to some warning signs that should have mitigated these high hopes even before Barak came to power. There was more than one indication that he was not going to associate himself, let alone reach out, to the peace movement. For example, in August 1997, representatives of all the larger peace organizations gathered for a work meeting, that is, a meeting that was expected to lead to practical decisions, with MK Barak in his Knesset office. The peace activists' mood was a blend of past frustration and hope for a better future:

> The last time they all sat together was almost two years ago . . . at the large peace rally at the end of which, it was not only Rabin who was shot, but as revealed in retrospect, so was the entire peace camp. Meanwhile, the rage was replaced with desperation, which in its turn changed to apathy; resistance to the government's policy today boils down to crying havoc, moaning and endless debates amongst the good lads and lasses of the peace movement (Kim 1997).

This was mixed with "a sense of revival, that the lingering process of wound-licking would end at last, and that the new leader of the opposition would give a green light to wide public opposition to the government" (ibid.). The peace activists' expectations from this meeting did not materialize, however; they were greatly disenchanted at its end. A relatively minor disappointment was that representatives of the different peace SMOs failed to rally around one work plan; each of them came forward with his or her organization's own proposals. Most of these plans were neither innovative nor wide enough in scope to justify combining all the forces of the peace movement. The major disappointment, however, was caused by Barak's negative attitude. He listened to what they had to say but expressed no real interest in leading a cooperative effort of all components of the peace camp, nor did he seem to be interested in close cooperation between the Labour party and the peace movement, although the peace activists were ready to keep a very low profile to not impair the electoral prospects of Barak and his party. At the end of the meeting, he decided to appoint a committee to discuss what should be done, yet without committing himself to any further cooperation with the peace movement. In

---

[69] Indeed, the 1999 election of Ehud Barak, whose campaign appeals included photos of him as commander of the operation to retake the hijacked Sabena aircraft, his foot planted on the head of a dead Palestinian terrorist, presaged a readiness on the part of the public to "give peace a chance" while maintaining the broadest possible margin of security.

fact, the committee that he appointed did not include even one representative of Labour. In other words, Barak decided on behalf of the peace movement who would sit on a committee, of which he and his party were not a part (ibid.).[70]

Among his other motivations, it seems that Barak was reluctant to let himself or his party be associated in the public mind with the peace movement because he was already "contaminated" with a leftist image after being asked during a press interview what he would have done had he been born a Palestinian. His much criticized, and probably much regretted, answer was direct: "If I were the right age, I guess I would join one of the terrorist organizations" (Drucker 2002, 23). In fact, in a survey conducted in 1999, almost one half (49%) of the respondents defined Barak as being on the left, and 32% put him in the center, with only 9% putting him on the right (Peace Index, July 1999).

Still, for many peace activists who were not aware of this unfortunate meeting or preferred to ignore it, Barak seemed by far preferable for the nation and the movement to his opponent, Netanyahu. Many were hopeful that once he became Prime Minister, his attitudes would be less affected by electoral considerations, the national climate of opinion would become less hawkish, and government policy on the Palestinian issue would change for the better. There is evidence that the optimism of several quite experienced peace activists rose in mid-1999 almost to the level of the early 1990s, and some even hoped that the time for the movement to take off had arrived. Other veteran peace activists were so captivated by Barak's abilities that they openly downgraded extraparliamentary activism: "It is impossible to do democracy outside of the political parties. In extra-parliamentary movements, which are informal, it is very difficult to change the leadership because of their voluntary nature.... Peace Now wanted to present an alternative but realized that there wasn't one" (Yuli Tamir, in Shchori 1999).

It should be noted that most activists of the radical fringe peace groups never fell for Barak's magic touch and argued that the gap between the man and real peace making was too huge to be bridged by hopes. This was only an insignificant minority, however; the entire left gave their votes to Barak.

As indicated in the graph in Appendix 2, general public opinion at the time of the elections and immediately following them was deeply divided about the Oslo process, but the number of those who supported and believed in it reached the highest level between May and August 1999. Apparently, the majority were not bothered by the slow pace of the negotiations with the Palestinians – the August 1999 Peace Index survey indicated that 49% thought that the negotiations were progressing at the right speed, 18% thought that they were being conducted too slowly, and 12.5% judged their pace as too rapid. Members of the peace movement became quite worried, however, when they saw that Barak's government was doing practically nothing to stop or even slow

---

[70] It should perhaps be mentioned here that the way Barak handled the peace activists was not unique in any way, but rather symptomatic of his problematic people skills, an issue discussed in detail in Drucker 2002.

down the construction of new outposts in the West Bank or the expansion of existing settlements there.[71] Another concern of the peace movement concerned Barak's priorities: he opted for achieving a peace agreement with Syria over reaching a settlement with the Palestinians.[72]

It was apparent that Barak, much like Rabin, was not at all sympathetic to the peace movement or its arguments, which of course contributed to the peace activists' growing frustration and their alienation from him and his government. Still, in the first months of his term, it looked as though the peace train were moving rapidly, with the government locomotive pulling it full strength ahead. The motivation and prospects for recruiting massive public support for peace protests were therefore very low. Furthermore, again as in Rabin's days, those who remained in the movement hesitated to openly and fiercely criticize Labour government's policy:

Shalom Achshav was not oriented and, in my opinion, is still not oriented to being critical and acting as a protest movement. That was true when the left was in power – from Rabin, through the Peres period, to the Barak period. When the government is "bad," i.e., right-wing, then it's easier for us. This is what explains the difference in protest in the times when Peres, Netanyahu, and Barak were in power, when more or less similar things were happening in terms of the building in the settlements, the terror attacks, and political behavior. In the end, all three didn't implement Oslo (Moriah Shlomot, in Hermann 2005, 19).

Thus, from late 1999 to mid-2000, the peace movement was actually in limbo. On one level, the formal peace process showed some signs of recovering, a mirage that fully covered the horizon with the IDF pull-out from Lebanon in May 2000. On another level, the harsh realities of the occupation were self-evident: the Settlement Watch team of *Shalom Achshav*[73] repeatedly revealed expanded construction, and teams of *b'Tselem* time after time exposed gross violations of Palestinian human rights by Israeli authorities and security agencies.

---

[71] Paradoxically, Barak was in fact the only Israeli prime minister since the signing of the DOP who did not make any practical territorial concessions to the Palestinians. Despite his pro-peace rhetoric, the Settlement Watch reports indicate that the expanding of the settlements also was accelerated during his term of office.

[72] Public opinion at the time lay in between: the majority, 57.5%, wanted the efforts to reach an agreement to be conducted simultaneously with the Syrians and the Palestinians; 17% wanted to see preference given to the Syrian channel, and 14% to the Palestinian one (Peace Index, June 1999).

[73] The Settlement Watch project was launched by *Shalom Achshav* in 1990, with the aim of monitoring and protesting "the building of settlements, including housing tenders, expropriation of lands, budget allocations, and the like [...] in the West Bank and East Jerusalem" (http://www.peacenow.org.il). The project was based on the assumption that knowing the facts was a precondition to a meaningful debate on the future of Israel's control of the territories and its costs. Settlement Watch established itself as a highly professional and reliable source of information in this regard. Its annual report is widely circulated and read by journalists and experts in and outside of Israel.

A development on the level of general public opinion, which significantly restricted the room for maneuvering that was open to the peace movement, was the disappearance of the political left – the dovish camp in the public's terms. Thus, while in former years it was very much "in" in certain circles to affiliate oneself with this political camp, this was no longer the case by the end of the 1990s. Ongoing Palestinian terror against Israeli civilians contributed much to the deterioration of its attractiveness, and even more to that of the peace movement, in the public eye. This growing resentment of the peace camp agenda was clearly expressed in an article about a Supreme Court decision, in response to an appeal by several peace and human rights groups that asked the court to limit the means used by security authorities when investigating Palestinians suspected of being involved in terrorist activities:

The dovish mentality is normally tender, humane and highly considerate of the other. This is fine. However, in a confrontation situation, particularly in the region in which we live, being dovish calls for another state of mind. Israeli doves should be equipped with iron thorns, because if they only offer – with a smile – olive branches, they are doomed to turn into doves grilled on a skewer. I am a dove but I want to go on living. I want peace but am also ready to fight for it and not just the easy way – by demonstrating and blowing nice slogans into the air. I am ready to fight for it the hard, sometimes cruel, way that puts serious moral dilemmas on my doorstep daily. I refuse to find refuge in some wishy-washy position, and the hell with everything else, as long as I save my soul (Dankner 1999).

Another related phenomenon on the public opinion level was the mounting blurring of the differences between left and right on issues relating to Israeli-Palestinian relations during these years. Indeed, both political camps had become almost equally disillusioned with the government's unsuccessful peace efforts (with the right being able to take the "we told you so" approach). At the same time, many people of the right came to realize that to have some claim in the region, the Israeli side would have to make substantial territorial and other compromises to the Palestinians. In other words, although the left gradually lost its appeal, on the moderate right, growing erosion in the belief in the "not an inch" postulate was also noticeable. In other words, the traditional division between the Israeli left and the right started to get blurred. By definition ideology based, this prevalent conceptual ambiguity presented the peace movement with an unfavorable POS.

Furthermore, in light of the ongoing sluggish and low-profile peace activism, the availability of external financial resources further decreased. Even *Shalom Achshav*, in the past better off than most Israeli peace groups, now had to knock on the door of potential donors each time that the group wanted to organize a large demonstration,[74] in the hope that they would write a check so that the demonstration could take place. The lack of resources available to

---

[74] Despite financial and other obstacles, the 2003 demonstration was eventually organized under the slogan "Get out of the territories for the sake of Israel" and attracted a large crowd although only limited media attention, and exerted no influence over the government's policies.

them aggravated the competition between the various peace movements and other social grassroots actors, which in its turn raised the class issue to the surface. A classic outcome of the association between the peace agenda and bourgeois economic interests was placed bluntly on the table at a meeting in 2002 between activists of the *haKeshet haMizrachit* (The Mizrahi Democratic Rainbow) and top peace activists (Pundak, Hirschfeld, Savir, and others). The former argued that "Oslo people" were "a group of detached, arrogant and estranged men, who travel all over the world but are never ready to go down to Dimona and Yeruham [poverty-stricken Israeli development towns in the south – TH]. They failed to understand that had they addressed the entire public and not only their own class, peace would have received wide support and not appeared to be in the interests of the rich only." The "Oslo people," on their part, answered that the social activists were also in fact an elite group, detached from the working classes that they pretended to represent, and that many of them lived in exclusive neighborhoods and not in Yeruham or Dimona (Leibovitz-Dar 2002). In retrospect, it appears that the disagreement over the expected outcomes of future peace treaties and over the Israeli labor market was fueled by the competition between the two endeavors for funding. This rivalry became fiercer during the deepening economic crisis in Israel in the late 1990s and the early 2000s, and when external donations to Israeli civil society organizations dried up, following the deterioration of the international image of Israel because of its reactions to the Palestinian *intifada*.

Another concern typical of this period was that only few people would show up for demonstrations, as indeed happened more than once. Of note, the funding available to the more radical groups, which had always been relatively limited, proved more solid and less prone to fluctuation in the late 1990s and early 2000s, because their donors never expected them to organize massive protest events nor actually to bring about policy changes. Thus, as these organizations did not carry out costly activities, the impact on their level of activity of the declining availability of funds from donors, if and when it occurred, was considerably milder than in the case of the moderate and mass-based peace SMOs.

In the late 1990s and early 2000s, a new generation of people who had been young high school students when Rabin was assassinated,[75] and, of course, even younger when the Oslo DOP was signed, began to develop some political interest and awareness. Few of them found it in the peace movement. Most of those who opted for the peace activism option arrived at that point with completely different cognitive and affective "luggage" than that of the older generation of

---

[75] In the wake of Rabin's assassination, for days the square where it took place was filled with mourning youth ("candle youth" as they were referred to by the media because of the many candles they lit). In retrospect, however, it appears that mourning for the dead leader and his peace policy was not enough to bring these masses into the peace movement, because the results of the next election all indicated that the young voters preferred the parties of the center and the right to those left of center.

peace activists. In fact, from these newcomers' point of view, *Shalom Achshav*, which, as already mentioned, epitomized the entire peace movement in the eyes of many, was as shabby, old-fashioned, over-institutionalized, and therefore mistrusted, as all the mainstream political parties. This is how a young activist explained it:

Personally, in the 1990s I wasn't very involved politically. I did go to the big Peace Now demonstrations, but I didn't have a lot of friends there, and also I didn't feel at home because it's a large movement and it was hard for me as a new activist to integrate or connect with it. Joining Peace Now would have meant connecting with a generation that's a lot older than I am. There's also a generation gap between me and my friends on one hand and New Profile on the other, since there too, pardon me for saying this, most of the activists are relatively older women.... I witnessed the collapse of the peace movement. In the first weeks after the *intifada* broke out there were two large demonstrations. One was in the plaza of the Tel Aviv Museum. When [Labour MK] Yael Dayan came on stage to speak, the public simply booed her, and she left. That really shocked me because as I see it, the left has become totally confused. The young generation, people we can perhaps call the postmoderns of the left, since they don't really belong to either the old or the new left and don't use the same concepts, are really looking for a new agenda (Guy West, in Hermann 2005, 72).

The generation gap between the older and newer peace activists was highly visible and problematic in terms of their ability to cooperate. This was due to their different sources of inspiration, as indicated by a prominent figure of the old guard:

The new generation is coming to political or social activism as if after twenty years of a political vacuum.... The new group finds its reference point in the Seattle-Geneva-Porto Alegre global phenomena and the anti-globalization movement, not their local forbearers.... It would only be a partial exaggeration to state that while the older generations developed from the local anti-occupation/ anti-colonial struggle to an internationalist world outlook, the new generation is taking the opposite tack: from the global struggle against injustice to the struggle against Israeli occupation of the Palestinian territories and the war against Iraq. Another characteristic of the newer layer of antiwar activists is its lack of strong ideological culture or motivation. This works in parallel with a very strong ethical motivation and a more intuitive sense of what is just and unjust.... The new generation has no problem in rejecting the concept of a Jewish state (Warschawski 2003, 15; 30).

Some newcomers to the peace movement were critical not only of the moderate peace organizations but also of the more radical older groups, which they considered leftovers from the New Left of the 1970s. These newcomers could not sympathize with what they viewed as the middle-aged radicals' fascination with the idea of being social outcasts, since they themselves did not enter peace activism because they were alienated with the national collective, although some of them were highly critical of the capitalist ethos and consumerist society. Their typical modus operandi was therefore keeping one foot in the mainstream (e.g., holding on to their jobs in high-tech companies or in the electronic media or focusing on academic studies) while also engaging part time in anti-occupation activities. The means of communication and self-expression that they preferred were also significantly different than those favored by the former generation of Israeli peace activists. Instead of meetings and long ideological discussions, they opted for heavy use of cyberspace for the dissemination of uncomplicated, even simplistic in the eyes of the old guard, anti-occupation messages, but also for cultural events and even techno-music parties under an anti-occupation banner (e.g., the "Rave against the Occupation," which took place in 2002). Finally, by and large, they were much more global in their self-identity and connections than the older generation. In other words, they no longer feared the implications of being openly connected to international bodies such as the anti-globalization campaign, although most of these were very unfriendly to Israel, particularly after the outbreak of the second *intifada*, which is about the time that the balance within the peace movement began to change in favor of the younger-age cohort.

As long as the formal peace negotiations were still going on, the peace movement somehow muddled through. When Barak announced in June 2000 that he was going to Camp David at the invitation of U.S. President Bill Clinton to meet with Arafat and try to close a deal, a Peace Headquarters was quickly set up with the aim of organizing a massive demonstration in support of him, thinking in terms of bringing 700,000 demonstrators to Tel Aviv's city square (Moriah Shlomot, in Hermann 2005, 54). The veteran activists had in mind the highly successful demonstration organized by *Shalom Achshav* in 1978, on the eve of Prime Minister Begin's trip to Camp David for a summit meeting with Egyptian President Saadat, hosted by then U.S. President Jimmy Carter. Eventually, however, fearing that the turnout might be too small, it was decided to give up the idea of a mass demonstration.[76] Another factor that led to this decision was the realization within the peace movement that, this time, the Palestinian side was going to Camp David against their will, and therefore a demonstration would probably be looked upon negatively by their Palestinian counterparts. In retrospect, there are still some who believe that it was wrong not to hold the demonstration:

I feel that in not acting on this plan, we betrayed our role. I'm not so naïve as to think that if we had organized such a demonstration the results would have been substantially different, but I think things have a dynamic of their own that should be encouraged. Barak went to Camp David alone with a divided government. It could be that more

---

[76] On the eve of the Barak's departure, Israeli public opinion was almost equally divided between those who were still somewhat hopeful that the process would bear fruit – 46% – compared with 53% who didn't believe in it. A similar stalemate prevailed in response to the question to which extent the Palestinian authority was really interested in making peace with Israel (48% said it was, and the same percentage argued that it was not). On the question of whether an agreement based on the two-state solution would mean the end of the conflict and the end of demands by the Palestinians, however, 36% took the position that it would, although the majority – 56% – thought that such an agreement would not be the end of it (Peace Index, June 2000).

real public support for him at that time would have done something – at least that was our role, even if it wouldn't have changed the reality (Moriah Shlomot, in Hermann 2005, 54).

With the Camp David meeting in July 2000 a colossal failure, and Barak's return, furious, empty-handed, and declaring all former understandings and agreements "null and void," the sky actually fell on the peace movement. For some reason, however, for certain highly experienced activists, it did not feel like the end of everything, and the movement did not act as if there were a state of emergency:

Right after the failure of Camp David, there were those who blamed Barak for every-thing, and there were others who simply had trouble comprehending what had hap-pened. At least in the first weeks, we spent long hours trying to understand what had actually happened at Camp David, what was proposed, and so on, but we weren't able to arrive at a clear picture. If I remember rightly, and correct me if I'm wrong, we didn't change anything at all as a result of the failure of the summit, since even if we didn't accept Barak and Clinton's version, we still didn't think all was lost, and we expected the negotiations to be renewed (Galia Golan, in Hermann 2005, 51).

At the same time, word was going around that Barak had spoken in private about his determination to crack down politically on the peace movement, because its existence interfered with his massive effort to promote the "there is no [Palestinian] partner" agenda (or media spin, as others see it).[77] The "there is a Palestinian partner but perhaps no Israeli one" position of the peace move-ment, which before may have not been to his liking but basically conformed to his policy, turned into a real thorn in Barak's side now, after the failure to reach an agreement, which he attributed to clear Palestinian reluctance to end the conflict.[78] From Barak's point of view, the peace movement's insistence on there being a partner on the other side, not to mention accusations from the more radical peace activists that he was insincere in his declarations about putting an end to the occupation and readiness to pay the necessary territorial price for peace, were not only false but politically detrimental. Public opinion was clearly on his side on these matters.

The interpretation of Camp David's consequences adopted by the peace movement was certainly incompatible with both the official position and gen-eral public opinion. In fact, some of those holding more moderate views within the peace movement believed that Barak's offers forever broke some taboos and

---

[77] For a discussion of the Barak "no partner" spin, see Rachamim 2005. As noted in retrospect by Barak's spokesperson in the Camp David period, however, in fact negotiations with the Palestinians did not end on July 25, 2000, but continued until almost the last minute of his term of office (Gadi Baltiansky, in Rachamim 2005, 16).

[78] In a public opinion survey taken immediately after Barak's return from Camp David, 67% of the Jewish respondents put the responsibility for the failure on the Palestinian side, 13% on both sides to the same extent, and 12% on Israel. Of the respondents, 44% perceived Barak's negotiating positions as too soft, 35% as adequate, and only 9% as too hard (Peace Index, July 2000).

that once they were put on the table, could never really be null and void. Hopelessly optimistic, they invested this summit with some tremendous educational if not political value:

At Camp David, even Barak recognized that the only way to live here together is to read history, not only as the story of the Jewish people returning to their land after protracted suffering and their persecution and destruction in the Holocaust, not only as the story of the Jewish people building a new and egalitarian home here, but also as the story of hundreds of thousands of Palestinians who were chased out of their homes so that we could establish a state, and the story of millions of refugees who dream of returning to their land (Golan-Agnon 2005, 211).

In due course, many opted for a less benevolent explanation of Barak's conduct at Camp David; however, members and supporters of the peace movement were apparently among the very first in Israel who shouted that the emperor, if not completely naked, was not fully dressed:

A large question mark is at the heart of Barak's narrative: What happened to the Palestinians? What changed their positions so drastically? Barak admits that his proposition did not fully correspond to the Palestinian expectations.... This spin portrays the Palestinians as a capricious bride who, because of a torn hem in her wedding dress, runs out of the hall and thereby ruins her life. Her victims, apart from herself, of course, are the generous bridegroom (Barak) and the wealthy best man (Clinton), who are left to deal with the guests and the shame (Rabinowitz 2001, 34).

The gap between Barak and the remaining hard core of the peace movement became so wide that by the end of his short term of office, their relationship had become as bitter as it had been during the Netanyahu years and would be during Sharon's first term in office. Here again, the emerging wall-to-wall anti-Oslo national consensus could be seen. Moshe Arens, former Defense Minister from the Likud party, reacted to the criticism of those representing the peace movement's views by saying:

In the last 20 years, the doctrine, if not the dogma, of those who refer to themselves as the peace camp was the "peace now" concept. It was based on the assumption that the Israeli-Arab conflict can be resolved now; that a solution to this problem can be found if Israel were just generous in making concessions. The implementation of this doctrine started in Oslo – eight years ago.... Israel is recovering today from this schizophrenic spell that has lasted over ten years. One public sector, the "peace camp", deluded itself and insisted that significant concessions will bring peace.... Now after all these years, a wide consensus has been established. The fact that Arafat rejected Barak's disgraceful concessions is the ultimate proof that this was not a road that could lead to peace (Arens 2001).

In October 2000, the second Palestinian *Al-Aqsa intifada* erupted, encouraged by, yet not totally a result of, the provocative visit of then MK Ariel

Sharon to the Temple Mount on September 28, 2000.[79] It took some time
before the gravity of this new development in Israeli-Palestinian relations was
fully grasped, with the violent episodes of the first few days widely perceived
in Israel as sporadic and probably transitory. By and large, it took weeks, even
months, before it was clear that the violent conflict had returned in full. This
is apparently true of the peace movement as well, although in retrospect, some
peace activists said that they were expecting it at any moment because of the
ongoing occupation and Israel's maltreatment of the Palestinian population.

What deeply shocked the Jewish public in early October were the massive
and quite violent demonstrations in some Israeli Arab towns and villages, in solidarity with the revolting Palestinians in the territories. The Israeli authorities'
reaction to its Arab citizens' protest was harsh and immediate, with security
forces moving in at full strength. Thirteen Arab Israelis participating in the
demonstrations were shot dead.[80] The events inflamed the entire country. Jewish public opinion at large considered the riots as the ultimate proof, if any
were needed, of the deep disloyalty of Arab Israeli citizens to their state and of
their being a fifth column, which coordinated its attack on Israel from within
the Green Line with the campaign that the Palestinians launched at about the
same time from the outside. Arab Israelis, on the other hand, saw the fierce
conduct of the security forces as the ultimate proof, if any were needed, that
the state and the Jewish majority did not view them as citizens but as enemies
and therefore used the same practices against them that it had used for years
in the territories.[81] The internal Jewish-Arab rift became deeper than it had
ever been before, and the peace movement, which for years had avoided making this a major issue on its agenda for a variety of reasons, could no longer
ignore it.

This was an extremely difficult choice for the peace movement, because
expressing solidarity with the Arab sector was almost unavoidable if it were
to maintain its ideological integrity. At the same time, against the prevalent
climate of opinion among Jewish Israelis in the fall of 2000, such open support
for the Arab sector's pain and anger could have caused huge damage in terms
of its already problematic public image at home. Therefore, the movement did
not come out with an unequivocal act, like a mass demonstration in solidarity with the Arab Israeli sector. Instead, many peace activists opted for verbal
condolences to the bereaved families and individually organized visits of individual members and delegations to Arab villages and colleagues. This limited

---

[79] For a moderate left-wing interpretation of the interaction between these two events see
http://www.beilin.org.il. For a right-wing view, see http://hn.150m.com.

[80] One Jewish Israeli was killed as well when his car was stoned by demonstrating Arabs.

[81] An enquiry committee to look into these violent events and their roots, the Orr Committee,
was appointed in November 2000. Its report was submitted in September 2003. The report
included sharp criticism of the conduct of the police in this specific case, but beyond that, it also
emphasized that in general the State of Israel treated its Arab citizens in a discriminating and
faulty way. One of the Orr committee's main recommendations was that the State reexamine
its relations with this sector and invest more resources in improving them.

response should also be understood in light of the shock that more than a few activists experienced when witnessing the Arab disturbances. The shock was not so much because of the demonstrators' openly expressed solidarity with their brothers in the territories, but mainly because of the means they used – blocking roads and stoning passing cars. It seemed that the domestic Israeli societal fabric was very close to being torn apart, and with it, the ability of the peace activists to rally together – Jews and Arabs – around the two-state solution:

What I remember most strongly from the day the clashes broke out with the Israeli Arabs is the feeling that maybe everything – and I stress everything, the whole concept of two states – had basically collapsed. Before we knew about the number killed and the effect that it had, I thought this might be a signal that there were no more 1967 lines, that if the Israeli Arabs were taking part in the struggle, then maybe the struggle wasn't about two states, and then where did we stand as a movement whose main message, all these years, was two states and a return to the Green Line borders? (Moriah Shlomot, in Hermann 2005, 55).

These events created severe tension within the mixed Jewish-Arab organizations, particularly in the women's peace groups:

October 2000. I, personally, felt like after the military coup d'état in Chile. There were some women amongst us who were angry with the Arab women, and blamed them for the fact that they could not drive safely anymore. There were, however, Palestinians[82] who protested against the Jewish women demanding to know: "Where were you when we needed you?" We tried hard to maintain some solidarity within the group, but it was very difficult.... Suddenly it is your Jewish identity that determines who you are, with no relation to your positions and the meaning that you yourself attribute to it, and you are limited within the boundaries of your nationality even if against your will (Tauberman, in Isachar 2003, 60).

This sense of alienation based on different national identities was openly stated by an female Arab Israeli activist: "When we decided a month later [after the October 2000 clashes between the Israeli police and Arab protesters – TH] to hold the first meeting of *Bat Shalom*, I hesitated whether or not to go.... I felt that my friendship with each of them as individuals was not damaged. However, as a body, I saw them as part of the Israeli-Jewish collective" (Abu Hussein 2003, 113).

It took a while for the peace organizations to respond to the October 2000 events in terms of clarifying and amending their attitudes toward the Arab Israeli sector. The change was not great even when the full meaning of the events was internalized. The Zionist organizations faced a particularly severe

---

[82] The term that one uses to refer to the Arab minority in Israel often reflects one's political positions: the traditional, more conservative term is "Israeli Arabs." Then there are those who prefer the semi-legal term "Arab citizens of Israel." Israelis of the left and many of the Arab sector prefer the term "Israeli Palestinians," whereas the radicals make do with the simple title "Palestinians," thereby obliterating all differences between those living in Israel and those living in the occupied territories, viewing them as an integral national entity.

dilemma because they had supported maintaining Israel as a Jewish state, whereas the majority in the Arab Israeli sector demanded to make Israel a "state of all its citizens." In early 2001, however, they made some attempt to reach out to the Arab sector. For example, in March of that year, *Shalom Achshav* participated for the first time in events commemorating *Yom haAdama* (Land Day) of 1976. The reason for this change was explained by the then Secretary General of the movement: "Taking part in Land Day events this year is our answer to the question 'where have you been', posed by Israeli Arabs after the events of last October.... We are ready to join in certain parts of their civil struggle but even they understand that there is a limit to how far we can go with this" (Moria Shlomot, in Galili 2001). The difficulty that moderate peace activists had in determining how far to go when expressing solidarity with the Arabs was observed by a journalist reporting on the upcoming commemoration event: "In order to set themselves apart from the radical left, the [Peace Now] movement's activists intend to stay at the margins of the demonstration with the slogan: Equality – yes, deprivation and discrimination – no" (Galili 2001).

As expected, the radical left reacted to what they viewed as sitting on the fence of the moderate peace groups with sharp criticism:

The events of October-November 2000 were some sort of a declaration on the status of the Green Line as a factor in defining the Israeli political agenda. They forced the Israeli left to present a clear-cut position regarding the status of Israeli Palestinian citizens and of Palestinians living in the West Bank and Gaza.... But the Israeli left behaves as if it has just lost its agenda;... it deals with the liberal rights of Israeli Palestinian citizens; their right to life, their right to demonstrate, their right to free speech. This is indeed what it should be doing; however, it still does not dare to deal with their collective rights as a national minority within a sovereign Jewish state and with the demands of this minority for land and cultural autonomy. This avoidance is particularly offensive today when the state is reacting, not as a liberal body, but as a Jewish state (Shenhav, 2001, 209).

As shocking as the domestic Jewish-Arab crisis was for the peace movement, the major rupture occurred when the full meaning of the events of the October 2000 *intifada* in the territories was grasped:

The overall reaction [to the early October events] was confusion; I remember only one person who actually moved to the right, and eventually also left us. I can't speak for everyone, but as I see it, at least on the formal and public level, there was a gradual break between those of us in the peace movement and our interlocutors on the Palestinian side, though we continued to talk with most of the Palestinians with whom we had personal friendships.... [Later on – TH], with guests from abroad, we went to Ramallah and met with Mustafa Barghouti. At least for me, and I think for the others too, this was the first time that we heard what the Israeli side had really offered at Camp David, or at least what the Palestinians understood had been offered to them. And only then did we begin to understand why the *intifada* broke out (Galia Golan, in Hermann 2005, 52).

And indeed, *confusion, bewilderment,* and *disorientation* were the words used by many to characterize the state of mind of the peace camp after the outbreak of the *intifada*:

At this junction between support for a peace agreement and emotional disbelief in reconciliation, the peace camp is sitting today. It is not true that there is no peace camp, it just doesn't know exactly how to phrase its renewed appeal to the public. In recent years, it dealt with moves towards reconciliation based on the assumption that peace is already here. Now it has to go back to the basics, in a climate of opinion in which the word peace has lost its meaning (Galili 2002a).

The more common metaphor to describe the Israeli Jewish public reaction following the outbreak of the *intifada* is an "earthquake" (e.g., Bar-Tal and Halperin 2007). The thesis presented here, however, maintains that this metaphor does not accurately describe the overall feeling because it implies that Jewish Israeli public opinion at that time had positive expectations of the Palestinian side that were shattered by the wave of violence that began in October. The fact of the matter, however, is that the outbreak of the *intifada* was in a way, almost a corrective experience for many in Israel, because from their perspective, the world was once again behaving as expected – the Palestinians were attacking and the Jews were fighting back. This attitudinal stability is manifested in the fact that in March 2001, 72% of the Jewish respondents maintained that the Palestinians would destroy Israel if they could (Peace Index, March 2001), whereas in February 2000, eight months before the *intifada* started, the percentage was 69%, a statistically insignificant gap. In other words, the extreme violence used by the Palestinians – in particular, the lynching of two Israeli soldiers on October 12, 2000 – added only slightly, if at all, to this perception.

Apparently, the Jewish Israeli public has a complete, tried-and-true repertoire of practical and emotional tools for dealing with such familiar dismal circumstances, but not for dealing with a situation in which the external threat is dramatically reduced, as seemed to be the case in the early Oslo decade. When the Oslo process was proceeding apace, Israeli society experienced a troublesome sense of disorientation, as if the sun had begun to set in the morning and rise at night. As already indicated, the public's faith in the process, which had never skyrocketed, began to erode severely within months of Barak's election, so that the "there is no partner" spin following his return empty-handed from Camp David in the summer of 2000, having "offered everything and been turned down," only struck a familiar chord. So, too, did the explanation for the *intifada* that erupted shortly thereafter: this was the Palestinian leadership's clever way of obtaining what it had failed to gain through negotiations. In fact, 40% of the Jewish respondents to the March 2001 Peace Index survey opted for this explanation. The larger group, 53%, however, opted for the alternative explanation: that the *intifada* was meant only to cause Israel damage and casualties and not to create a better bargaining position for the Palestinians in the context of future peace negotiations. Therefore, the outbreak of the *intifada* was indeed traumatic, yet hardly an emotional or cognitive earthquake; rather, it confirmed the most deeply held concepts and beliefs of the Israeli public regarding the murderous nature of the other side.[83] For many who, during the Oslo years, had been torn between support for the idea and ongoing skepticism regarding Palestinian intentions, the *intifada* resolved this cognitive dissonance and pushed them to the hawkish right. It did not cause a majority of Israeli Jews to ponder whether Israel itself had contributed in any way to the gathering Palestinian anger that led to its eruption.

The approach recommended by the peace movement, that is, trying to prevent terrorists from carrying out their deadly missions but at the same time continuing negotiations with the Palestinian Authority and reducing to a minimum the Israeli actions that interfered with the normal life of the Palestinian population, were not accepted by the government nor favored by public opinion. The number of checkpoints and closures sharply increased, at least partly under the policy of collective punishment. Needless to say, the number of Palestinian casualties by far exceeded that of Israelis killed by Palestinians. Public opinion at that time regarding the challenge posed by the Palestinians was clearly unreceptive to accommodating policies: in November 2000, 78% of the Jewish respondents argued that the Palestinians did not value human life and therefore continued with the *intifada* despite the large number of casualties on their side. An even larger percentage – 87% – argued that the Palestinians were well aware of the high value that the Jews place on human life and therefore used violence to erode the resolution of Israeli society (Peace Index, November 2000). Taken with the almost 60% who at the time felt a high threat to their own lives and the lives of their relatives (versus 40% who did not), any advocacy entailing elements of compassion for the other side was doomed to fail.

Signals from the top echelons were very confusing, so that the peace movement was in a difficult position when it came to creating a new agenda that would fit the new situation. On one hand, most politicians, including some from Labour, which remained in power until early February 2001, placed full responsibility for the escalation of violence on the Palestinians, and mainly on Arafat personally. Any means, they said, that could prevent even one suicide bombing should be used to save Israeli lives, even if this caused suffering on the Palestinian side, a point accepted by the general public. The media cooperated with this propaganda campaign almost in full (Dor 2001). On the other hand, however, formal negotiations between Israeli delegates and Palestinian officials actually continued while violence raged throughout the land. Despite

---

[83] In the December 2000 Peace Index survey, when asked to characterize the Palestinian people on a scale from 1 – non-violent, to 5 – extremely violent, 72% (!) placed the Palestinians in positions 4 and 5, e.g., characterized them as violent or extremely violent. As early as March 1995, 60% of the respondents put the Palestinians in these two categories, a fact that also suggests that the *intifada* was not a major earthquake.

the mantra of "there is no partner," these talks were held in the open with some highly visible peaks: the Sharm El Sheikh summit in mid-October and the Taba talks in January 2001, just days before the elections, which, in the eyes of many, contributed to Barak's defeat (Beilin 2001, 219).[84]

In February 2001, Sharon defeated Barak by an unprecedented margin. In many respects, this marked the end of the Oslo decade – more than the failed Camp David meeting of summer 2000, and more than the outbreak of the *intifada* in October of that year, which are usually taken as turning points. It also marked the political collapse of the Israeli left, of which the peace movement is an integral part. This is how an Israeli author who had moved toward the right described the significance of the elections, the day after the results came in:

It can be stated without any doubt that more than the results reflected the public's confidence in the right, they reflected its desire to punish the left. The left was punished because it insisted on continuing to sell the same merchandise it had sold before the earthquake – the false formula stating that salvation would come if we just pull out of the territories – although it was quite clear that the product was basically defective. The public punished the left for this deceit. For trying to advertise a false reality, which stood in total opposition to actual experience and common sense. Furthermore, the left was punished for stubbornly insisting on a failed perception that inflicted a catastrophe on us all, revealing that it has lost its survival instincts, which luckily enough, most of us maintain (Megged 2001).

The Dark Tunnel Zone

The last two years of the Oslo process, which are discussed here, marked a low point not only in the situation of the peace movement but also in the overall regional situation. The *intifada* developed into a full-blown violent clash between Israeli and Palestinian societies. The rising number of Palestinian terrorist attacks, which culminated in the 2002 Passover suicide bombing at the Park Hotel, opened the way to two massive Israeli military incursions of the West Bank, and made the entire country, from the Mediterranean to the Jordan River, one war zone. This completely obliterated the distinction between the front and the civilian back lines, and swept away the cognitive differentiation between territories within and outside of the Green Line, on which the peace movement's platform was based. The Israeli citizens' sense of personal security and hence the overall public mood deteriorated to unprecedented lows. In May 2001, 82% of the Jewish respondents to the Peace Index survey said that their personal safety had deteriorated since the beginning of the peace process. Also

---

[84] This argument could be empirically challenged, because in the Peace Index survey of November 2000, a majority of 56% (as against 39%) thought that as long as Barak was Prime Minister, he was entitled to conduct negotiations with the Palestinians, even if the elections were already around the corner. Also, before the elections, the public was still split exactly down the middle regarding the best means to deal with the *intifada* – 40% preferred military means while 40% favored political ones.

in that survey, 80% expressed their belief that even if the Palestinians eventually signed a permanent peace agreement with Israel, they could not be trusted to stop the armed struggle or give up on the territories left in Israeli hands that they feel are theirs.

The fear and anxiety about terrorism naturally increased even more the already-wide legitimization for the IDF to take whichever steps it considered proper to win this round. In April 2002, 86% supported or strongly supported the massive IDF operation called "Defense Wall," which actually meant reoccupation of large parts of the Palestinian territories. Although 86% maintained that the operation served the security interests of Israel well, its cost in terms of losing the support of international public opinion was also clear. Thus, only 32% considered it beneficial in this regard, whereas 54% reported that it damaged Israel's diplomatic interests (Peace Index, April 2002). Reoccupation of Palestinian cities, from which the IDF had withdrawn in accordance with the Oslo accords, was also strongly supported in these years, with the number of supporters significantly increasing: in October 2001, 68% of the respondents in the Peace Index survey supported the takeover of Palestinians cities, and in June 2002, 80% favored such a move. Moreover, over 70% supported or strongly supported the prolonged stay of the soldiers in the Palestinian towns and cities after the second IDF operation in June. Of the respondents, 67% maintained that only a very small minority of the Palestinians opposed suicide bombings, and 56% argued that making the life of the Palestinian population less difficult by reducing the number of checkpoints, for example, would not help to decrease terrorist attacks (Peace Index, June 2002). It is not surprising, therefore, that the Jewish Israeli public also strongly endorsed the policy of targeted killings. For example, in October 2001, 77%, and in January 2002, 73% supported or strongly supported the use of this means (see Peace Index surveys for these months).

At the same time, apparently, as so often happens in situations of increased external threat, the level of national cohesion significantly increased. This sense of togetherness accounted for the seemingly strange fact that despite the many casualties and the fear, Jewish Israelis by and large felt capable of dealing well with the challenge of the *intifada*: 61% believed that Israeli society was more able than the Palestinians to endure a long confrontation, with only 12% believing that the Palestinians were more able (Peace Index, June 2002). As mentioned previously, the means that the public was ready to let the government use in its struggle against Palestinian terrorists were almost unlimited. Indeed, the government, now headed by Ariel Sharon, was completely absorbed with conducting the battle against the Palestinians, undermining Arafat's authority, and planning the route of the soon-to-be-launched construction of the separation barrier. The government conducted no dialogue whatsoever with the peace movement and did not even respond to its admittedly weak manifestations of protest.

It is also worth mentioning the highly negative influence, from the point of view of peace activism, of the change in the global climate of opinion regarding

the Arab world and Islam following the events of September 11, 2001. The War
on Terror launched by the United States against Islamic fundamentalism led to
the development of strong anti-Arab feelings and attitudes in the West. Hence,
Palestinian violence was now interpreted, or framed, by many in Europe and
the United States as less a liberation struggle and more as part of the global
Islamic Jihad. From the Israeli mainstream's point of view, this was seen as a
positive development, against the background of the highly critical position of
Europe and many in the United States of Israel's moves after the breaking out
of the *intifada*. Not surprisingly, the majority in Israel dismissed any alternative
framings to the now highly popular "clash of civilizations" theory (e.g., those
interpretations of the tragic event that pointed to the exploitation of third
world countries by the rich West or that highlighted the rise of fundamentalist
Islam and its growing popularity as repercussions of globalization). The Israeli
mainstream hoped in a sense that the events of September 11 would make the
world see the light and support Israel's heavy hand toward the Palestinians,
rather than criticize it. Many Jewish communities and individuals of liberal
views abroad, particularly in the United States, who in the past had been
inclined to support the Israeli peace movement, now moved to the right and
cut off their donations and other means of support.

The moderate peace groups were paralyzed when they faced the horror of
escalating Palestinian violence and harsh Israeli preventive measures on one
hand, and their growing realization that public opinion was rapidly turning
away from the peace agenda. The fact that Sharon, formerly the political pariah,
the man found by an official enquiry commission (The Kahan Commission,
1983) responsible for not preventing the Sabra and Shatila massacre, was
elected by such a large margin (62.3% compared with only 37.6% voting
for Barak) was their worst nightmare, and it materialized before their eyes.
The POS they faced in the early 2000s was so contracted in almost every
respect that, for quite a while, the activists were unable to pull themselves
together. Thus, the first large protest activity – a demonstration under the
slogan "No to an Unnecessary War" – was organized by *Shalom Achshav*
only in April 2001, 6 months after the *intifada* erupted and almost 3 months
after Sharon was elected. Although not catastrophic in terms of attendance,
the demonstration did not attract large enough numbers to signal significant
public dissatisfaction. In fact, the climate of opinion for peace activism became
so extremely unfavorable that after the elections, with the violence raging, some
in Israel even called for taking the "Oslo architects" to court (they were also
referred to as the "Oslo criminals"[85] for allegedly having jeopardized national
security):

The call to investigate the architects of the Oslo process is not new. However,
with each passing day, new reasons that reinforce its validity keep emerging, making such an investigation an immediate moral imperative – and an eventual political

[85] See, e.g., http://www.fresh.co.il.

inevitability.... The gamble that the creators of the Oslo concept took with the fate of the nation was manifestly unacceptable. Intelligence assessments warned that the dangers entailed in the policies they wished to embrace were grave and that the chances of success were slim. However, the Oslo gamblers... tried with ever-increasing desperation to bend reality to conform to their vision (or rather their fantasy), and impose upon it the rosy illusions of their wishful thinking (Sherman 2001).

The more radical peace groups and activists were no less depressed but much angrier than the moderate ones. As outcasts, with no constituency to lose on one hand, and so highly confident in their framing of the situation on the other, they came forward with unforgiving criticism of the Israeli side. No confusion was admitted in this tiny yet highly articulate and rather strident political camp. The reasons for the clarity of mind were explained in the introduction to a volume of articles by some central intellectuals of the radical peace camp (plus several Palestinian contributors), written in late 2000 and published in 2001, in which they elaborated – in real time – their reasoning regarding unfolding events. This introduction also reflects the dismissive, belittling attitude of the radical peace activists toward the moderate ones:

The authors of the articles in this book are not at all uncomfortable, as none of their conceptions collapsed.... The developments of recent months did not shake or cast any doubts over the [intellectual] framework and the major guidelines endorsed by the authors of this book – first because they never forgot that the situation was one of occupation; that this was the point of departure, and that the pattern of power and social relations between Jews and Palestinians also determined many of the patterns of relations between Jews and Palestinians and between Jews and Jews within the Green Line, which shaped the image of the others and the way their words and their deeds were perceived (Ofir 2001, 12).

A careful reading of this collection of articles suggests that this statement, claiming that the radical activists were not confused, was perhaps accurate on the individual level but less so on the collective level. This is because the interpretations put forward by the different authors do not really create a coherent narrative. Thus, some of the articles put forward deterministic logic to explain the *intifada* as the unavoidable antithesis to the defective Oslo logic, out of which clash the historical course of events was likely to change and eventually lead to real peace (e.g., Rabinowitz 2001, 36; Peled 2001, 46). Others (e.g., Reinhart 2001) were much more pessimistic and foresaw the conflict further deteriorating and being transformed at a later stage into an essentially religious one. Certain articles actually encouraged the Palestinians to use more force, because, according to the interpretation that they put forward, this was the only language that Israel and the Jewish Israelis understood and that could force the government into making the necessary concessions, that is, evacuating all the occupied territories and removing the settlements (Levy 2001, 91; 97). The common thread in almost all the articles,[86] however, was the view that it was Israel and Israel alone, because of its colonialist nature, apartheid-like practices, and opportunistic policies, that was responsible for shutting the window of opportunity on peace that was created when the Palestinians joined the Oslo process:

Seven years after Oslo, and nothing is left of the hopes and the dreams that so many developed about it. Once again, Israel missed a historical opportunity to achieve a just peace with the Palestinian people and be integrated into the Middle East. Instead, it turned this opportunity into another chapter of repression and control. . . . It is difficult to find a good explanation for this Israeli behavior, except its aversion to the idea of giving up the lands and water resources of the occupied territories (Reinhart 2001, 64).

Although by and large, the old moderate peace groups never fully recovered from the shock of the outbreak of the *intifada*, and the old radical ones radicalized their ideology to the point where they were completely at odds with overall public discourse in Israel, some new peace initiatives, new organizations, and innovative modes of operation emerged in the early 2000s. *Ta'ayush* ("partnership" or "life in common" in Arabic) was one of the most visible and in certain respects the most successful new peace organization at this time. Its uniqueness was evident from the beginning because, unlike most other peace organizations, it was founded jointly by Israeli Jews and Arabs and enjoyed much popularity in the Arab Israeli sector. The group was established in October 2000 in response to Sharon's provocative visit to the Temple Mount and the ensuing vicious cycle of violent Palestinian and Israeli reactions:

We – Arab and Jewish citizens of Israel – live surrounded by walls and barbed wire: the walls of segregation, racism, and discrimination between Jews and Arabs within Israel; the walls of closure and siege encircling the Palestinians in the occupied West Bank and Gaza Strip; and the wall of war surrounding all inhabitants of Israel. . . . In the fall of 2000 we joined together to form *Ta'ayush* . . . a grassroots movement of Arabs and Jews working to break down the walls of racism and segregation by constructing a true Arab-Jewish partnership. A future of equality, justice and peace begins today, between us, through concrete, daily actions of solidarity to end the Israeli occupation of the Palestinian territories and to achieve full civil equality for all Israeli citizens (http://taayush.tripod.com).

To avoid endless ideological arguments within the group, among moderates and radicals, Zionists, non-Zionists, and anti-Zionists, *Ta'ayush* declared itself from the start a nonideological, nonpartisan organization in the sense that it did not adhere to one peace ideology, neither moderate nor radical, that had to be followed and accepted by all activists or to any political party (Weingarten, in Isachar 2003, 96; Zackhem and Halevi 2004; Shulman 2007, 13). To let

---

[86] Except for the article by Prof. Ruth Gabison, who is not a member of the radical peace camp, in which she warned against the political and intellectual hazards of the growing distance between the radical camp and the Israeli Jewish collective, and its open identification with the Palestinian cause (Gabison 2001).

everyone on board, *"Ta'ayush* held on to several principles that did not give any activists second thoughts about joining: full civil equality within the borders of Israel, an end to Occupation, evacuation of the settlements, return to the 1967 borders and a just solution to the refugee problem" (Bdeir and Halevi 2002). Everyone – man or woman, Jew or Arab – who could ascribe to these principles, irrespective of individual nuances, was invited to take part in the organization's direct actions. The shared notion on which the group was actually based was joint Israeli-Palestinian nonviolent direct action in a crisis situation.

The three founders, one Arab and two Jews, had a great deal of experience in peace activism, and their vision for the new group aimed to avoid the pitfalls they had identified in peace organizations and activities with which they were familiar.[87] The name selected for the group pointed to rejection of the term *coexistence* so often used by other peace organizations:

The word *Ta'ayush* usually translates the term 'co-existence' but its real meaning is 'living together,' 'sharing life with one another'. The difference between living together and co-existence is perhaps not very significant for those who are not familiar with the dialogue groups, peace encounters, peace tents and creativity workshops that characterized the dialogue style of the nineties, but the difference is enormous. It means living together, struggling together against alienation, against the separation wall, discrimination and racism, mastery and patronism, humiliation and boycott, exploitation and occupation (Bdeir and Halevi 2002).

Ta'ayush's main aim was to end the occupation by direct humanitarian action, not – like the classic peace organizations – by demonstrations, paperwork, or big words:

From its earliest days, *Ta'ayush* has produced action only, neither manifestos nor ideological debates. The group that consolidated wanted to reverse the usual scale of priorities: after realizing that declarations do not always stand the test of 'moments of truth', action was chosen as the way to demonstrate a refusal to accept the repetition of incursions, and to be present where things took place. Direct, non-violent action was the path chosen, as well as decision-making by consensus (ibid.).

The group therefore organized large deliveries of food, blankets, clothes, medications, and other necessary items of which the Palestinians under the reoccupation and prolonged closures were in need. Working together with Palestinian relief NGOs, they used to meet near the checkpoints, where the packages were delivered by the Israeli Jewish and Arab activists to the Palestinian activists on the other side for distribution among the needy. The items delivered were often donated or bought with donations of Arab Israeli communities. Often the IDF soldiers and border policemen tried to prevent the deliveries from crossing the line between the two sides, and occasionally physical confrontations between the activists of both sides and the servicemen developed,

---

[87] This rich previous political experience was not necessarily typical of all *Ta'ayush's* activists. As Prof. David Shulman wrote in his autobiographical account of his participation in the group's activities, political activism was not on the list of his favorite pastimes (Shulman 2007, 13).

with the former trying to maintain their adherence to nonviolent resistance, not always with much success. For example, in April 2002, demonstrating without a permit near the A-Ram checkpoint in the Ramallah area, over 3,000 peace and human rights activists, many of them *Ta'ayush* members, faced a ruthless response from policemen and border guards, including shock grenades and tear gas. The police spokesperson stated that the demonstrators had attacked the policemen and thrown stones at them while trying to break though the checkpoint, but reports by journalists who were present refute these allegations (e.g., Ziegelman 2002).

Ta'ayush's other activities included helping Palestinian villagers, intimidated by the settlers, to pick olives, and protesting against the separation wall, which Israel had been constructing in keeping with the government decision of June 2002. They also saw their role as fighting all kinds of segregation and separation between Israelis and Palestinians, and – again an item missing from the agenda of most veteran peace organizations – between Jews and Arabs within Israel.

Ta'ayush succeeded beyond many people's expectations in bringing Israeli Arab and Jewish activists together in an egalitarian manner, although this was a challenge, "no easier than creating an egalitarian heterosexual partnership, even if both partners are willing. The patterns of mastery and ownership are strong, and like them, patterns of passiveness and surrender. It needed trying hard, and everyone tried hard" (Bdeir and Halevi 2002). The group's unique features apparently helped it to survive the worst years of the *intifada* without giving up even when facing the most dismal POS. Its humanitarian activities in 2001 and 2002 not only aided Palestinians who needed food and supplies but also helped to pull together the Arab Israeli sector and turn it toward a constructive course of action after the shock of the October 2000 events.

Nonetheless, eventually, the great promise of its establishment – to bring together a significant number of Israeli Jews and Arabs committed to peace even if of different views – failed to achieve its aim, with relations between the two groups souring along the way. In addition, despite its declared openness, as leading *Ta'ayush* activists admitted, the declared ideological pluralism proved to be practically unworkable. The well-known tension between the moderates and the radicals became highly divisive. Furthermore, the Jewish public failed to discern the nuances within the group, labeling everyone there unpatriotic, if not traitorous. Thus, the group was unable to avoid its position at the very edge of the political periphery because it was stigmatized as motivated by an Arab and pro-Palestinian agenda. Therefore, in terms of its ability to exert political influence within Israel and change the domestic climate of opinion, *Ta'ayush* was unable to avoid the destiny of many other well-intentioned, yet relatively ineffective, peace endeavors. Conversely, to be able to cooperate with the group, the Palestinians in the territories insisted that *Ta'ayush* put forward a clear-cut position in favor of their national cause. Last but not least, *Ta'ayush* seems to have suffered from the same problematic sociodemographic composition as other peace movements in terms of the Jewish audiences that it brought on board. Outsiders, namely people of non-Ashkenazi origin or not from the middle class or having high education, felt unwanted, as reflected in the sarcastic description of the experience of a young Mizrahi woman who attended one of its open meetings. Although humorous, the piece sharply criticizes the obstacles that the participants' exclusionist atmosphere created and that stand in the way of people who do not fit the classic profile of a peace activist but would like to join their endeavor:

Last Thursday evening I went to a meeting of *Ta'ayush* in Tel Aviv.... I arrived an hour late, as before that I attended a lecture at the vegetarians and naturalists movement.[88] The room was already full so I had to stand near the door and heard almost nothing.... Later on, a seat inside was made available.... The air was hot and thick and I got thirsty. I opened my bag, took out a bottle and drank the small amount of water that was still there. I noticed some people staring at me, but what was it – admiration? blame? jealousy? I thought that they envied me because they were thirsty, too. I thought that they might have been staring at me because my tight t-shirt had a Mei Eden logo on it,[89] suspecting that I was part of a marketing campaign for mineral water.[90] Somehow, I always feel a bit out of place in all these Green and peace organizations that I recently joined, in my politically incorrect outfit. I suppose that everybody at the meeting was against everything connected to globalization, or if this is all about Mei Eden, maybe they were just against advertisements or against the use of women as sex objects in ads. I had to leave the meeting early, as I didn't want to get home too late. The only people who use the taxi service to Lod late at night are drug addicts.[91] I got home all right, went to bed, and in the evening when I was watching TV it hit me. I asked my brother – don't they produce Mei Eden in the Golan Heights?[92]

Yes.

Oops.

Then I got it. I checked the "list of banned products that one should never buy" and there it was.[93]

As David Shulman sums up his account of his *Ta'ayush* activity, the participants were not demoralized but continued to see their role as important and of value:

We know our rivals, those close to us who sit apathetically in the government's offices or serve in the upper levels of command in the army, or simply stay at home doing nothing. We shall face them in every corner – in every house they demolish, in every olive tree they uproot, in every field they confiscate. We shall confront them time and again, nonviolently, we shall follow them and keep records and testify, and here and

---

[88] This allegedly irrelevant remark is meant create the association in the reader's mind between the peace activists and other, perhaps naïve or weird "do-gooders."

[89] Brand name of the most popular mineral water in Israel.

[90] This is also an ironic remark that refers to the peace activists' resentment of commercialism and also to the writer herself as wearing a sexy outfit that does not fit the code of conduct in a movement in which clothing is expected to be simple, not too tight, but often quite expensive.

[91] The writer reminds us that "she isn't like all the others there" – she lives in Lod, a peripheral, mixed Jewish-Arab town – and uses public transportation, not having a car of her own (implying that the others in the room do own a car).

[92] As the Golan Heights are in fact occupied territories, the more radical peace activists would not use any products made in this area.

[93] The list of "forbidden" goods was complied and disseminated by *Gush Shalom*.

there – stop them. They have the weapons, we have each other and some hope in the darkness (Shulman 2007, 200).

Not surprisingly, criticism of peace activities such as those conducted by *Ta'ayush* sharpened with the deterioration in the Israeli-Palestinian conflict, with the most acid comments coming from former supporters of the Oslo agenda. One such disappointed former supporter announced that the world-view of the peace movement in the early 2000s was the unfortunate result of defective thinking or, as he put it, "a faulty diskette":

Facts have no impact on the left.... This left never has doubts and no news can interfere with its view of the world. This left doesn't know when to stop and ask questions or reflect that perhaps what it said yesterday is no longer correct today. I do not doubt the unique qualities of these people . . . but taking them together and each one separately – they are made of the very same piece of cloth. Meeting them leaves one with the impression that they all have the same diskette implanted in their brains. They all speak the same language and dress uniformly when they go to demonstrations.... Even when it turned out that while negotiating peace Arafat was preparing the next *intifada*, this camp continued to give him full credit.... When you ask a normal leftist if anything changed for him lately, he turns on the diskette and with no hesitation, using the familiar wording, will . . . bring all kinds of evidence and signs that we, the Jews, are the ones to blame (Fogel 2003).

A few weeks before *Ta'ayush* came into being, another even more unique peace organization – Israel's *Indymedia* – was created. It was the local chapter of the international Indymedia (Independent Media Group), a virtual organization, which was set up in 1999 in Seattle, Washington, as an alternative media system.[94] The idea of creating a safe haven for alternative media reports in Israel was not totally innovative; it originated with the AIC, established in 1984. For many years, the AIC was almost the only important intellectual meeting place for the opinions of the non- and anti-Zionist peace camp. Some of the finest political publications of this group were published there, and some of the most nonconformist discussions of peace- and security-related matters

---

[94] Activists of the anti-globalization protest movement who gathered in Seattle thought that the mainstream media did not provide room for a variety of new opinions and ideas, or for non-conformist agendas like theirs, because it was too well connected to the state apparatus and to other economic, cultural, and political power centers. To handle the information dissemination problem, they developed an Internet-based media network where everyone could air their views by video, voice, or text, and could discuss them freely without censorship. What is more, unlike the regular media, the new system was also open to responses with no hierarchy between the original posting and the talk backs, thereby changing the communication process from top-down to two-way. This innovation proved highly successful – the responses were often a lot richer than the messages themselves. Actually, following *Indymedia* and similar non-conformist virtual media, the electronic editions of many of today's Internet editions of standard newspapers also offer a talk back option though which readers can respond to the journalists' articles. Studies of talk backs show that normally, only people with a strong interest in the subject or those with specific personality traits participate in this often very rough-edge dialogue. Therefore, the talk backs cannot be taken as representative of public opinion in any way. For example, talk backs in Israeli online newspapers are normally full of very much right of center and anti-peace responses, a proportion that does not reflect overall public opinion.

were conducted under the AIC's auspices. The AIC was oriented to old-style media, however; with the generational and circumstantial changes of the early 2000s, another means of disseminating information was needed to fulfill these functions. *Indymedia* Israel was established in August 2000. After facing some technical problems in converting the international Indymedia platform into Hebrew, the website became operable two days after Sharon went up to the Temple Mount. Although the site originally was not meant to be completely open to everyone, because of technical delays caused by the Jewish high holidays in September, it was decided to leave it open to all until the end of the holidays. Before long, the webmasters realized how much information about the visit and its backlash was reaching their site from all kinds of sources – individual and organizational – in Israel and abroad. The free discussion also revealed how many groups there were within the Israeli left, and how much they needed an electronic media platform of this sort to coordinate their efforts and get to know about each other's activities, information which in the past had been stopped by various media gatekeepers. Apparently, the past experience of veteran peace activists with these gatekeepers had not been good: "We worked, and we channeled a lot of information to the media. Very little of it got through to the public because of the newspaper editors, who didn't want to pass it on. Today there's an Internet site where information flows between organizations and from organizations directly to the public, without supervision and without mediation" (Diana Dolev, in Hermann 2005, 46). With the new virtual platform, the gates seemed much more open. Indeed, in due course, quite a few new groups, like the small anti-occupation and prosocial justice anarchist queer group *Kvisa Shchora* (Black Laundry) and *Rave Neged haKibush* (Rave against Occupation), which could never have developed in the framework of the classical peace movement and certainly not crossed the threshold of mainstream media, gained life based on services offered mainly by *Indymedia*.

The Internet platform offered by *Indymedia* was also used to disperse information on what was happening in the Palestinian territories during the *intifada* that was not reported by the mainstream media (Kazin 2001). What prevented it from turning into a new organizational pillar of Israeli peace activism, however, was the fact that the international Indymedia network was so fiercely anti-Israeli that at a certain point, some search engines excluded it for using highly derogative, even anti-Semitic descriptions of Israel and its policies. Like *Vaad haShalom haYisraeli* of the 1950s, *Indymedia* Israel was also caught between its global and local affiliations, with bridging the two becoming more and more difficult as the *intifada* and Israeli responses escalated. Also – as so often happens – with the expansion of activity, the core group underwent a rapid process of institutionalization, including finding themselves an office and office holders. The original activists, who were of the nonconformist, noninstitutionalized type, gradually dispersed because they no longer thought that they belonged there. Later, technical problems made Israel's *Indymedia* website often inaccessible, and it vanished for extended periods.

Two significant women's peace bodies also took off at the time of the *intifada* – *Koalitziat Nashim l'Shalom* (Coalition of Women for Peace) and *MachsomWatch*.[95] As we shall see, the two were very different (although *MachsomWatch* is a partner in the *Koalitzia*). The *Koalitzia* is a highly ideo- logical (although also highly pluralistic) and organizationally disciplined SMO, whereas *MachsomWatch* is much more flexible in both ideology and opera- tion (Resh 2005). Each of the two, using their specific strategies, proved quite immune to the fatal POS created by the *intifada*, and highly capable of crossing the stormy seas in which many other peace initiatives sank. At the same time, it should be noted that the *Koalitzia*, articulate and politically self-conscious as it was, remained almost invisible to the wider public, whereas the unprompted and less structured *MachsomWatch* received wide media coverage and can in fact take much credit for at least raising the national consciousness about the problems in the checkpoint system.

The *Koalitziat Nashim l'Shalom*, which brought together various auto- nomous women's peace organizations (not individual activists), was not the first of its kind. In 1987, a similar coalition, Women and Peace, which brought together individual Jewish and Arab feminists striving for peace, was estab- lished. The earlier coalition remained active, quite successfully maintaining close relations with Palestinian women in the Palestinian territories until the early 1990s. In other words, following the argument of resource mobilization theory on the value of preexisting organizations (even if defunct), when the *Koalitziat Nashim l'Shalom* was established in late 2000, it could indeed rely on an existing, relatively condensed, social, organizational, and ideological net- work. The organizations participating in the *Koalitzia* presented an interesting mélange of old and new, smaller and larger, institutionalized and not, closer and farther from the Israeli mainstream: *Bat Shalom, Tandi, MachsomWatch, haEm haChamishit, Nashim b'Shachor, NELED, Noga, WILPF* and *Profil Hadash*.[96] The organizations that joined the coalition agreed to cooperate on the basis of shared principles (listed here), but in all other realms, they main- tained their autonomy and were allowed to retain their unique ideological creeds. Each organization also maintained its individual structure and char- acter. In other words, they did not merge into one large organization but cooperated on a certain level and in regard to specific issues, while maintaining their particular agendas. Like its forerunner, the new coalition was also women only and was meant to bring a variety of feminist organizations and activists – Jewish and Arab Israelis of the left – under one roof, based on principles to be acknowledged by all participating bodies:

The Coalition of Women for Peace seeks to mobilize women in support of human rights and a just peace between Israel and its Arab neighbors, as we work to strengthen democracy within Israel. Our principles: An end to the occupation; The full involvement

[95] *Machsom* is the Hebrew word for *checkpoint*.
[96] All these organizations are listed in Appendix I.

of women in negotiations for peace; Establishment of the state of Palestine side-by-side with the state of Israel based on the 1967 borders; Recognition of Jerusalem as the shared capital of two states; Israel must recognize its share of responsibility for the results of the 1948 war, and cooperate in finding a just solution for the Palestinian refugees; Opposition to the militarism that permeates Israeli society; Equality, inclusion and justice for Palestinian citizens of Israel; Equal rights for women and all residents of Israel; Social and economic justice for Israel's citizens, and integration in the region (http://coalitionofwomen.org).

The feminist approach was put forward by the *Koalitzia* as a remedy for the protracted conflict:

Men, who are used to looking at the world through the sight of a rifle and the prism of macho hubris, always ran, and still run, the world. In Israel, this is even more true because the state is led by generals who view the other side as the enemy and try to defeat it. They assume problems are solved only by force. But we come and say, no, conflicts cannot be solved by force, not in the family and not between nations (Bitterman, in Isachar 2003, 146).

In addition to supporting the peace work of its member organizations, the *Koalitzia* organized mass rallies and human rights campaigns, tried to reach out to Mizrahi and Russian-immigrant women, and even handled advocacy activity. In recent years, it also conducted tours along the route of the Separation Barrier. The *Koalitzia* provided emergency supplies to Palestinian women and children in refugee camps and school supplies to thousands of Palestinian children. Twice a year, it holds public rallies calling for an end to the occupation, rallies that receive almost no media coverage despite their rather significant number of participants, probably because of the female character of these activities. In fact, the *Koalizia* organized several fairly large demonstrations of the caliber that in the past only *Shalom Achshav* was thought to be capable of organizing (the organizers claim as many as 10,000 participants on two occasions, although according to eyewitness accounts, these never reached more than a few thousand). With some of its members highly dedicated to the cultivation of international connections, the *Koalizia* was able to mobilize women in more than one hundred locations on five continents to hold solidarity vigils with the major events that it organized.

Given the gloomy objective POS facing it, the record of the *Koalizia* is quite impressive both as a peace organization and as a women's organization (a situation often referred to in sociology literature as *double marginality*). To this, one should add the relatively meager resources at its disposal and the difficulties involved in running such a multiparticipant endeavor. Even during the bloodiest phases of the *intifada*, it managed to maintain some relations with its Palestinian counterparts in the Palestinian territories at a time when many other Israeli peace organizations lost theirs. Finally, the *Koalitzia* succeeded in establishing a nonhierarchical and fairly, although not totally, harmonious work routine, a remarkable achievement considering the highly opinionated character of the figures involved and the variety of agendas that the different participating organizations brought with them. On the negative side, there is their inability to situate themselves as significant participants in the public discourse on peace-related matters. They also made no significant achievements in promoting more female participants on various levels of talks with the Palestinians or other diplomatic endeavors, as advocated by U.N. Resolution 1325.

Machsom Watch, the other significant women's peace organization of this era, was founded in January 2001, in response to repeated reports in the press about human rights abuses of Palestinians crossing army and border police checkpoints. As already mentioned, the military response by Israel to the *Al-Aqsa intifada* involved the prolonged closures of villages and towns on the West Bank and the setting up of numerous fixed and temporary checkpoints. Palestinians were unable to avoid these checkpoints, because to travel – not only out of the territories but also from one village to another or to the next town – they had to pass through one or more checkpoints. Too often, the merciless treatment that they experienced was not the direct outcome of security needs, but of the soldiers' misconduct. The accumulation of such misdeeds created what *Machsom Watch* called a "checkpoint culture," of which humiliation and brutality were an integral part.

The goals of *Machsom Watch* are threefold: (1) to monitor the behavior of soldiers and police at checkpoints, based on the working assumption that: "the army is the Israeli citizens' emissary, so we are responsible for the soldiers and how they act toward other people; we are responsible for the harm that their actions cause Israeli society"; (2) to ensure that the human and civil rights of Palestinians attempting to enter Israel are protected; and (3) to record and report the results of our observations to the widest possible audience, from the decision-making level to that of the general public, for the sake of the present and for the historical records of the *intifada* period.[97]

Going head on with the army in wartime is not easy, particularly not for women, and even more so for women who view themselves as an integral part of their national collective, even if they criticize specific government policies. *Machsom Watch*'s initial strategy for challenging this "checkpoint culture," without crossing societal red lines, was to take the witness position: stand near the checkpoints, observe how they were operated by Israeli security personnel, and report on every case of ill-treatment. Beyond the specific problems created by the maltreatment of Palestinians at the checkpoints, the very existence of checkpoints is perceived by *Machsom Watch* as the ultimate symbol of all the negative aspects of the occupation in terms of ongoing violations of Palestinians' human rights. Indeed, protecting human rights rather

---

97 http://www.machsomwatch.org/eng/. In recent years, the group expanded its witnessing activity: today, it also watches the conduct of the Israeli courts, in cases of Palestinians who are taken to court as active members in illegal – i.e., allegedly terrorist – organizations (Halevi and Shlonski 2008).

than a pure political peace agenda is what motivates many of the women in
MachsomWatch:

I remember the first time they took me on a patrol on Christmas Eve two and a half years
ago. We came to the Bethlehem checkpoint and stood there with the [*MachsomWatch*]
badge. A man in his forties came up to us; no one stopped him, the place was almost
empty, and he walked up to us with downcast eyes and said, "Thank you." I burst into
tears. Why does a person need to thank someone who basically has done nothing to help
him, why does he have to say thank you at all that he can get through? I think a lot about
the fact that life is actually time. Each of us gets fifty years, or a hundred years, depending
on genetics and health and luck. Yet we're robbing a whole population of time in their
lives – the hours that they stand at our checkpoints (Irit Sela, in Hermann 2005, 67).

Detailed reports of the observations were immediately posted on the *MachsomWatch* website and disseminated through the media: "Every time we get
back from the checkpoints exhausted and dirty, the first thing we do is to write
a report that describes what we saw and heard, and circulate it" (Irit Sela,
op. cit., 66). Later, the women who participated in these vigils also began to
try to actively help the Palestinians who were harassed by the soldiers or the
police, by telephoning the military commanders and calling their attention to
these violations. At the beginning, the reaction to these calls was dismissive,
but when the women who observed the checkpoints received positive media
coverage and showed persistence and resolution, and as the general public
became more aware and somewhat more sensitive to such unnecessary cases of
cruelty,[98] the IDF staff became more attentive.

MachsomWatch is a women-only organization and all their activities are
performed on a purely voluntary basis. Although its activity directly challenges
the dominant militaristic-macho discourse that prevails in Israeli society, many
of *MachsomWatch* members do not hold strong feminist or anti-militaristic
ideology. *Machsomwatchers* encompass a wide spectrum of ages and backgrounds, with, once again, a definite bias towards Ashkenazi, middle-aged,
professional, and secular[99] women. All members are Israeli, and the absolute
majority is Jewish.[100] Some of the women who participate in the vigils are even
mothers to sons and daughters who are serving or have served in the army, or
are married to military officers. Their party identification, if they have any, is

---

[98] In July 2001, 31% of the Jewish respondents to the Peace Index survey confirmed that as far as
they knew, such abusive events occur at the checkpoints frequently or very frequently; however,
in December 2003, 41% responded thus. In 2001, 44% maintained that the authorities should
take severe action against the perpetrators as though they had maltreated Jewish Israelis (33%
thought that they should be treated less severely than if the victims were Jewish); in 2003, the
percentage of those demanding severe punishment increased to 47%, and 28% opted for the
lighter option. In the earlier survey, 13% favored no severe punishment, compared with 18%
in the 2003 survey.

[99] With some rare exceptions of highly liberal religious women.

[100] A few Arab women have also taken part in some activities (e.g., Abu Hussein 2003, 111);
however, the inherent interaction with soldiers and IDF authorities is apparently a great
practical and psychological obstacle for the participation of Arab women in *MachsomWatch*
activities.

diverse from the center parties to the far left. Within this continuum, the group is politically pluralistic and puts forward a wide ideational framework of opposition to the occupation and a commitment to human rights. The group is also diversified in terms of members' former and parallel political experience, and some women testify to having none: "Personally, up to that time [the beginning of the *intifada*] my level of activity and knowledge was very low. So *MachsomWatch* is very important to me because I haven't yet figured out for myself whether I didn't know because they didn't want me to know, or because I didn't want to know (Daphna Banai, in Hermann 2005, 45).

The initiative, which began with 3 women, now boasts 500 participants all over the country, each of whom has a regular 3- to 5-hour shift at a specific checkpoint. The organizational structure of *MachsomWatch* is very simple. It has four branches: the Jerusalem branch, which was set up at the beginning of the *Al Aqsa intifada*, the Tel Aviv branch, a southern group stationed in the Tarkumia and Hebron area, and a relatively new group stationed at checkpoints in the northern region. The different branches coordinate their activities through an open and nonhierarchical procedure. The Tel Aviv and the Jerusalem branches hold monthly meetings. The southerners and the northerners are freer groups and participate in these meetings when and if they wish. Once a month, there is a meeting of the organizing body, with everyone invited to attend. The organizing body includes eight elected members. Once a year elections are held for the chairs of the Jerusalem and Tel Aviv branches and their deputies. This medium level of institutionalization, which is in a way an imperative because of the organization's activity type, one that necessitates significant coordination, is carefully maintained: "We're afraid of processes in large bodies, because there's still something personal among us, some mutual human respect among the participants. We trust each other, even if not all the others do things exactly as I do them. But we recognize that different ways of doing things are valid. When a body begins to be very large, to gather power, it starts to gather weakness" (Irit Sela, in Hermann 2005, 69).

Possibly because most women participating in *MachsomWatch* activities are not classic political protesters, because they are basically ideological mainstreamers and well integrated into the Jewish Israeli sociodemographic center (and probably even more because they point to very basic human rights violations in a civilized, even classically feminine manner), their activities today are fairly consensual, much more so than when they began to operate, and their voice is often heard in mainstream media. Indeed, here and there they have been harassed by settlers and denounced by people on the right for lowering the morale of the soldiers at the checkpoints, who are "only doing what they were told." Still, it seems that they have succeeded in delivering their message better than other peace organizations. Apparently, *MachsomWatch* managed to perforate the curtain of silence and to influence public discourse about the checkpoints and the closures.[101]

---

[101] *MachsomWatch*'s message against the maltreatment of Palestinians by soldiers was strongly supported by the *Shovrim Shtika* (Breaking the Silence) group of ex-soldiers discussed below.

Although the organizations discussed here put forward innovative frame-works for action and tactics that suit the unfolding circumstances, ideologically the most interesting upshot of the political developments of the early 2000s was the unprecedented swelling – less in numerical terms and more in terms of higher visibility and growing legitimacy – of the refusal phenomenon. The centrality of military service in Israeli society and the controversial nature of the appeal over the years by certain peace groups to potential servicemen and women to refuse the draft when called have already been discussed. Refusal to serve during the *Al-Aqsa intifada* period was somewhat different. First, this time, there were indeed few – but clearly more than in the past – cases of refusal based on pacifist arguments. Second, there were many more cases than in the past of refusal by reserve soldiers who were politically mainstreamers but strongly oppose the practices of the Israeli government and the IDF in the Palestinian territories. The argument that, although not intentionally or openly brought together pacifist refuseniks and those advocating refusal on the grounds of political opposition to the state's policies stated that when one is called for service in the armed forces, as a moral agent, one should consider whether the activities that he or she is asked to perform when in uniform are morally justified. As already mentioned, for the pacifist, a rare justification for using military force might be, for example, in defense of the weak and the help-less when they are ferociously attacked by a stronger, evil party. Those who are not pacifists do not deny the possibility of justified use of military force in the service of the national interest. In fact, most of them define a defensive war as a just war, but in special circumstances, when the use of force is offensive or can be replaced by nonviolent – for example, political – means, or when its aim is to repress others, then, they argue, a moral person should refuse to play a part in it.

In the early 1990s, with the prospects of ending the growing conflict, the taboo on discussion of the socio-political functions of military service was somewhat modified. For the first time, it was legitimate to discuss to what extent universal conscription was really universal,[102] and whether it was really a direct outcome of objective security needs or just another means of social control.[103] It was even suggested, for the first time ever, that military service

---

[102] As already mentioned, the draft is not really universal, because ultra-Orthodox Jews and Arab Israeli citizens are almost automatically exempt. Many other Jewish men and women are also exempt for medical, psychological, and social reasons, however. As of today, only about 60% of the Jewish-Israeli 18-year-old age group is actually drafted into the army and serves the designated 3 years in full.

[103] The views of the Jewish Israeli public concerning military service have undergone rapid change since the early 1990s. Whereas in the past, military service was a sine qua non for good citizenship, in the April 2001 Peace Index survey, almost one-third (31%) of the Jewish respondents supported abolishing universal conscription and making the IDF a professional army (59% disagreed and were almost equally split between those who believed that universal conscription is critical to maintaining a strong army, and those who believed that everyone should take a part in the defense of the country). Of the respondents 49% (as opposed to 42%) supported the idea of introducing the option of civil service for people who, for whatever reason, do not want to join the army.

was a tool used by the ruling Ashkenazi elite for (ab)using the underprivileged Mizrahi sector. Radical Mizrahi activists, who were also often involved in peace activism, maintained that Mizrahi Jews were not only used by the state of Israel as human shields, but that the state also set them against the Arabs:

The State actually encourages the Mizrahi [Jews] to block crossroads only when this is aimed against the Arabs; it is even ready to turn a blind eye on stoning and tire burning in pogroms against the Arabs, and even on calls to kill Arabs. It even sometimes supplies them [the Mizrahi –TH] with uniforms and weapons. As of today, we, the Mizrahi as a collective, still do not have the 'right' to resign from our role as 'Arab haters', which is the pillar of our national identity (Chetrit 2001, 291).

In practice, throughout the years, many Mizrahi youngsters indeed avoided military service, because they felt deeply alienated from the state. Because of their low educational level, minimal political awareness, and lack of connections to the media, however, their protest was never framed in political-ideological terms and therefore remained in the realm of social deviation. The conscientious objectors of the early 2000s were mostly from the better-off and more articulate societal groups – classic supporters of the peace process.[104]

Since the outbreak of the *Al-Aqsa intifada*, and particularly after the reoccupation of Palestinian areas by Israeli military forces in mid-2002, the number of Israelis declaring their refusal to serve in the occupied territories dramatically increased (by Israeli standards), from a few hundred throughout the first 55 years of the state's existence, to over 500 refuseniks between October 2000 and early 2003.[105] Many symposia were organized at the time to discuss the legitimization and significance of the refusal phenomenon, and numerous reports and articles were published in the newspapers and the electronic media. Whereas in the past, Jewish Israeli public opinion strongly opposed refusal, at the time under discussion here, a significant minority of the Israeli public viewed

---

[104] Although the refusal of men was much more significant in number and – for obvious reasons – in potential effects on the functioning of the IDF, it is worth noting that the refuseniks also included several women. Although universal conscription in Israel also relates to women, implementation has been considerably more lenient in their case. First, only women with high personal qualifications were actually drafted. In addition, based on an agreement reached with the Orthodox leadership in the early days of the state, Israeli law acknowledged the right of women to declare that they were religiously observant and therefore exempt. Also, unlike men, Israeli women in general were always offered the legal right to conscientious objection based on moral grounds. Indeed, over the years, several hundred women used this legal loophole and asked for exemption based on mainly pacifist grounds. With the emergence of the refusal movement in the early 2000s, however, the authorities closed this half-open door, and women refuseniks, who based their refusal on political grounds, were often treated as harshly as the men.

[105] As of this writing, the number of political conscientious objectors is about 1,000. Leaders of the refusal movement maintain, however, that this number is only the tip of the iceberg, because a much larger number of draftees, in the thousands, prefer to use different legal loopholes not to serve in the territories without making a case out of it and risk being sent to jail.

refusal as a legitimate right (23% in the Peace Index survey of February 2002, and 20% in the September and December 2003 Peace Index surveys).[106]

The following quotation reflects the sort of criticism of the state expressed by those refusing to serve in the early 2000s, in protest of the means used by Israel to overcome the Palestinian *intifada*:

I can state unequivocally that the state of Israel has reached an unprecedented moral ebb. The critical deterioration phase that began in the days of Barak's "most generous offer" [at the July 2000 Camp David summit – TH] was just another effort to impose a unilateral agreement on the Palestinian people. Today, the level of militarization and racism among the Israeli Jewish public is coming very close to fascism. The oppression of any critical thinking, acquiescence with the crimes of the occupation, the deification of the military and the slow inculcation of principles of 'ethnic cleansing' are all elements of overall social degeneration. To all these, the systematic hounding of the Palestinian citizens of Israel, the hateful violence against peaceful protesters and the overall mercilessness toward the weak and the 'other' should be added (Matar 2004, 133).

The author of the quote above was one of five young Israelis who, because of their pacifist criticism of the occupation, refused to be drafted into the IDF when they reached draft age.[107] Their case received much media and public attention, and views on this kind of refusal were extremely divided. Of note, however, is that the majority of refusal acts were carried out not by young people who had not yet been mobilized but by soldiers in the reserves. Indeed, the fact that among the refuseniks were fighters from elite units – the Israeli commando and Air Force pilots – made the protest much more visible, nationally distressing, and of course, much more contested. Thus, the bulk of refuseniks in the *Al-Aqsa intifada* period were not motivated

---

[106] Interestingly enough, although perhaps not surprisingly, the legitimization at that time for conscientious objection by people on the right (27% in February 2002), in the then-hypothetical case that they would refuse to take part in evacuating Jewish settlements, was somewhat higher than the legitimization for left-wing refusal. As is mentioned later, the implementation of the disengagement plan was indeed accompanied by a heated debate within the right-wing national-religious political camp as well as in wider circles of the Israeli public over the justification of soldiers who politically opposed this move to refuse to take part in it.

[107] They were court martialed in 2004 and sent to jail for 1 year. In mid-2003, a forum of parents whose children refused to serve was established. The organization of such a forum was a highly nonconsensual step. It should be noted, however, that its goals were phrased very cautiously, without declaring the parents' solidarity with the act of refusal: "The parents' forum is not a political organization in the usual sense of the word. It is composed of people who belong to different parts of the Israeli political spectrum. All parents are committed to defending the civil and human rights of their children. There are parents who support draft resistance in principle, on philosophical or political grounds, and others who view the forum as mainly a personal support group for their children and for themselves. The group is bound together by virtue of the fact that all have a son who refuses to serve in the IDF for moral reasons" (from a message circulated through the *Profil Hadash* email list on June 2, 2003).

by pacifist ideas. Most of them did not challenge Israel's way of conducting political negotiations with the Palestinians or the expansion of the settlement project, nor did they relate to the state's relations with Arab Israelis.[108] They also did not share a belief in any one solution to the conflict. Their initial act of refusal was usually motivated by their disapproval of Israel's mode of conduct in the territories; for example, the targeted killings, but in most cases they expressed readiness to take part in defensive military missions. This position was best exemplified in the "Combatants Letter," published and widely circulated in January 2002. That letter served as the basis for the new *Ometz l'Sarev* (Courage to Refuse) organization, which stated, among other things:

We, combat officers and soldiers who have served the State of Israel for long weeks every year, in spite of the dear cost to our personal lives, have been on reserve duty in the Occupied Territories, and were issued commands and directives that had nothing to do with the security of our country, and that had the sole purpose of perpetuating our control over the Palestinian people.

We, whose eyes have seen the bloody toll this Occupation exacts from both sides,

We, who sensed how the commands issued to us in the Occupied Territories destroy all the values that we were raised upon,

We, who understand now that the price of Occupation is the loss of IDF's human character and the corruption of the entire Israeli society,

We, who know that the Territories are not a part of Israel, and that all settlements are bound to be evacuated,

We hereby declare that we shall not continue to fight this War of the Settlements.

We shall not continue to fight beyond the 1967 borders in order to dominate, expel, starve and humiliate an entire people.

We hereby declare that we shall continue serving the Israel Defense Force in any mission that serves Israel's defense

(http://www.seruv.org.il)

One of the organizers of the letter described the crisis of confidence that led to the wave of refusal, when he explained why, after many years during which he had performed his military duties fully, in 2000, he could not take it anymore:

The number of dead on both sides was mounting. The public got the explanations in the newspapers: Barak offered them everything, the Arabs do not want peace, but only to push us all into the sea. Let the IDF do its job and win, the various spokespersons pleaded.... But for the first time, even I didn't buy this. I didn't buy the explanation that soldiers were being killed in the territories 'for the sake of security', I didn't buy the explanation about the unavoidability of the occupation; nor did I buy the oppression

---

[108] For clearly psychological reasons, however, some of these refuseniks became much more radical in their criticism of Israeli politicians and policies in the context of the conflict after they were fiercely attacked and even ostracized by family members, friends, and the media because of their initial refusal.

and humiliation, and I also could not understand how I, the good and moral officer, had taken part in such actions (Zonenschein 2004, 140–141).

This expanding phenomenon gained national attention and deeply disturbed the authorities. Thus, for example, in February 2002, the very mainstream Israel Democracy Institute (IDI) organized a symposium on "The Right to Refuse," with the participation of top IDF officers (with no refuseniks on the panel, however). Surprisingly, the representatives of the military were not of one opinion but divided among themselves on this issue. Thus, the Commander of the Southern Command was rather moderate in his attitude towards the refuseniks: "People are saying 'no more', and their words are hard and problematic. This calls for serious examination, as the phenomenon may well spread and effect wider groups and perhaps spread among the youth, as well. . . . Thus far," he added, "no one has asked them what they are actually asking for" (Shchori 2002). Another high-ranking reserve officer called for greater tolerance for the pacifist refuseniks and even for opening options to alternative civil service. The Commander of the IDF Education Corps presented a much tougher position, however, maintaining that indeed the refuseniks "should not be hanged [metaphorically speaking, of course – TH] but one should be very firm with them" (ibid.). Later, in January 2004, IDF Chief of Staff, Moshe (Boggy) Ya'alon, in referring to the refusal phenomenon, went so far as to declare that the weakest link in the national defense was the Israeli public and its "lack of endurance." Israelis, he said at a press conference, were no longer prepared to fight for their ideals and to risk their lives, because since September 2000 there had been no consensus on what the fighting was all about (in Marcus 2004).

In retrospect, however, it seems that these concerns of the authorities were by and large somewhat exaggerated, because what seemed at the time to be an emerging wave of refusal did not turn into a tsunami, as the main activists had perhaps hoped. Actually, it faded out without shaking the foundations of the collective view of military service, although it could be one of the multiple causes for the recently much-discussed cracks in the universal conscription. The most trivial reason for the decline in the refusal movement was the ongoing and highly violent Palestinian *intifada*, which, in general, increased Israelis' sense of patriotism and support for the military forces. There were also other reasons, however, that were mainly related to relations within the peace camp. First, tensions developed between those who signed the "Combatants Letter," which attracted the widest public and media attention, and those who refused but did not sign it nor join the signers' group, for example, the pacifist refuseniks. The former, who expressed their patriotism and strong adherence to Zionism, were naturally somewhat better accepted by the general public than the individual refuseniks, whose criticism of Israel and often of the Zionist project was generally much more blatant. In fact, even the military authorities were careful in their handling of the acts of the *Ometz l'Sarev* group because of their professed loyalty to the system at large, including to the IDF. Second, the group of signers chose not to define themselves as a political movement and certainly not as a peace movement. On the contrary, they repeatedly emphasized their nonpolitical character and tried to set themselves apart from the more radical peace groups that also supported conscientious objection, such as *Yesh Gvul* and *Profil Hadash*. The spokesperson of *Ometz l'Sarev* explained why they did not view themselves as a peace movement:

I think we're a movement for ending the occupation more than we're a peace movement. Traditionally, whoever sees himself as peace loving is drawn to optimism of that kind. We, on the other hand, are motivated by a feeling of revulsion that can't wait and doesn't allow us to go on with our lives.... The words don't interest us; politics isn't our area at all. As long as the soldiers behave the way they do in the field, and recently there is also a slight utilitarian basis – as long as our soldiers are getting killed – we'll call for refusal, with no connection to this or that political program.... In other words, it's right to say that we're not a peace movement in the normal sense of the term. We're a pretty large group of people who saw very problematical things, which motivated us to action, more than the hope for a future that's a little better (Diamant, in Hermann 2005, 61).

Another activist of *Ometz l'Sarev* put it in terms that were even more specific: "There is no doubt that our profile is different from *Yesh Gvul*'s.... We belong to the center. Our protest does not come from the margins. *Yesh Gvul* is clearly identified politically, to the point where they have lost some of their ability to influence the general public" (Amit Mashiah, in Galili 2002b). *Ometz l'Sarev*'s unwillingness to identify with the peace movement and the groups that expressed more radical criticism of military service was met with a cold shoulder by the latter, who openly doubted the new refuseniks' commitment to peace. The more moderate peace movements and political parties, that is, Meretz, distanced themselves from *Ometz l'Sarev* because they traditionally denounced the refusal idea: "Meretz dissociated itself from them, and the peace movements are avoiding the issue of refusal as if it were a landmine that threatened to blow up in their faces" (Galili 2002b). This complicated situation created a schism within the anti-occupation camp; however, it apparently did not save *Ometz l'Sarev* from being pushed to the periphery much more rapidly than had originally been expected. As one journalist correctly forecast, "The aspiration to be the avant-garde of refusal and, at the same time, the darling of the Israeli ethos, is not really feasible, though it is not entirely mistaken as a tactic on the Israeli scene.... So the refusers want to have it all: to be beautiful, to be right, to protest" (Galili 2002b).

The propensity of newcomers like the refusenik group to dissociate themselves from the "traditional" peace movement so as not to be stigmatized and ostracized was even more apparent in the case of *haMifkad haLeumi* (literally: The National Census), which emerged in 2002. *HaMifkad haLeumi*, the Israeli side of a civil initiative, intended to change the climate of opinion among Jewish Israelis. Its very patriotic Hebrew name, carefully chosen by some of the best public relations experts in Israel, who voluntarily helped this initiative in its first steps, was meant to create an immediate link to the national consensus and save the new endeavor from the fringe stigma of the peace movement. To further catch the eye and heart of the Jewish Israeli mainstream, they designed a logo that incorporated elements of Israel's national emblem and colored it in the national colors – blue and white. The new initiative's name was also intentionally different from its English, rather neutral, name, The People's Voice, which emphasized the initiative's grassroots nature and was meant to win the hearts and minds of people outside Israel. Unlike *Yozmat Geneva* (the Geneva Initiative), the second new style initiative that gained public momentum about a year later, and which was strongly connected with the traditional peace movement (if only because of the person who led it – Yossi Beilin), *haMifkad haLeumi* distanced itself from even moderate peace organizations such as *Shalom Achshav*, but did so in a way that would enable peace activists to come on board as well. This allegedly constructive ambiguity strategy was reflected on the initiative's website in the FAQs section, which said

Q: Is the People's Voice linked in any way to peace campaigns or other social movements?
A: The People's Voice is an independent initiative, but since its goal is to get a significant proportion of Israel's population to sign on to the Statement of Principles, it will strive to join forces with any other movement prepared to adopt this document in its entirety and assist in the effort (http://www.mifkad.org.il)

Everyone familiar with the fate of peace activism in Israel could see the strategy behind these strategic choices: "Past attempts by political and social movements to speak to Israeli society in universal terms have failed dismally; when these movements began to speak in terms derived from the Zionist ethos, people began to listen" (Galili 2002b). Indeed, to avoid being labeled as collaborators with the enemy, *haMifkad haLeumi*, led by Ami Ayalon, former commander of the Navy and former head of the General Security Agency (*Shabak*), did not define itself as an Israeli-Palestinian endeavor but rather opted for an alliance between separate Palestinian and Israeli endeavors. The two sides were brought together by a statement of principles signed by Ayalon and Prof. Sari Nusseibeh, president of Al Quds University in East Jerusalem and an independent Palestinian political activist, on July 27, 2002, which stated

Two states for two peoples: Both sides will declare that Palestine is the only state of the Palestinian people and Israel is the only state of the Jewish people.
Borders: Permanent borders between the two states will be agreed upon on the basis of the June 4, 1967 lines, UN resolutions, and the Arab peace initiative.
Jerusalem: Jerusalem will be an open city, the capital of two states. Freedom of religion and full access to holy sites will be guaranteed to all.
Right of return: Recognizing the suffering and the plight of the Palestinian refugees, the international community, Israel, and the Palestinian State will initiate and contribute to an international fund to compensate them.

The Palestinian State will be demilitarized and the international community will guarantee its security and independence.

End of conflict: Upon the full implementation of these principles, all claims on both sides and the Israeli-Palestinian conflict will end.

(http://www.mifkad.org.il)

The idea of the initiative was to present to the general public – not only the classic pro-peace audience – a short document that outlined the features of final status without going into too much detail as to how to get there. The underlying concept was a classic strategic planning model, or "reverse engineering," going backward from the desired end to the point of departure. It was believed that a highly publicized media campaign, which would get the support of many thousands on the Israeli side, would signal to the Palestinians that despite the hostilities and killings, the silent majority still wanted peace, and vice versa – the Israelis would see that many Palestinians were interested in getting back to the negotiation table to reach a permanent peace. The dilemma with which the organizers had to struggle was how to create such a popular wave in support of the resumption of negotiations and the signing of an accord, when the facts on the ground appeared so antithetical to the cause of peace. The initiative's manifest aim was to encourage hundreds of thousands (perhaps even more than a million) of Israelis and Palestinians to sign the document and in this way create a wave of pro-peace public opinion that would eventually make the leaders of both sides reconsider their hard-line positions. These signatures, to be collected by means of the Internet, signing booths, telephone, "snail mail," and the like, would be presented to the authorized decision makers in the hope that this would push them into renewing negotiations and eventually arriving at an agreement along the lines of their statement.

Beyond its careful middle-of-the-road self-positioning and avoidance of any protest ambience, the considerable resources available, the support of central figures in Israeli society, and indeed the patriotic image that it had so carefully constructed, helped the initiative to take off while the *intifada* was in full swing. There were placards of *haMifkad haLeumi* all over the country, and the number of people who were ready to put its sticker on their cars was unprecedented. The two leaders of the endeavor became welcome guests on television talk shows and popular lecturers in and outside the region. Money from various sources poured in, and the events organized by the initiative were well attended by dignitaries as well as by the general public. Less than a year after the formal launching of the signing campaign, about 375,000 signatures of Israelis and Palestinians had been collected. The lists were presented to the president of Israel at a small ceremony.

The organizers' and supporters' expectations were that if enough signatures were collected, decision makers would lend an ear to this bottom-up call for resumption of negotiations. This did not happen, however. Furthermore, replacing the classic means of protest by merely asking the average citizen to sign a political document seemed less successful than had been thought originally. Considering the resentment toward peace activism at the time, asking one merely to sign a document, an act that could be performed in private, was a good strategy under the circumstances. However, this one-off action was apparently unable to produce enough political commitment to carry the expected wave of pro-peace public opinion.

It should also be noted that traditional peace SMOs did not join the *Mifkad haLeumi* initiative. First, on the ideological level, only a few, in what was by then a rather radicalized peace movement, could identify with the basic statement of principles, because the statement defined Israel as a Jewish state, not as a state of all its citizens. They also did not want to support a declaration of principles that said nothing about Israel's responsibility for the Palestinian catastrophes – the *nakba* of 1948 and the *naksa* of 1967. The document completely rejected the right of return and did not demand the removal of all Jewish settlements in the territories (the phrasing intentionally opened a window for some significant border corrections, which would have included many settlements within Israel's sovereignty). Second, the fact that *haMifkad haLeumi* was headed on the Israeli side by an ex-general was abhorrent to many peace activists – mainly to women peace activists – because they took it as proof that the endeavor did not offer a real alternative to the mainstream security ethos. Finally, many peace activists were simply offended by the *Mifkad*'s reluctance to associate with them and therefore did not reach out to the group, particularly as they were used to being active beyond merely signing a document such as the Ayalon-Nusseibeh platform. Nevertheless, many of them did sign it in private.

Paradoxically however, neither the initiative's efforts to set itself apart from the peace movement nor the movement's detachment from it, prevented it from being stigmatized as leftist or peacenik. Thus, *haMifkad haLeumi* missed some of its target audiences: the religious or residents of development towns, for example, who steered clear of it in the same way they had stayed away from the peace camp. Moreover, the thousands of signatures collected among Palestinians were not enough to convince the wider Israeli public that the majority of Palestinians wanted a peace agreement with Israel and were willing to relinquish their violent struggle. Therefore, despite its tactical achievements, the *Mifkad* failed in its main mission – to create a cognitive earthquake that would force the leaders into making a strategic move in the direction of peace making.

It seems that the various innovative techniques used by the different elements of the peace movement in the early 2000s – from sharpening their criticism by means of opting for new media and methods, to relinquishing mass protest and focusing on conscience raising – did not change the movement's very limited political influence. These techniques did not improve the movement's positioning in the national political arena, which was dominated by the "no partner" formula. This general state of mind dictated that "anyone who tried to portray a more complicated picture, was denounced as supporting the enemy" (Benvenisti 2007). The objective realities within and outside of Israeli society apparently stood in too-sharp contradiction to the peace agenda put forth by the peace movement, in terms of the level of violence and the mounting mistrust of the Palestinian side. Thus, even people with a basically positive disposition toward the idea of territorial withdrawal became more and more skeptical and began to develop the reasoning that eventually led to the unilateral disengagement from Gaza in the summer of 2005:

The mistake of the left was and still is the connection it established between the demand for a [territorial] withdrawal and the argument regarding the desire for peace that allegedly exists on the other side. As has now been proved beyond a doubt, the other side in general lacks 'compassion' and 'humanity' and even 'critical rational thinking'.... This connection on the part of the left lessened Israelis' readiness to withdraw.... Instead, the Israeli political left should now explain that the downward spiral to war can only be halted by a unilateral change on our side. We must withdraw from the West Bank and Gaza, not because of the 'humanity' of the Palestinians, not necessarily because their demands are justified, and irrespective of their willingness or unwillingness to reach an agreement with us. The main reason for such a withdrawal is the limits of Israel's power. The citizens of Israel should understand before it gets too late, that the Green Line demarcates the perimeter of Israel's capabilities. Any effort to use force beyond it will inflict disaster on us (Leibovitz 2001).

The Dead-End Point

In January 2003, Ariel Sharon led the Likud party to a second overwhelming electoral victory – the number of seats that his party held now more than doubled: from 18 to 38! This electoral victory was nourished by Sharon's almost unprecedented popularity among the public, mainly because of the way he organized the Israeli defense forces' crackdown on the second Palestinian *intifada* in 2001 and 2002 (although the terror attacks, in particular the suicide bombings, did not stop). Another positive input in his public status was the green light that he gave (in April 2002) – clearly in contrast with his personal adherence to the notion of Greater Israel – to begin the construction of the Separation Barrier, a defensive measure that a majority of the Jewish Israeli public wholeheartedly supported,[109] and to which the peace movement objected from day one.[110] Even the overall dismal economic situation that prevailed in Israel

---

[109] In June 2002, 57% of the Jewish Israeli public supported the construction of the fence, although its route was still unknown, whereas 34% opposed it. The remainder had no clear opinion. It is interesting to note that the level of support among the voters of the center and left-of-center parties was considerably higher (75%) than that of voters for right-wing parties – 47% (Peace Index, June 2002). This is because for center-left voters, the barrier was a means for redemarcation of the Green Line. The right-wingers' lower level of support could be explained by their perception of the barrier as the border between Israel and a future Palestinian state, to whose establishment they objected. A year later, in June 2003, the level of support for the fence reached 60% and in February 2004, 83%, which indicates that many on the right also changed their view and now supported its construction.

[110] Paradoxically, perhaps, the Palestinian positions regarding the barrier were less negative than those of the Israeli peace movement. Actually, the Palestinian critics focused more on its route, which did not correspond to the Green Line, than on its construction.

at the time and the various corruption allegations raised against Sharon and members of his family before the elections could not erode his strong public position. Thus, there was no chance that peace activists' criticism of his policies, which were highly favored by the general public, could harm him politically.

Winning so many parliamentary seats enabled Sharon to establish his dream coalition, leaving out the ultra-orthodox parties and Labour, the leader of which, Amram Mizna, strongly opposed Sharon's harsh policies and practices vis-à-vis the Palestinians. The electoral fiasco experienced in the 2003 elections by the parties of the left,[111] was clearly the result of the public's support for noncompromising positions in the context of the Israeli-Palestinian conflict. Thus, a few days after the election day, a plurality (38%) of a representative sample of the Jewish population in Israel held that this defeat was mainly the result of these parties' position on the conflict, whereas the second explanation was their leaders (20%), and in third place (13%), their snobbery and detachment from the average citizen (Peace Index survey, January 2003).[112] Against this background, the chances that the peace movement would regain momentum in terms of mass activities and political visibility were very limited. As is shown here, however, despite this belligerent national state of mind and the dead end in Israeli-Palestinian relations, several new and unique peace initiatives emerged between 2003 and 2006. These and other peace activities were conducted in this period in a different environment and thus with a different state of mind, because in December 2003, Sharon declared his plan for unilateral disengagement from Gaza.

Not only did the national arena dramatically change because of this policy shift, but the peace movement was also severely shaken by it. The moderate organizations and groups openly supported the disengagement plan, with many of their activists dramatically reducing their resentment toward Sharon personally. The radical groups and activists, however, strongly and fiercely opposed the plan and presented it as more evidence of Sharon's evil personality. Indeed, many moderate peace activists did not like the unilateral rationale underlying Sharon's plan, and an even larger number of them supported the plan but did not actually believe that Sharon was really able or willing to dismantle the Jewish settlements in the Gaza Strip. A cautious, undeclared alignment emerged between the prime minister and the moderate Israeli peace camp, however, while his relations with the radical peace groups dramatically deteriorated. As his relations with the settlement movement and its supporters on the right hit rock bottom,[113] a strange, unspoken anti-Sharon/anti-disengagement

---

[111] The Labour party experienced a severe electoral defeat in the 2003 elections – losing 7 seats in the Knesset (from 26, it dropped to only 19).

[112] Of interest, in the same survey, when asked for the source of the Likud's victory, 40% pointed to its leader, Sharon, whereas only 22% connected the victory to the party's position on the conflict.

[113] The split within the right between Sharon's supporters and those who opposed the disengagement plan was so severe that in November 2005, against the background of the strong opposition that he faced within the Likud party, Sharon left it and, together with other top

solidarity was created between the radical left and the radical right. In a way, then, the disengagement plan tore apart the peace movement, a blow from which it has not recovered.

As the negotiations with the Palestinians were completely paralyzed in the early 2000s, a situation that changed only very little after the death of President Arafat in November 2004,[114] although his successor – Mahmud Abbas (Abu Mazen) – was widely considered in Israel to be much more moderate and not supportive of terrorism against Israelis, the peace activists' efforts in 2003–2004 were not aimed at any concrete peace plan but at minimizing the damage caused by the recent reoccupation of the territories and, in particular, by the separation barrier, or *the Wall*, as most peace activists refer to it. Thus, since the beginning of its construction in mid-2002, the barrier, which was widely supported by the general public, as noted previously, became a major target in the thinking and activity of the radical peace camp. The moderate groups, mainly *Shalom Achshav*, did not take an active part in this struggle, although individual activists did so. In April 2003, a new conflict-related but not self-declared peace group was created – *Anarchistim Neged haGader* (Anarchists against the Wall [AATW]).

It started with a few radical leftist activists, professing direct action tactics, in cooperation with Palestinians who objected to the construction works. With some local people, they put up a "protest tent" in the Palestinian village of Mes'ha in Samaria (the northern part of the West Bank), where the barrier was about to be erected. Apparently, in response to the sharp criticism of the Israeli peace movement's alleged patronizing of the Palestinians, the *Anarchistim* considered cooperation with the locals to be highly significant: "All of AATW's work in Palestine is coordinated through villages' local popular committees and is essentially Palestinian led" (http://www.awalls.org). The new group's dissatisfaction with the traditional means used by other peace activists, which they considered too soft, is also reflected elsewhere in the same text: "We believe that it is possible to do more than demonstrate inside Israel or participate in humanitarian relief actions. Israeli apartheid and occupation isn't going to end by itself [sic] – it will end when it becomes ungovernable and unmanageable. It is time to physically oppose the bulldozers, the army and the occupation" (ibid). Furthermore, as anarchists, and contrary to all other peace organizations in Israel, the AATW opposed the two-state solution ("Two States for Two Nations – Two States too Many" as they put it – Federazione dei Comunisti Anarchici 2004, 5) as well as the one, binational state model favored by

Likud and Labour politicians (including Shimon Peres, one of the founding fathers of the Oslo process), established the new Kadima party.

[114] The public good wishes by certain peace activists to Arafat when he was on his deathbed (e.g., Frankenthal 2004) and the warm words in his memory by others after he passed away (for example, by Uri Avneri in Shavit 2004a), were strongly condemned by many in Israel (e.g., http://www.inn.co.il), because these were perceived as additional evidence of the peace activists' disloyalty to their own nation and even of siding with the Palestinian leader who was perceived as archenemy of Israel and of the Jews.

the radical Israeli peace activists. This is because as anarchists, they considered the state, any state, as the real source of conflict between people and groups. In fact, they criticized all Israeli peace organizations for giving in to the state's logic – which they basically opposed – when shaping their solutions to the conflict:

We do not need to promote a political programme, be it that of the Geneva Accords or some alternative. Instead, we must put the demand for an entirely different way of life and equality for all the inhabitants of the region on the agenda. Even if we act in an independent (local) way, we still have to remember that as long there are States and as long as the capitalist system continues to exist, every improvement we manage to achieve will be partial and under permanent threat. Thus, we have to see our struggle as part of the struggle being carried on throughout the whole world against the world capitalism and call for a revolutionary change based on the abolition of class oppression, exploitation, and aim towards building a new society – a classless anarchist-communist society. A society in which there will be no State coercion, where organized violence will be abolished, where chauvinism will be inexistent, and where all other evils of the capitalist era will be removed (ibid., 66).

The first tent vigil in Mes'ha lasted for 4 months, during which – according to the organizers – thousands of Israelis and international visitors came to express their solidarity with this anti-Wall protest. On December 26, 2003, one (Jewish) protestor from the group was shot by IDF soldiers while demonstrating near the construction site and was severely wounded. The *Anarchistim* expected that this tragic event would help them to promote their cause. The military court, however, decided – as it would decide in most future cases when anti-Wall protestors were injured by the security forces – that the soldiers were in the right. Also, not surprisingly, the protestors were unable to prevent the construction of the barrier at this location. By physically confronting the soldiers and other security forces and bulldozers, however, they did succeed at one point to open a gate in the fence, an act that they considered a tactical achievement, although the gate was closed shortly afterwards.

The *Anarchistim* claimed even greater success in another Palestinian village, Budrus, where they reported that direct action led to a permanent change in the barrier's route. Here again, as in other locations, the activists' efforts to dismantle parts of the barrier were confronted vigorously by the military forces in the area, including the use of live ammunition. The army contested the protestors' and the media reporters' argument that the soldiers had been brutal and maintained that their lives had been put in danger by the demonstrators. In this case, although the military personnel again were acquitted of the use of unnecessary force, the military court did not accept all the IDF's defense arguments and stated that the forces should have been better prepared to handle such acts of defiance without having to use excessive means.

In this context, it is interesting to bring into the picture the AATW claim that even in these tense situations, the IDF and other Israeli security agencies carefully differentiate between Jewish and non-Jewish protestors, treating the former much less harshly than the latter. Non-Jewish protestors, mainly Palestinians but also Arab Israelis, the AATW homepage argued, are intentionally killed or wounded: "Even though many Israeli activists have been wounded at the demonstrations, some of them seriously, it is the Palestinians who have paid the highest toll. To date, 10 Palestinian demonstrators have been killed in demonstrations against the barrier and thousands have been wounded" (op. cit.). In fact, it is maintained by AATW that the mere presence of Jewish Israelis at the protest provides the Palestinian protestors with a certain amount of protection, at least from the soldiers and the border policemen, although not necessarily from the settlers who often show up in the area and contribute to the escalation of the confrontation. This observation is sustained by evidence from other peace activists who participated in these and other joint Jewish-Palestinian protest activities (e.g., Shulman 2007, 182). Although not one of the manifest goals of any Israeli peace group, the activists seemed to adhere to logic similar to that which motivated the foreign ISM activists who served as human shields for Palestinians (http://www.palsolidarity.org).

From 2005 to the time of this writing, AATW and many of its supporters have conducted weekly demonstrations in the Palestinian village of Bili'in (and in the nearby village of Na'alin), which, according to the Oslo agreements, are located in Palestinian-controlled area B – west of the Palestinian city of Ramallah and east of the Jewish town of Modi'in. Bili'in was selected by the anti-barrier protestors because the construction route there leaves 70% of the agricultural lands on the "wrong" (i.e., Israeli) side of the barrier. This means that, once construction is finished, the farmers will be unable to reach and cultivate their lands. Furthermore, on parts of these confiscated lands, new Jewish neighborhoods, belonging to the Jewish town of Modiin East/Ilit, have been built. This act of confiscating Palestinian lands and then building Jewish homes on them seems to sustain the anti-barrier activists' argument that its construction is not only – perhaps not even mainly – security motivated, but is in fact a means of annexing Palestinian lands to Israel (e.g., Shulman 2007, 176).

In time, the ongoing Bili'in campaign developed into a long series of symbolic interactions between the anti-barrier protesters and representatives of the state of Israel – the IDF and the border police – with the participation of international human rights and ISM activists,[115] as well as individual Israeli peace activists belonging to various groups. Unlike most other protest actions by Israeli peace groups, which were mostly conducted within the limits of the law, all the *Anarchistim*'s actions, those of Bili'in included, were defined at the outset as direct action that does not stop at (or stopped by) the legal limits. The scene becomes a battlefield on which IDF soldiers and border policemen fight the defiant anti-barrier activists, who try to stick to nonviolent means, if

---

[115] For inside information about the close cooperation between ISM and the *Anarchistim*, see Ayalon 2006. The ideological and tactical proximity between the two organizations – AATW and ISM – is also evident in the content and style of their respective homepages.

only because they recognize their strategic and tactical inferiority. The clashes and in particular the army's forceful ways of dealing with the weekly confrontations are often extensively covered by Israeli and international media. The reports mainly favor the protestors and are highly critical of the soldiers' conduct, with headlines like "Savage Attack on Peaceful Palestinian-Israeli Demo" (http://www.scoop.co.nz, April 29, 2005). The symbolic nature of the actions relates to their timing (which is known in advance, usually on Friday mornings) as well as to the "rules of conduct," but not to the growing risk involved in taking part in them, in terms of being physically hurt, even killed, or prosecuted. In fact, the clashes between the protestors and the soldiers often reach the courts, with the legal statistics at the time of this writing (as reported on the AATW homepage) being 63 indictments, 13 convictions, 9 acquittals, 24 plea bargains, and 9 cases withdrawn. All of these legal procedures were extremely costly.

Being anti-state in general and anti-Zionist in particular, at home the *Anarchistim* are widely considered disloyal to the national cause and thus as a political pariah.[116] Thus, having no positive public image within Israel to save, they have never refrained from seeking donations wherever possible and by whichever means possible, including through media channels known to be strongly anti-Israeli, such as *Indymedia* (e.g., http://barcelona.indymedia. org). The practical achievements of this ongoing struggle were mostly nominal, although in some places the route of the wall was changed by court order. The wall has, however, become a solid fact. Apparently, this relative failure of the anti-Wall activists' struggle, and the relative success of the state in constructing the separation barrier resulted from the fact that the conflict has become, for both sides, not only a conflict about a barrier and its route but a struggle over sovereignty and national identity (Ben Eliezer and Feinstein 2007).

In sharp contrast to AATW, which is a classic example of a revolutionary social movement, the next peace endeavor to appear was the "respectable" *Yozmat Geneva* (The Geneva Initiative). *Yozmat Geneva* was of a hybrid nature – formally a grassroots endeavor but in practice with a highly elitist composition and with strong connections to the political as well as to the military establishments. To start with, its leader, Yossi Beilin, was (and still is) a parliamentarian and an ex-minister, and so were at least 7 of its 34 Israeli originators. Several others were former MKs and former ministers. The other members of the original *Yozma* group manifested similar mainstream characteristics: they were high-ranking retired IDF commanders, successful businessmen, or intellectuals of the highest standing, all having access to top Israeli and international decision makers and dignitaries. In a way, the similarity between the original team of the Peres Center for Peace and that of *Yozmat Geneva* is striking (not less symbolic is the fact that both NGOs' offices are located in Tel Aviv, very close to IDF headquarters). Many of the founding members of the *Yozma* were

---

[116] In fact, one of their own leaflets was – apparently ironically – subtitled, "This Leaflet is Distributed by Israeli National Traitor Anarchists."

members of the Labour and the Meretz parties.[117] Another hybrid facet of the *Yozma* was its interface with the consensus.

Although strongly opposed by the political right and by many center-leaning Israelis, opposition that caused it to experience some rough times in terms of public standing, the *Yozma*, much like its core group members, was ideationally located deep within the Zionist perimeter. *Yozmat Geneva* therefore was strongly rejected by many Palestinians and by certain non-Zionist or anti-Zionist components of the Israeli peace movement. From the outset, *Yozmat Geneva* – unlike the *Mifkad haLeumi* – declared itself to be a joint Israeli-Palestinian endeavor. Its main aim was to fight the despair and hopelessness that prevailed in the early 2000s on both sides. Its founders intended to do so by proving that although the Oslo peace talks had stopped and achieved no mutually acceptable solution to the conflict, it was in fact possible to put forward what they referred to as a model for an agreed-on peace treaty.[118] The entire endeavor was based on a highly detailed, carefully constructed, and relatively long (47-page) document, composed, like the *Hamifkad Haleumi*, by an Israeli team headed by Yossi Beilin and a Palestinian team headed by a key Palestinian political figure – Yasser Abd-Rabbo.[119] The establishment nature of the initiative was further sustained by the fact that several members of the negotiating teams had been involved in the past in formal Israeli-Palestinian rounds of negotiations; in particular, the Taba talks, which took place just before the 2001 elections. By defining their blueprint as a model, the *Yozmat Geneva* people aimed to indicate that it was not a final peace agreement document. In addition, they wished to clarify that they were not authorized negotiators on behalf of their nations, a critical point that was nonetheless raised against them immediately after the *Yozma* became public knowledge.

The basic document was overtly based on the Clinton parameters of 2000 (http://www.geneva-accord.org). The document outlined the final status agreement, touching on all central issues (although according to its critics, it was rather equivocal on some crucial issues, mainly the Palestinian refugees' right of return). The document related to the end of the conflict and the end of all claims; mutual recognition of the Israeli and Palestinian right to two separate states; a final agreed-on border; a comprehensive solution to the Palestinian refugee problem, under which refugees would be entitled to compensation for

[117] In 1996, the Meretz party, led at that time by Yossi Beilin, adopted the Geneva Initiative's document as its political platform in the Israeli-Palestinian context.

[118] Originally, the document was widely referred to as *Heskem Geneva* (The Geneva Accord), implying a formal document. Because of the extensive criticism of its initiators' lack of authority to sign any agreement on behalf of their collectives, since they were neither elected by the public nor appointed by the state's leaders, the title was changed to *Yozma* (Initiative), a more neutral term bearing no formal connotations. The slogan used by the Israeli *Yozmat Geneva* still says "Say Yes to the Agreement," however, with the explanation that it refers not necessarily to the Geneva initiative but to *any* peace agreement.

[119] Several observers in Israel (e.g., Avineri 2003) noted that although the Israeli team included nonofficial personnel and opposition politicians, the Palestinian team was, in fact, semiofficial.

their refugee status and for loss of property and would have the right to return to the State of Palestine or absorption within Israel only if Israel approves; large settlement blocks and most of the settlers annexed to Israel, as part of a 1:1 land swap; recognition of the Jewish neighborhoods in Jerusalem as the Israeli capital, including the Jewish neighborhoods in East Jerusalem, and recognition of the Arab neighborhoods of Jerusalem as the Palestinian capital; a demilitarized Palestinian state; a comprehensive and complete Palestinian commitment to fighting terrorism and incitement; and an international verification group to oversee implementation (http://www.geneva-accord.org).

The *Yozmat Geneva* campaign was launched on December 1, 2003, at a festive ceremony in Geneva. Sustained by strong and highly professional public relations machinery from its inception, the *Yozma* campaign received wide attention within and outside of Israel, significantly more than any other Israeli or Israeli-Palestinian peace endeavor to date, including the Ayalon-Nusseibeh campaign, which seemed to have established a record in this regard. In addition to the highly professional way in which the *Yozma* was built and marketed,[120] several other reasons for this exceptional local and international interest can be identified: first, unlike most former peace initiatives, which were mostly ignored by the political establishment, *Yozmat Geneva* was attacked by PM Sharon as "subversive" shortly before it was publicized[121] and therefore gained public attention from its inception. Second, as mentioned before, the high-profile composition of the initiative's core group, with none of its members suspected of being non- or anti-Zionist, politically naïve, or an extremist, invested the campaign with a highly respectable image. Third, the organizers worked tirelessly to gain the blessing of prominent world leaders – from Nelson Mandela to Bill Clinton and Kofi Annan. Their success in gaining open support from prominent international figures helped them not only to get the attention and support of international public opinion but also to raise their visibility and credentials at home. Fourth, owing to its extensive funding, public exposure to the Geneva document was also very wide – before the signing ceremony, millions of copies

---

[120] Still, the initiative was not flawless from this perspective: the length of the document was clearly an obstacle, because very few read it from cover to cover or even began to read the text because of its length. Furthermore, as one peace activist noted at a meeting of representatives of other peace groups with Yossi Beilin, a few hours before he left for the Initiative's inauguration ceremony: "My mother and her lady friends like the Initiative's ideas very much, but they have no clue what they are asked to do in order to express their solidarity with it. The *Mifkad Leumi* asked them to sign its document, what does the *Yozma* ask its supporters to do?" This question caught Beilin unprepared and his reply was ambivalent, something like, "We will have to think about it" (based on notes of the author who was present at the meeting).

[121] Sharon's argument was that not only should no negotiations have been held with the Palestinians at that specific time because of their support for terror but also that only authorized decision makers were legally allowed to negotiate with the Palestinians, and the Initiative's people were not in such a position. The fact that several MKs of the opposition were involved in the negotiations was taken as an even better basis for labeling the Initiative as "subversive." He also refused to allow the representatives of the Initiative into his residence when they came to present him with the signed document, based on this same argument, its being subversive.

had already been printed and mailed to every home in Israel.[122] Although most Israelis found the document itself far too long and complicated to read, they were aware of its existence and related to it in one way or another.[123]

Following the publication and dissemination of the document and the Initiative's inauguration ceremony, two parallel NGOs for the promotion of the endeavor were created – one Israeli and one Palestinian. Initially, public gatherings of different sizes and kinds were also organized. The truth of the matter, however, is that neither side invested efforts in really encouraging the development of a massive grassroots movement as a backbone for the initiative. This strategic decision can be attributed to the dismal experience of earlier similar peace initiatives in relying on large numbers.[124] Furthermore, as mentioned previously, the Israeli team was composed mainly of professionals – people with long experience in formal diplomatic and other negotiation channels. Although they invested significant resources in mobilizing public support, they seemed not to have been eager to bring nonprofessional people on board.

Even this limited mobilization effort was only partly successful, however; the Clinton plan enjoyed some success but never gained extensive public support in Israel. In mid-2002, only 35% of the Jewish public supported the entire Clinton "package," and 57% opposed it (Peace Index survey, May 2002).[125] Support decreased, however, when these parameters were brought under the *Yozmat Geneva* umbrella – only about 25% supported the initiative in October 2003 and about 30% a month later.[126] Lower support for the same items can probably be attributed to the problematic image of the *Yozma*.

The reactions of the media and political actors in Israel were extensive and mixed: some applauded the *Yozmat Geneva* as timely (e.g., Barnea 2003),[127] courageous and potentially effective. Others, mainly on the political right, de-legitimized it as an unauthorized, if not illegal, move by a civil society organization, which undermined the Israeli government's efforts to work effectively with the Palestinians. MK Shaul Yahalom of the religious, right-wing Mafdal party went so far as to maintain in October 2003 that participation in the *Yozma* amounted legally to treason, for which the penalty is death. Of the interviewees in that month's Peace Index survey, 13.5% agreed with this view, whereas a large majority – 77.5% – opposed it. In the same survey, however,

---

[122] On the Palestinian side, the document was not as widely disseminated: it was published in the newspapers, and reactions to it were mostly rather unenthusiastic.

[123] According to the November 2003 Peace Index survey, 86.5% of Israeli Jews had heard about the Geneva document, and 32% had expressed support for it.

[124] This neglect of the grassroots aspect was not well taken by veteran peace activists, who viewed it as a major defect of the *Yozma*, which they therefore thought was not representative (see, e.g., Amir 2004).

[125] It should be noted, however, that individual items in the Clinton plan enjoyed much higher public support throughout the years.

[126] E.g., Peace Index surveys, October and November 2003.

[127] Barnea, one of the most prominent journalists in Israel, defined the initiative as "Sharon's punishment for being enslaved in the 'there-is-no one-to-talk-to' misconception" (Barnea 2003).

61% said that such agreements lie outside the legitimate prerogative of citizens' initiatives such as Geneva, and only 31% considered this legitimate. MK Dr. Yuval Steinitz of the Likud characterized the initiative as "dangerous" and said that it served the interests of one person only – Palestinian leader Yassir Arafat.[128] Another prominent politician of the right, MK Prof. Uzi Landau, said, "This stupid initiative is bad for peace, bad for security and bad for the State of Israel. It serves only one party: the enemy. It lacks any formal standing, but it is eroding Israel's public position and gives the Palestinians a better starting point for additional demands, even better than that given them by Barak after Camp David" (Landau 2003). Others were perhaps milder in their opposition but still highly critical; it was often maintained even by Labour politicians that the Geneva Initiative negotiating team had given in to the Palestinians' demands on the most important issues, on which official Israeli negotiators at Camp David and Taba had refused to compromise (e.g., Angel 2003).

Another issue, which provoked extensive public disapproval, was the financing of *Yozmat Geneva*. Although some leading Israeli businessmen contributed generously, the fact that the initiative received vast financial support from external bodies that included the Swiss and the Japanese governments as well as the EU had a negative impact on its public image. *Yozmat Geneva* was portrayed by its opponents as a vehicle for the promotion of foreign interests and not necessarily Israeli ones:

How come no journalist checked where Yossi Beilin had three million shekel for producing and distributing the booklet to every household in Israel? . . . Indeed infiltration by foreign states, subversion and exerting influence over politicians are not new phenomena. History books are full of descriptions of politicians who were bought by foreign powers, but in our country, everything is permissible if it is 'for the sake of peace' (Leshem 2003).

The topic of financing was so central to public discourse at that time that the *Yozma* covered this issue in the FAQs section of its website:

Q: Where does the money for financing the Geneva Campaign headquarters come from?
A: The Geneva Campaign headquarters is operated by a non-profit company registered with the Companies Registrar. The company gets donations from individuals and institutions in Israel and other countries, and these are directed to various activities, naturally under the full supervision of lawyers and accountants. Every person or institution that believes in the need to promote peace between the Israel and the Palestinian people and in the need to give the two peoples new hope that reality can be changed can make a donation, as long as it is done legally (http://www.heskem.org.il).

---

[128] At a symposium on December 29, 2003, organized by the Tami Steinmetz Center for Peace Research, Tel Aviv University, http://likudnik.co.il.

The main target of criticism, however, was the refugee clause in the document, which – according to critics and contrary to the *Yozma* leaders' statements – accepted the Palestinians' claim to the right of return to Israel, not only in principle but also in practice. All of the critics pointed to U.N. Resolution 194, which is mentioned in the *Yozma* document as the point of departure for a just and attainable solution to the conflict and which states that refugees be allowed to return to their homes when the hostilities end (e.g., Avineri 2003). Shlomo Ben Ami, a well-known historian and former Labour MK and Foreign Minister, stated that although the Geneva document did not endorse the right of return, the clause was problematic: "The [Clinton] plan does not grant actual right of return, but the architects of the Geneva Initiative distorted the principles of the plan when they agreed to translate them into accepting a number of refugees equal to the average number that third countries agree to accept" (Ben Ami 2007).

Again, it appears that to relieve the concerns of its potential supporters, the *Yozma* clarified this in the FAQs section of its homepage:

The term 'right of return' does not appear at all in the accord. Also, there is no discussion of the question of how the refugee problem was created and only possible solutions that appear in President Clinton's model (see chapter 7, article 4) – refugees can remain in their present host countries and get financial compensation, return to the State of Palestine or relocate to third countries that will take part in the rehabilitation efforts. Israel, together with other third countries, will take part in the refugee rehabilitation endeavor. It was clearly stated in the accord that only Israel will decide upon the number and the identity of the refugees who will be allowed to enter its territory, and will take into consideration for this purpose the number of refugees that other countries will be ready to absorb. Another article states that this suggested solution will replace the US resolution on this matter and that after the agreement is signed, the sides to it will have no further claims (http://www.heskem.org.il).

The moderate Zionist peace camp basically supported the *Yozma*, although *Shalom Achshav*, for example, never joined it in the organization of any public event and, in its publications and statements, always put Geneva on an equal footing with the Ayalon-Nusseibeh document, leaving its supporters to decide which document they preferred. The radical peace camp was split in its reactions. Although some of its central activists were cautiously positive about its bilateral element, which again positioned the Palestinians as suitable partners for peace talks particularly later, against the background of Sharon's declaration of his plan for unilateral disengagement from Gaza (e.g., Peter 2004), others fiercely opposed it:

If the State of Israel and the Palestinian Authority reach a "peace" agreement, it will not result from an Israeli wish for "security" for its citizens and a Palestinian wish for "independence." It will be – more than anything else – a part of the configuration of the international powers' interests as such concepts are alien to their way of thinking. The Geneva Accords, initiated by politicians and businessmen, if signed and applied as intended (two different things), will be the expression of these interests, as will any other political agreement one can imagine (http://www.fdca.it/wall/media/anarwall_EN.pdf, 64).

Another criticism of the Geneva Initiative put forward by the radical left was that the *Yozma* document did not and could not in any way reflect the real aspirations of the Palestinian people, although perhaps its Palestinian signers could live with it (e.g., Dreznin 2004). The critics defined it as misleading because it went much too far in giving in to Israeli-Jewish demands – a mirror image of the argument by mainstream critics of the initiative! For example, the radical left said that the document acknowledged the basic postulate of the Zionist creed – the right of the Jewish people to a state in Israel/Palestine, a notion that has always been rejected by the Palestinian liberation movement. The main criticism by the radical peace camp was of what they considered relinquishing the refugees' actual right of return (e.g., Amir 2004).

Was *Yozmat Geneva* a success or did it fail? In terms of visibility and viability, it seems to have been a success story, particularly considering the overall contracted POS that the peace movement faced in the early 2000s. Its representatives are often interviewed in the media on developments in Israeli-Palestinian diplomatic relations or when a new peace proposal is put forward; its offices are active (and run by paid staff); it is well known and highly respected abroad; and it conducts many joint activities with Palestinians as well as conferences and workshops for the Israeli public. At the same time, *Yozmat Geneva* was never adopted as a platform by any party except, in certain respects, Meretz; it did not grow into a vast grassroots movement; and it was never incorporated into national policy regarding the conflict and its resolution. Public opinion about it did not improve much. Nevertheless, by its very existence, *Yozmat Geneva* apparently set in motion – unintentionally – the adoption of the unilateral logic that nourished the unilateral disengagement plan.

On December 18, 2003, shortly after *Yozmat Geneva* was announced and some – particularly but not exclusively on the left – argue, precisely because of that,[129] Ariel Sharon, in the prime minister's traditional speech delivered at the annual Herzliya Conference,[130] proposed his unexpected Gaza Disengagement

---

[129] Surprisingly, the linkage between Geneva and the unilateral withdrawal was established by Sharon's closest aide, attorney Dov Weisglass. It was made in a press interview given in October 2004, at which Weisglass actually said that it was the growing visibility and support for *Yozmat Geneva* that had driven Sharon to launch his disengagement plan (Shavit 2004). Weisglass' comment was circulated and extensively publicized by the peace camp in general, and by Geneva supporters in particular (http://www.nrg.co.il). Still, it is unclear to what extent this was more than a slip of the tongue or an off-the-cuff remark. The critics maintain that such a strategic move, with the costs it entailed in terms of Sharon's popularity among the political right, was enormous and that it therefore seems quite unlikely that he would have opted for it only to pull the rug out from under the Geneva campaign.

[130] The Herzliya conference is an annual event organized by the Institute for Policy and Strategy (IPS) of the Interdisciplinary Center (IDC). For more information on the conferences, see http://www.herzliyaconference.org/Eng/.

plan.[131] In his speech, he cited four reasons for the disengagement: security, economics, political considerations (i.e., Israel's international relations), and demography (Israel's need to rid itself of the highly populated Palestinian Gaza Strip). Contrary to the bilateral rationale of the Oslo process, this plan was based on unilateral logic that made any dialogue with the Palestinians redundant. In practice, the plan included pulling IDF forces out of Gaza and certain areas in North Samaria, and the evacuation of all Jewish settlements and settlers (approximately 8,000 people) from these areas. The implementation of the plan was set for summer 2005, long enough to prepare for it properly but also remote enough for the opposition to organize against it. The main opposition expected was naturally from the settlers and their supporters. Never before, in the context of the Olso process, had settlements been removed, not in its heyday in the early-mid 1990s, not even after the traumatic February 1994 massacre of Palestinian worshippers by a Jewish settler at the Tomb of the Fathers in Hebron (which many in Israel considered a golden opportunity to remove the extremist settlers from the heart of the town where they had caused numerous problems for the Palestinian residents of the area).

The right-wing opposition to Sharon's plan was extremely intense; in fact, it was the largest,[132] most diversified (including demonstrations, petitions, passive resistance, burning tires, etc.), and the most prolonged (almost a year long) grassroots campaign in Israel's history. Although the protestors were concerned about the upcoming evacuation, they were much more alarmed that this limited evacuation could serve as a precedent for extensive future evacuations on the West Bank. They were even more shocked because they viewed Sharon as their patron: he was known as the founding father of the settlement project. Those who opposed the plan on a security basis were taken aback, because Sharon had previously been highly reluctant to make any concessions to the Palestinians until they proved their resolution to fight terrorism against Israel and Israelis. Now he was giving up lands with no Palestinian concessions whatsoever. Sharon's announcement came as a shock not only to his voters at home but also to many Jews in the Diaspora:

Apparently, the disengagement plan caught the Jews [in the Diaspora – TH] unprepared. They read in the newspapers about his intention to leave Gaza and were particularly shocked at his intention also to evacuate the settlers. For years, they heard a completely

---

[131] "The term *disengagement* was thought up by a clever PR man. It was meant to create a false image in the mind of the Israeli public, which was fed up with Gaza, as if the evacuation of the soldiers and the settlers would enable us to turn our backs on the Strip and its Palestinian residents and rid ourselves of the violence and the demands they put forth" (Ben Yishai 2007).

[132] Shortly before the implementation of the disengagement plan and the evacuation of the settlements by the IDF, in mid-July 2005, the right wing, orange opposition organized a massive protest at Kfar Maymon, on the Israeli side of the border with the Gaza Strip. At the rally, which lasted three days, tens of thousands of protestors of various ages, places of residence, income, ethnic origin, gender, education, and party affiliation took part. Despite the prevalent expectation that the protest would turn violent, it did not, and after some very tense hours, the protestors obeyed the security forces and returned home.

different tone from official Israeli bodies, and they always adopted the Israeli position as if were the word of God.

It so happened, that Sharon changed but the Jews did not. The person who elevated the settlements to near sanctity and managed to persuade them that Israel could not exist without the settlements, that Tel Aviv would not survive without Netzarim.... Now they are called upon to completely change their views, and they don't know what to think (Ben Simon 2004).

Public opinion at home on this move was indeed split, but not down the middle – despite the massive protest, at all times support for the disengagement was significantly higher than opposition to it. The unilateral aspect was particularly popular among Israeli Jews who had become completely disillusioned with the Palestinians as partners for a peace dialogue because of the apparent failure of the Oslo process and the bloodshed of the *intifada*. They were also very much influenced by the leaders and the media. In December 2003, shortly after Sharon's speech, 59% of a random national sample of Jewish Israelis were in favor of an immediate unilateral disengagement, whereas only 29% preferred to wait for the opportunity to reach an agreement with the Palestinians (the remainder had no clear opinion; Peace Index survey, December 2003). Between Sharon's announcement in December 2003 and the implementation of the disengagement in August 2005, at which time the support for the plan stood at 57% (Peace Index survey, July 2005), public attitude toward it fluctuated – ranging from a peak of 68% in June 2004 to a low point of 54% in June 2005. At no point was support lower than or equal to the opposition, however. According to all of the studies performed at the time (and according to common wisdom), location on the left-right continuum was closely linked to one's views on the disengagement plan. A similar correlation could be found between one's self-definition on the secular-religious scale and one's views on the disengagement plan.[133] Most Jewish Israelis at the center and left of center, who defined themselves as being secular, favored the plan, whereas almost all of those located on the right side of the political spectrum, and defining themselves as ultra-Orthodox and Orthodox, strongly opposed the move.

Public support for the disengagement plan was mainly rooted in the Israelis' growing unwillingness to pay the mounting cost of Israel's presence in Gaza in terms of human lives, mainly of Israeli soldiers (55%), and much less so (22%) in a desire to end the occupation (Peace Index survey, December 2003). Opponents of the plan explained their position first by their concern that the Palestinians would interpret the unilateral withdrawal as the outcome of their armed struggle – that is, that Israel ran away under fire, the way the Israeli withdrawal from South Lebanon in 2000 was interpreted by Hezbollah and others. The second reason given by those who opposed the disengagement was that the withdrawal would encourage more Palestinian terrorism against Israel, and the third reason was that the move was strategically dangerous, that is, it would reflect on Israel's regional positioning. Only a tiny minority (11%)

---

[133] Support for the plan in the Arab sector was extremely high – over 85% – at all times.

attributed their opposition to the fact that it could be a precedent to a massive withdrawal on the West Bank, and even fewer raised the Greater Israel motif as their main reason (ibid).

The support for the pullout from Gaza also rested upon the growing awareness in Israel of the ugly facets of the occupation. This was reflected in the vast media coverage of a new group of former soldiers, *Shovrim Shtika* (Breaking the Silence), which emerged in 2004 and exposed atrocities against the Palestinian population in which they took part when on active service. They testified verbally and showed pictures that they had taken of instances in which they had humiliated, beaten, detained, and terrified Palestinians for no real security reason. These testimonies, as well as the readiness of simple soldiers with no political agenda, and certainly not a peace agenda, to come forward openly and repent for what they had done, shocked the Israeli public. The customary public refusal to listen to the peace groups' descriptions and to evidence of army brutality was now severely reduced, because the stories told by these former soldiers could not be attributed to disloyalty to the nation or to their acting in the service of "others." The fury with which the army reacted added credibility to these testimonies, which indeed achieved their aim – the silence was broken.[134]

By and large, the Zionist left and the moderate peace groups, despite their long-term dislike of Sharon himself, supported the disengagement plan from its inception to its implementation. Indeed, they never organized any pro-disengagement rallies, but their position was clear from various media interviews and articles and from the silence in the streets – no protest against it was organized nor were advertisements placed in newspapers or elsewhere. There were different reasons for this support – many former supporters of the peace agenda had now become disillusioned with the chances of conducting a fruitful dialogue with the Palestinians and therefore adopted the unilateral reasoning. Others viewed the evacuation of the settlements in Gaza and northern Samaria as a first step toward ending the occupation and to a much larger settlement evacuation on the West Bank. The moral justification for removing the Gaza settlements and settlers – which all of the sections and groups of the peace movement had always considered evil because of the inhuman treatment of

---

[134] Of interest here is another peace initiative of a different kind that entailed no protest aspect, launched in September 2004 – a joint Israeli-Palestinian radio station (initially web operated but later a regular radio channel, 107.2 FM) called *Radio Kol Hashalom l'Lo Gvulot* (Radio All for Peace without Borders). The Hebrew name of the station was a tribute to the legendary Voice of Peace radio station, which in the 1970s was one of the very few pro-peace voices in the Middle East. Operated by a joint team of young Israelis and Palestinians, All for Peace can be heard in Israel and the Palestinian territories. The trilingual (Arabic, Hebrew, and English) program focuses on matters related to the conflict and ways for its resolution as well as news programs, Western and Middle Eastern music, and programs for youth. The station is located in East Jerusalem and, although its sponsors are local (the Israeli *Givat Haviva* Jewish-Arab Center and the *Palestinian Biladi-Jerusalem Times*), its activities are financed by external bodies, among others, the Rich Foundation, the EU, and the United States Institute of Peace (http://www.allforpeace.org).

their Palestinian neighbors – was also highlighted (e.g., Sarid 2005). In a rather representative way, a central activist of *Shalom Achshav* stated the logic of supporting the disengagement:

There is no doubt that from the diplomatic and the security points of view, the Disengagement plan is full of pitfalls, most of which are still repairable.... At the same time, the central significance of the Disengagement plan is not diplomatic nor military. Its central significance is domestic, and its implementation will play a critical role in the shaping of the Israeli society as democratic, by following majority will as expressed in the decisions made by the government and the Knesset. This is a historical move, which will have a critical role in shaping Israeli society for many generations (Oppenheimer 2005).

Now that it seemed that the government was, in a way, serving the peace movement's logic – that the occupation of Gaza and the settlements there were a security and diplomatic liability rather than an asset for Israel – the peace camp had to redefine its own role and its positioning vis-à-vis the authorities, much as it had in the early 1990s. The most important task was to prepare a fierce campaign against Sharon if he tried to use his plan as leverage to deepen Israel's hold on the West Bank by intensifying settlement activities there, as well as by taking President Bush's "road map for peace" off the regional and international agenda (Etkes 2005). Others, however, were more concerned with the long-term consequences of supporting the plan in terms of the peace process at large and of the peace movement's viability if it joined forces, even if for only one historical moment, with a right wing government, as expressed by the coordinator of the *Shalom Achshav* student cell at the Hebrew University:

The left is governed today by a conspiracy of silence; it is not allowed to criticize the Disengagement plan.... This way, the left becomes a full partner in the blindness which Sharon is trying to inflict on the Israeli public. I have heard no criticism whatsoever by the Zionist left regarding the disengagement;... there is no discussion of the diplomatic freeze that will only deteriorate after the plan is implemented; no concern about strengthening the settlement project, as Sharon and Dov Weisglass said publicly; no fear of the continuation of military control over Gaza and northern Samaria; of suppressing 1.5 million Palestinians or the unavoidable strengthening of Hamas and the Islamic Jihad. The left has to criticize and warn, and even more important, put forward an alternative. It is unacceptable that the Geneva Initiative and the Road Map are no longer part of the vocabulary of the Zionist left wing parties and organizations since the day the Disengagement plan made the headlines. The left has to go back to the basic conceptions that it held during the last few decades and not surrender to dictates, such as the no partner conception created by unsuccessful leaders like Netanyahu, Barak and Sharon (Zinger 2004).

Indeed, there were certain politicians and activists in the moderate peace camp who were unhappy with the basic logic of Sharon's plan. They argued that not only would its implementation divide the nation but it would also destroy the bilateral rationale, as in fact it pushed the Palestinians out of the picture and diminished the prospects for 'normal' future peace talks and agreements: "The trauma of the disengagement from Gaza will indeed create a schism but will resolve nothing, if Israel does not rid itself of the prevalent discourse about 'fences', 'disengagement', and 'unilateralism'. As proven by its relations with Lebanon, Jordan and Egypt, Israel can achieve no better security than that offered by internationally acknowledged borders" (Ben Ami 2005).

In contrast to the silence of the moderate peace camp, the radical peace groups fiercely opposed the disengagement plan from day one. Their opposition was based on various grounds, with the common thread being ad hominem: that in no way should the left/peace camp support any plan by Sharon, because the man could not mean well. The first argument was that this move was basically meant to create a deep and unbridgeable split between the two parts of the Palestinian-controlled territories – the West Bank and the Gaza Strip, a classic "divide and conquer" strategy. It was predicted that this would lead to civil war between Palestinian political parties [as indeed occurred in 2006–2007 – TH]. Moreover, the division of the Palestinian territories would, in a way, legitimize the continuation of the Israeli occupation and settlement on the West Bank, because the Palestinians would already have a state in Gaza. This is a "war crime," argued some writers on the radical left, and therefore decent people should steer clear of the plan and its initiator (e.g., Bar'am 2004).[135]

Another argument of the radical left was that even after withdrawal from the Gaza Strip, Israel would not relinquish its control over the border area and access points – ground, air, and sea – thereby in fact maintaining its domination over the lives and well-being of residents of Gaza. Gaza, they foresaw, would turn into one big prison, in which the local population would starve, become violent because of distress, and be exposed to various human rights violations (http://www.hagada.org.il). Sharon's cynicism, it was also argued, was beyond imagination: once out of Gaza, Israel under his leadership would refuse to take any responsibility for what would happen there, although in fact it would be responsible for developments there, by allowing or not allowing people and goods into and out of the Strip. The sole purpose of the planned disengagement was to perpetuate the occupation and not to disengage from the territories but from a future dialogue with the Palestinian leadership (Gojanski 2003). Instead of referring to the plan by its formal name – the disengagement plan – some radicals therefore gave it an ironic alternative name – the Stay Put Plan (in Hebrew, *Tochnit haHishaarut*; e.g., Gat 2005).

---

[135] Later, in the light of the anti-disengagement protest of the right, Bar'am changed his position somewhat and maintained that despite his negative views past and present on Sharon, the left should side with him and with Labour to block the settlers and their allies. The historical analogy he used, apparently to justify this change of mind, was Spain during the civil war: "In order to stop Fascism, the local left tried to join forces with the liberals and the social-democrats which were ready to support the republic despite their anti-revolutionary positions. When the left deserted this course,... the internal balance of the anti-Fascist alignment was destroyed" (Bar'am 2005).

Following the interview with Dov Weisglass (see note 129), Uri Avneri of *Gush Shalom* analyzed what he considered to be Sharon's motivation for launching the plan:

Things are crystal clear: the 'Disengagement plan' is meant to freeze the peace process for decades...to take the Palestinian state idea off the table forever. A dozen small settlements will be dismantled in order to leave almost all settlers on the West Bank intact. Israel will 'relinquish' the Gaza Strip, which covers 1.3% of the land, in order to finally take over the West Bank, which is 16 times as large. The Gaza Strip will be disconnected from the world on the ground, the sea and the air, and so will the 7–8 Palestinian enclaves which will be created on the West Bank. Why then did 'Dubbi' [Weisglass – TH] expose this plan – after all, this means spitting in the face of the Labour Party – exactly when Sharon is in need of its support? The answer is simple: Sharon wants to win the right, and could not care less for the left (Avneri 2004).

As in similar past situations, it was the moderates who were most fiercely criticized by the radicals: "The Israeli left decided to commit suicide. It is no longer committed to its members. It is only committed to Sharon" (Reinhart 2005). Other commentators taking the same position were more detailed but no less derisive:

In fostering the illusion that the disengagement plan is a first step towards the ending of the occupation, the left today is supporting a plot which is only meant to deepen [Israel's – TH] foothold on the West Bank.... The left argues that, as such, it could never oppose the evacuation of settlements and that the disengagement sets a precedent. This suggests that Sharon is actually implementing the left's programme, but is this really the case? It becomes clearer and clearer that after phase A of the disengagement, in which the settlers will be evacuated from the Gaza Strip, which will then turn into a ghetto surrounded by Israeli battalions, Sharon will turn to phase B: the annexation of large parts of the West Bank.... The left has adopted an equivocal position: on one hand, opposition to the occupation and on the other hand, support for the disengagement. A paradox! This is because the disengagement sustains the occupation; it doesn't weaken it.... The refuseniks and the peace activists should differentiate between their persistent and just struggle against the occupation, against the Wall, against the checkpoints, and their support for Sharon. The disengagement is a major political move in Israel's occupation policy, not a move that opens the door to peace (Nader 2005).

Others took this opportunity to accuse the moderate peace activists of not fighting strongly enough against the settlers and their settlement project and of waking up only when almost everyone else in Israel was condemning the settlers' anti-disengagement protest:

Good morning to the Israeli left! After what seems to be eternal hibernation, it is starting to make some sounds of awakening. Only when the wind blows in its direction, and not by itself, does the extra-parliamentary left dare to come out of the closet in which it has been hiding for more than four years. One should perhaps welcome these signs of awakening, but it is impossible not to hold it accountable for its disgraceful silence, ongoing cowardice and leaving the street to the mercy of the right and the settlers.... The soft voices made by the Zionist peace camp cannot absolve it of its responsibility: its silence made it a collaborator with whatever the government has been doing all these damned years.... Now, under the auspices of a Prime Minister of the right, the left is suddenly reminded that it also has something to say, but a weak, pale echo of Sharon's words (Levy 2005).

Certain radical left critics even called on refuseniks, who were not ready to serve in the territories because of their anti-occupation positions, to refuse to take part now in the evacuation of the settlements in the Gaza Strip:

While the entire country is shivering with fear at the threat of massive refusal by the people on the right, the voice of the left, is, as usual, unheard.... What will the refuseniks of the left do when they are called upon? Will they joyfully join the battalions that will surround *Neve D'kalim* [one of the Jewish settlements in Gaza to be evacuated – TH] or will they stick to their refusal? On the face of it, there is no question here whatsoever. It is obvious and expected that the refuseniks of the left will celebrate this day, and take part in the evacuation effort.... obvious, expected, and yet, automatic. Totally wrong, though. Every person of the left in his right mind should – immediately, urgently and with no excuses – disengage from the disengagement.... The reason why the refuseniks of the left should continue to refuse to serve in the territories – not even in the context of the evacuation of *Katif* [another Jewish settlement area in the Gaza Strip – TH] – is that cooperation with any military move in the territories pulls the rug from under the feet of the political aims of the left.... No, one should not lend a hand to a plan that will permanently bury the chance for peace.... The Gush Katif settlers are preparing a 'mini civil war' so that the lesson will be clear to everyone – if this is what happens when trying to evacuate 8,000 settlers in the Strip, the evacuation of a quarter of a million settlers from the West Bank is totally unthinkable (Landau 2005).

The successful and rapid implementation of the disengagement plan with no bloodshed, especially in view of the prevalent fear of massive, violent resistance by the settlers and their supporters,[136] further boosted Sharon's image as a resolute and trustworthy leader in the eyes of the Israeli and the international public. The fact that he promised to evacuate the settlements and kept his word indeed cost him the support of the right, but won him the admiration of many in the center and even on the left. His conduct was so highly appreciated that even some hard-core leftists changed their views of him. Haim Hanegbi, of the very radical left, wrote an article just before the 2006 elections in which, to the great shock of his co-leftists, he stated that he was going to vote for Sharon in the upcoming election (in which, because he fell ill, Sharon was not a candidate)

Perhaps now, as he reaches 80, grandpa Ariel finally understands how hopeless the never ending war against the Palestinians is, a war he has been conducting all his life, as they, the sons of this land, will stick to it until the bitter end ... and perhaps this knowledge stimulated Sharon to uproot ten settlements all at once: the courage he manifested in public promises much good for the Israelis, and also for the Palestinians. Is there anyone else in the old parties – Labour and Likud – who has such courage? (Hanegbi 2005).

---

[136] In the Peace Index survey of July 2005, which was conducted only days before the implementation of the disengagement plan, over one-third (35.8%) of the respondents expected that it would involve serious bloodshed and violence.

Obviously, this reversal by Hanegbi did not reflect the left's general state of mind and was very negatively viewed by others in this camp (e.g., Bar'am 2005). Still, this turnabout reflected the confusion, disorientation, and internal disintegration of the peace camp in the face of the dead end that it had reached. Its efforts to influence the course of events and maintain its presence as a coherent and relevant voice in the political discourse on national security matters had stalled. Since then and to the time of this writing, the peace movement can be described as being in deep hibernation or in a coma.

The unexpectedly quick and relatively nonviolent implementation of the disengagement plan in August 2005 marked a significant change in the opportunities structure for Israeli extraparliamentary activism. The failure of the largest-ever grassroots campaign ("Orange") to prevent Israel's military pull-out from the Gaza Strip as well as the evacuation of all settlements and settlers from this area (Meir and Rahav Meir 2006) signaled to all extraparliamentary groups, organizations, and activists, right and left, that they could not effectively challenge the decisions of a resolute government, particularly one that enjoyed the support of the majority of the public. Furthermore, against the background of the enormous resources that were invested in the implementation of the disengagement process, everyone in Israel came to realize that the state was much stronger than any grassroots movement, not merely a counter-movement, as many activists would like to think or as certain social movements theoreticians argue (e.g., Hoover and Kowalewski 1992). This realization, in its turn, eroded the motivation of peace and other social activists to launch new campaigns in protest of government policies and decisions. The best proof of this changed POS came a year later, in summer 2006, with the apparent inability of the anti-Second Lebanon War movement to take off (see Hermann forthcoming, 2009a).

The Second Lebanon War was launched by Israel on July 12, 2006, hours after Lebanese Hezbollah militants snatched two Israeli soldiers and killed three others in a cross-border attack. The declared aims of the war were: the release of the two soldiers, a full cease-fire along the border with Lebanon, the deployment of the Lebanese army in South Lebanon, and the removal of Hezbollah's units and artillery from South Lebanon. Israeli Jewish[137] public opinion was strongly supportive of this strategic move by the government.[138] In fact, throughout the 33 days of fighting, a solid majority of approximately

---

[137] Despite the nineteen Arab casualties and the significant damage caused by Hezbollah's missiles and rockets on several Arab towns and villages in the north of Israel, many among the Israeli-Arab population apparently held, if not pro-Hezbollah, then anti-Israeli sentiments (see, e.g., Kashua 2006). These opinions were uttered only behind closed doors, because their public expression might have further aggravated the already tense relations with the Jewish majority (see e.g., Al Jazzeera 2006).

[138] For daily measurements of the public sentiments and attitudes toward the ongoing war, see Shavit, Yaar, Hermann, and Adler 2006.

90% justified the launching of the war.[139] Even when the first reservations about the government's conduct of the operation began to be made in public in mid-August 2006, the level of support for the government remained at about 75%. At that time, the level of the public's optimism about Israel's ability to achieve the war's aims was somewhat lower, about 50%, still quite impressive under the circumstances (see Shavit, Yaar, Hermann, and Adler 2006).

This massive public support for the government's decision to launch the war indicated a comprehensive national consensus, against which the few peace activists who differed and opposed the war did not have much chance of mobilizing a large enough number of citizens to start a significant antiwar protest campaign. Beyond the public opinion impediment, which made visible protest acts rather unfeasible, organizing a massive antiwar protest was not a strategically rational option either during the fighting. While the entire northern part of Israel was being heavily bombarded by Hezbollah's artillery (forty-four civilians were killed), such a protest would have been widely considered as unpatriotic and apparently would have further eroded the peace movement's public standing.

Several antiwar demonstrations and rallies were organized here and there, mostly by the Israeli Arab parties and organizations joined by the more radical peace groups. The first demonstration took place in Tel Aviv as early as July 16, 2006, only 4 days after the war began. According to the organizers' report, approximately 300 people, mostly Israeli Arabs but also a few Jews, attended the rally (according to the police report, attendance was much smaller). The second antiwar demonstration took place on July 22 and was attended by 3,000 to 4,000 people, again with minor participation of Israeli Jews, a fact that, against the background of the specific Israeli political scene, clearly undermined the political relevance of this act. It seems that the demonstrators had gathered at these two events not only to signal their opposition to the war but also in the hope that the war would revive the peace movement in general; however, this did not happen. No significant pro-peace or antiwar grassroots activity has developed, and the movement at large remains comatose. It did not recover even when well-known authors Amoz Oz, A. B. Yehoshua, and David Grossman, who had sided with the government at the beginning of the war, issued a public statement on August 10, 2006, in which they urged the government not to launch a massive ground operation in Lebanon and to do its best to end the war as soon as possible (Yudilevitch 2006).[140]

---

[139] One year later, in July 2007, when the criticism of the government's performance during the war was already widespread and intense, a majority of 57% (as opposed to 39% who disagreed) of the Jewish public justified in retrospect the decision to launch the war in 2006 (see, Peace Index survey, July 2007).

[140] Tragically, two days after the three authors issued this statement, David Grossman's son, Uri, was killed in Lebanon during the ground operation launched on August 12, 2006.

Quite unexpectedly, the peace movement did not awaken even when the soldiers' protest movement, which eventually failed, seemed to be gaining momentum after the war. The main reason that many former peace activists, who had taken part in soldiers' protests in 1973 and/or in the antiwar activities in 1982, did not join forces with the new soldiers' protest campaign was not support of the Second Lebanon War or appreciation of the top leaders of the state who launched it, but the fact that, from their point of view, the campaign was politically incorrect. It seemed to enjoy the support of the Orange anti-disengagement, right-wing political camp. For example, Yariv Oppenheimer, then director general of the largest peace movement, *Shalom Achshav*, explained in several media articles (e.g., Oppenheimer 2006) and interviews that this soldiers' protest should not be supported because it was not authentic and honest but a means for the Israeli political right, in particular for Netanyahu, to topple the Kadima-Labour–headed coalition government of Ehud Olmert:

This is not a green, but an orange protest. It is the protest of right-wingers who are trying to instigate a political revolt. Were they authentically just protest-oriented, they would not be so much after the heads of the Prime Minister, the Defense Minister and the IDF Chief of Staff, but would have called for a formal inquiry commission. Meanwhile, Netanyahu sits quietly by while they are doing his job (in Bengal 2006).

Oppenheimer's negative political framing of the the post-Second Lebanon War soldiers' protest invited much criticism against him and his movement. Some of the reactions were very crude and brutal,[141] whereas others were more sophisticated, although not less unkind:

Shalom Achshav under Oppenheimer's leadership turned from a distinguished movement into one infected with the same disease that the public detects these days in the upper echelons of our political establishment: political parochialism, a narrow focus of interest, cynicism and detachment from the general good and the state's well being (Lebel 2006).

The cold shoulder turned toward the soldiers' protest campaign was not unique to either Oppenheimer or *Shalom Achshav*; the more radical peace groups and activists did not cooperate with this campaign either. Their resentment was also based on the political "color" of the campaign, which they disliked, but even more so on the campaigners' open support for military service. The fact that the protesting soldiers criticized the decision-making process prior to and during the war, but not the very use of military force as a means for dealing with regional problems and actors disqualified them as even ad-hoc allies in the eyes of the more radical members of the peace camp:

The arguments of the protestors focus on two issues only, because their perspective is as narrow as that of a simple soldier in the reserves: IDF unpreparedness for the war

---

[141] See, e.g., http://www.shalomnow.com, or http://www.omedia.co.il

and its premature termination. However, the first issue is the individual fault of many of them, and the second is an unworthy cause. There are much heavier questions: why did we launch this war in the first place?, how could it have been prevented?, why is war the one and only language that we talk?, what are the limits of the use of the force that we are allowed to use? and where are we heading now? These questions are not addressed at all by the new movement (Levy 2006).

The detachment from the protesting soldiers by the peace movement at large might have helped it to maintain its political creed but at the same time contributed to its already prevalent external (and perhaps even internal) image as politically passé. Its political irrelevance became even more visible to many in Israel when a year later a new peace initiative – the Annapolis Plan – was placed on the table by the American administration. In November 2007, the American administration made another effort to revive the Middle East peace talks by convening an international (35-state) conference at the U.S. Naval Academy in Annapolis, Maryland. The event opened with a joint Israeli-Palestinian understanding document, read by the host, U.S. President George W. Bush. The document, authorized by the government on the Israeli side, was not supported on the Palestinian side by the Hamas-led government but only by President Abu Mazen of the losing Fatah party. It began

We express our determination to bring an end to bloodshed, suffering and decades of conflict between our peoples, to usher in a new era of peace, based on freedom, security, justice, dignity, respect and mutual recognition, to propagate a culture of peace and non-violence, and to confront terrorism and incitement, whether committed by Palestinians or Israelis (http://www.mfa.gov.il).

The declared target of this extensive diplomatic move, apparently a last effort by President Bush at the end of his second term in office to leave behind some legacy of peace, was to launch the peace talks in December 2007 and reach a permanent peace agreement by the end of 2008. This seemed a rather unfeasible aim at the time it was proffered, since all Islamist Arab states and movements, including Hamas, strongly opposed the conference and the new peace effort. In Israel, too, the level of support and optimism was not impressive: the parties and movements of the Israeli political right rejected the initiative, and the public was at best indifferent, if not skeptical.[142]

As to the peace movement, once again it was split between the more radical groups that opposed the Annapolis Plan as not being well enough prepared to be a suitable point of departure for a successful peace process, and for reiterating the two-state formula as its baseline, which they opposed. These

---

[142] In the Peace Index surveys of October and November 2007, about 75% of the respondents said that they did not follow the preparations for the conference nor the reports about it when it took place. In November, after the conference was over, about two-thirds said that it had failed to explore the basic conflict of interests between Israel and the Palestinians, and 62% estimated that it also failed to promote peace between the two sides.

critics envisaged a failure even before the conference began and warned that the repercussions of another failure would be devastating:

It is almost guaranteed that what happened after the Camp David conference in 2000 will happen again this time, e.g., that a third *intifada*, the shape and extent of which it is difficult to predict, will break out. One of its results, however, will surely be the total collapse of the Palestinian Authority and the take-over of all Palestinian territories by Hamas (Avneri 2007).

Other activists and groups opposed the Annapolis Plan because of its host, President Bush, whom they considered a hopeless warmonger and held to be guilty of the Iraq war and its aftermath:

Peace is a highly cherished value for us, and therefore we unconditionally welcome any negotiations between Israel's representatives and representatives of the Palestinians and the Arab states. The problem, in our opinion, is, however, that Annapolis is not at all a peace conference. Rather, its main aim is to create an alignment of forces that will support the aggressive American polices in the region. Bush, who is irresponsibly threatening us with a third world war and who has forbade Israel in the last two years to negotiate peace with Syria, will never be the one to bring us peace. On the contrary, he is preparing the ground for further military steps by himself or his regional allies (Daud and Tan'ami 2007).

The more radical peace activists aimed their criticism at Israeli Prime Minister Olmert. They argued that his real yet hidden motivation for going to Annapolis was not to bring peace but to maintain his feeble government at any cost.[143] As one person in the audience of a public symposium organized by *Gush Shalom* on November 21, 2007, put it a few days before the Annapolis conference:

It is absolutely clear that Olmert is only interested in his government's survival. After Annapolis, we [Israel – TH] will conduct the negotiations slowly in order not to jeopardize the coalition, and then, when the designated election date gets closer, Olmert will accelerate the pace because then he will be in need of an agenda that includes peace (http://zope.gush-shalom.org).

Although the general tone in these small and radical political circles was indeed negative, not everyone was as pessimistic and antagonistic, as suggested by the following statement by Haim Bar'am:

We saw in *Ha'aretz* the full list of conference participants. It was embellished with the flags of all these states and if nothing else, perhaps at least, in a way, it educated the "thoughtful people" who read this newspaper. Hundreds of millions of Muslims were represented at Annapolis by their governments. So the Israelis, who were indoctrinated for years and years to think about every Muslim as a half crazy fundamentalist terrorist, learned now that, in fact, most Muslims want to achieve peace (Bar'am 2008).

---

[143] A majority (61%) of the Jewish respondents in the March 2008 Peace Index survey said that Olmert did not truly intend to reach a peace agreement by the end of 2008, the target date of the Annapolis Plan.

Members of the moderate Zionist peace groups were apparently also somewhat skeptical but largely more positive. They saw Annapolis as a rare, perhaps the last, window of opportunity, which if closed prematurely with no agreement, would bury their preferred two-state solution.[144] Thus in October 2007, when the conference was announced, *Shalom Achshav* and *Yozmat Geneva* launched a joint campaign, under the slogans, "Olmert – The Time Has Come to Choose," and "Say Yes to a Peace Agreement." To their target audience, they explained, "The Annapolis Conference holds great potential, representing a unique opportunity. Peace Now and the Geneva Initiative are launching this campaign to press the Government of Israel to turn this conference into the beginning of a significant negotiating process leading to the creation of a Palestinian state and the end of the Israeli-Palestinian conflict" (http://www.peacenow.org.il).

The campaign thus had a dual aim: to urge the government to join the Annapolis process as well as to prepare Israeli public opinion for the upcoming conference and the resumption of the peace talks, which if successful would be followed by the signing of a peace agreement and by extensive Israeli withdrawal from the West Bank. Aware of Israeli's prevalent disbelief in peace and in the Palestinian side following the collapse of the Oslo process, the supporters of Annapolis did not risk calling for large peace demonstrations, because low attendance would have politically backfired. Thus, while *Shalom Achshav* called for a pro-Annapolis rally on November 24, 2007, the designated location in Jerusalem – Paris Square, opposite the Prime Minister's Residence – could not host more than the few hundred demonstrators, who indeed showed up, but this situation did not leave much hope for future, larger events. Also several ads in support of the Annapolis process, signed by well-known academics, journalists, intellectuals, industrialists, show business celebrities, and other public figures, were placed in major Israeli newspapers to create pro-Annapolis hype. This did not happen, however, mostly because, for a variety of domestic, regional, and international reasons, the Annapolis Process did not take off, and the peace momentum was not regained. Still, the fact that the moderate peace groups went along with the Annapolis path and engaged with the highly unpopular Olmert was counterproductive in terms of their public image. They were accused of allegedly supporting a corrupt politician's plan to divert domestic and international attention from his wrongdoings by launching a doomed-to-fail peace process, of – as in the case of Sharon and his disengagement plan – being fooled by a basically right-wing politician who had no motivation to conclude a peace agreement, and of turning a blind eye to the interests of the Palestinians, for whom the Annapolis Plan was a dictate that they had to obey because of their weakness.

June 2007 witnessed many, mainly small, events organized by various Israel peace organizations (sometimes together with their Palestinian counterparts) to mark 40 years of occupation since the June 1967/Six Day War (e.g., Bowen

---

[144] For one blueprint for the Annapolis peace plan negotiations, see the Geneva Accord 2008.

2007). For example, on June 12, *Gush Shalom* organized a protest march in Tel Aviv under the slogan: "40 Years of Occupation! 40 Years of Despair!" with the participation of several dozen marchers (http://zope.gush-shalom.org). At this event, Nurit Peled-Elhanan spoke. Peled-Elhanan is laureate of the Sakharov Prize of the European Parliament for Human Rights and Freedom of Thought and a bereaved mother whose daughter was killed by a Palestinian act of terror. She is also the daughter of Mati Peled, a retired IDF General who became an academic and a peace activist. In her speech she said, among other things:

> For forty years now, racism and megalomania have dictated our lives. Forty years during which more than four million people do not know the meaning of freedom of movement. Forty years in which Palestinian children are born and raised as prisoners in their homes that the Occupation converted into a prison, deprived at the outset of all the rights that human beings are entitled to because they are human. Forty years during which Israeli children are educated in racism of the type that has been unknown in the civilized world for decades. Forty years during which they have learned to hate the neighbors just because they are neighbors, to fear them without knowing them, to see a quarter of the citizens of the State as a demographic danger and an enemy within, and to relate to the residents of the ghettos created by the policy of occupation as a problem that must be solved.... And this evening we must ask where we take our shame? How will we remove the disgrace? But first and foremost, how is it that the shame does not keep us from sleeping at night? How do we consent to have half our salaries used for the execution of crimes against humanity?... This evening we must appeal to the world for help in ridding ourselves of the shame. This evening we must explain to the world that if it wants to rescue the people of Israel and the Palestinian people from the imminent holocaust that threatens all of us it is necessary to condemn the policy of occupation, the dominion of death must be stopped in its tracks (http://www.kibush.co.il).

A photo exhibition focusing on 40 years of occupation of the city of Hebron in the West Bank was organized by an independent art school in Tel Aviv with the participation of Israeli Jewish, Arab, and Palestinian photographers, some of whom were also peace activists (http://www.archijob.co.il). In Hebron itself, *Shalom Achshav* organized an anti-occupation vigil with the participation of about 300 people. The IDF tried to prevent the vigil from taking place for "security reasons." The organizers appealed to the Supreme Court, which overturned the IDF prohibition. The numerous mainstream media discussions, articles, reports, and symposia on the prolonged occupation were almost all critical of Israel's mode of conduct in the territories. In a rather concerted fashion, exemplifying the marginality of the peace movement in Israeli public discourse today, the occupation is presented as perhaps an undesirable but, under the circumstances, unavoidable reality. Very few voices expressed the same kind of criticism that the various peace groups tried to disseminate, that it was Israel's fault that the occupation had not yet ended and that the settlements were allowed to flourish and become a huge obstacle to any peace agreement and a thorn in the side of the Palestinians.

The Path Strewn with Obstacles (1993–2008) 239

It is perhaps suitable to end this chapter with some observations and comments related to the peace movement and published in mid-2008, when *Shalom Achshav*, the epitome of the Israeli peace movement, celebrated its thirtieth anniversary. Very few of these were gratifying. The selected examples brought here represent the prevalent disposition outside and within the movement 15 years after the Oslo process appeared on the horizon and, for a short time, warmed the cold hearts of many Middle Easterners. The first observation is by Dr. Mordechai Kedar, a disillusioned peace activist, who focused on what he considered the two main fallacies of the peace movement at large: first, the movement constantly refers to "occupied territories," although in fact, according to his analysis, these territories legally belong to no one. The Gaza Strip had been occupied by Egypt, and the West Bank had been occupied by Jordan until the Six-Day War, and therefore this territory cannot be termed as "occupied."[145] Second, the movement's agenda placed the concept of the "Palestinian People" in the center, whereas, according to Kedar, history and the present reality tell us that there is no such people. These two false concepts, he argued, not only damaged the movement's political chances but also distorted the national discourse and opened the door to unfeasible and unjustified peaceful solutions to the conflict. Kedar went on to "expose" the linguistic and factual/historical ignorance of most peace activists, who, he argued, not only do not read or speak Arabic but also totally misread the Arabs' real intentions. Furthermore, the peace activists see only the darker sides of the Jewish settlers and of the Israeli right-wingers, while always highlighting the bright side of the Arabs. Finally, Kedar argued that peace activism is highly beneficial financially and accused the activists of living on generous donations from foreign anti-Israeli organizations (Kedar 2008).

A completely different, but in a way no less gloomy "birthday greeting" came from Hedva Isachar, a feminist peace activist, who attended the rather fancy (and probably costly) thirtieth anniversary rally:

The event came with the slogan "30 years leading to peace." So heartrending, so naïve. To what peace have we led? and what exactly are we celebrating here tonight? Are we gathered here to honor the long empty "Peace"? or to pay tribute to the typically Israeli "Now," – confrontational, demanding immediate satisfaction – a "Now" that has lasted more than half of the state's lifespan until it lost its flexibility? Can we justify being smug only because of the "miracle" of the movement's survival? Because it is a peace brand name, famous worldwide, which is able to attract frequent donors? Because of nostalgia for the 1980s? (Isachar 2008).

---

[145] In the Peace Index survey of March 2008, only 32% of the Jewish respondents defined the West Bank as an "occupied territory." If the two-state solution is implemented, 65% favored a closed border.

6

A Path Finder – Exploring New Ways or Getting Lost?

As explained at the outset, the assumption underlying this analysis is that the balance sheet of a social movement is determined by a complicated set of interactions among its basic ideological and operative features, the political opportunity structure (POS) that it faces (on whose nature it has almost no influence), and its reading or the framing of the POS. It has also been maintained that the conventional understanding of the POS by social movement theoreticians as referring mostly to systemic features, such the level of state repression exerted in the specific political system, the structure of the ruling elite, or the stability of the system, is lacking. This is because it missed a crucial factor – the societal one, namely, general public opinion, against which background social movements develop and that they all address, whether as their direct target or as a means of influencing decision makers. This composite, state-centered, and proximate POS in its turn determines the myriad openings and constraints that affect the bottom line of the balance sheet, that is, the movement's success or failure.

When studying a specific movement, the analyst must examine the entire repertoire of factors and highlight the most relevant components of the POS that, in the specific case under investigation, provide the best explanation. Analysts should not automatically follow the "shopping list" that the classic POS theorem puts forward. Indeed, it appears that in the case of the Israeli peace movement between 1993 and 2008, the most influential components of the POS were not all "classical" POS factors:

1. The drastic changes, first positive and later negative, in relations between Israel and the Palestinians. At first, with the launching of the peace talks, when these relations were positive, the raison d'être for the movement was in doubt as authorized decision makers took on the role of peacemaking. Later, when these relations soured, the movement's political relevance was further undermined. This is because while the peace movement advocated strengthening these relations and accelerating

negotiations to reach an acceptable formula for a peace agreement on the ground, Israeli-Palestinian relations went from hopeful to hopeless, and diplomatic negotiations slowed down until they hit a dead end with the escalating violence.

2. The detachment between the movement and the governments in power. In the case of Labour, this stemmed from the party's efforts to disassociate itself, as a left-to-center party, from the movement, fearing that conformity between the official postulates of the Oslo process and the peace movement's agenda, let alone the social proximity between the peace activists and the party's leaders would de-legitimize it and the process. According to classic POS theories, the greater legitimacy awarded to the Oslo agenda, which was very close to the peace movement's ideas, together with Labour's political comeback in the early 1990s and again at the end of the decade, should have presented the peace movement with a set of expanded opportunities and facilitated its work. These realities actually worked in the opposite direction, however; they weakened it almost to the point of demise. In the case of the Likud governments, on the other hand, the detachment stemmed from the sharp contrast between the party's right-wing ideology and the dovish agenda of the peace movement. The socioeconomic background of Likud voters was also antithetical to that of the peace movement's activists. In any case, although the 1990s were the first time that peace had ever appeared on the regional horizon, there was hardly a moment when the peace movement and the political establishment, be it headed by either Labour or of Likud, found a common denominator or conducted any kind of constructive dialogue.

3. The deep and continuing alienation between the peace movement and most of the Israeli Jewish public. The prevalent antagonism of large segments of the Israeli public toward the peace movement, even among those who were basically pro-Oslo and ready to make territorial and other concessions to reach an agreement, is interpreted here more as the outcome of the negative public image of the movement, and less as a direct result of substantial ideological disagreements. In other words, the gaps were sociological and socioeconomic no less than they were political. Indeed, the peace movement was widely perceived either as dangerously naïve, or – what upset Israelis more – disloyal to the national collective. Furthermore, the movement was also often taken as representing a specific socioeconomic and sociodemographic sector: elitist, secular, liberal, and wealthy, which was trying to promote its specific class agenda. They believed that in practice, although not on the declarative level, the movement had closed its gates to Israelis of other sociodemographic and socioeconomic profiles. Instead of admitting to this, its adversaries maintain, the movement tried to conceal its particularist interests by packaging and marketing its peace agenda as universally sound and as a sine qua non for just and moral thinking, thereby presenting the others

as immoral and anti-peace. Obviously, the general public's resentment of the peace movement could not be divorced from the political establishment's antagonistic approach to it. It made perfect sense to assume that were one or more of Israel's prime ministers openly appreciative of the movement or were its agenda ever embraced by a mainstream political party, the public would have been significantly less suspicious, at least concerning its loyalty to the national interest.

If this reading of deficient peace movement public relations is correct, it implies that the problem lies only in part in the clash between the movement's peace vision and the reality. In other words, the explanation that the movement failed only because it was politically wrong is oversimplistic. It is argued here that even if the official peace process had been – or will be in the future – successful, the movement itself might still be unable to move from the political periphery to the center and gain wide acknowledgment. This assumption is sustained by the puzzling yet empirical lack of correlation, discussed in detail in the previous chapters, between the situation on the level of the peace talks and the peace movement's positioning vis-à-vis the Jewish Israeli mainstream in the years discussed here.

Based on this, it would be simplest to come forth with a one-line conclusion to this book: despite the promising developments in the early 1990s, by the mid-2000s, the bottom line of the Israeli peace movement's balance sheet was negative. Those who would concur with such a conclusion would probably, as conclusive support for their verdict, mention the fact that today, not only is it unclear whether a permanent peace agreement between Israel and the Palestinians can be reached in the foreseeable future, but that the peace movement itself is currently barely noticeable in the public arena. The same is true if the Israeli peace movement is examined against the matrix of the four patterns of success defined by Gamson (1990, 25–29). First, the movement obviously failed to influence national policymaking; second, it came very close to total demise; third, in terms of gaining legitimacy as a valid representative of social interests, it also did not go far; and fourth, as mentioned, it certainly never became sufficiently threatening to the authorities for them to try and stop it, motivated by concern that it would grow into a significant political power.

However, as this concluding chapter shows, the picture is considerably more complex. It is suggested here that if more sophisticated and insightful success/failure measures are employed, the bottom line becomes less clearly negative. A more suitable tool to assess the Israeli peace movement's achievements seems to be the one put forth by Rochon and Mazmanian (1993), who suggested when assessing the outcomes of a movement's activity to pay more attention to (1) the movement's long-term effects on policy (i.e., not necessarily on specific and immediate policy decisions), and (2) its contribution to changes in societal values and the national mindset. Indeed, no one would deny that gaining direct access to the policy-making process is the most effective way of realizing a social movement's aims. As exemplified by Rochon and

Mazmanian's analysis of the American Nuclear Freeze movement, changing the relevant social values that in the long run would alter the outcomes of the policy-making process is no less rewarding in terms of the bottom line of a social movement's effectiveness. In fact, changing specific policies without changing social values might prove to be a Pyrrhic victory (op. cit., 77). By the slower and less visible process of societal value changing, the movement gains influence over the future political scene, although as an organization, it might never be credited for the change or for influencing future policies made under a different collective mindset.

The following discussion therefore suggests that, indeed, in terms of its direct impact on Israeli policy making regarding the resolution of the conflict with the Palestinians and of positioning itself at the political center, the Israeli peace movement cannot make much of a claim to fame. The same goes for its rather difficult relations with the mainstream and its apparent inability to obtain wide public support. Nevertheless, as is discussed in more detail below, its balance sheet is much less negative than appears at first sight if the long-term policy-making process and value changing are introduced into the analysis. This is because its very presence and persistence introduced some new notions and ideas into national security discourse and opened it up to less particularistic, less rigid, and more universal ways of thinking about the regional arena and its players. Its rather evasive but highly important contribution can be found in the alteration of the Israeli climate of opinion about the Middle East conflict.

As the weaker points of Israeli peace activism are more visible and widely discussed, these are considered first.

Effecting National Policy

The similarity between the conceptual pillars of the official Oslo agenda and those of the peace movement's agenda is almost self-evident. It is also clear that it was the peace movement, well ahead of the Rabin government and the Israeli mainstream, that openly adhered to ideas such as the two-state solution and territories for peace. Naturally, supporters of the movement would suggest causal relations between the two, that is, claim influence over the outlook of the mainstream and the government regarding the resolution of the Israeli-Palestinian conflict and the transformation of the national policy preference. Others, however, either ignore the similarity or argue that the strategic shift implied by the Oslo process mainly reflected changes in global and regional realities that necessitated policy changes. In other words, they deny the existence of a causal relationship between the peace movement's advocacy and the Oslo transformation. As has been noted, people on the right often do recognize this influence but, naturally, view it as highly negative.

Because the political arena is not a scientific laboratory in which control can be maintained over the various inputs, neither side can unequivocally confirm their case. The fact that throughout the period, all Israeli policy makers – Labour and Likud – avoided direct contact with the peace movement, and leaders on both sides often criticized it as unpatriotic and even as undermining Israel's security, suggests that if there were a causal relationship, it was certainly not on the level of direct influence over the concrete decisions made. The same goes for the variety of the people-to-people programs and dialogue activities, which today most analysts seem to consider as having low practical impact:[1]

> In spite of the hopes activists had, today it's clear that these [people-to-people] programs were little more than an isolated 'bubble' in a troubled sea: P2P activities had no impact on the troubled political process; they were virtually ignored by local and international policymakers; and they were unable to mobilize substantial segments of the two peoples.... Optimally, bottom-up activities like P2P should be an organic component of a sustained top-down political process... but in the Israeli-Palestinian conflict, P2P wasn't given a chance to be an effective tool for conflict resolution (Herzog and Hai 2005, 9–10).

This has clearly been the case since the summer of 2000. As Liel notes, "generally speaking the Palestinian-Israeli people-to-people efforts have so far failed, as have the private track two initiatives" (Liel 2005–6, 21). In other words, not only did the movement fall short in pushing the decision makers into action in what it considered the right direction, but it also failed to promote successful extraparliamentary/grassroots peace-related endeavors.

Relations with the Political Establishment

As already stated, one of the most salient changes in the POS facing the Israeli peace movement in the period under investigation resulted from shifts in the alignments of the ruling elite, which in turn affected the peace movement's ability to find influential allies within the political establishment. Indeed, despite the cold shoulder it received from the upper echelons, during the terms in office of the two Labour governments discussed here, the peace movement had more allies within decision-making circles. Paradoxically, however, it appears that the closer the ruling party was to the peace movement ideologically, the less able the movement was to achieve political voice and mobilize public support. This was the outcome of the peace movement's much-discussed hesitation to openly criticize Labour so as not to indirectly help their right-wing rivals, as well as of the Labour governments' need to disassociate themselves from the peace movement to avoid being stigmatized as unpatriotic or naïve. In other words, the operational conditions under Labour governments were in certain respects worse than under the Likud.

On the other hand, when the Likud was in power, the peace movement felt in its right place, that is, in the opposition, and indirectly received more support from Labour-affiliated bodies (although not directly from the party or its leaders). Therefore, the movement felt free to condemn the decision makers

---

[1] For a comprehensive collection of views on the value and outcomes of people-to-people activities, see Abu-Zayyad and Schenker 2006.

and was also backed by various internal and external bodies that opposed these governments. This seemingly biased treatment of the different governments regardless of their actions, although understandable, seems to have further damaged the movement's image as fair and even made it subversive in the eyes of many because it sometimes cooperated with external bodies.[2] Paradoxically, it was not praised by anyone in the mainstream for siding with the government over the disengagement plan, since once again its support could have well led to contamination of the plan with a defeatist image.

Establishing Facts on the Ground

Perhaps second only to its failure to gain access to the national decision-making process and to conduct fruitful people-to-people projects, the peace movement's most salient weakness was the difficulty it had in going beyond transient acts of protest: "Our greatest failure, and the success of *Gush Emunim*, is on the ground. While we settled in the hearts, the right settled on the hills" (Tzali Reshef, in Shavit 2002). In a country where the fundamental ethos is one of deeds (i.e., the pioneer and fighter role models) and not of words,[3] the fact that the peace movement could not justify its existence through constructive deeds is a major blemish on its public record. Similarly, besides its development of – in the eyes of many, a rather abstract – pro-peace agenda, the peace movement was always in a sense a negative movement, because it mainly aimed at preventing certain decisions or actions. Thus, it adopted a position *against* the settlements, *against* the occupation, *against* the government's policies, *against* the Lebanon War, and *against* the separation barrier. One of *Shalom Achshav*'s central figures admitted that it was always a reactive movement, a problematic pattern of behavior. Waiting for *the* right moment actually paralyzed the group, and meanwhile life went on (Arnon, in Galili 2002a). There is much truth in this argument because traditionally, and in sharp contrast with the pro-active settler movement – the peace movement's main political rival, *Shalom Achshav* and most other peace groups always reacted to already-decided and often

---

[2] This issue of external cooperation and mainly funding made the peace movement a main target of criticism. The most visible example is the NGO Monitor project, which states its mission as follows: "Until recently, however, these NGOs, which receive significant financial support from generous donors, philanthropic institutions, and government budgets, have not themselves been subject to independent and critical analysis. NGO Monitor, therefore, was founded to promote accountability, and advance a vigorous discussion on the reports and activities of humanitarian NGOs in the framework of the Arab-Israeli conflict." (http://www.ngo-monitor .org/ngo-monitor/mission.htm)

[3] It should be noted that some critics even argue that the movement lacks a deep spiritual message that might perhaps have compensated for its practical impotence: "For the Peace Movement, conflict resolution provides a technical procedure for demarking secure borders, creating new economic markets, and constructing a new regional order. Concerns about deeper spiritual values and humanistic peace concepts preoccupy peace groups only minimally. They offer little to challenge the arguably warped religious message of the right-wing opponents of the peace process" (Newman 1997, 422).

already-implemented policies. Obviously, one can argue that this movement was *for* peace, *for* mutual respect, *for* reconciliation, and *for* the end of bloodshed. Against the background of the unfolding events of the 1990s, however, the constructive parts of its plan were not widely considered tangible – nonviolent modes of conflict resolution, peaceful coexistence, a positive peace in which both sides fully materialize their human and material capital – might have seemed desirable to most Israelis but was less down-to-earth than the settlement project or the separation barrier.

The definition of the peace movement as one of many words but few deeds went hand-in-hand with the image of peace activists' as spoiled bourgeoisie, who preach naïve ideas from their cozy offices in the ivory tower of academia or from their comfortable city homes, but are unwilling to make real personal sacrifices to translate their ideas into practice. Paradoxically, the peace activists' ongoing obedience to the law, that is, by applying for a permit for each demonstration or not entering areas closed by the IDF, strengthened the peace activists' feeble image not as good citizens, but as being not sufficiently committed to their cause, compared with the settlers and the protesters of the right. The latter were more respected by many in Israel, including many of their ideological opponents, because they overtly challenged the authorities and were willing to risk being beaten by policemen and having soldiers imprisoned.[4] When peace activists did clash with the police and the army, for example, over the separation barrier, public reaction was quite hostile toward the protestors. This in its turn sustains the argument that in terms of its public image and popularity, the peace movement was playing a no-win game.

Reaching Out to the Jewish-Israeli Public

The previous discussion suggests that a major impediment on the way to gaining political influence was the peace movement's inability to reach out to the majority of the Jewish Israeli public and the wide conceptual gaps between its agenda and the general public's preferences about various aspects of Israeli-Palestinian relations. As discussed in various sections of this book, there is more than one explanation for this.

First, there is the cognitive gap. The peace message was apparently the victim of the "war culture"[5] – a characteristic typical of ethno-national collectives engaged in a protracted conflict – that predominated in Israel. Groups like

---

4 It should be mentioned, however, that the violence by right-wing protestors in the context of the unilateral disengagement of 2005 and the ensuing events in 2006 severely damaged their public image, which suggests that such "self-sacrifice" is appreciated by the Israeli public only to a point.

5 "Many people in such [protracted] wars do not live in the war zone, but all are affected by the custom of violence. This does not mean that large numbers of people become engaged in violent actions. It does not even mean that they acquiesce in the violent actions of others. It means that violence and its effects work their way into the very fabric of society and become part of normal life" (Darby 2001, 126).

the peace movement, that put forward a political solution, are cognitively and emotionally inconsistent with such a culture. Thus, they often find themselves conducting a "dialogue of the deaf" with the rest of society, because their basic interpretation of reality is at odds with the prevalent one. In the case here, the Israeli peace movement first confronted the basic interpretation of the conflict as "zero sum" and as the sole fault of the Arab side. It also challenged the view shared by most Jewish Israelis that there was nothing, or very little, that Israel could and can do to reduce the level of violence, as according to the prevalent narrative, all Israel's military actions were conducted in self-defense. The movement's call for an understanding of, even if not for complying with, the needs and rights of the other side, defined by the mainstream as the enemy, contradicted the basic war culture state of mind, which ignores the other side's miseries and suffering.

Assuming that certain constituencies were indeed ideologically beyond the reach of the peace movement, it is still puzzling why was it not able extensively to mobilize those segments that would have fitted in, and even more, why it lost the support of so many of its supporters when the Oslo process did not make the expected progress. Apparently, the answer to these questions does not lie in an unsuitable POS in terms of relations with the authorities, and certainly not in the trivial explanation about the inherent contradiction between the "objective" reality and the movement's allegedly "naïve" agenda, because the discrepancy on these levels was considerably wider in pre-Oslo days, during the first *intifada*. At that time, however, the peace movement flourished. It is suggested here that, to a considerable extent, the mobilization difficulties in the years under investigation, and in particular in the late 1990s and early 2000s, were caused by the massive ideological shift on the part of still-active and new components of the movement toward a radical moralistic and universalistic outlook. Whereas in the 1980s and the early 1990s, the moderates were the majority and the center of gravity of the entire peace movement, the internal balance of power changed in favor of the radicals in the late 1990s and early 2000s. Their version of the peace agenda stood in dramatic contrast with the realistic and indeed nationalist worldview of the collective's relations with the outside world in general and with Palestinians in particular, that dominated Jewish Israeli thinking on the subject. In fact, it also contradicted the agenda of the former leading organization of the movement, *Shalom Achshav*, which, as noted, shrank dramatically in size and influence.

This trend of radicalization and its upshot turned the peace movement's state of mind into something close to that of a sect, leading it to claim a monopoly on the truth. This sectarianism also had a noticeable linguistic aspect. Based on their radical interpretation of the reasons for the collapse of the peace process and the harsh disapproval of Israel's conduct vis-à-vis the Palestinians in terms of impairing their basic national and human rights, some peace groups began to use alternative language. The use of the term "The Apartheid Wall" has already been mentioned, as well as the "Apartheid Roads" for the roads constructed on the West Bank for the use of settlers only, to minimize contact with the Palestinians. Other examples are more striking: for example, in various discussion forums, the Israeli Defense Forces (IDF) is labeled the Israeli Offence Forces (IOF). Army officers, active and retired, are often referred to as "war criminals," as were certain politicians (Sharon, in particular). One peace organization even sent lists of Israeli officers whom they considered criminals under international law, so that authorities in other countries could detain them when they left Israel. Other peace groups joined Israel's critics in Europe and the United States and openly called for boycotting Israeli products, and for international economic and other sanctions to be taken against Israel in the hope that, as in the case of South Africa, this would force Israel to change its policies and end the occupation. Finally, overt support by several peace groups of the July 2004 Hague International Tribunal's decision critical of the Separation Barrier, against the background of extremely high public support for its construction on one hand and mounting criticism of Israel for this construction in Europe and in other parts of the world on the other, contributed greatly to the widening gap between the movement and the general public.

Second, as has been explained in detail, this alienation between the movement – made up of mostly Ashkenazi, secular, urban, middle-class, highly educated activists – and large sectors within the Jewish Israeli public, also had identifiable socio-economic origins: "It is very easy to ridicule them. The right, like the far left, love to mock this upper tenth percentile tribe which committed the sins of arrogance, hubris and disillusion" (Shavit 2002). To name but a few sectors that remained completely estranged from it – the religious and especially the ultra-Orthodox communities, residents of settlements and development towns, residents of poor neighborhoods in large cities, people in non-kibbutz agricultural communities, people of lower education and income, and newcomers from the republics of the former Soviet Union and from Ethiopia. To these one should add the younger age cohorts of the Israeli general public, which in general – as seen in numerous surveys and studies – tend more to the right than older age groups with similar sociodemographic characteristics. This in its turn led to aging and energy loss of the peace movement, in contrast to the forever-young sociodemographic profile of the right-wing settler grassroots organizations.

The peace groups were always aware of the socioeconomic impediment; in fact, they constantly tried to overcome it in a variety of ways. Almost every new peace group, on emerging, aspired to break this invisible yet solid separation wall. In most cases, however, as was shown, these initiatives were short-lived. Furthermore, efforts to bring together people of the peace movement and social activists who concentrated on domestic affairs also usually failed, mainly because the correlation between peace activism and class became highly apparent in the period discussed here. This association was not completely baseless or imagined; for example, following the signing of the peace treaty between Israel and Jordan, several factories were moved by their owners (who openly declared their support for the peace agenda, although not necessarily for the peace movement), from certain already unemployment-stricken development towns in the south, to the east side of the Jordan river, where labor costs were significantly lower than in Israel. Quite naturally, people who were laid off because of that, as well as others fearing the same fate if relations with the Palestinians and the Arab world improved, highly resented peace advocacy. To them, it was obvious that people of the middle and upper-middle classes, in which most peace activists were positioned, were not going to lose their jobs following any peace treaties signed in the future; on the contrary, they could only profit from the opening of the borders and the emergence of a New Middle East. This was fertile ground for the emergence of strong feelings of deprivation and nourished anti-peace-movement sentiments.

Later, when following the collapse of the negotiations the flow of financial assistance from outside of the country to the movement dried up, the lack of resources forced peace groups to choose between efforts to change the perhaps unchangeable reality of their limited societal appeal, or invest them all in peace activities with their crowd. Such a brave strategic decision was never made by any peace SMO or at least was never openly put on the table. Thus, the discrepancy between the sweet talk by many peace organizations about social justice and distributive justice when it came to the Palestinians vis-à-vis Israel and the reality in which many Israelis already suffered from outcome of the Oslo agreements (and enjoyed no peace dividends), only aggravated them.

Beyond the money-peace association, another connection between the peace message and its carriers was quite common in the attacks on women's peace activism. This leads us to another marketing deficiency of the Israeli peace movement: the feminine/feminist image of the movement that, in the eyes of many, diminished its legitimacy as a partner to security discourse. The fact that most Israeli women, including most of those involved in peace activism, lacked combat experience made the movement, in which women have always been a majority, seem irrelevant to the security debate and undermined its political efficacy.[6] As the definition of security in Israel today is still highly conservative, relating only to the militaristic aspects (Newman 2006), alternative perceptions such as human security, heralded by the peace movement, feminists, ecologists, and the like, are often almost automatically disqualified.

Relations with Arab Israeli Citizens and the Palestinians in the Territories

On the face of it, Israel's Arab citizens and the Palestinians should have been highly supportive of the peace movement. After all, had the movement's agenda been fully adopted by the authorities, the Israeli negotiators would have been far more sensitive to the interests and needs of both Palestinians and Arab Israelis. Furthermore, the negotiations would have taken into consideration the attitudes and aspirations of the Arab citizens of Israel and not only of the Jewish majority. Still, although the frequency of interaction between peace

---

[6] Even members of the movement are sometimes quoted as concurring with this argument (see, e.g., Lemish and Barzel 2000, 154).

activists and individuals from the Arab Israeli sector and Palestinians by far exceeded those conducted by other segments of Jewish Israeli society, these relations did not develop into effective political alliances either with Israel's Arab citizens or with the Palestinians in the territories.

Why was no alliance with Israeli Arab citizens established? First, as mentioned, most Israeli peace groups primarily addressed the Jewish majority, and refrained from openly reaching out to the Arab Israeli minority or focusing on its grievances, so as not to undermine their main mobilization endeavor. Second, in a sense, there was a hidden but erroneous assumption in the peace movement's agenda that once the external conflict was resolved, domestic Jewish-Arab friction would automatically lessen drastically. When peace was seen on the horizon, the Jewish public's attitudes towards Arab Israeli citizens did not improve. On the contrary, the mainstream's insistence on maintaining the Jewish character of Israel and the rejection of the state of all its citizens concept only increased in the early 1990s with the progress in the peace talks. Arab Israelis were not only highly frustrated because of this but also accused the peace activists of promoting an illusion.

Another obstacle in the way to creating such a political alliance was the fact that the agenda of the peace groups was at best irrelevant and sometimes unacceptable to the Arab Israeli sector. For example, they have no immediate interest in a discussion of the right to conscientious objection because Arab Israelis are automatically exempt from military service, or the problem of if and how Israel's national security is best protected vis-à-vis the Arab world, which Arab Israeli citizens do not fear and of which they feel an integral part. Clearly, the basically favorable view by moderate peace organizations toward the Zionist idea, considered by Arab Israelis (and all other Palestinians) as the source of their national historical catastrophe and their current second-class-citizen status within the Jewish-democratic state, minimized the chances of creating a real alliance here. Finally, as locals, Arab Israelis were always much more aware than the Palestinians in the territories of the marginal political status of the peace movement in the Jewish Israeli political arena. Based on this awareness, the Arab Israeli sector had little motivation to associate itself with the movement, particularly against the background of the conceptual points of contention mentioned above.

The reasons that the Israeli peace movement had difficulty allying itself effectively with the Palestinian side were similar, although not identical. Between the late 1970s and the mid-1990s, as was stated previously, many dialogue activities took place in Israel and abroad, and there were many Track II meetings that brought together Israeli peace activists and pro-peace Palestinians. In those years, some very close Israeli-Palestinian relations on both the personal and the organizational levels developed, some even strong enough to survive the political ups and downs of the ensuing years as well as the violence exerted by each side against the other (see, e.g., Salem 2007). Even in better times, however, no real political partnership was consolidated. To start with, there was no equality between the two sides in terms of their relative situation and hence their interest in such a partnership and their ability to work toward it. Somewhat paradoxically, although not surprisingly, most of the time, Israeli peace activists were significantly more eager than their Palestinian counterparts to cooperate, sometimes to the point of turning a blind eye to the Palestinians' ongoing political unwillingness or emotional inability to normalize relations. This was much like the case of the New Middle East vision, which fascinated some Israelis but terrified most Palestinians and Arabs, who did not like the idea of being embraced too strongly by Israel's much more advanced and powerful industry. Here as well, the Israeli side was too keen on publicly expressing friendship and unity, whereas the Palestinian participants were always more reserved. This gap became more acute in the 1990s.

Why were Palestinians less enthusiastic than Israeli peace activists about working together after 1993 than before the signing of the Oslo Accords? First and above all, although they reached out to the Palestinians, Israeli peace activists still belonged to the occupying force. Apparently, in this context, the Palestinians thought that the Israeli peace movement was not critical enough of the Israeli governments' conduct of the negotiations and not active enough in launching massive protest activities when full implementation of the various Oslo agreements was repeatedly delayed. Second was the unfulfilled Palestinian demand for strong action by the peace movement in relation to the failure – or refusal – of all Israeli governments to make life easier for the Palestinians in the territories, even in the better days of the Oslo process. As has been explained, for domestic reasons and particularly at such times, the movement was not in a position to organize massive anti-government protests, yet this explanation was not good enough for the Palestinians, as at least in the early stages of the Oslo process, they did not correctly assess the movement's loss of power and the resources available to it. They therefore felt betrayed and never regained trust in the movement.[7]

The paucity of parallel peace endeavors on the Palestinian side, particularly during the first two segments of the Oslo road but in fact also in the years before and after, was one of the main problems that faced the Israeli peace movement. Whereas there were individual Palestinians and Palestinian organizations that participated in joint activities with Israeli peace organizations, in almost all cases they did not define themselves as Palestinian peace activists or organizations even when the word peace appeared in their names (mainly because this proved very appealing to external donors and international foundations). Furthermore, whatever they called themselves, all the Palestinian activists and organizations emphasized their loyalty first to the Palestinian national cause and were never ready to openly criticize their national leadership. This fact created

---

[7] This sense of disappointment was not unique to the case study discussed here. Apparently it often happens that nongovernmental social actors create an image of effectiveness, while in reality their ability to make a real change is much more limited: "NGOs, now so widely praised, can anticipate becoming victims of the current unrealistic expectations and being abandoned as rapidly and as widely as they have been embraced" (Fisher 1997, 445).

a structural imbalance with the Israeli peace organizations, which publicly declared their commitment to universalistic values (i.e., justice, nonviolence, universal right to self-determination) and repeatedly denounced their own government. For example, there were certainly no Palestinian parallels to the cries at Israeli peace demonstrations that their Prime Minster (mostly Sharon) was a murderer. This was closely related to one of the weaknesses mentioned above: from the point of view of the Israeli public, this imbalance was very difficult to accept and led to the deepening conviction that the Israeli peace organizations were both disloyal and blind to the true nature of their Palestinian counterparts.

Later, the majority of Palestinians who had been involved in Track II or people-to-people activities failed to grasp fully the traumatic effects on many peace activists of the dreadful terrorist attacks on Israeli civilians. Without necessarily justifying terrorism against civilians, these Palestinians assumed that unlike most other Jewish Israelis, the peace activists would acknowledge the connection between the standstill in the peace process together with the miserable living conditions in the territories, and the use of violence, even suicide bombings by some Palestinian militants. Although these Palestinians did not expect Israeli peace activists to support these activities, they at least expected them to understand the motivations of the perpetrators. Thus, Israeli peace organization members often thought they were truly responsible and were willing to respond positively to the requests of their Palestinian counterparts to condemn Israeli occupation practices. It was extremely rare, however, for Palestinian peace organizations to come out openly against terror activities, even suicide bombings against Israeli civilians. On the few occasions when they did so, their statements often included expressions of empathy, not with the acts per se, but with the underlying circumstances. This was a grave mistake, because in reality the effect of violence on at least moderate Israeli peace activists was the exact opposite of increased solidarity with the Palestinians' suffering leading to terror. When faced with terror, instead of putting pressure on the Israeli government to remove the closures and the checkpoints in the territories and to resume the talks, many Israel peace activists renounced their peace agenda and politically turned right.

This acute gap in the two sides' interpretations of the situation widened with the outbreak of the *Al-Aqsa intifada*, when the peace movement shrank drastically, but the Palestinians still expected it to go head on with Barak and then with Sharon and lead a massive anti-government protest. When the Palestinians realized that this was not to be, they were left with no motivation to overcome their long-standing reservations with the peace movement and continue with the few remaining joint activities. From the early 2000s onward, the Palestinians drastically reduced their participation in joint activities and sought another "horse" on the Israeli side on which to put their money:

The disconnection initiated by the Palestinians originated in their lost hope that the 'peace process' would lead to the end of the occupation and in their disappointment in what seemed to them to be the betrayal of the peace camp that embraced the theses of the right.... The result is that the direct, non-establishment connection was broken off and we find ourselves many years back (Benvenisti 2001).

The split between the Palestinians and the peace movement deepened further in the 2000s. Mainstream Palestinians moved from their original – difficult for Israeli Jews to swallow – demand that Israel formally recognize the Palestinian refugees' right of return, to a demand for the actual implementation of return, even if on a limited or symbolic scale. Except for the non-Zionist factions of the Israeli peace movement, and a very few in more 'mainstream' peace organizations (i.e., Yossi Beilin and some of his followers in *Yozmat Geneva*), this demand for Israeli recognition of the right of return was widely rejected by most peace activists, who on that specific matter saw eye to eye with the mainstream: the acknowledgment of Israel's responsibility for the creation of the refugee problem, let alone the actual return of millions of Palestinians to Israel within the Green Line, was tantamount to destroying the Jewish character of the state of Israel, if not its physical annihilation. This unqualified rejection strengthened the Palestinian view that the Israeli peace movement was indeed part of the occupation system and conceptually not very different from the Jewish Israeli Zionist mainstream. The following declaration issued by a Palestinian NGO regarding the refugee issue exemplifies the Palestinians' reaction:

The Palestine Right to Return Coalition (PRRC) upholds the inalienable right of Palestinian refugees to return home as an integral component of a just and viable peace.... PRRC strongly condemns the statement published in the Israeli newspaper *Ha'aretz* (2 January 2001) by "Peace Now" and other self-proclaimed Israeli "peace camp" which calls for Palestinians to abandon their inalienable right of return. The call by the so-called Israeli "peace" movement for the abrogation of the Palestinian refugees' right to return home is a clear manifestation that racism and exclusive formulation are in fact an integral part of most Israeli organizations that uphold Zionism.... These Zionist groups acknowledge the creation of Israel as the instigator of the expulsion and dispossession of the Palestinian people, but their proposed solution is to transfer the Palestinian refugees to whatever land the Israeli administration allocates as the Palestinian state. In the name of a Zionist-defined "peace," these groups support the racist and oppressive Israeli occupying power in denying Palestinians their rightful ownership of the land from which they were expelled. These "peace" advocates call for a "positive conclusion" that maintains the formula of an exclusive racist Jewish state. The statement made by the so-called Israeli "peace" movement exposes their racist position and represents the imbalance of power that allows them to co-opt and monopolize the term "peace" and define it within an oppressive and racist framework (Al-Awda 2001, http://www.al-awda.org).

The Israeli peace movement has also been directly criticized by leading Palestinian figures. For example, renowned intellectual Edward Said claimed to have been verbally attacked by the audience after he gave a lecture on the reasons for the failure of the Oslo process, as seen from the Palestinian side: "My opponents were in every case people who described themselves as supporters of Peace Now (i.e., liberal Jews) and hence of peace with the Palestinians" (Said

2000, 4). Admittedly, more than once, the more radical Israeli peace activists backed up these Palestinian feelings:

For years, we [*Gush Shalom*] have felt ourselves to be part of a wider peace camp – a distinct, radical part, but a part nevertheless. At the annual Rabin memorial rallies, at the beginning of each November, we felt quite at home distributing leaflets and stickers to hundreds of thousands filling Rabin square. Still we were always aware that many of the crowd there regarded withdrawal from the occupied territories not as the beginning of a new common future but as "getting rid of Arabs" so as to preserve the Jewish majority in Israel, and/or an act of generosity for which the Palestinians must be eternally grateful.... We realized that we could not trust them in times of extreme tension and nationalist polarization, when passions run high and fragile bridges across the national and ethnic divide are stretched to the breaking point and beyond. For the time being, we are on our own again, the hardcore of the peace camp, counting ourselves lucky when attendance at a protest action can be measured in hundreds rather than dozens (Keller 2000).

Some radical Israelis went even further and dismissed the entire effort of the peace movement: "There is no [real – TH] peace movement in Israel. This is why we need sanctions [on Israel – TH]. If there were a peace movement in Israel, I would not call for sanctions. Unfortunately, there is no peace movement in Israel. There is no peace movement to talk about and therefore the occupation will not come to an end" (Pappe 2005). Whereas most moderate peace activists often thought that the Palestinians contributed their share to the failure of the peace process and thereby to the continuation of the occupation, because of their sense of guilt about Israel's conduct, their criticism of the Palestinian side was expressed much more subtly and never aimed at their counterparts in the Palestinian pro-peace organizations:

Other obstacles [by Israel to reaching an agreement] included Israeli insensitivity to the suffering of an entire people possessed of a collective pride and struggling to gain national liberation from continuing occupation; Palestinian insensitivity to the influence of terrorism on the Israeli public; the destructive effect of anti-Israeli incitement and propaganda; and an immature Palestinian political system which employed double talk and generally performed in a negligent and unprofessional manner.... The fault was not the unwillingness of Israeli and Palestinian communities to reach an agreement, but poor management of the process. If the two sides can recognize and learn from their mistakes, it should be possible to renew the negotiations and to reach a Permanent Status Agreement: the first leg on the long and difficult journey to reconciliation between the two peoples and peace between the two states (Pundak 2001, 45).

This soft treatment of the Palestinians, as noted, was rooted in Israeli peace activists' authentic feeling that their country was the more guilty party, and their fear that the already sour relations with the Palestinian side would be cut off. The Israeli public viewed this as just another manifestation of the peace movement's pro-Palestinian position and general irrationality. The practical choice with which the movement was presented was therefore a very difficult, almost zero-sum choice: to leave behind either their public at home or their public on the other side. In recent years, the peace movement mainly handled this critical dilemma through denial. The result was massive loss of both publics.

Intramovement Relations

Another characteristic that weakened the movement in the 1990s and the 2000s was the ongoing inability by the various bodies composing it to put aside their differences and at least coordinate their messages and activities, if not consider mergers. Several rather workable coalitions were created, as discussed previously, but in light of the bleak background against which they operated and their difficulties in cooperating with other political actors, governmental and nongovernmental, much more intramovement cooperation was needed, particularly as very few of the created coalitions survived the strong divisive factors. The organizational and individual sense of uniqueness within each peace group, as well as their insistence on retaining their pure ideologies, produced internal rivalries and heated disputes, which wasted energy and resources and damaged the movements' public image. From the point of view of external observers, these splits seemed unreasonable, because from the outside the ideological and operative differences between the various peace organizations seemed minimal and insignificant. Certain peace activists realized this and were embarrassed:

Everyone is talking about the left's taste for splitting, the internal controversies.... From the outside, we all look alike. We are all lefties, although we like to think that many ideological disagreements set us apart. I always feel that I do not belong. The categories that were developed to define exactly in which box each of us belongs are even more diversified than the darn overall categories. Zionist, non-Zionist, anti-Zionist, post-Zionist, frustrated post-Zionist. These categories are really not good for me (Golan-Agnon 2005, 158).

Still, the relationships between the various Israeli peace organizations can be divided into two categories: cooperative and competitive-confrontational. Full-fledged antagonism rarely developed. Naturally, the closer the organizations were in their ideological positions and strategic goals, the easier it was for them to cooperate, even if only on an ad hoc basis. Ideological proximity was not always enough to produce collaboration, however. The highest level of cooperation was reached between the women-only peace organizations and among the peace-human rights organizations; the effective and viable *Koalitziat Nashim* and the ad-hoc coalitions formed by *Rofim l'Zchuyot ha'Adam, b'Tselem, haVaad haZiburi Neged Inuyim* (the Public Committee against Torture), and *haVaad Neged Harisat Batim* have already been mentioned. This sort of cooperation was also often facilitated by the overlapping affiliations of these organizations' top activists, who belonged to several such organizations and to the same social networks. Similar familial relations, with all the complexities invested in such interactions, also developed between the older and younger refusenik organizations – *Yesh Gvul* and *Ometz l'Sarev*. Reasonably conducive work relations were established between *Shalom Achshav* and *East for Peace*, as well as with the *Hug Horim Shakulim*.

Less significant, but still noteworthy, cooperation – based on the shared Zionist creed of these movements – existed among certain secular peace organizations, mainly *Shalom Achshav*, and the religious ones – *Oz v'Shalom* and *Netivot Shalom*. Although in terms of their peace vision and Zionist self-definition, these peace organizations were not far apart, the liberal, universalist views of the secular peace organizations and the particularist religious tenets held by the religious ones were difficult to reconcile so that they could serve as the basis for formulating a common operational rationale. Observance of the Sabbath and the holidays made it difficult to schedule joint activities, as noted previously.

As far as other like-minded peace groups were concerned, gender effects often stood between the women's and the mixed-gender peace groups, even when their respective perceptions of peace per se were almost identical. Cooperation was thus reduced in these cases because of seemingly trivial but in fact quite influential differences in the value hierarchy of the potential partners. Competitive-confrontational relations did develop between the moderate and the radical components of the peace movement, a division that corresponded in many ways to the division between the Zionist and the anti- or non-Zionist organizations. Frequent attacks by groups such as *Gush Shalom* or *Ta'ayush* on *Shalom Achshav* for its alleged overcompliance with the Jewish Israeli mainstream should be understood in this context.[8] Owing to their small size and despite their severe ideological reservations about it, most of these peace organizations did join *Shalom Achshav*'s organized demonstrations and rallies, acknowledging the importance of large masses for gaining political influence and visibility. Paradoxically, speakers of consensus-oriented peace organizations, for example, *haMifkad haLeumi* initiative (and, in the past, also the leaders of *Dor Shalom*) often accused *Shalom Achshav* of misconduct in the other direction – that they adopted an extremist platform, thereby reinforcing the image of peace activism as nonpatriotic. It is not clear to what extent these attacks reflected a real ideological dispute or were merely tactics in the context of competitive mobilization efforts. They clearly played into the hands of the peace movement's opponents, however, and exemplified the negative influence of internal tensions on the peace movement's ability to function effectively on the national political level.

To summarize the above, the bottom line of the negative side of the balance sheet is that in terms of establishing itself as a major participant in the national security debate, gaining direct access to the national decision-making system, and consolidating stable alignments with powerful political actors within Israel and with the Palestinian peace movements, the Israeli peace

---

[8] An anecdotal illustration of these tensions is the following: When we asked a central activist in the Alternative Information Center which political body in Israel he considered the absolute antithesis to his organization, he immediately responded, *Shalom Achshav*.

movement between 1993 and 2008 cannot point to many significant achievements.

As argued earlier, however, the other more successful side of the movement's balance sheet includes more than one item. Uri Avneri, a devoted and often disputed peace activist, who is also a practiced observer of the Israeli political scene, captured the gist of the matter:

You may ask – indeed, you must ask: What has the Israeli peace movement achieved? On the face of it – nothing. On the contrary, since the Oslo agreement, the situation of the Palestinians has worsened from year to year. The economic misery is deepening even further. Every day people are being killed. The construction of the monster Wall is continuing. The racist settlements are spreading rapidly. Just now we learned that the Jordan Valley – a third of the West Bank – is being cut off from Palestinian territory and practically annexed to Israel. The victory of Hamas in the Palestinian elections is a result of these actions. All this is happening in plain view. But below the surface a contrary process is at work. Fifty years ago, only a handful of people in Israel and around the world recognized the existence of the Palestinian people. Even 32 years ago, Golda Meir could declare that "there is no such thing as a Palestinian people." Nowadays there is no normal person in Israel and the world who denies the existence of the Palestinian people and its right to a state of its own. That is a victory for the tenacious Palestinian struggle, but also for the Israeli peace movement (Avneri 2006).

This impressionistic and perhaps somewhat biased but enlightening assessment can be analytically divided into several items on the movement's success list, still bearing in mind the difficulties of establishing causal relations when assessing the impact of a social movement.

Modifying the Jewish Israeli Discourse on Peace and Security

Despite the obvious fact that the Oslo process, strongly supported as it was by most peace groups at the time of its launching, failed to bear the expected fruit, a permanent peace agreement, there are strong indications that deep cognitive changes in Israel regarding the Palestinians, the conflict, and the ways to resolve it have occurred on the Jewish Israeli side. By and large, it appears that the screen of nonrecognition, epitomized by Golda Meir's statement that Avneri mentioned, about the nonexistence of a Palestinian people, almost disappeared. Israelis who oppose the peace talks, much like those who support them, today acknowledge the Palestinian national entity, even if they define it as inherently evil or hostile. Furthermore, "concepts such as a 'viable' Palestinian state and the need for 'contiguity' became standard phrases, to say nothing of 'territorial compromise', or 'land for peace' which once had been anathema for right wing governments. . . . Gone were the ideas of Greater Israel and even claims of the need for 'territorial depth' for Israel's security" (Golan, 138). As a result, deeply rooted past taboos, such as on the establishment of an independent Palestinian state or making massive territorial concessions, were significantly shattered, as seen in declarations of Israeli leaders from all major parties[9] and in public opinion polls. Thus, compared with a tiny minority of 5% to 10% in the 1980s, a stable majority of about two-thirds of the Jewish Israeli public in recent years supported the establishment of such a state. Likewise, determining that the Green Line, that is, the pre-1967 war borders, with some modifications would be the permanent borders between Israel and Palestine, which was once widely considered a maximalist and unacceptable Palestinian demand, is today accepted by many politicians of the center and even somewhat right-of-center, as well as by many in the Israeli public. Although the role of the peace movement in paving the way for these changes cannot be established in an uncontested causal manner, it does seems quite substantial.

No less important, the peace movement was one of the first to openly raise a doubt concerning overreliance on strategic military superiority as the ultimate means to guarantee Israel's national security in the long run. Indeed, although the conceptualization of national security held by most Israeli decision makers is still heavily military oriented, some movement in the direction of conceptualizing it in human security terms can be detected in the 1990s and 2000s. On the level of public discourse, such arguments are heard even more often. Although usually contested and not widely embraced because they are considered naïve, they are rarely described today as being subversive or irrelevant.

Furthermore, one should recall that the various peace groups advocated the political channel for conflict resolution when this was a highly unpopular idea. For many years, most mainstream political actors, including Labour, considered this irrelevant because of the allegedly zero-sum nature of the conflict. Today, the added value of a political solution to the conflict is widely acknowledged. The peace movement also first highlighted the correlation between the huge security budget burden and Israel's inability to find enough resources to sustain satisfactory advanced social services. Even if the movement did not succeed in gaining the political support most of the Jewish Israeli public for transferring considerable budgets from security to social purposes, it may well claim credit for the fact that: "People are more ready now, in spite of all the anger they feel towards the Palestinians, to listen to explanations about the situation. And they're making the connections between the economic situation and the political situation. A lot more should be done to reach these people, these organizations, and through them, to reach the street" (Baskin and al Qaq 2002, 11).

This contribution to national security discourse did not escape the opponents of the peace movement of the political right who, as was shown earlier, attributed to it the highly successful promotion of the "two states for two peoples" formula. Nor was this unnoticed by the leaders of the peace movement. Apparently, to some extent, this lifted their low morale in the face of other political letdowns: "The success of the peace movement has been in the struggle

---

[9] Even Prime Minister Sharon openly accepted this in May 2002, in the face of strong opposition from his own Likud party caucus.

for the Israeli conscience. Despite all the crises and the difficulties, the Israeli public today accepts positions that we put forward 20 years ago, and which were then considered marginal. The great majority of Israelis does not want territories, does not want occupation and does not want settlements" (Tzali Reshef in Shavit 2002). Another former activist summarized this contribution of the peace movement as follows:

> The insistent advocacy of the peace movement gradually led many people, both in the center and on the left, to modify their views and accept the need for mutual recognition and compromise. The idea that the occupation is a political, financial, and moral liability rather than a strategic asset, and that Palestinian self-determination is inevitable, gradually gained greater currency.... Recent opinion surveys and policy preferences of the current Labor government strongly suggest that the movement was successful in gradually moving the 'middle' towards compromise and reconciliation (Bar-On 1996, 323–324).

Increasing the Level of Political Pluralism

Beyond introducing these specific themes relating to the conflict into Israeli public discourse, the peace movement should also be credited for its ability to take a step back from the mainstream and to rethink some formerly uncontested values and postulates. The movement's peace-oriented discourse also helped to elaborate on the multidimensional significance and outcomes of the ongoing occupation far beyond the security realm. For example, architecture analyses currently take into consideration the broad spatial effects of occupier-occupied relations (see, e.g., Weizman 2007). In the highly mobilized and consensus-oriented Jewish Israeli society and under the pressure of external conflict, such voluntary critical distancing was not easy, nor did it go unnoticed. Although people of the radical left often undermine this achievement by stating that the peace movement did not go far enough in its criticism of Israeli politics, relatively few political actors were able to do this over time in the way that the moderate peace groups did, and to mobilize significant public support. Putting its content aside for a moment, the ongoing challenge to highly consensual values put forward by the peace movement was a precedent that paved the way for other bodies and groups to dare to examine and challenge other pillars of the national consensus critically and openly. In other words, it is argued here that the peace movement's prolonged opposition to the mainstream, despite its limited direct political influence and other difficulties, considerably increased the level of pluralism of the Israeli political system, expanded the perimeter of the public debate over national security matters, and thereby contributed to the maturing of Israeli democracy.

Influencing Specific Policies

It has already been mentioned that in the period discussed here, the Israeli peace movement was mostly unable to pressure Israeli policymakers into following its concrete political recommendations. There were some exceptions to this generalization, however; cases in which it did influence, even if indirectly, the conduct of the authorities. In the negative direction, one might argue that enacting the 1986 law that prohibited contacts between Israeli citizens and PLO officials was actually a reaction to numerous meetings by peace movement activists with Palestinians. As no one else met or wanted to meet with Palestinians at that time, it is not unfeasible to view causality here, although the influence was not in the desired direction. A similar case was the toughening of IDF policies vis-à-vis conscientious objectors against swelling political refusal in the early 2000s. Indeed, as mentioned, these refuseniks often did not identify openly with the peace movement, yet, willing or not, the authorities and the public identified them with it. Whereas until the early 2000s, ways were found to exempt youngsters who refused to serve on pacifist grounds, and political conscientious objectors were perhaps punished by the army authorities but not severely, the increase in the number and visibility of those who challenged conscription or service in the occupied territories brought in its wake toughening of the authorities' treatment of the refuseniks.

At least in two cases, however, peace initiatives seem to have a rightful claim to some positive credit for encouraging policy changes: the withdrawal of the IDF from South Lebanon in mid-2000 under Prime Minister Barak of Labour, and Likud Prime Minister Sharon's unilateral disengagement plan in 2005. Neither leader ever confirmed that he had been motivated by peace activities, so once again the causal linkage cannot be stated beyond a doubt. Still, the overall impression is that the activities of the *Arba Imahot* movement by its agents or allies in government corridors encouraged the decision to pull out of Lebanon. This understanding is even shared by knowledgeable figures such as General (ret.) Ami Ayalon, leader of *haMifkad haLeumi*, who testified: "I ask you: why in the end did we leave Lebanon? It was not the government's will to get out; it was the public that forced it to do so" (Ayalon 2002, The Davis Project, 27/6).

The second case is that of *Yozmat Geneva* (the Geneva Initiative) and Prime Minister Sharon's plan for unilateral disengagement. Beyond other factors, the high visibility of the Geneva agenda in late 2003 seems to have pushed Sharon toward the decision to opt for a pullout from Gaza, motivated by concern that if the government did nothing, *Yozmat Geneva*'s popularity would increase and eventually make its plan a significant political opposition.

Improving Israel's External Image

The variety of peace activities conducted alongside Israel's formal behavior vis-à-vis the Palestinians seems also to have contributed to the creation of a more heterogeneous and positive image of Israeli society in international public opinion. Particularly for those highly critical of Israeli policies in the territories, continuous local peace activism signaled that perhaps not everyone in Israel approved of the ongoing occupation or agreed to take part in it. This in turn prevented out-and-out denouncement of Israeli society and mitigated the efforts of Israel's opponents to initiate a successful pro-sanctions campaign or launch a comprehensive boycott of Israeli products or of Israeli academia.[10]

The existence of many peace organizations also sustained the argument that despite its conduct in the territories, the comparison to South Africa during the Apartheid regime is incorrect. This is because basically Israel is a democratic society, in which even severe opponents of the government's policies can express criticism without being persecuted or prosecuted. The nicer, liberal, and universalist other face of Israel presented by the peace movement was especially attractive to liberal Jewish audiences in the West, and in particular in the United States. This Jewish sector was torn between basic support for the existence of a Jewish state in the land of Israel and identification with the Jewish Israeli community there on one hand, and on the other hand, their liberal beliefs, which led them to strongly support the Palestinian demand for national self-determination and a state, which made them very critical of the occupation. The existence of the Israeli peace movement enabled these audiences to hold on to both their identification with Israeli Jews (if not with the state) and their liberal outlook. Furthermore, it facilitated their relations with non-Jewish liberal circles in different countries. Instead of having to choose between expressing their extreme criticism of Israel or supporting Israel and its code of conduct, of which they basically disapproved, they could show empirical evidence that not all Israeli Jews cooperated with the occupation. In recent years, this encouraged the establishment of organizations such as the Jewish Voice for Peace (http://www.jewishvoiceforpeace.org) of the San Francisco Bay, which cooperated closely with Israeli peace activists, particularly with the more radical local groups (the moderate, American Zionist peace groups sought to push toward bringing an end to the occupation by influencing U.S. policy makers in Washington).

Magnifying Silenced Voices and Public Sectors

In the theoretical section, it was mentioned that social movement activists often do little more than act for the sake of acting, instead of sitting at home doing nothing but complaining about things being done the wrong way "out there." Indeed, the Israeli peace movement was quite successful in offering an outlet for the peace activists' frustration and dissatisfaction with official policies. Social movement theory tells us that beyond attaining actual political influence, the expressive function of social activism is one of the highest motivations of people who become involved in it. The fact that the peace movement was there for people who did not sympathize with the government's conduct and with the mainstream's support for official positions and actions, even in the most difficult days of terror and counter-violence, was extremely important. With all

---

[10] Clearly, the movement's rivals see it differently and blame the movement for smearing Israel by publically criticizing it and "investing it with a non-human, even demonic image" (Kedar 2008).

its ups and downs, over the years the peace movement provided a stable framework for expressing nonconformist views on foreign and security matters, and even more, enabled the critics of the government to organize protest demonstrations and rallies as well as other activities, which made their reservations about the official positions visible to many others. This outlet was highly important to those whose views had no representation in the government and who were greatly disliked by other Israelis. Therefore, they stayed in the movement even when it lost momentum and was severely denounced. This burning urge to be active, even when they knew that these actions would have minimal impact, was described as follows by a veteran peace activist: "The activists share one common characteristic – the drive to do something, the drive to act. It might be a sort of escapism, but this is how we manage to maintain our sanity. If we give up – we will become clinically depressed.... Sitting down and doing nothing is irresponsible" (Harel 2003, 37). Even their critics often expressed admiration for these peace activists' resolution: "[T]here is something impressive in their political *tzumud*.[11] There is something impressive in the Sisyphean insistence of Tzali Reshef and Janet Aviad [leaders of *Shalom Achshav* – TH] and those dwindling crowds to stand in the squares with their torches again and again" (Shavit 2002).

In particular, the peace movement was successful in giving a voice to two sectors: those on the left side of the political spectrum, whose electoral achievements were so meager in recent years that they had almost no parliamentary representation. This in turn encouraged their rivals not to consider the peace movement's ideas seriously but to dismiss them as just a fig leaf covering these groups' inability or refusal to come to terms with their electoral predicament. The other was Israeli women, who were traditionally widely excluded from public discourse on peace and security. Despite the criticism mentioned earlier, of certain peace groups for silencing women activists, the peace movement was perhaps the best political safe haven for women in Israel. Women there rose to leadership positions, and in number they constituted well over half of the participants in various peace activities (Hermann and Kurtz 1995).

This book began by stating a theoretical aim regarding the potential of social movements in general. Now seems to be the right stage to determine whether this analysis of the Israeli peace movement can produce any insights into the questions presented there. What are the relevant components of the political opportunity structure? To what extent can a social movement take off and gain influence on the political scene when it comes to high politics – matters such as peace making? What are the criteria for correctly assessing its achievements?

On the first issue, which is directly related to the reservations presented in the theoretical section about the working hypotheses of the political process school

---

[11] *Tzumud* is the term normally used to describe the Palestinian resolution not to give up on their lands, irrespective of what suffering this insistence entails. Here the author uses it in a very unconventional way to praise the persistence of the Israel peace activists but through this use, hints at loyalty to the Palestinian cause.

of social movement theory, it seems that two general conclusions stem from this analysis of the Israel case. First, it suggests that, ironically and contrary to the commonly held assumption, the ascendance to power of an administration or government that is ideologically closer to the movement does not necessarily create an expanded POS in terms of offering a better operational environment and easier access to the political power center and to the decision-making process. In fact, it seems that the opposite is true. Indeed, professional politicians as such are not usually eager to share their achievements with other political players, and therefore they would rather appropriate a movement's successful ideas than give it credit for developing them. When the decision makers are part of the same or a nearby political camp, however, the urgency not to give credit is greater because they face the danger of being accused of being puppets on a string, that is, manipulated by extra-parliamentary forces, a highly problematic situation in a strictly representative democracy (although less so in more participatory systems). We can expect this disassociation to be particularly noticeable when the movement's public image is not quite respectable, but more revolutionary, because beyond their other concerns, decision makers worry about being contaminated.

On the movement's side of the equation, apparently when leaders appear to pursue an agenda similar to that of national policy, its mobilization appeal decreases dramatically. Even the more devoted activists think that they can take it easy and let the officials handle the matter at stake. Quite naturally, when activists trust the people in power, their motivation to launch protest campaigns lessens, even if the policies shaped and the actions taken are not exactly to their liking. Furthermore, apparently because the natural state of most social movements is opposition to the authorities, when they find themselves on the same side of the fence with the government, the demobilization vector again seems to grow stronger. Open ideological friction with the party in power and with its leaders could be detrimental to the movement's agenda but better serve the movement as an organization, because its activists' sense of commitment and enthusiasm for protest will increase and not rapidly dissipate. In other words, sometimes the ideological interests of a social movement and its organizational ones are, if not antithetical, then at least not fully corresponding.

Second, the Israeli case suggests that the focus of POS theories on the political establishment level is indeed incomplete. The opinion of the general public seems no less important a factor in the POS facing a social movement than the policies of the political elite, the composition of the elite, and the government's readiness to use repression. The conceptual affinity between the movement and the general public determines the former's location – whether in the center or on the periphery – of the political arena. In fact, particularly in cases when the use of violent means is not an acceptable option for the social movement, the government need not use repression when the general public in effect isolates or ostracizes the social activists. Clearly, it is the general public that sets the movement's mobilization capacities and the resources available to it. It is the public, more than the political establishment that defines the movement as respectable or revolutionary, thereby increasing or reducing its chances of political success. The movement's public relations determine the movement's ability to gain the ear of decision makers. The pluralist school maintains that they are motivated by electoral considerations and are therefore more attentive to the stronger voices, the larger groupings, and the wealthier agents in society and shape their policies in a way that will conform with those actors' outlooks and interests. A social movement with no public behind it is doomed to failure, no less and perhaps much more than if the financial or organizational resources available to it are insufficient.

The case of the Israeli peace movement sustains the theoretical differentiation not only between the state-centered and proximate POS, but also within the latter category between policy-specific opportunities and group-specific ones. In addition to the clearly significant correlation between the degree of expansion (or alternatively, contraction) of the POS and the movement's agenda compared with other "industries" in the same political framework, the specific human composition and political agenda seem to determine the movement's fate both in terms of its relations with the authorities and its positioning vis-à-vis the general public. As to the entire spectrum of social movements in Israel in these years, the peace movement faced a less favorable POS than, for example, the large NGOs that provided food or legal advice to the needy. Although they were indirectly critical of the authorities' welfare policies, in most cases the NGOs lacked protest elements. In addition, the issue at stake was considered less politically divisive. But even within the peace movement, there were significant differences in the status of the different peace groups/SMOs. The authorities' readiness to let certain citizens' groups run their own shop while using severe and even violent means against others depends much on the extent to which the activists are sociodemographically and politically close to, or far from, the sociopolitical center and its agenda. Hence, the potential for repression by the authorities was significantly lower for the moderate, Zionist peace organizations since their agenda could be included within the Zionist perimeter and because their activists often had the same profile as the elite and socially networked with it, although this did not necessarily increase the authorities' propensity for political cooperation. The POS was much less convenient for the radical anti-Zionist peace groups, for those that advocated conscientious objection, and of course for those that had a significant number of Arab activists. The authorities and the general public defined these organizations as revolutionary; that is, they called for a radical transformation of the political system and therefore the use of repressive measures was significantly higher in their case. As the Israeli case suggests, the picture is more complicated from the public's point of view, where the social proximity of social activists to the elite can actually harm their public image. This stems from the fact that the authenticity of the criticism and the protest can be questioned on the assumption that those close to the center would never act in a way that would in any way threaten the stability of the prevailing sociopolitical order.

As for the movement's agenda and composition as a precondition to gaining political visibility and public influence, the Israeli case suggests that to conduct a constructive dialogue with the mainstream – the leaders and the public – and to be considered politically relevant, the movement's agenda should share at least some common postulates with the mainstream about the framing of the situation and the acceptable and unacceptable solutions to the conflict to which it relates. Naturally, this is very difficult for the more purist activists and for radicals, who basically renounce the mainstream agenda and would like to see their own alternative program implemented. On the other hand, the case of moderates who get too close to the mainstream or are too compliant is also problematic, because this conflicts with the movement's raison d'être and undermines its mobilization potential.

The human composition of the movement's leadership also appears to be highly significant: not everyone with an authentic agenda can achieve results, just as the cause might be. To gain a foothold in the public discourse on social and political issues, speakers on its behalf should be knowledgeable and qualified challengers of those representing the establishment and its policies. On the other hand, those with the expertise necessary to gain access, that is, proper education, self-confidence, available time and other resources, are less likely to come up with an alternative outlook or innovative solutions.

When it comes to the definition of relevant public opinion according to foreign policy-making theories, our case seems to sustain the assumption presented in the theoretical section, that organized public opinion in the shape of a social movement, if persistent and long lasting, can introduce some critical value changes into the overall climate of opinion, which in turn might affect the policy-making process and the values and precepts underlying unorganized public opinion. Indeed, surveys can miss these organized grassroots groups. The students of foreign policy-making processes should therefore adopt other methods, for example, ethnographic techniques, which could reveal inputs into the processes they are studying but that are not reflected in the archival study of formal documents, content analysis of politicians' memoirs, or public opinion polls.

Finally, our case study sustains the view that it is problematic to judge a social movement's achievements mainly on the basis of its direct influence on specific policies or decisions, because this is not what most civil society organizations excel at. Even when convinced of the truth of the movement's arguments, politicians tend to be very careful not to respond immediately, so as not to be accused of being manipulated. The strength of such civil society actors, if any, is more discernible on the level of cultivating the ground for collective cognitive change and introducing new ideas and new options into the collective repertoire, which in turn can change national policies. The origins of climate of opinion changes are very difficult to discern and link to one or another factor or actor. Hence, social movements that introduce such change find it extremely difficult to prove their impact. Even if activists do not ask for credit for the change, any organization must show proof of its efficacy to raise funds, maintain its activists, and certainly to expand its mobilization capabilities. If such a connection between the change and the movement is not established and recognized, it might well be widely considered as a failure, which is exactly the way most people view the Israeli peace movement today.

While not ignoring its weaker sides, this book has tried to do the Israeli peace movement some justice and state that as wearying and unrewarding as the journey has been, along the way it has scattered some sweet hopes for peace, which might be followed by many others in the future.

Appendix 1: List of Israeli Peace Groups

Name	Name (E)	Website	Year Established
Ad Kan	Enough Is Enough		2002
haAguda l'Zchuyot haEzrach b'Yisrael	Association for Civil Rights in Israel, The (ACRI)	http://www.acri.org.il/english-acri/engine/index.asp	1972
Agudat haMifgash haBein Dati	Interfaith Encounter Association, The	www.interfaith-encounter.org	Late 1950s
Anarchistim Neged haGader	Anarchists Against the Wall (AATW)	http://www.awalls.org/	2003
Anshei Dat l'Maan haShalom	Clergy for Peace		1988
Arba Imahot	Four Mothers	http://www.4mothers.org.il/	1997
Atid Acher	Different Future, A	http://www.adifferentfuture.org/	2005
b'Tselem	B'Tselem: The Israeli Information Center for Human Rights in the Occupied Territories	http://www.btselem.org/English/	1989
Baderech el haSulcha	Sulha Peace Project	www.sulha.com	2000
Bat Shalom	Daughter of Peace – Israeli branch of the Jerusalem Link	http://www.batshalom.org/	1993
Beit haGefen	Vine House, The	http://civilsociety.haifa.ac.il/orgDet.asp?lang=eng&orgid=5	1963
Beit haTikva	House of Hope		1978
Besod Siach	Besod Siach – Open Discussion Groups	http://www.coexnet.org.il/site/common/index.php?where=organization%2Fprofile.php&id=68	1993
Bitterlemons	Bitterlemons	http://www.bitterlemons.org/index.html	2002
Bnei Avraham	Sons of Abraham		1996
Brit Shalom	Peace Alliance	http://www.britshalom.org/background.htm	1925

(continued)

Name	Name (E)	Website	Year Established
Brit Shivyon	Equality Covenant		
Brit Zedek v'Shalom	Jewish Alliance for Peace	www.btvshalom.org	2002
Bustan	Bustan	http://www.bustan.org/	1999
Bustan Shalom	Peace Garden		1999
Dai l'Kibush	End the Occupation		1987
Derech haShivyon	Way of Equality, The		1996
Dor Shalem	Entire Generation, An		1995
Dor Shalom	Peace Generation		1995
Du Kiyum	Negev Coexistence Forum	http://dukium.org/	1997
Ecopeace	Friends of the Earth Middle East (FoEME)	http://www.foeme.org/	1998
haEm haChamishit	Fifth (5th) Mother, The	http://coalitionofwomen.org/home/hebrew/organizations/the_fifth_mother	2002
haForum l'Haskama Ezrachit	Citizen's Accord Forum between Jews and Arabs in Israel, The (CAF)	http://www.caf.org.il/Index.asp	2000
haForum l'Shalom v'Tsedek Chevrati	Forum for Peace and Social Justice		
haGesher	Bridge, The		1975
Gesher l'Shalom	Bridge to Peace		1975
Gisha	*Gisha* – Legal Center for Freedom of Movement	http://www.gisha.org/	2005
Gush Shalom	Peace Bloc	http://zope.gush-shalom.org/home/he	1992
Hal'aa haKibush	Down with the Occupation		1985
Halonot	Windows–Channels for Communication	http://www.win-peace.org/	1991
Hayalim Neged Shtika	Soldiers against Silence		1982

Hitkarvut – Ma'arav Yerushalayim	Dialogue Groups – Rapprochement	http://www.rapprochement.org/	1988
Horim Neged Schika	Parents against Erosion		1983
Horim Neged Shtika	Parents against Silence		1984
ha'Igud ha'Yisraeli shel Rofim l'Meniat Milchama Garinit	Israel Association of Physicians for the Prevention of Nuclear War Union		
Ihud			1942
Imahot l'Maan Shalom	Mothers 4 Peace	http://www.moms4peace.com/	2002
Imahot Neged Shtika	Mothers Against Silence		1982
Imut	Mental Health Workers for the Advancement of Peace		1988
Indymedia	Indymedia Israel	https://israel.indymedia.org/	1999
IPCRI	Israel-Palestinian Center for Research and Information IPCRI	http://www.ipcri.org/	1988
Ir Amim	Ir Amim [City of Nations]	http://www.ir-amim.org.il/eng/	2004
Ir Shalem	Ir Shalem – Jerusalem (Front of Peace Now)		1995
Irgun haNashim haBeinleumi l'Shalom b'Mizrach haTichon	International Women's Commission (IWC)	http://www.iwc-peace.org/	2005
Irgun Sarvanei Milchama b'Yisrael	Association of Israeli War Resisters – Branch of WRI		1947
Isha l'Isha	Woman to Woman – Haifa Feminist Center	http://www.haifawomenscoalition.org.il/	1983
Kav Adom	Red Line		1988
Kav l'Oved	Workers Hotline	http://www.kavlaoved.org.il/	1989
haKav haYarok	Green Line, The – Students Draw the Line		2002

(*continued*)

269

Name	Name (E)	Website	Year Established
Keshev	*Keshev* – The Center for the Protection of Democracy in Israel	http://keshev.org.il/Site/default.asp	1998
haKoalitsia l'Peula Lo Alima	Coalition for Non-Violent Action		2004
Koalitziat Nashim l'Shalom	Coalition of Women for Peace	http://coalitionofwomen.org/home/english	2000
Kol ha'Isha	Women's Voice		1994
Kvisa Shchora	Black Laundry	http://www.blacklaundry.org/eng-index.html	2001
Knutsat Dialog D'heisha-Yerushalayim (Beit Shmuel)	Deheisha-Jerusalem Dialogue (Beit Shmuel)		
Lo b'Shmi	Not In My Name	http://www.nimm.org/	2000
Lochamin l'Shalom	Combatants for Peace	http://www.combatantsforpeace.org/default.asp?lng=eng	2005
Machon Arik	Arik Institute	http://www.arikpeace.org/	2004
Machon baNegev l'Estrategiyot shel Shalom u'Pituach	Negev Institute for Strategies of Peace and Development	http://www.nisped.org.il/	1998
haMachon haYehudi Aravi l'Shalom – Givat Haviva	Jewish Arab Center for Peace	http://www.givathaviva.org.il/english/peace/welcome.htm	1963
MachsomWatch	Machsom Watch	http://www.machsomwatch.org/	2002
Magazin baKibush	Occupation Magazine	http://www.kibush.co.il/	2004
Mabut baChaim	Peace Begins Within Me	http://www.eolife.org/about.php	2003
Mapat baShalom	Peace Quilt		1989
Martzim Neged baShlita haKfuya b'Shtachim	Lecturers Against Imposed Rule in the Territories		1987
Mate baShalom shel haZafon	Peace Movement Coordinating Committee in Haifa & the North		1988

Mate Tnuot haShalom	Peace Movement Headquarters		1997
Mechuyavut l'Shalom v'l'Tsedek Chevrati	Commitment to Peace and Social Justice	http://www.commitment.org.il/article_page.asp?id=65&scid=14	1998
haMercaz haBeinleumi l'Shalom	International Center for Peace		1982
haMercaz l'Informazia Alternativit	Alternative Information Center, The	http://www.alternativenews.org/	1984
haMerkaz haYehudi-Aravi l'Kidum Kalkali	Jewish-Arab Center for Economic Development, The		1998
Merkaz Peres l'Shalom	Peres Center for Peace	http://www.peres-center.org/	1997
haMifkad haLeumi	People's Voice (The Ayalon-Nusseibeh Initiative)	http://www.mifkad.org.il/	2003
Mishmarot haShalom	Guards of Peace		1995
Mishmarot Shalom	Peace Guards		1995
Mishpachot Shakulot Nifgaot Terror l'maan haShalom	Association of Bereaved Families in the Middle East, The (Parents' Circle)	http://www.parentscircle.israel.net/	1995
haMizrach el haShalom	East for Peace		1983
Moatsa Bein Datit Mitaemet b'Yisrael	Inter-religious Coordination Council in Israel, The (ICCI)	http://www.icci.co.il	1991
haMoatsa baYisraelit l'Shalom Yisrael-Falestin	Israeli Council for Israeli-Palestinian Peace		1975
haMoatsa l'Shalom u'Bitachon	Council for Peace and Security, The	http://www.peace-security-council.org/	1988
haMoked l'Haganat haPrat	Center for the Defense of the Individual (*HaMoked*)	http://www.hamoked.org.il/index_en.asp	1988
Nashim b'Shachor	Women in Black		1988
Nashim b'Lavan	Women in White		1997

(continued)

Name	Name (E)	Website	Year Established
Nashim Bonot Tarbut Shalom	Engendering Peace		2000
Nashim l'maan Asirot Politiot	Women for Political Prisoners (WFPP)		1988
Nashim l'maan Kdushat haChayim	Women for the Sanctity of Life		1996
Nashim Neged Plisha l'Levanon	Women Against the Invasion of Lebanon		1982
Nashim v'Shalom	Women and Peace		1989
Neled	We Will Give Birth		1989
Netivei Achva	Friendship's Way		1983
Netivot Shalom	Paths for Peace	http://www.netivot-shalom.org.il/parsha.php	1982
Neve Shalom	Oasis for Peace	http://www.nswas.com/	1977
Nisan	Nisan Young Women Leaders	http://www.nisan.org/	1995
Nitsanei Shalom	Interns for Peace	http://mpdn.org/interns.htm	1976
Ohel haShalom	Peace Tent, The		2005
Ometz l'Sarev	Courage to Refuse	http://www.seruv.org.il/english/default.asp	2002
Osim Shalom	Osim Shalom		1983
haOt	Sign, The		2002
Oz v'Shalom	Strength and Peace	http://www.netivot-shalom.org.il/parsha.php	1976
Oz v'Shalom/Netivot Shalom	Courage and Peace	http://www.netivot-shalom.org.il/parsha.php	1976
Palestinaim v'Yisraelim l'maan e Alimut	Palestinians and Israelis for Non-violence – Branch of IFOR	http://www.ifor.org/	1997
Pe Echad	One Voice	http://www.onevoicemovement.org/	2002
Profil Hadash	New Profile	http://www.newprofile.org/	1998
Proyekt Schunat Volfson	Wolfson Community Project – Acre		1990
Radio Kol haShalom – l'Lo Gvulot	Radio All for Peace	http://www.allforpeace.org/default.aspx	2004

Hebrew	English	URL	Year
Reshet	Network – Coordinating Organization	http://www.coexnet.org.il/site/common/index.php?where=about/en/index.php	1983
Reshet haShutfut haYehudit-Aravit b'Yisrael	Coexistence Network in Israel		2002
Reshet Nashim l'Shalom	Women's Network for Peace		1982
Reut / Sdaka	Friendship		
Rofim l'Zchuyot ha'Adam	Physicians for Human Rights	http://www.phr.org.il/phr/	1988
Shalom Achshav	Peace Now	http://www.peacenow.org.il/site/he/homepage.asp	1978
haShana baEsrim v'Achat	21st Year, The		1988
Shani – Nashim Neged haKibush	Women Against the Occupation		1988
Shministim	New High-School Refuseniks Movement, The	http://www.shministim.org/	2004
Shomrei Mishpat – Rabanim l'maan Zchuyot haAdam	Rabbis for Human Rights (formerly – Rabbinic Human Rights Watch)	http://www.rhr.israel.net/	1989
Shovrim Shtika	Breaking the Silence	http://www.shovrimshtika.org/index.e.asp	2004
Shutafut	Partnership		1977
Shuvi	Shuvi [Come back]	http://www.shuvi.org/	2004
Shvil baZahav	Middleway	http://www.middleway.org/	2002
Studentim l'maan haShalom	Student Union for Peace		1996
Ta'ayush	Ta'ayush [Partnership]	http://www.taayush.org/	2000
haTnua l'Tziyonut Acheret	Movement for Another Zionism		1975
Truat Nashim Demokratit Yisraelit	TANDI – Movement of Democratic Women for Israel	http://coalitionofwomen.org/home/english/organizations/tandi	1948
baVaad haYisraeli Neged Harisat Batim	Israeli Committee Against House Demolition	http://www.icahd.org/eng/	1996

(continued)

Name	Name (E)	Website	Year Established
haVaad haZiburi Neged Inuyim	Public Committee Against Torture in Israel	http://www.stoptorture.org.il/eng/	1990
Vaad haShalom haYisraeli	Israeli Peace Committee		1950
haVaad l'Dialog Yisraeli-Falestinai	Committee for Israeli-Palestinian Dialogue		1986
haVaad l'Maan Beita	Committee for Beita		1988
haVaad l'Solidariut im Hevron	Hebron Solidarity Committee		1993
haVaad l'Solidariut im Bir Zeit	Committee for Solidarity with Bir Zeit		1981
haVaad Neged haMilchama b'Levanon	Committee against the War in Lebanon	http://www.israeli-left-archive.org/?site= localhost&a=p&p=about&c=israelic &cct=1&qto=3&l=en&w=utf-8	1982
haVaad Neged haYad haKasha	Committee against the Iron Fist		1986
Vaad haYotsrim	Committee of Jewish and Arab Creative Artists		1988
WILPF	WILPF – Israeli Branch	http://www.wilpf.org/	1983
Yaldei haMizrach haTichon	Middle East Children's Alliance	www.mecaforpeace.org	1988
Yaldei Yisrael	Peace Child Israel	http://www.mideastweb.org/peacechild/	1988
Yesh Din	There Is Justice	http://www.yesh-din.org/site/index.php	2005
Yesh Gvul	There Is a Limit	http://www.yeshgvul.org/	1982
Yisraelim Mitoch Bchira	Israelis by Choice / Immigrants Against Occupation		1988

	Name	URL	Year
haYom haShvi'i	Seventh (7th) Day, The	http://www.7th-day.co.il/hayom-hashvie/	2002
Yozmat Kopenhagen	International Alliance for Arab-Israel Peace (The Copenhagen Initiative)	http://www.pforp.net	1995
Yozmat Geneva	Geneva Initiative	http://www.geneva-accord.org/HomePage.aspx?FolderID=11&lang=en	2003
Zochrot	Remembering	http://www.zochrot.org/	2002
	Care and Learning – In Defense of "Children Under Occupation"	http://www.rightlivelihood.org/mer_khamis_speech.html	1987
	Israel-Palestinian Science Organization (IPSO)	http://www.ipso-jerusalem.org/	2004
	Jerusalem Link, The	http://www.batshalom.org/english/jlink/	1994
	Jerusalem Peace Makers	www.jerusalempeacemakers.org	2004
	Just Vision	www.justvision.org	2003
	Middle East Citizen's Assembly (MECA)		
	Oznik Media	http://www.oznik.com/	2000
	Palestinian Israeli Health Care Group		1997
	Peace Research Institute in the Middle East (PRIME)	http://www.vispo.com/PRIME/	1998

Appendix 2: Israeli Jewish Public Support for the Oslo Process (1994–2008)

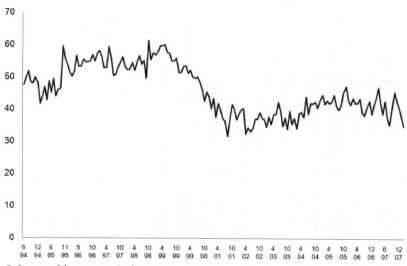

Oslo monthly support index (June 1994–December 2007)

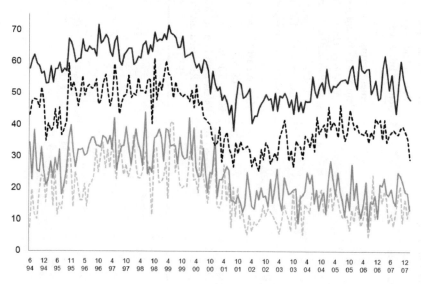

--- Ultra-orthodox ——Orthodox --- Traditional ——Secular

Oslo monthly support, in percentages, by levels of religious observance (June 1994–December 2007)

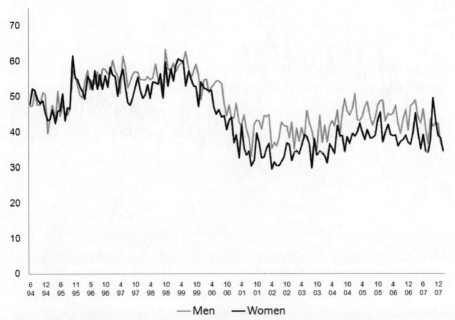

Oslo monthly support, in percentages, by gender (June 1994–December 2007)

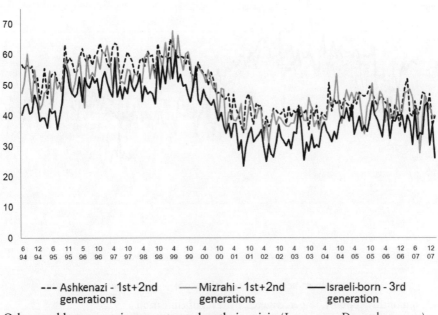

Oslo monthly support, in percentages, by ethnic origin (June 1994–December 2007)

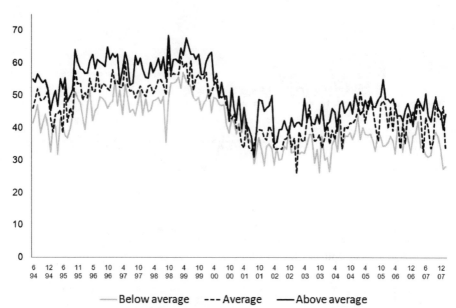

Oslo monthly support, in percentages, by income (June 1994–December 2007)

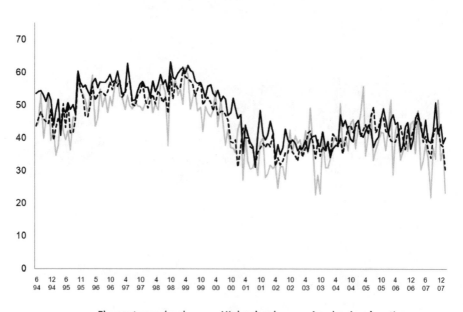

Oslo monthly support, in percentages, by level of education
(June 1994–December 2007)

Bibliography

Books, Reports, and Journal Issues

Abbas, Mahmud. 1995. *Through Secret Channels: The Road to Oslo*. Reading, UK: Garnet Publishing.

Abu Nimer, Mohammed. 1999. *Dialogue, Conflict Resolution, and Change: Arab-Jewish Encounters*. Albany, NY: SUNY.

Abu-Zayyad, Ziad, and Hillel Schenker, eds. 2005/2006. *People-to-People: What Went Wrong & How to Fix It? Palestine-Israel Journal*. Vol. 12 (4)–13 (1).

Al Mahdi, Amin. 2001. *The Other Opinion*. Tel Aviv: Hakibbutz Hameuhad [Hebrew].

Alinsky, Saul. 1972. *Rules for Radicals*. New York: Vintage.

Almond, Gabriel. 1950. *The American People and Foreign Policy*. New York: Harcourt, Brace.

Alpher, Joseph, and Ghassam Khatib, eds. 2007. *Peacemakers or Peace Industry? Bitterlemons*. 28 May. http://www.bitterlemons.org/previous/bl280507ed19.html (accessed May 2008).

Alpher, Joseph, Ghassan Khatib, and Charmaine Seitz, eds. 2007. *The Best of Bitterlemons – Five Years of Writings from Israel and Palestine*. Bitterlemons.org.

Aminzade, Ronald R., Jack A. Goldstone, Doug McAdam, Elizabeth J. Perry, William H. Sewell, Sidney Tarrow, and Charles Tilly. 2001. *Silence and Voice in the Study of Contentious Politics*, Cambridge Studies in Contentious Politics. Cambridge, UK: Cambridge University Press.

Arian, Asher. 1995. *Security Threatened: Surveying Israeli Opinion on Peace and War*. New York: Cambridge University Press.

———. 1996, 1997, 1998. *Public Opinion on National Security* (Survey Results). Tel Aviv: Tel Aviv University, The Jaffee Center for Strategic Studies.

Aristophanes. 1990. *Lysistrata*. Edited with an Introduction and Commentary by Jeffrey Henderson. New York: Oxford University Press.

Arnon, Arie, and Saeb Bamya, eds. 2007. Economic Dimensions of a Two-State Agreement between Israel and Palestine. Marseilles, Tel Aviv, Bethlehem: Aix Group.

Ashkenazi, Moty. 2003. *A War Will Break Out at 6 P.M.* Tel Aviv: Hakibbutz Hameuchad [Hebrew].

Avneri, Uri. 1986. *My Friend the Enemy*. London: Zed Books.

Azoulay, Ariella, and Adi Ophir. 2008. *This Regime Which is Not One – Occupation and Democracy Between the Sea and the River (1967–).* Tel Aviv: Resling [Hebrew].

Bar-Levav, Avriel, ed. 2006. *Peace and War in Jewish Culture.* Jerusalem: Zalman Shazar Center for Jewish History [Hebrew].

Bar-On, Mordechai. 1996. *In Pursuit of Peace: A History of the Israeli Peace Movement.* Washington, DC: US Institute of Peace.

Bar-Siman-Tov, Yaacov, ed. 2003. *As the Generals See It: The Collapse of the Oslo Process and the Violent Israeli-Palestinian Conflict.* Jerusalem: The Leonard Davis Institute for International Relations, Hebrew University of Jerusalem [Hebrew].

————, ed. 2005. *The Israeli-Palestinian Conflict 2000–2005: The Shift from a Peace Process to a Violent Confrontation.* Jerusalem: The Jerusalem Institute for Israel Studies.

Baskin, Gershon, and Zakaria al Qaq. 2002. *Yes PM – Years of Experience in Strategies of Peace Making: Looking at Israeli-Palestinian People-to-People Activities, 1993–2002.* Jerusalem: IPCRI.

Bechor, Guy. 1996. *Constitution for Israel.* [Huka Le'Ysrael]. Jerusalem: Keter [Hebrew].

Begin, Ze'ev Benyamin. 2000. *A Sad Story.* Tel Aviv: Miskal – Yediot Aharonot Books [Hebrew].

Beilin, Yossi. 1997. *Touching Peace: From Oslo Accord to Final Agreement.* Tel Aviv: Miskal – Yediot Aharonot Books and Chemed Books [Hebrew].

————. 2001. *Manual for a Wounded Dove.* Tel Aviv: Miskal – Yediot Aharonot Books [Hebrew].

————. 2004. *From Hachula to Geneva.* Tel Aviv: Yediot Aharonot [Hebrew].

Bell, Daniel. 1960. *The End of Ideology.* New York: Free Press.

Ben Ami, Shlomo. 2004. *A Front without a Rearguard: A Voyage to the Boundaries of the Peace Process.* Tel Aviv: Miskal – Yediot Aharonot Books and Chemed Books [Hebrew].

Ben Meir, Atalya. 2005. *Oslo: Failure of Folly.* Tel Aviv: Tamuz Publishing [Hebrew].

Ben-Porat, Guy. 2006. Global Liberalism, Local Populism: Peace and Conflict in Israel/Palestine and Northern Ireland. Syracuse, NY: Syracuse University Press.

Ben Porat, Shayke. 1996. *Conversations with Yossi Beilin.* Tel Aviv: Hakibbutz Hameuchad [Hebrew].

Bentsur, Eytan. 1997. *The Road to Peace Crosses Madrid.* Tel Aviv: Yediot Aharonot Books [Hebrew].

Benziman, Uzi, ed. 2006. *Whose Land is it?* Jerusalem: The Israel Democracy Institute.

Boggs, Carl. 1986. *Social Movements and Political Power: Emerging Forms of Radicalism in the West.* Philadelphia, PA: Temple University Press.

————. 2000. *The End of Politics: Corporate Power and the Decline of the Public Sphere.* New York: The Guilford Press.

Braverman, Irus. 2006. *Illegalism in East Jerusalem: An Examination of the House-Demolition Phenomenon in Light of Trends in Planning, Law, and Society.* Tel Aviv: The Tami Steinmetz Center for Peace Research, Tel Aviv University.

Brock, Peter. 1972. *Pacifism in Europe to 1914.* Princeton, NJ: Princeton University Press.

Buber, Martin. 1988. *One Land for Two People.* Tel Aviv and Jerusalem: Schoken [Hebrew].

Buechler, Steven M., and F. Kurt Cylke, eds. 1997. *Social Movements: Perspectives and Issues.* Mountain View, CA: Mayfield Publishing Company.

Chacham, Ronit. 2003. *Breaking Ranks: Refusing to Serve in the West Bank & Gaza Strip*. New York: Other Press.

Chatfield, Charles, ed. 1973. *Peace Movements in America*. New York: Schocken Books.

Chen, Michael. 2000. *The Guards of Peace and Democracy, November 4th, 1995: Annals of a Project Organization*. Tel Aviv: Ramot, Tel Aviv University [Hebrew].

Cohen, Asher, and Bernard Susser. 2000. *Israel and the Politics of Jewish Identity: The Secular-Religious Impasse*. Baltimore, MD: The Johns Hopkins University Press.

Cohen, Bernard C. 1973. *The Public's Impact on Foreign Policy*. Boston, MA: Little, Brown.

Cohen, Raymond, 1997. *Negotiating across Cultures*. Washington DC: United States Institute of Peace.

Cortright, David. 1993. *Peace Works: The Citizen's Role in Ending the Cold War*. Boulder, CO: Westview Press.

Coy, Patrick G., ed. 2001. *Political Opportunities, Social Movements and Democratization*, Research in Social Movements, Conflicts and Change, Vol. 23. Oxford: Elsevier/JAI.

Dahl, Robert. 1971. *Polyarchy: Participation and Opposition*. New Haven, CT: Yale University Press.

Dalton, Russell J. 1988. *Citizen Politics in Western Democracies: Public Opinion and Political Parties in the United States, Great Britain, West Germany, and France*. Chatham, NJ: Chatham House.

Darby, John. 2001. *The Effects of Violence on Peace Processes*. Washington, DC: United States Institute of Peace Press.

Darby, John, and Roger MacGinty, eds. 2003. *Contemporary Peace Making: Conflict, Violence and Peace Processes*. London: Palgrave Macmillan.

DeBenedetti, Charles. 1990. *An American Ordeal: The Antiwar Movement of the Vietnam Era*. Syracuse, NY: Syracuse University Press.

della Porta, Donatella. 1995. *Social Movements, Political Violence and the State: A Comparative Analysis of Italy and Germany*. New York: Cambridge University Press.

della Porta, Donatella, Hanspeter Kriesi, and Dieter Rucht, eds. 1999. *Social Movements in a Globalizing World*. New York: St. Martin's Press.

Dershowitz, Alan. 2004. *The Case for Israel*. New York: John Wiley & Sons, Inc.

Dor, Daniel. 2001. *Newspapers under the Influence*. Tel Aviv: Babel [Hebrew].

Dorman, Michael. 1974. *Confrontation: Politics and Protest*. New York: Delacorte Press.

Dowty, Alan. 1998. *The Jewish State: A Century Later*. Berkeley, CA: University of California Press.

Drucker, Raviv. 2002. *Harakiri – Ehud Barak: The Failure*. Tel Aviv: Yediot Aharonot Books and Chemed Books [Hebrew].

du Toit, Pierre. 2001. *South Africa's Brittle Peace: The Problem of Post-Settlement Violence*. Houndmills, UK: Palgrave Macmillan.

Eder, Klaus. 1993. *The New Politics of Class: Social Movements and Cultural Dynamics in Advanced Societies*. London: Sage.

Eichenberg, Richard C. 1989. *Public Opinion and National Security in Western Europe*. Ithaca, NY: Cornell University Press.

Eisenstadt, Samuel Noah. 1967. *Israeli Society*. New York: Basic Books.

Enderlin, Charles. 2003. *Shattered Dreams: The Failure of the Peace Process in the Middle East, 1995–2002*. New York: Other Press.

Entman, Robert M. 2003. *Projections of Power: Framing News, Public Opinion, and U.S. Foreign Policy.* Chicago, IL University of Chicago Press.

Eshel, Nimrod. 1994. *The Seamen's Strike.* Tel Aviv: Am Oved [Hebrew].

Everson, David H. 1982. *Public Opinion and Interest Groups in American Politics.* New York: Franklin Watts.

Everts, Philip, and Pierangelo Isernia, eds. 2001. *When the Going Gets Tough: Public Opinion and the International Use of Force.* London: Routledge.

Feige, Michael. 2002. *One Space, Two Places: Gush Emunim, Peace Now and the Construction of Israeli Space.* Jerusalem: Magnes Press [Hebrew].

Flapan, Simha. 1987. *The Birth of Israel: Myths and Realities.* New York: Pantheon.

Gamson, William A. 1990. *The Strategy of Social Protest.* 2nd ed. Belmont, CA: Wadsworth.

————— 1992. *Talking Politics.* New York: Cambridge University Press.

Gerner, Deborah J. 1991. *One Land, Two People: The Conflict over Palestine.* Boulder, CO: Westview Press.

Gidron, Benjamin, and Hagai Katz. 1998. Defining the Nonprofit Sector: Israel, Johns Hopkins Comparative Nonprofit Sector Project Working Papers. Baltimore: Johns Hopkins University Institute for Policy Studies.

Gidron, Benjamin, Stanley N. Katz, and Yeheskel Hasenfeld, eds. 2002. *Mobilizing for Peace: Conflict Resolution in Northern Ireland, Israel/Palestine, and South Africa.* New York: Oxford University Press.

Giugni, Marco G., Doug McAdam, and Charles Tilly, eds. 1999. *How Social Movements Matter.* Minneapolis: University of Minnesota Press.

Golan, Galia. 2007. *Israel and Palestine – Peace Plans from Oslo to Disengagement.* Princeton, NJ: Markus Weiner Publishers.

Golan-Agnon, Daphna. 2005. *Next Year in Jerusalem: Everyday Life in a Divided Land.* New York: The New Press.

Goren, Nimrod. 2004. *Going against the Wind: The Role of NGOs in Jerusalem under an Ongoing Conflict.* Jerusalem: Jerusalem Institute for Israel Studies.

Grinberg, Lev. 2007. *Imagined Peace, Discourse of War: The Failure of Leadership, Politics and Democracy in Israel 1992–2006.* Tel Aviv: Resling [Hebrew].

Grossman, David. 2003. *Death as a Way of Life: Israel Ten Years after Oslo.* New York: Farrar, Straus & Giroux.

Gurr, Ted Robert. 1970. *Why Men Rebel.* Princeton, NJ: Princeton University Press.

Hagan, Joe D. 1993. *Political Opposition and Foreign Policy in Comparative Perspective.* Boulder, CO: Lynne Rienner.

Halabi, Rabah, ed. 2000. *Identities in Dialogue: Arab-Jewish Encounters in Whahat Al-Salam/Neveh-Shalom.* Tel-Aviv: Hakibbutz Hameuchad [Hebrew].

Halevi, Hava, and Hagit Shlonsky. 2008. *Membership and Activity in an Unauthorized Association: The Military Courts during 2008.* Machsomwatch [Hebrew].

Hashana Ha'esrim Ve'achat. 1988. *A Covenant against the Occupation.* Jerusalem.

Haskell, John. 2001. *Direct Democracy or Representative Government? Dispelling the Populist Myth.* Boulder, CO: Westview Press.

Hasson-Rochlin, Yona. 2007. Parenthood to Soldiers in Israel as a Political Resource. MA thesis, Democracy Studies, The Open University of Israel, Raanana [Hebrew].

Hay, Colin. 2007. *Why We Hate Politics.* Cambridge: Polity Press.

Heller, Joseph. 2003. *From Brit Shalom to the Ihud: Judah Leib Magnes and the Struggle for a Binational State in Palestine.* Jerusalem: Magnes [Hebrew].

Hermann, Tamar. 1989. *Between the Peace Covenant and Peace Now: The Pragmatic Pacifism of the Israeli Peace Movement in a Comparative Perspective. PhD diss.*, Tel Aviv University [Hebrew].

———. 2005. *The Israeli Peace Movement Looks in the Mirror: The Oslo Process and Its Effects on the Movement.* A summary of discussions at meetings of activists (5 May, 8 June 2004). United States Institute of Peace [also available in Hebrew].

Herzog, Shira, and Avivit Hai. 2005. *The Power of Possibility: The Role of People-to-People Programs in the Current Israeli-Palestinian Reality.* Tel Aviv: Economic Cooperation Foundation and Friedrich-Ebert-Stiftung.

Hirschfeld, Yair. 2000. *Oslo: A Formula for Peace.* Tel Aviv: Am Oved [Hebrew].

Hirschman, Albert O. 1970. *Exit, Voice, and Loyalty: Responses to Decline in Firms, Organizations, and States.* Cambridge, MA: Harvard University Press.

Holsti, Ole R. 2004. *Public Opinion and American Foreign Policy.* Revised ed. Ann Arbor, MI: University of Michigan Press.

Horovitz, David, ed. 1996. *Yitzhak Rabin: Soldier of Peace.* London: Halban.

Horowitz, Dan, and Moshe Lissak. 1978. *Origins of the Israeli Polity: Palestine under the Mandate.* Chicago, IL: Chicago University Press.

———. 1988. *Trouble in Utopia: The Overburdened Polity of Israel.* Albany, NY: SUNY.

Hurwitz, Deena R., ed. 1992. *Walking the Red Line, Israelis in Search of Justice for Palestine.* Philadelphia, PA: New Society Publishers.

Inglehart, Ronald. 1977. *The Silent Revolution: Changing Values and Political Styles among Western Publics.* Princeton, NJ: Princeton University Press.

Isaac, Rael Jean. 1976. *Israel Divided: Ideological Politics in the Jewish State.* Baltimore, MD: The Johns Hopkins University Press.

Isachar, Hedva, ed. 2003. *Sisters in Peace: Feminist Voices of the Left.* Tel Aviv: Resling [Hebrew].

Joffe, Lawrence. 1996. *Keesing's Guide to the Mid-East Peace Process.* London: Cartermill.

Johnston, Hank, and Bert Klandermans, eds. 1995. *Social Movements and Culture,* Social Movements, Protest, and Contention Series, Vol. 4. Minneapolis: University of Minnesota Press.

Kabalo, Paula. 2007. *The Story of a Civic Association – Shurat Hamitnadvim.* Tel Aviv: Am Oved [Hebrew].

Kacowicz, Arie M. 2004. *Rashomon in Jerusalem: Mapping the Israeli Negotiators' Positions on the Israeli-Palestinian Peace Process, 1993–2001.* Jerusalem: The Leonard Davis Institute for International Relations, Hebrew University of Jerusalem.

Kaminer, Reuven. 1996. *The Politics of Protest: The Israeli Peace Movement and the Palestinian Intifada.* Brighton, UK: Sussex Academic Press.

Kaplan, Temma. 1997. *Crazy for Democracy: Women's Grassroots Movements.* New York and London: Routledge.

Karif, Moshe. 2005. *The Easterner: The Story of the Mizrahi Democratic Rainbow Party and the Fight for Social Equality in Israel, 1995–2005.* Tel Aviv: Globs.

Karsh, Efraim. 2003. *The Oslo War: An Anatomy of Self-Delusion,* Mideast and Security Studies Series, No. 55. Ramat-Gan: The BESA Center for Strategic Studies [Hebrew].

Kemp, Adriana, David Newman, Uri Ram, and Oren Yiftachel, eds. 2004. *Israelis in Conflict: Hegemonies, Identities and Challenges.* Brighton, UK: Sussex Academic Press.

Kidron, Peretz, ed. 2004. _Refusenik!_ Tel Aviv: Xargol [Also available in English as: _Refusenik!: Israel's Soldiers of Conscience_, New York: Zed Books].

Klandermans, Bert, Hanspeter Kriesi, and Sidney Tarrow, eds. 1988. _From Structure to Action: Comparing Social Movement Research across Cultures._ Greenwich, CT: JAI Press.

Klandermans, Bert, and Suzzanne Staggenborg, eds. 2002. _Methods of Social Movement Research._ Minneapolis: University of Minnesota Press.

Knoke, David, and James H. Kuklinski. 1982. _Network Analysis:_ Newbury Park, CA: Sage.

Kornhauser, William. 1959. _The Politics of Mass Society._ New York: The Free Press.

Kowalewski, David, and Dean Hoover. 1995. _Dynamic Models of Conflict and Pacification: Dissenters, Officials, and Peacemakers._ Westport, CT: Praeger Publishers.

Kurtzer, Daniel C., and Scott B. Lasensky. 2008. _Negotiating Arab-Israeli Peace: American Leadership in the Middle East._ Washington, DC: United States Institute of Peace Press.

Lahat, Golan. 2004. _The Messianic Temptation._ Tel Aviv: Am Oved [Hebrew].

Lake, Anthony, ed. 1976. _The Vietnam Legacy: The War, American Society, and the Future of American Foreign Policy._ New York: New York University Press.

Landau, Yehezkel. 2003. _Healing the Holy Land: Interreligious Peacebuilding in Israel/Palestine_, Peaceworks Series No. 51. Washington, DC: United States Institute of Peace.

Lebel, Udi, and Gideon Doron. 2005. _Politics of Bereavement._ Tel Aviv: Hakibbutz Hameuhad [Hebrew].

le Bon, Gustave. [1895] 1960. _The Crowd: A Study of the Popular Mind._ New York: Viking Press.

Lehman-Wilzig, Sam N. 1990. _Stiff-Necked People, Bottle-Necked System: The Evolution and Roots of Israeli Public Protest, 1949–1986._ Bloomington, IN: Indiana University Press.

———. 1992. _Wildfire: Grassroots Revolts in Israel in the Post-Socialist Era._ Albany, NY: SUNY.

Leon, Dan, ed. 2004. _Who's Left in Israel: Radical Political Alternatives for the Future of Israel._ Brighton, UK: Sussex Academic Press.

Leonard David Institute. _What Went Wrong? Oral History Project, 2002–3._ Jerusalem: Leonard David Institute, The Hebrew University [unpublished].

Levy, Yagil. 2007. _From the 'People's Army' to the 'Army of the Peripheries.'_ Jerusalem: Carmel [Hebrew].

Lewis, Samuel and Kenneth W. Stein. 1991. _Making Peace among Arabs and Israelis: Lessons from Fifty Years of Negotiating Experience._ Washington DC: United States Institute of Peace.

Lippmann, Walter. 1922. _Public Opinion._ New York: Free Press.

Lustick, Ian. 1980. _Arabs in the Jewish State: Israel's Control of a National Minority._ Austin, TX: University of Texas Press.

Makovsky, David. 1996. _Making Peace with the PLO: The Rabin Government's Road to the Oslo Accord._ Boulder, CO: Westview Press.

Margolis, Michael, and Gary A. Mauser, eds. 1989. _Manipulating Public Opinion: Essays on Public Opinion as a Dependent Variable._ Pacific Grove, CA: Brook/Cole.

Marsh, David, and Gerry Stoker, eds. 2002. _Theory and Methods in Political Science._ New York: Palgrave-Macmillan.

McAdam, Doug. 1982. *Political Process and the Development of Black Insurgency, 1930–1970*. Chicago, IL: University of Chicago Press.

McAdam, Doug, John D. McCarthy, and Mayer N. Zald, eds. 1996. *Comparative Perspectives on Social Movements: Political Opportunities, Mobilizing Structures, and Cultural Framings*, Cambridge Studies in Comparative Politics. New York: Cambridge University Press.

McCarthy, John D., and Mayer N. Zald. 1973. *The Trend of Social Movements in America: Professionalization and Resource Mobilization*. Morristown, NJ: General Learning Corporation.

Meir, Yedidya, and Sivan Rahav-Meir, 2006. *Days of Disengagement – Conversations about the Israeli Evacuation from the Gaza Strip*. Tel Aviv: Miskal [Hebrew].

Meital, Yoram. 2006. *Peace in Tatters: Israel, Palestine, and the Middle East*. Boulder, CO: Lynne Rienner Publishers.

Meyer, David S. 1990. *A Winter of Discontent: The Nuclear Freeze and American Politics*. New York: Praeger Publishers.

Michael, Kobi, and David Kellen, eds. 2007. *Stabilizing the Israeli-Palestinian Conflict: Considerations for a Multinational Peace Support Operation*. Jerusalem: The Harry S. Truman Institute for the Advancement of Peace.

Morgan, Michael, and Susan Leggett, eds. 1996. *Mainstream(s) and Margins: Cultural Politics in the 90s*. Westport, CT: Greenwood.

Morris, Benny. 2001. *Righteous Victims: A History of the Zionist-Arab Conflict, 1881–2001*. New York: Vintage Books.

Mutz, Diana C. 1998. *Impersonal Influence: How Perceptions of Mass Collectives Affect Political Attitudes*. New York: Cambridge University Press.

Netanyahu, Benjamin. 1993. *A Place among the Nations*. New York: Bantam Books.

Netivot Shalom. 1982. *This Is Our Position*. Jerusalem [Hebrew].

Newman, David, ed. 1985. *The Impact of Gush Emunim: Politics and Settlement in the West Bank*. London: Croom Helm.

Noelle-Neumann, Elisabeth. 1993. *The Spiral of Silence: Public Opinion – Our Social Skin*. Chicago, IL: University of Chicago Press.

Norell, Magnus. 2002. *A Dissenting Democracy: The Israeli Movement 'Peace Now.'* London: Frank Cass.

Ofir, Adi, ed. 2001. *Real Time: The Al-Aqsa Intifada and the Israeli Left*. Jerusalem: Keter [Hebrew].

Olson, Mancur. 1965. *The Logic of Collective Action: Public Goods and the Theory of Groups*. Cambridge, MA: Harvard University Press.

Page, Benjamin I., and Robert Y. Shapiro. 1992. *The Rational Public: Fifty Years of Trends in Americans' Policy Preferences*. Chicago, IL: University of Chicago Press.

Palgi, Arie. 1979. *Peace and Nothing More*. Tel Aviv: Sifriat Poalim [Hebrew].

Peleg, Ilan, ed. 1997. *The Middle East Peace Process: Interdisciplinary Perspectives*. Albany, NY: SUNY.

Peres, Shimon. 1993. *The New Middle East*. New York: Henry Holt and Company.

———. 1995. *Battling for Peace. A Memoir*. Edited by David Landau. New York: Random House.

Peri, Yoram. 1983. *Between Battles and Ballots: Israeli Military in Politics*. Cambridge Middle East Library. New York: Cambridge University Press.

———. 2005. *Brothers at War: Rabin's Assassination and the Cultural War in Israel*. Tel Aviv: Miskal [Hebrew].

Piven, Frances Fox, and Richard Cloward. 1977. *Poor People's Movements: Why They Succeed, How They Fail*. New York: Vintage.

Portugali, Juval. 1996. *Implicate Relations: Society and Space in the Israeli-Palestinian Conflict*. Tel Aviv: Hakibbutz Hameuchad [Hebrew].

Rabinovich, Itamar. 1999. *Waging Peace: Israel and the Arabs at the End of the Century*. New York: Farrar, Straus and Giroux.

Rachamim, Yechezkel, ed. 2005. *No One to Talk To: A Critical Review of the Media-Politician Connection*. Tel Aviv: Tel Aviv University, The Chaim Herzog Institute for Media, Politics and Society.

Reshef, Tzaly. 1996. *Peace Now*. [Shalom Achshav]. Jerusalem: Keter Publishing House [Hebrew].

Rochon, Thomas R. 1988. *Mobilizing for Peace: The Antinuclear Movements in Western Europe*. Princeton, NJ: Princeton University Press.

Rosenwasser, Penny. 1992. *Voices from a "Promised Land": Palestinian and Israeli Peace Activists Speak Their Hearts*. Willimantic, CT: Curbstone Press.

Ross, Dennis. 2004. *The Missing Peace: The Inside Story of the Fight for Middle East Peace*. New York: Farrar, Straus and Giroux.

Rothstein, Robert L., Moshe Ma'oz, and Khalil Shikaki, eds. 2002. *The Israeli-Palestinian Peace Process – Oslo and the Lessons of Failure: Perspectives, Predicaments and Prospects*. Brighton, UK: Sussex Academic Press.

Russett, Bruce. 1990. *Controlling the Sword: The Democratic Governance of National Security*. Cambridge, MA: Harvard University Press.

Said, Edward W. 2000. *The End of the Peace Process: Oslo and After*. New York: Pantheon Books.

Sasson-Levi, Orna. 1995. *Radical Rhetoric, Conformist Practices: Theory and Praxis in an Israeli Protest Movement. Shain Working Paper No. 1*. Jerusalem: Hebrew University [Hebrew].

Savir, Uri. 1998. *The Process: 1100 Days That Changed the Middle East*. New York: Random House.

_____. 2006. *Peace First*. Tel Aviv: Miskal – Yediot Aharonot Books and Chemed Books [Hebrew].

Schedler, Andreas, ed. 1997. *The End of Politics? Explorations into Modern Antipolitics*. New York: St. Martin's Press.

Sedaitis, Judith, and Jim Butterfield, eds. 1991. *Perestroika from Below: Social Movements in the Soviet Union*. Boulder, CO: Westview Press.

Shafir, Gershon, and Yoav Peled, eds. 2000. *The New Israel: Peacemaking and Liberalization*. Boulder, CO: Westview.

Shamir, Jacob, and Michal Shamir. 1993. *The Dynamics of Israeli Public Opinion on Peace and the Territories*, Research Reports Series, No. 1. Tel Aviv: The Tami Steinmetz Center for Peace Research, Tel Aviv University.

_____. 2000. *The Anatomy of Public Opinion*. Ann Arbor, MI: University of Michigan Press.

Shamir, Shimon, ed. 2005. *Citizen Diplomacy in Track-2: Is There a Role for Citizens in Conflict Resolution?* Tel Aviv: Ramot, Tel Aviv University.

Shamir, Yitzhak. 1994. *Summing Up: An Autobiography*. London: Weidenfeld and Nicholson.

Sharoni, Simona. 1995. *Gender and the Israeli Palestinian Conflict: The Politics of Women's Resistance*. Syracuse, NY: Syracuse University Press.

Sharp, Gene. 1984. *Non-Violent Resistance*. Jerusalem: Mifras Publishing House [Hebrew].

Shaw, Randy. 2001. *The Activist's Handbook: A Primer*. Berkeley, CA: University of California Press.

Shenhav, Yehouda. 2003. *The Arab-Jews: Nationalism, Religion and Ethnicity*. Tel-Aviv: Am Oved [Hebrew].

Sher, Gilead. 2005. *Within Reach: The Israeli-Palestinian Peace Negotiations, 1999–2001*. London: Routledge/Taylor & Francis.

Shulman, David. 2007. *Dark Hope: Working for Peace in Israel and Palestine*. Chicago, IL: University of Chicago Press.

Small, Melvin, and William D. Hoover, eds. 1992. *Give Peace a Chance: Exploring the Vietnam Antiwar Movement*. Syracuse, NY: Syracuse University Press.

Smelser, Neil J. 1963. *Theory of Collective Action*. New York: Free Press.

Smith, Daniel. 1988. *Uncle Shem Wants You – Pacifism, Conscientious Objection and Draft Resistance in Israel 1987*. Wilmington, OH: Wilmington College.

Sobel, Richard. 2001. *The Impact of Public Opinion on U.S. Foreign Policy since Vietnam: Constraining the Colossus*. New York: Oxford University Press.

Sprinzak, Ehud. 1986. *Every Man Is Right in His Own Eyes: Illegalism in Israeli Society*. Tel Aviv: Sifriat Poalim [Hebrew].

Tarrow, Sidney. 1983. *Struggling to Reform: Social Movements and Policy Change During Cycles of Protest, Western Societies Paper No. 15*. Ithaca, NY: Cornell University, Center for International Studies.

———. 1994. *Power in Movement: Social Movements, Collective Action, and Politics*, Cambridge Studies in Comparative Politics. New York: Cambridge University Press.

Taub, Gadi. 2007. *The Settlers*. Tel Aviv: Miskal [Hebrew].

The Chicago Council on Public Affairs. 2007. *World Public Opinion 2007*. Chicago, IL: The Chicago Council on Public Affairs and WorldPublicOpnion.org.

The Geneva Initiative, 2008. *An Agreement within One Year*. Tel Aviv (March) [Hebrew].

Tilly, Charles. 1978. *From Mobilization to Revolution*. Reading, MA: Addison-Wesley.

Turner, Ralph H., and Lewis M. Killian. 1957. *Collective Behavior*. Englewood Cliffs, NJ: Prentice-Hall.

———. 1972. *Collective Behavior*. 2nd ed. Englewood Cliffs, NJ: Prentice-Hall.

Walch, Jim. 1999. *In the Net: An Internet Guide for Activists*. New York: Zed Books.

Walzer, Michael. 1977. *Just and Unjust Wars: A Moral Argument with Historical Illustrations*. New York: Basic Books.

Watson, Geoffrey R. 2000. *The Oslo Accords: International Law and the Israeli-Palestinian Peace Agreements*. Oxford: Oxford University Press.

Webster, Frank, ed. 2001. *Culture and Politics in the Information Age: A New Politics?* London: Routledge.

Weizman, Eyal. 2007. *Hollow Land: Israel's Architecture of Occupation*. London: Verso.

Wittkopf, Eugene R. 1990. *Faces of Internationalism: Public Opinion and American Foreign Policy*. Durham, NC: Duke University Press.

Yishai, Yael. 2003. *Civil Society in Israel: Between Mobilization and Pacification*. Jerusalem: Carmel [Hebrew].

Yaar, Ephraim, and Zeev Shavit, eds. 2001. *Trends in Israeli Society*. Tel Aviv: The Open University [Hebrew].

Yonah,Yossi, Yonit Naaman, and David Machlev, eds. 2007. *Rainbow of Opinions: A Mizrahi Agenda for Israel.* Jerusalem: November Books.

Yuchtman-Yaar, Ephraim, and Yohanan Peres. 2000. *Between Consent and Dissent: Democracy and Peace in the Israeli Mind.* Lanham, MD: Rowman & Littlefield Publishers.

Zait, David. 1985. *Zionism through Peace.* Tel Aviv: Sifriat Poalim [Hebrew].

Zald, Mayer N., and John D. McCarthy, eds. 1987. *Social Movements in an Organizational Society: Collected Essays.* New Brunswick, NJ: Transaction Books.

Zaller, John R. 1992. *The Nature and Origins of Mass Opinion.* New York: Cambridge University Press.

Articles and Chapters in Books

Abramov, Etty. 2004. Say Hello [Peace] Nicely. *Tel Aviv Magazine,* 22 October [Hebrew].

Abu Hussein, Mariam. 2003. In *Sisters in Peace: Feminist Voices of the Left,* edited by Hedva Isachar, 110–115. Tel Aviv: Resling [Hebrew].

Abu Nimer, Mohammed. 1997. Dialogue and National Consensus in the Pre-Madrid Period: Dilemmas of Israeli and Palestinian Peace Activists. In *Critical Essays on Israeli Society, Religion, and Government,* edited by Kevin Avruch and Walter P. Zenner, 30–52. Albany, NY: SUNY.

Adams, Nina. 1992. The Women Who Left Them Behind. In *Give Peace a Chance: Exploring the Vietnam Antiwar Movement,* edited by Melvin Small and William D. Hoover, 182–195. Syracuse, NY: Syracuse University Press.

Adir, Stephen. 2001. The Origins of the Protest Movement against Nuclear Power. In *Political Opportunities, Social Movements and Democratization,* edited by Patrick G. Coy, 145–178. Oxford: Elsevier/JAI.

Akzin, Benjamin. 1955. The Role of Parties in Israeli Democracy. *The Journal of Politics* 17 (4):507–545.

———. 1970. The University as a Source of Deterioration. *Yediot Aharonot,* 12 June [Hebrew].

Aldrich, John, H., Christopher Gelpi, Peter Feaver, Jason Reifler, and Kristin Thompson Sharp. 2006. Foreign Policy and the Electoral Connection. *Annual Review of Political Science* 9: 477–502.

Algazi, Yosef. 2003. A Legend with an Unhappy End. *Ha'aretz,* 2 November [Hebrew].

Aloni, Shulamit. 2007. No Peace without Third-Party Intervention. *Palestine-Israel Journal,* 14 (4):63–68.

Al-Jazzeera. 2006. Arab-Jewish tensions rise in Israel. 9 August. http://english.aljazeera .net/archive/2006/08/2008491518145202.html (accessed May 2008).

Aminzade, Ronald R., and Doug McAdam. 2001. Emotions and Contentious Politics. In *Silence and Voice in the Study of Contentious Politics,* by Ronald R. Aminzade, et al., 14–50. Cambridge, UK: Cambridge University Press.

Amir, Shmuel. 2004. Requiem for an Initiative. *The Left Bank Magazine,* 13 March. http://www.hagada.org.il/hagada/html/modules.php?name=News&file=print& sid=1994 (accessed May 2008) [Hebrew].

Amital, Yehuda. 1983. Political or Educational Message. In *Torah, Zionism and Peace,* 3–8. Jerusalem: Netivot Shalom [Hebrew].

Angel, Orna. 2003. Found a Partner? *Ynet,* 19 October. http://www.ynet.co.il/articles/ 0,7340,L-2796988,00.html (accessed May 2008) [Hebrew].

Arens, Moshe. 2001. Good-Bye to the Concept. *Ha'aretz*, 6 February [Hebrew].

———. 2007. Who Wants Such a State? *Ha'aretz*, 5 July [Hebrew].

Asheri, Ehud. 1996. The Campaign over the Street. *Ha'aretz*, 7 October [Hebrew].

Avineri, Shlomo. 2003. The Geneva Lies. *Ynet*, 1 December. http://www.ynet.co .il/articles/1,7340,L-2827655,00.html (accessed May 2008) [Hebrew].

Avneri, Uri. 1998. What Is Political Influence? *Ha'aretz*, 3 April [Hebrew].

———. 2004. Thank You, Dubbi. *Hagada Hasmalit*, 23 October. http://www.hagada .org.il/hagada/html/modules.php?name=News&file=print&sid=2812 (accessed May 2008) [Hebrew].

———. 2006. An Extraordinary Conference. *Gushad* [Gush Shalom Electronic Bulletin], 28 February.

———. 2007. The Catastrophe after Annapolis? *Walla*, 12 October. http://news.walla .co.il/?w=//1179931 (accessed May 2008) [Hebrew].

Ayalon, Ami. 2003. The Broken Dream: Analyzing the Israeli- Palestinian Process. In *As the Generals See It: The Collapse of the Oslo Process and the Violent Israeli-Palestinian Conflict*, edited by Yaacov Bar-Siman-Tov, 5–12. Jerusalem: The Leonard Davis Institute for International Relations, Hebrew University of Jerusalem [Hebrew].

Ayalon, Uri. 2004. Resisting the Apartheid Wall. http://www.fdca.it/wall/media/ anarwall_EN.pdf (accessed May 2008).

———. 2006. From Bakunin to Bi'liin: The Anarchists against the Wall and Anarchist Theory. Seminar paper for "Social Movements and Political Protest in Israel," The Open University of Israel, Raanana [Hebrew].

Baker, Akram. 2007. More a Fraud Than a Friend. In *Peacemakers or Peace Industry? Bitterlemons*, edited by Joseph Alpher and Ghassam Khatib. 28 May. http://www .bitterlemons.org/previous/bl280507ed19.html (accessed May 2008).

Bar'am, Haim. 2005. Moreh Nevochim [Teaching the Perplexed]. *Kol Ha'ir*, July. http://www.hagada.org.il/eng/modules.php?name=News&file=article&sid=11 (accessed May 2008).

———. 2005. Three Pedagogical Stories. *Hagada Hasmalit*, 23 December. http://www .hagada.org.il/hagada/html/modules.php?name=News&file=article&sid=4168 (accessed May 2008) [Hebrew].

———. 2007. Annapolis Days. *Hagada Hasmalit*. http://www.hagada.org.il/hagada/ html/modules.php?name=News&file=article&sid=5785 (accessed May 2008) [Hebrew].

Barnea, Nahum. 2003. The Geneva Message. *Ynet*, 13 October. http://www.ynet.co .il/articles/0,7340,L-2788778,00.html (accessed May 2008) [Hebrew].

Bar-On, Mordechai. 1998. The Historians' Debate in Israel and the Middle East Peace Process. In *The Middle East Peace Process: Interdisciplinary Perspectives*, edited by Ilan Peleg, 21–40. Albany, NY: SUNY.

Bar-Tal, Daniel. 2004/2005. The Influence of Events and (Mis)Information on Israeli-Jewish Public Opinion: The Case of the Camp David Summit and the Second Intifada. *Palestine-Israel Journal* 11 (3 & 4). http://www.pij.org/details.php?id=306 (accessed May 2008).

Barak, Oren. 2005. The Failure of the Israeli-Palestinian Peace Process, 1993–2000. *Journal of Peace Research* 42 (6):716–736.

Baskin, Gershon. 2002. The Oslo Peace Process – Lessons Learned, 8 December. http://www.ariga.com/5763/2002--12-08-gbaskin.shtml (accessed May 2008).

Baum, Dalit. 2006. Women in Black and Men in Pink – Protesting against the Israeli Occupation. *Social Identities*, 12 (5):563–574.

Bdeir, Azmi, and Yasmine Halevi. 2002. Taayush – Seen from the Inside. September. http://taayush.tripod.com/new/inside-look-eng.html (accessed May 2008).

Bechor, Guy. 1998. The Establishment of the First Arab Peace Movement Will Be Declared Today in Cairo. *Ha'aretz*, 22 April [Hebrew].

Bell, Christine, and Catherine O'Rourke. 2007. The People's Peace? Peace Agreements, Civil Society, and Participatory Democracy. *International Political Science Review* 28 (3):293–324.

Bellin, Eva. 1994. Civil Society: Effective Tool of Analysis for Middle East Politics? *PS: Political Science and Politics* 27 (3):509–510.

Ben Benyamin, Sari. 1997. The Interest of the Entire Public. *Ha'aretz*, 8 September [Hebrew].

Ben Eliezer, Uri and Yuval Feinstein. 2007. The Battle over Our Homes: Reconstructing/Deconstructing Sovereign Practices around Israel's Separation Barrier on the West Bank. *Israel Studies* 12 (1):171–192.

Ben Simon, Daniel. 2004. Sharon Changed, the Jews Didn't. *Ha'aretz Online*, 7 July. http://www.panim.org.il/press/haaretzsharon.htm (accessed May 2008) [Hebrew].

Ben Yishai, Ron. 2007. The Disengagement Two Years Later: The Withdrawal That Failed. *Ynet*, 14 August. http://www.ynet.co.il/articles/0,7340,L-3436595,00.html (accessed May 2008) [Hebrew].

Ben-Ami, Shlomo. 2005. Back to the Oslo Pitfalls. *Ha'aretz*, 17 March. http://www.haaretz.co.il/hasite/pages/ShArtPE.jhtml?itemNo=553177&contrassID=2&subContrassID=3&sbSubContrassID=0 (accessed May 2008) [Hebrew].

———. 2007. Back to the Clinton Plan. *Ha'aretz*, 20 March. http://www.haaretz.com/hasen/spages/839139.html (accessed May 2008).

Benda, Julien. 1941. Pacifism and Democracy. *Foreign Affairs* 19 (4):693–701.

Bengal, Maya. 2006. This is Orange, not Green Protest. *NRG*, 24 August. http://www.nrg.co.il/online/1/ART1/469/470.html (accessed May 2008) [Hebrew].

Ben-Eliezer, Uri. 1998. State versus Civil Society? A Non-Binary Model of Domination through the Example of Israel. *Journal of Historical Sociology* 11 (3):370–396.

Benvenisti, Meron. 1998. Needed: A Grey Struggle. *Ha'aretz*, 22 October [Hebrew].

———. 2001. Waiting for Only a Sign. *Ha'aretz*, 27 April [Hebrew].

———. 2007. The Party Spoiler Role. *Ha'aretz*, 17 August [Hebrew].

Bercovitch, Jacob and S. Ayse Kadayifci. 2002. Conflict Management and the Israeli-Palestinian Conflict: The Importance of Capturing the "Right Moment." *Asia-Pacific Review* 9 (2):113–119.

Bitterman, Dita. 2003. In *Sisters in Peace: Feminist Voices of the Left*, edited by Hedva Isachar, 146–151. Tel Aviv: Resling [Hebrew].

Blee, Kathleen, and Vera Taylor. 2002. Semi-Structured Interviewing in Social Movement Research. In *Methods of Social Movement Research*, edited by Bert Klandermans and Suzzanne Staggenborg, 92–117. Minneapolis: University of Minnesota Press.

Blumer, Herbert. 1960. Social Movements. In *New Outline of the Principles of Sociology*, edited by Alfred McClung Lee. New York: Barnes & Noble.

Bourdieu, Pierre. 1993. Public Opinion Does Not Exist. In *Sociology in Question*, 149–157. London: Sage.

Breuer, Mordechai. 1978. The Religious Camp and the Struggle for Peace. *International Problems: Society and Politics* 34:6–10.

Brin, Shlomo. 2001. Oslo: Our Lost Hope. *Meimad* 23 (December):1–4 [Hebrew].

Brown, Sam. 1976. The Defeat of the Antiwar Movement. In *The Vietnam Legacy: The War, American Society, and the Future of American Foreign Policy*, edited by Anthony Lake, 120–128. New York: New York University Press.

Bowen, Nicholas. 2007. Protests to mark 40 years of Israeli occupation. *IMEMC News*, 4 June. http://www.imemc.org/article/48735 (accessed May 2008).

Burstein, Paul. 1999. Social Movements and Public Policy. In *How Social Movements Matter*, edited by Marco G. Giugni, Doug McAdam and Charles Tilly, 3–21. Minneapolis: University of Minnesota Press.

———. 2003. The Impact of Public Opinion on Public Policy: A Review and an Agenda. *Political Research Quarterly* 56 (1):29–40.

Burstein, Paul, and April Linton. 2002. The Impact of Political Parties, Interest Groups, and Social Movement Organizations on Public Policy: Some Recent Evidence and Theoretical Concerns. *Social Forces* 81 (2):380–408.

Calhoun, Craig. 1998. Community without Propinquity Revisited: Communication Technology and the Transformation of the Urban Public Sphere. *Sociological Inquiry* 68 (3):373–397.

Chaitin, Julia, Fida Obeidi, Sami Adwan, and Dan Bar-On. 2002. Environmental Work and Peace Work: The Palestinian-Israel Case. *Peace and Conflict Studies* 9 (2):64–94.

Chetrit, Sami Shalom. 2001. On Mizrahi-Palestinian Cooperation in Israel. In *Real Time: The Al-Aqsa Intifada and the Israeli Left*, edited by Adi Ofir, 288–297. Jerusalem: Keter [Hebrew].

———. 2004. The New Mizrahim: The Radical Mizrahi Discourse and the Mizrahi Democratic Rainbow Coalition [Hebrew]. http://www.notes.co.il/sami/4532.asp (accessed May 2008).

Chittick, William O., and Keith R. Billingsley. 1989. The Structure of Elite Foreign Policy Beliefs. *Western Political Quarterly* 42 (2):201–224.

Converse, Philip E. 1964. The Nature of Belief Systems in Mass Publics. In *Ideology and Discontent*, edited by David E. Apter. New York: Free Press.

———. 1970. Attitudes and Non-Attitudes: Continuation of a Dialogue. In *The Quantitative Analysis of Social Problems*, edited by Edward R. Tufte. Reading, MA: Addison-Wesley.

Coy, Patrick G. 2001. Introduction: Political Opportunities, Social Movements, and Democratization. In *Political Opportunities, Social Movements and Democratization*, edited by Patrick G. Coy, vii–xi. Oxford: Elsevier/JAI.

Cygielman, Victor. 1995. No, Oslo Is Not Dead. *Palestine-Israel Journal* 2 (1):3–4.

Daloomy, Ariel. 2005. The Israeli Refusniks: 1982–2003. *Israel Affairs* 11 (4):695–716.

Dankner, Amnon. 1999. Reflections of a Leftist GSA Fan. *Maariv – New Year's Eve Supplement*, 10 September [Hebrew].

———. 2003. Why Is the Left Rejected? *Maariv Online*, 9 June [Hebrew].

Daud, Anwar and Nitzan Tan'ami. 2007. The Annapolis Connference – Why We do not Welcome it. *Hagada HaSmalit*, 12 November. http://www.hagada.org.il/hagada/html/modules.php?name=News&file=article&sid=5751 (accessed May 2008) [Hebrew].

Davidi, Efraim. 2000. Protest Amid Confusion: Israel's Peace Camp in the Uprising's First Month. *Middle East Report* 217:36–39.

Dayan, Arye. 1998. To: Prime Minister Menachem Begin. *Ha'aretz Weekend Supplement*, 30 January [Hebrew].

della Porta, Donatella. 1999. Political Protest, Protesters, and Protest Policing: Public Discourse in Italy and Germany from the 1960s to the 1980s. In *How Social Movements Matter*, edited by Marco G. Giugni, Doug McAdam and Charles Tilly, 66–96. Minneapolis: University of Minnesota Press.

Diani, Mario. 1992. The Concept of Social Movement. *The Sociological Review* 40 (1):1–25.

———. 2001. Social Movement Networks: Virtual and Real. In *Culture and Politics in the Information Age: A New Politics?*, edited by Frank Webster, 117–27. London: Routledge.

———. 2002. Network Analysis. In *Methods of Social Movement Research*, edited by Bert Klandermans and Suzzanne Staggenborg, 173–200. Minneapolis: University of Minnesota Press.

Dolev, Omri. 1998. A Whole Generation Is Looking for Itself. *Ha'ir*, 29 March [Hebrew].

Downton, James, and Paul Wehr. 1998. Persistent Pacifism: How Activist Commitment Is Developed and Sustained. *Journal of Peace Research* 35 (5):531–550.

Dreznin, Andre. 2004. The Right of Return: The Illusion of the Israeli Peace Camp. *Hagada Hasmalit*, 5 July. http://www.hagada.org.il/hagada/html/modules.php?name=News&file=article&sid=2436 (accessed May 2008) [Hebrew].

Einwohner, Rachel L. 2001. Protester/Target Interactions: A Microsociological Approach to Studying Movement Outcomes. In *Political Opportunities, Social Movements and Democratization*, edited by Patrick G. Coy, 207–227. Oxford: Elsevier/JAI.

Eisinger, Peter K. 1973. The Conditions of Protest Behavior in American Cities. *American Political Science Review* 67:11–28.

Eldar, Akiva. 2001. How Much to the Left? *Ha'aretz*, 10 May [Hebrew].

———. 2009. Crisis in a Phone Booth. *Ha'aretz*, 12 May [Hebrew].

Elizur, Uri. 2001. The Intellectual Brother of "Trust Me." *Yediot Aharonot Weekend Supplement*, 2 March [Hebrew].

Espanyoli, Nabila. 2003. In *Sisters in Peace: Feminist Voices of the Left*, edited by Hedva Isachar, 27–32. Tel Aviv: Resling [Hebrew].

Etkes, Dror. 2005. And What after the Disengagement? *NRG*, 25 February. http://www.nrg.co.il/online/1/ART/875/915.html (accessed May 2008) [Hebrew].

Federazione dei Comunisti Anarchici (FDCA). 2004. We Are All Anarchists against the Wall! http://www.fdca.it/wall/media/anarwall_EN.pdf (accessed May 2008).

Feige, Michael. 1998. Peace Now and the Legitimation Crisis of "Civil Militarism." *Israel Studies* 3 (1):85–111.

Fisher, William F. 1997. Doing Good? The Politics and Antipolitics of NGO Practices. *Annual Review of Anthropology* 26:439–464.

Fogel, David. 2003. The Faulty Diskette of the Left. *Maariv Online*, 15 May [Hebrew].

Frankenthal, Yitzhak. 2001. Enough with the Loss of Life. *Ha'aretz*, 6 June [Hebrew].

———. 2002. The Ethics of Revenge. By a father who lost his son to terror; a speech made by the Chairman of the Families' Forum, at a rally in Jerusalem on Saturday, July 27, 2002, outside the Israeli Prime Minister's residence. *Tikkun Magazine* [Hebrew].

———. 2004. Arafat, I Wish You a Full Recovery. *Ynet*, 30 October. http://www.ynet.co.il/articles/0,7340,L-2997192,00.html (accessed May 2008) [Hebrew].

Fried, Meital. 1999. A New Organization Is Calling for Withdrawal from Lebanon – Red Line: We Shall Not Refrain from Using Violence. *Ha'aretz*, 1 March [Hebrew].

Gabison, Ruth. 2001. *Personal Soul Searching*. In *Real Time: The Al-Aqsa Intifada and the Israeli Left*, edited by Adi Ofir, 169–178. Jerusalem: Keter [Hebrew].

Galili, Lily. 1996. One Jerusalem, but for Two People. *Ha'aretz*, 9 August [Hebrew].
———. 1997a. In the Name of the Mother. *Ha'aretz*, 20 January [Hebrew].
———. 1997b. The Short Question Stage. *Ha'aretz*, 26 March [Hebrew].
———. 1997c. Withdrawal without Borders. *Ha'aretz*, 8 September [Hebrew].
———. 2001. For the First Time Peace Now Will Take Part in the Land Day. *Ha'aretz*, 2 March [Hebrew].
———. 2002a. In "Disgust Heights" Settlement, We Shall Restore the Peace Movement's Shambles. *Ha'aretz*, 14 January [Hebrew].
———. 2002b. Every Man Has a Red Line. *Ha'aretz*, 4 April. http://refusals.homestead.com/EveryMan040402.html (accessed May 2008).
———. 2003. Giving up on the Entrance Ticket. *Ha'aretz*, 5 September [Hebrew].
Galili, Orit. 1997. Dor Shalem [an Entire Generation] Does Not Know Where to Go. *Ha'aretz*, 23 May [Hebrew].
Gamson, William A., and David S. Meyer. 1996. Framing Political Opportunity. In *Comparative Perspectives on Social Movements: Political Opportunities, Mobilizing Structures, and Cultural Framings*, edited by Doug McAdam, John D. McCarthy and Mayer N. Zald, 275–290. New York: Cambridge University Press.
Gat, Yoram. 2005. The Stay Put Plan. *Hagada Hasmalit*, 7 January. http://www.hagada.org.il/hagada/html/modules.php?name=News&file=article&sid=3081 (accessed May 2008) [Hebrew].
Gelb, Joyce, and Vivien Hart. 1999. Feminist Politics in a Hostile Environment: Obstacles and Opportunities. In *How Social Movements Matter*, edited by Marco G. Giugni, Doug McAdam and Charles Tilly, 149–181. Minneapolis: University of Minnesota Press.
Gidron, Benjamin, Michal Bar, and Hagai Katz. 2002. Characteristics of Israeli Organized Civil Society. *Israeli Sociology* 4 (2):369–400 [Hebrew].
Giugni, Marco G. 1998. Was It Worth the Effort? The Outcomes and Consequences of Social Movements. *Annual Review of Sociology* 24:371–393.
———. 1999. How Social Movements Matter: Past Research, Present Problems, Future Developments. In *How Social Movements Matter*, edited by Marco G. Giugni, Doug McAdam and Charles Tilly, xiii–xxxiii. Minneapolis: University of Minnesota Press.
Golan, Galia. 2008. Reflections on Mistakes on Israel's 60th Anniversary. *New Horizons Online* 43 [Hebrew].
Gold, Dore. 1993. Changing Political Dynamics between Israelis and Palestinians. In *Political and Structural Arrangements in the New Era of Israeli-Palestinian Relations*, 55–60. Jerusalem: Jerusalem Center for Public Affairs and the Konrad Adenauer Stiftung.
Goldner, Melinda. 2001. Expanding Political Opportunities and Changing Collective Identities in the Complementary and Alternative Medicine Movement. In *Political Opportunities, Social Movements and Democratization*, edited by Patrick G. Coy, 69–102. Oxford: Elsevier/JAI.
Goodwin, Jeff, and James M. Jasper. 1999. Caught in a Winding, Snarling Vine: The Structural Bias of Political Process Theory. *Sociological Forum* 14 (1):27–54.
Gozansky, Tamar. 2003. "Disengagement" for the Purpose of Permanent Annexation. *Hagada Hasmalit*, 24 December. http://hagada.org.il/hagada/html/modules.php?name=News&file=article&sid=1689 (accessed May 2008) [Hebrew].
Gubser, Peter. 2002. The Impact of NGOs on State and Non-State Relations in the Middle East. *Middle East Policy* 9 (1):139–148.

Gutwein, Daniel. 2002. Post-Zionism and the Middle Class: Their Rise and Fall? *New Directions* 6:12–34 [Hebrew].

Halperin, Irit. 2007. Between the Lines: The Story of Machsom Watch. *Journal of Humanistic Psychology* 47:333–339.

Hanegbi, Haim. 2005. Why I Will Vote for Sharon. *Ha'aretz Weekend Supplement*, 16 December [Hebrew].

Hara, Noriko, and Pnina Shachaf. 2008. A Comparative Analysis of Online Peace Movement Organizations. In *Social Information Technology: Connecting Society and Cultural Issues*, edited by Terry Kidd and Irene Chen, 52–67. Hershey, PA: Idea Group. http://eprints.rclis.org/archive/00012154/ (Accessed May 2008).

Harel, Amos. 2004. On the Number of IDF Draftees. *Ha'aretz*, 30 July [Hebrew].

Harel, Judith. 2003. In *Sisters in Peace: Feminist Voices of the Left*, edited by Hedva Isachar, 33–38. Tel Aviv: Resling [Hebrew].

Helman, Sara, and Tamar Rapoport. 1997. Women in Black: Challenging Israel's Gender and Socio-Political Orders. *British Journal of Sociology* 48:681–700.

Hermann, Tamar. 1993a. Contemporary Peace Movements: Between the Hammer of Political Realism and the Anvil of Pacifism. *Western Political Quarterly* 46 (1):869–893.

———. 1993b. From Unidimensionality to Multidimensionality: Some Observations on the Dynamics of Social Movements. *Research in Social Movements, Conflicts and Change* 15:181–202.

———. 1995a. New Challenges to New Authority: Israeli Grassroots Activism in the 1950s. In *Israel: The First Decade of Independence*, edited by S. Ilan Troen and Noah Lucas, 105–124. Albany, NY: SUNY.

———. 1995b. The Rise of Instrumental Voting: The Campaign for Political Reform. In *The Elections in Israel 1992*, edited by Asher Arian and Michal Shamir, 275–298. Albany, NY: SUNY.

———. 1996. Do They Have a Chance? Protest and Political Structure of Opportunities in Israel. *Israel Studies* 1 (1): 144–170.

———. 2001. Contending Narratives: The Israeli Peace Movement's Role in the Oslo Process. In *Global Politics: Essays in Honour of David Vital*, edited by Abraham Ben-Zvi and Aaron S. Klieman, 237–266. London: Frank Cass.

———. 2002. The Sour Taste of Success: The Israeli Peace Movement, 1967–1998. In *Mobilizing for Peace: Conflict Resolution in Northern Ireland, Israel/Palestine, and South Africa*, edited by Benjamin Gidron, Stanley N. Katz and Yeheskel Hasenfeld, 94–129. New York: Oxford University Press.

———. 2004. Citizens' Protest on Security-Related Issues in Israel – the Case of 1973–4. In *Thirty Years Later: Challenges to Israel since the Yom Kippur War*, edited by Anat Kurtz, 65–75. Tel Aviv: Jaffee Center for Strategic Studies [Hebrew].

———. 2005a. Normalizing the Abnormal. 3 October. http://www.bitterlemons.org/previous/bl31005ed36.html#isr2 (accessed May 2008).

———. 2005b. The Binational Idea in Israel/Palestine: Past and Present. *Nations and Nationalism* 11 (3):381–402.

———. Forthcoming 2009a. The Calm After the Storm: Ineffectual Protest After the 2006 Lebanon War as an Indication of Changing Patterns Of Citizens' Political Participation in Israel. In *Decisions at National Turning Points*, edited by Moshe Lissak et al. Jerusalem: Van Leer Institute.

———. Forthcoming 2009b. "Realistic Nonviolence – The Israeli Four Mothers Movement." In *Non-Violent Movements and the Middle East Conflict*, edited by Maria Stephan. Boston: International Center on Non-Violent Conflict.

Hermann, Tamar, and Gila Kurtz. 1995. Prospects for Democratizing Foreign Policy-making: The Gradual Empowerment of Israeli Women. *Middle East Journal* 49:449–466.

Hermann, Tamar, and Ephraim Yuchtman-Yaar. 2002. Divided yet United: Israeli-Jewish Attitudes toward the Oslo Process. *Journal of Peace Research* 39 (5):597–617.

———. 2005. When the Policymaker and the Public Meet: Sharon, Israeli Public Opinion and the Unilateral Disengagement Plan. *Palestine-Israel Journal* 11 (4):93–100.

Herzog, Hanna. 1998. Women's Status in the Shadow of Security. In *Security Concerns: Insights from the Israeli Experience*, edited by Daniel Bar-Tal, Dan Jacobson and Aaron S. Klieman, 329–346. Greenwich, CT: JAI Press.

Herzog, Shira, and Avivit Hai. 2005/2006. What Do People Mean When They Say 'People-to-People'?: Origins, Definitions, Goals and Methods. *Palestine-Israel Journal* 12–13 (4, 1):8–15.

Hetsroni, Amir. 1998. All We Were Saying Was Give Peace a Chance: The Future of Israeli High School Peace Activists. *Peace and Conflict: Journal of Peace Psychology* 4 (3):237–355.

Holsti, Ole R. 1992. Public Opinion and Foreign Policy: Challenges to the Almond-Lippmann Consensus. *International Studies Quarterly* 36 (4):439–466.

Isachar, Hedva. 2008. Thirty Years to (Peace) Now. *Hagada Hasmalit*, 12 April. http://www.hagada.org.il/hagada/html/modules.php?name=News&file=article&sid=5962 (accessed May 2008).

Hoover, Dean, and David Kowalewski. 1992. Dynamic Models of Dissent and Repression. *Journal of Conflict Resolution*, 36 (1):150–182.

Jennings, M. Kent. 1987. Residues of a Movement: The Aging of the American Protest Generation. *The American Political Science Review* 81 (2):367–382.

Karpel, Dalia. 1999. The Symmetry of Bereavement. *Ha'aretz Weekend Supplement*, 23 April, 35–37 [Hebrew].

Kashua, Sayed. 2006. Oh, My Country My Motherland. *Walla*, 10 August. http://news.walla.co.il/?w=//960693 (accessed May 2008) [Hebrew].

Kaufman, Edy. 1988. The Intifadah and the Peace Camp in Israel: A Critical Introspective. *Journal of Palestine Studies* 17 (4):66–80.

Kaufman, Ilana. Forthcoming. Mitigating Tension or Institutionalizing Control? Activity of Israeli women vis a vis the Palestinian Population and Israeli Soldiers at West Bank Checkpoints.

Kazin, Orna. 2001. *Bypassing Consensus. Ha'aretz*, 24 January [Hebrew].

Kedar, Mordechai. 2008. Why Is There no Peace? Because of Peace Now, 21 April. http://www.omedia.co.il/Show_Article.asp?DynamicContentID=17555&MenuID=813 &ThreadID=1030 (accessed May 2008) [Hebrew].

Keller, Adam. 2000. The Other Israel: Israelis Protesting the Occupation. *Radical Philosophy Review* 3 (2):173–187.

Kessler, Paul. 2002. The Ongoing Struggle of the Israeli Peace Camp. *European Judaism* 35 (2):146–149.

Kim, Hannah. 1997. Where Has the Protest Disappeared? *Ha'aretz*, 22 August [Hebrew].

Kimche, David. 2003. Winning over Public Opinion. *Bitterlemons-international* 1 (5). 7 August. http://www.bitterlemons-international.org/previous.php?opt=1&id=5#20 (accessed May 2008).

Kitschelt, Herbert P. 1986. Political Opportunity Structures and Political Protest: Anti-Nuclear Movements in Four Democracies. *British Journal of Political Science* 16 (1):57–86.

Klandermans, Bert, and Suzzanne Staggenborg. 2002. Introduction. In *Methods of Social Movement Research*, edited by Bert Klandermans and Suzzanne Staggenborg, ix–xx. Minneapolis: University of Minnesota Press.

Kleidman, Robert. 1999. Comparative Perspectives on Social Movements: Political Opportunities, Mobilizing Structures, and Cultural Framings. *Social Forces* 78 (2): 838–840.

Kleiman, Hannah. 2001. Oslo Was a Medication (but Too Weak a One). *Tzomet Hasharon*, 7 September [Hebrew].

Koopmans, Ruud, and Dieter Rucht. 2002. Protest Event Analysis. In *Methods of Social Movement Research*, edited by Bert Klandermans and Suzzanne Staggenborg, 231–259. Minneapolis: University of Minnesota Press.

Kriesi, Hanspeter. 1996. The Organizational Structure of New Social Movements in a Political Context. In *Comparative Perspectives on Social Movements: Political Opportunities, Mobilizing Structures, and Cultural Framings*, edited by Doug McAdam, John D. McCarthy and Mayer N. Zald, 152–184. New York: Cambridge University Press.

Landau, Idan. 2005. Clear-Headed Refusal. *Ynet*, 15 March. http://www.ynet.co.il/articles/0,7340,L-3058656,00.html (accessed May 2008) [Hebrew].

Landau, Uzi. 2003. Anti-State of Israel. *Ynet*, 14 October. http://www.ynet.co.il/articles/0,7340,L-2790679,00.html (accessed May 2008) [Hebrew].

———. 2003b. The Left's Genetic Code. *Jerusalem Post*, 27 October. http://www.israelunitycoalition.org/news/article-old.php?id=2640 (accessed May 2008).

Laskier, Michael M. 2000. Israeli Activism American-Style: Civil Liberties, Environmental and Peace Organization as Pressure Groups for Social Change, 1970s–1990s. *Israel Studies* 5 (1):128–152.

Lebel, Udi. 2006. *Protest Now*. NRG, 18 October. http://192.118.0.136/online/1/ART1/492/915.html (accessed May 2008) [Hebrew].

Lebrecht, Hans. 1999. Peace Center Opening Draws Dignitaries. http://www.pww.org/past-weeks-1999/Israeli%20peace%20center.htm (accessed May 2008).

Lederach, John Paul. 2003. Cultivating Peace: A Practitioner's View of Deadly Conflict and Negotiation. In *Contemporary Peace Making: Conflict, Violence and Peace Processes*, edited by John Darby and Roger MacGinty, 30–37. London: Palgrave Macmillan.

Leibovitz, Illia. 2001. The Mistake of the Israeli Left. *Ha'aretz*, 17 August [Hebrew].

Leibovitz-Dar, Sara. 2002. Oslo Is Still Far from Ofakim. *Ha'aretz*, 1 February [Hebrew].

Lemish, Dafna, and Inbal Barzel. 2000. "Four Mothers": The Womb in the Public Sphere. *European Journal of Communication* 15 (2):147–169.

Lerman, Debbie. 2003. In *Sisters in Peace: Feminist Voices of the Left*, edited by Hedva Isachar, 72–76. Tel Aviv: Resling [Hebrew].

Leshem, Moshe. 2003. Where Does the Money Come from, Yossi? *Gamla Shall Not Fall Again*, 17 December. http://www.gamla.org.il/article/2003/dec/l3.htm (accessed May 2008) [Hebrew].

Levy, Gideon. 1997. The Establishment of the Committee against Uprooting Trees. *Ha'aretz Weekend Supplement*, 23 May [Hebrew].

———. 2001. Only by Force. In *Real Time: The Al-Aqsa Intifada and the Israeli Left*, edited by Adi Ofir, 90–98. Jerusalem: Keter [Hebrew].

———. 2005. Good Morning Left! *Ha'aretz*, 13 February. http://www.haaretz.co.il/hasite/pages/ShArtPE.jhtml?itemNo=539421&contrassID=2&subContrassID=3&sbSubContrassID=0 (accessed May 2008) [Hebrew].

_____. 2006. Enough of You, Cry-Babies. *Haaretz*, 27 August. http://www.haaretz.co .il/hasite/spages/755155.html (accessed May 2008) [Hebrew].

Levy, Yagil. 2005. The War of the Peripheries: Social Mapping of IDF Casualties in the Al-Aqsa Intifada. *Theory and Criticism* 27:36–69 [Hebrew].

Levy Yagil, and Shlomo Mizrahi. 2008. Alternative Politics and the Transformation of Society-Military Relations: The Israeli Experience. *Administration & Society* 40 (1):25–53.

Liel, Alon. 2005/2006. People-to-People: Telling the Truth About the Israeli-Palestinian Case. *Palestine-Israel Journal* 12–13 (4, 1):19–21.

Lofland, John. 1993. Theory-Bashing and Answer-Improving in the Study of Social Movements. *The American Sociologist* 24 (2):37–58.

Lord, Amnon. 2002. The Raided Cossacks. *Ynet*, Opinions, 27 May [Hebrew].

Luz, Ehud. 2006. The Jewish Religion: A Constraint or a Catalyst for the Use of Force. In *Peace and War in Jewish Culture*, edited by Avriel Bar-Levav, 247–76. Jerusalem: Zalman Shazar Center for Jewish History [Hebrew].

Machover, Moshe. 2005. Zionism: A Major Obstacle. 19 September. http://www .kibush.co.il/show_file.asp?num=8683 (accessed May 2008).

Maney, Gregory M. 2001. Rival Transnational Networks and Indigenous Rights: The San Blas Kuna in Panama and the Yanomami in Brazil. In *Political Opportunities, Social Movements and Democratization*, edited by Patrick G. Coy, 103–144. Oxford: Elsevier/JAI.

Maoz, Ifat, and Roy Eidelson. 2007. Psychological Bases of Extreme Policy Preferences: How the Personal Beliefs of Israeli-Jews Predict their Support for Population Transfer in the Israeli-Palestinian Conflict. *American Behavioral Scientist* 50 (11):1476–1497.

Marcus, Jonathan. 1996. Toward a Fragmented Polity? Israeli Politics, the Peace Process, and the 1996 General Election. *Washington Quarterly* 19 (4):19–36.

Marcus, Yoel. 2004. On Stamina and Strategic Myopia. *Ha'aretz*. 13 January. http://www.minfo.gov.ps/Int_press/english/13-01-04.htm (accessed May 2008).

Matar, Haggai. 2004. Facing Absolute Evil. In *Refusenik!*, edited by Peretz Kidron, 133–135. Tel Aviv: Xargol [Hebrew].

Mazali, Rela. 2003. In *Sisters in Peace: Feminist Voices of the Left*, edited by Hedva Isachar, 21–26. Tel Aviv: Resling [Hebrew].

McAdam, Doug, John D. McCarthy, and Mayer N. Zald. 1996. Introduction – Opportunities, Mobilizing Structures, and Framing Processes: Toward a Synthetic, Comparative Perspective on Social Movements. In *Comparative Perspectives on Social Movements: Political Opportunities, Mobilizing Structures, and Cultural Framings*, edited by Doug McAdam, John D. McCarthy and Mayer N. Zald, 1–22. New York: Cambridge University Press.

McCarthy, John D. 1996. Constraints and Opportunities in Adopting, Adapting and Inventing. In *Comparative Perspectives on Social Movements: Political Opportunities, Mobilizing Structures, and Cultural Framings*, edited by Doug McAdam, John D. McCarthy and Mayer N. Zald, 141–51. New York: Cambridge University Press.

Megged, Eyal. 2001. The Left and Its Punishment. *Ynet*, 29 January [Hebrew].

Mehulal, Malka. 1998. White Days. *Al Hasharon*, 2 January, 44–46 [Hebrew].

Melucci, Alberto. 1995. The Process of Collective Identity. In *Social Movements and Culture*, edited by Hank Johnston and Bert Klandermans, 41–63. Minneapolis: University of Minnesota Press.

Meyer, David S. 1999. How the Cold War Was Really Won: The Effects of the Antinuclear Movements of the 1980s. In *How Social Movements Matter*, edited by Marco

G. Giugni, Doug McAdam, and Charles Tilly, 182–203. Minneapolis: University of Minnesota Press.

Meyer, David S., and Debra Minkoff. 2004. Conceptualizing Political Opportunity. *Social Forces* 82 (4):1457–1492.

Miller, Warren E., and Donald E. Stokes. 1963. Constituency Influence in Congress. *American Political Science Review* 57 (1):45–56.

Misgav, Uri. 2001. We've Already Been to This Movie, but We Left in the Middle. *Ha'ir Weekly Magazine*, 30 August, 50–52 [Hebrew].

Moore, Kelly. 1999. Political Protest and Institutional Change: The Anti-Vietnam War Movement and American Science. In *How Social Movements Matter*, edited by Marco G. Giugni, Doug McAdam and Charles Tilly, 97–118. Minneapolis: University of Minnesota Press.

Muhlbauer, Varda. 2001. Israeli Women and the Peace Movements. *Peace Review* 13 (2):287–293.

Naaman, Dorit. 2006. The Silenced Outcry: A Feminist Perspective from the Israeli Checkpoints in Palestine. *NWSA Journal* 18 (3):168–180.

Nader, Nir. 2005. The Disengagement Plan and the Confusion of the Left. *Haoketz*, 23 June. http://www.haokets.org/archive.asp?PublisherID=124&ArticleSearch=&ArticleSearchType=3&ResponseWriterName=&ResponseSearch=&Response SearchType=3&FindExactValue=on (accessed May 2008) [Hebrew].

Nasser-Najjab, Nadia. 2005. Oslo Dialogue: An Evaluation. *Palestine-Israel Journal* 12–13 (4):22–33.

Newman, David. 1997. Conflicting Israeli Peace Discourses. *Peace Review* 9 (3):417–424.

––––––. 2002. How Israel's Peace Movement Fell Apart. *The New York Times.* 30 August. http://www.obermayer.us/aer/articles/peace/NYT0830Newman.htm (accessed May 2008).

––––––. 2006. In the Name of Security – in the Name of Peace: Environmental Schizophrenia and the Security Discourse in Israel/Palestine. In *Globalisation and Environmental Challenges: Reconceptualising Security in the 21st Century*, edited by Hans Gunter Brauch, et al. Berlin: Springer-Verlag.

Newman, David, and Tamar Hermann. 1992. A Comparative Study of Gush Emunim and Peace Now. *Middle Eastern Studies* 28 (3):509–530.

Nissan, Mordechai. 1994. The PLO and the Israeli Left: The Common Aim. *Nativ*, February, 5–11 [Hebrew].

Offe, Claus. 1985. New Social Movements: Challenging the Boundaries of Institutional Politics. *Social Research* 52 (4):817–868.

––––––. 1990. Reflections on the Institutional Self-Transformation of Movement Politics: A Tentative Stage Model. In *Challenging the Political Order*, edited by Russell Dalton and Manfred Kuechler, 232–250. New York: Oxford University Press.

Ofir, Adi. 2002. Jewish-Arab Coexistence: The Politics of Rationality. *Democratic Culture* 6:9–35 [Hebrew].

Oppenheimer, Yariv. 2005. Disengagement or the End of Democracy. *Ma'ariv*, 10 June. http://www.nrg.co.il/online/1/ART/944/572.html (accessed May 2008) [Hebrew].

––––––. 2006. The (Res.) *Orange Agenda*. Ynet. 24 August. http://www.ynet.co.il/articles/0,7340,L-3295156,00.html (accessed May 2008) [Hebrew].

Orbach, Uri. 2004. The Fashionable Left. *Ynet*, Opinions, 5 March [Hebrew].

Oron, Haim. 1993. *The Knesset Protocols*, 30 August, 7756 [Hebrew].

Orr, Akiva. 1994. 1993 – Palestine: Occupied Territory to Become a Bantustan. In *Israel: Politics, Myths and Identity Crises*, edited by Akiva Orr, 160–170. Boulder, CO: Pluto Press.

Owen. 2003. Talkback Item. *Ma'ariv Online*, 2 May [Hebrew].

Oz, Amos. 2005. The Devil's Progress. *The Guardian Review*, 3 September, 4–5.

Oz V'Shalom. 1975. *Platform*. Jerusalem.

Page, Benjamin I., and Jason Barabas. 2000. Foreign Policy Gaps between Citizens and Leaders. *International Studies Quarterly* 44 (3):339–364.

Papo, Aharon. 1996. Democracy? Democaricature! *Nativ*, January, 26–27 [Hebrew].

Pappe, Ilan. 2005. There Is No Peace Movement in Israel. An interview given to Silvia Cattori, 4 June.

Peled, Yoav. 1992. Ethnic Democracy and the Legal Construction of Citizenship: Arab Citizens of the Jewish State. *American Political Science Review* 86 (2):432–442.

———. 2001. Don't Be Right, Be Smart. In *Real Time: The Al-Aqsa Intifada and the Israeli Left*, edited by Adi Ofir, 46–56. Jerusalem: Keter [Hebrew].

Peled, Yoav, and Gershon Shafir. 1996. The Roots of Peacemaking: The Dynamics of Citizenship in Israel, 1948–1993. *International Journal of Middle East Studies* 28 (3):391–413.

Peleg, Ilan. 2004. Jewish-Palestinian Relations in Israel: From Hegemony to Equality? *International Journal of Politics, Culture, and Society* 17 (3): 415–437.

Peleg, Ilan and Dov Waxman. 2007. Losing Control? A Comparison of Majority-Minority Relations in Israel and Turkey. *Nationalism & Ethnic Politics*, 13 (3): 431–463.

Peleg, Michal. 1996. What's Hiding in the Donuts of the Rabbi from Shenkin Street. *Ha'ir*, 15 November [Hebrew].

Peleg, Samuel. 2002. If Words Could Kill: The Peace Process and the Failure of Public-Political Discourse. *State and Society* 2 (3):421–444 [Hebrew].

Penkar, Dorit. 2003. From the Employment Bureau to Politics and Back. *Mitsad Sheni* [On the Other Hand], January, 10–12 [Hebrew].

Peri, Yoram. 2002. Civil-Military Relations in Israel in Crisis. In *Military, State, and Society in Israel: Theoretical & Comparative Perspectives*, edited by Daniel Maman, Eyal Ben-Ari and Zeev Rosenhek, 107–136. New Brunswick, NJ: Transaction Books.

Peter, Danny. 2004. In Favor of Geneva, and yet.... *The Left Bank Magazine*, 4 February. http://hagada.org.il/hagada/html/modules.php?name=News&file=article &sid=1840 (accessed May 2008) [Hebrew].

Pinchas-Cohen, Hava. 2001. Mother Peace: The Fifth Mother. *Panim* 17:44–50 [Hebrew].

Pundak, Ron. 2001. From Oslo to Taba: What Went Wrong? *Survival* 43 (3):31–45. http://www.peres-center.org/media/Upload/61.pdf (accessed May 2008).

Rabin, Yitzhak. 1993. *The Knesset Protocols*, 21 September [Hebrew].

Rabinowitz, Dan. 2001. End of Conflict or Recycled Violence? In *Real Time: The Al-Aqsa Intifada and the Israeli Left*, edited by Adi Ofir, 33–45. Jerusalem: Keter [Hebrew].

Rappaport, Meron. 2002. The Peres Center without Peace. *Yediot Aharonot Weekend Supplement*, 20 September [Hebrew].

Reinfeld, Moshe. 1998. The Peace Movements Claim That They Were Discriminated against Compared to the Right in Financing the Jubilee Events. *Ha'aretz*, 8 April [Hebrew].

Reinhart, Tanya. 2001. Murderous Peace. In *Real Time: The Al-Aqsa Intifada and the Israeli Left*, edited by Adi Ofir, 57–68. Jerusalem: Keter [Hebrew].

——. 2003. The Complex Art of Simulation. *Yediot Aharonot*. 6 June. http://www.globalresearch.ca/articles/REI306A.html (accessed May 2008).

——. 2005. The Israeli Left Is Opting for Suicide. *Yediot Aharonot*, 23 March. http://fromoccupiedpalestine.org/node/1504 (accessed May 2008).

Resh, Nura. 2005. Machsomwatch: Women, Protest and the Fight for Human Rights in Israeli Occupied Territories. Paper read at 37th World Congress of the International Institute of Sociology, July 5–9, at Stockholm, Sweden.

Risse-Kappen, Thomas. 1991. Public Opinion, Domestic Structure, and Foreign Policy in Liberal Democracies. *World Politics* 43 (4):479–512.

Rochon, Thomas R., and Daniel A. Mazmanian. 1993. Social Movements and the Policy Process. *Annals of the American Academy of Political and Social Science* 528:75–87.

Rogers, Richard, and Anat Ben-David. 2008. The Palestinian-Israeli Peace Process and Transnational Issue Networks: The Complicated Place of the Israeli NGO. *New Media & Society* 10:497–528.

Rosenau, James N. 1992. The Relocation of Authority in a Shrinking World. *Comparative Politics* 24 (3):253–272.

Rubinstein, Danny. 1997. In Copenhagen Arabs and Israelis Established the "International Alliance for Israeli-Arab Peace." *Ha'aretz*, 31 January [Hebrew].

Salem, Walid. 2007. Joint Activism in Jerusalem: Is a Joint Community-Based Agenda Possible? *Palestine-Israel Journal* 14 (4):68–72.

Samet, Gideon. 1997. Strange Hesitation on the Road to War. *Ha'aretz*, 15 September [Hebrew].

Sarid, Yossi. 2005. The Shock of Return. *Ha'aretz*, 18 July [Hebrew].

Search for Common Ground. 1998. Focus: International Alliance for Arab-Israeli Peace. *Bulletin of Regional Cooperation* 7 (4):11.

Sewell, William H. 2001. Space in Contentious Politics. In *Silence and Voice in the Study of Contentious Politics*, by Ronald R. Aminzade, et al., 51–88. Cambridge, UK: Cambridge University Press.

Shadmi, Ariela. 2003. In *Sisters in Peace: Feminist Voices of the Left*, edited by Hedva Isachar, 131–136. Tel Aviv: Resling [Hebrew].

Shahal, Moshe. 1993. Address. In *Proceedings of the Conference on Political and Structural Arrangements in the New Era of Israeli-Palestinian Relations*, 12–24: Jerusalem Center for Public Affairs and the Konrad Adenauer Stiftung.

Shavit, Ari. 2002. Tzumud [Holding on to Land], Rehavia Style. *Ha'aretz Weekend Supplement*, 8 November [Hebrew].

——. 2004. The Big Freeze: Interview with Dov Weisglass. *Ha'aretz Magazine*. 8 October. http://fromoccupiedpalestine.org/node.php?id=1433 (accessed May 2008).

——. 2004b. Missing Arafat: Uri Avnery Interviewed. *Ha'aretz*, 18 November. http://www.zmag.org/content/print_article.cfm?itemID=6686&sectionID=107 (accessed May 2008).

——. 2007. Leaving the Zionist Ghetto: Interview with Avraham Burg *Ha'aretz Online*, 8 June. http://www.haaretz.com/hasen/spages/868385.html (accessed May 2008).

Shchori, Dalia. 1999. Knesset Now, Peace Later. *Ha'aretz*, 1 February [Hebrew].

——. 2002. The Debate on the Right of Refusal Reaches the Top of the IDF. *Ha'aretz*, 7 February [Hebrew].

Shenhav, Yehouda. 2001. The Red Line of the Green Line. In *Real Time: The Al-Aqsa Intifada and the Israeli Left*, edited by Adi Ofir, 204–212. Jerusalem: Keter [Hebrew].

Sherman, Martin. 2001. A State is a Business. *Ynet*, 12 July [Hebrew].

Shikaki, Khalil. 2002. Ending the Conflict: Can the Parties Afford It? In *The Israeli-Palestinian Peace Process – Oslo and the Lessons of Failure: Perspectives, Predicaments and Prospects*, edited by Robert L. Rothstein, Moshe Ma'oz and Khalil Shikaki, 37–46. Brighton, UK: Sussex Academic Press.

Shiloah, Tzvi. 1994. Labor: From Zionist Activism to Leftist Defeatism. *Nativ*, February, 24–27 [Hebrew].

Sinai, Ruth. 1998. The Movement Has Sunk in the Lebanese Mud. *Ha'aretz*, 7 January [Hebrew].

Sinnott, Richard. 2000. Knowledge and the Position of Attitudes to a European Foreign Policy on the Real-to-Random Continuum. *International Journal of Public Opinion Research* 12:113–137.

Smooha, Sammy. 1997. Ethnic Democracy: Israel as an Archetype. *Israel Studies* 2 (2):198–241.

Snow, David A., and Robert D. Benford. 1988. Ideology, Frame Resonance and Participant Mobilization. In *From Structure to Action: Comparing Social Movement Research across Cultures*, edited by Bert Klandermans, Hanspeter Kriesi and Sidney Tarrow, 197–219. Greenwich, CT: JAI Press.

———. 1992. Master Frames and Cycles of Protest. In *Frontiers in Social Movement Theory*, edited by Aldon D. Morris and Carol M. Mueller, 133–155. New Haven, CT: Yale University Press.

Snow, David A., and Danny Trom. 2002. The Case Study and the Study of Social Movements. In *Methods of Social Movement Research*, edited by Bert Klandermans and Suzzanne Staggenborg, 146–172. Minneapolis: University of Minnesota Press.

Stav, Arie. 1996. Praising the Dead, Condemning the Living. *Nativ*, January, 3–13 [Hebrew].

Suh, Doowon. 2001. How Do Political Opportunities Matter for Social Movements: Political Opportunity, Misframing, Pseudosuccess, and Pseudofailure. *The Sociological Quarterly* 42 (3):437–460.

Tamari, Salim. 2005/2006. Kissing Cousins: A Note on a Romantic Encounter. *Palestine-Israel Journal* 12–13 (4, 1):16–18.

Tarrow, Sidney. 1996. States and Opportunities: The Political Structuring of Social. Movements. In *Comparative Perspectives on Social Movements: Political Opportunities, Mobilizing Structures, and Cultural Framings*, edited by Doug McAdam, John D. McCarthy and Mayer N. Zald, 41–61. New York: Cambridge University Press.

———. 2001. Silence and Voice in the Study of Contentious Politics: Introduction. In *Silence and Voice in the Study of Contentious Politics*, by Ronald R. Aminzade, et al., 1–13. Cambridge, UK: Cambridge University Press.

Shavit, Yossi, Ephraim Yaar, Tamar Hermann, and Irit Adler. 2006. Israeli Public Opinion about the War – Part 1(19/7–6/8). *Public Opinion* 11, Tel Aviv University, The B. I. and Lucille Cohen Institute for Public Opinion Research, August. http://www.bicohen.tau.ac.il/ (accessed May 2008).

———. 2006. Israeli Public Opinion about the War – Part 2 (19/7–13/8). *Public Opinion* 12, Tel Aviv University, The B. I. and Lucille Cohen Institute for Public Opinion Research, August. http://www.bicohen.tau.ac.il/ (accessed May 2008).

Taub, Gadi. 1996. Running Away from Responsibility. *Ha'ir*, 10 November [Hebrew].

The Alternative Information Center. 1996. Round Table: The Israeli Left Two Years after Oslo. *Mitsad Sheni* [On the Other Hand], January, 3–7 [Hebrew].

Tilly, Charles. 1999. From Interactions to Outcomes in Social Movements. In *How Social Movements Matter*, edited by Marco G. Giugni, Doug McAdam and Charles Tilly, 253–70. Minneapolis: University of Minnesota Press.

Touraine, Alain. 1985. An Introduction to the Study of Social Movements. *Social Research* 52 (4):749–787.

Tzror, Rino. 1997. We Shall Defeat Hopelessness. *Ha'ir*, 19 September [Hebrew].

Warner, Michael. 2002. Publics and Counterpublics. *Public Culture* 14 (1):49–90. http://www.newschool.edu/gf/publicculture/backissues/pc36/warner.html (accessed May 2008).

Warschawski, Michael. 2001. The Party Is Over: An Open Letter to a Friend In "Peace Now." *Radical Philosophy Review* 3 (2):141–145.

———. 2003. Porto Alegre in Tel Aviv. *News from Within* XI (2):15, 30.

———. 2005. A Commentary from Israel: Peace Camp – Dead or Alive? *Machsom*, 21 August. http://www.solidarity-us.org/node/38 (accessed May 2008).

Weimann, Gabriel. 1985. Terrorists or Freedom Fighters? Labeling Terrorism in the Israeli Press. *Political Communication and Persuasion* 2 (4):433–445.

Weitz, Gidi. 1998. Peace Now Is Falling Apart. *Kol Ha'ir*, 28 August [Hebrew].

Wittner, Lawrence S. 2007. How the Peace Movement Can Win. *Foreign Policy in Focus*. FPIF Discussion Paper, 26 April. http://fpif.org/fpiftxt/4177 (accessed May 2008).

Wolfsfeld, Gadi. 2003. The Role of the News Media in Peace Negotiations: Variations over Time and Circumstance. In *Contemporary Peace Making: Conflict, Violence and Peace Processes*, edited by John Darby and Roger MacGinty, 87–100. London: Palgrave Macmillan.

Yasoor-Borochovitch, Dalit and Helena de Sevillia. 2007. The Influences of Gender Identities on Women's Human Rights Organizations: The Case of Machsom Watch. *Social Issues in Israel* 3, 136–165 [Hebrew].

Yiftachel, Oren. 1999. Ethnocracy: The Politics of Judaizing Israel/Palestine. *Constellations: International Journal of Critical and Democratic Theory* 6 (3):364–390.

Yitzchak, Yoav. 2001. How the European Union Meddles in Israeli Politics. *Israel Resource Review*. 27 June. http://israelbehindthenews.com/Archives/Jun-27-01.htm#EU (accessed May 2008).

Young, Nigel. 1986. The Peace Movement: A Comparative and Analytical Survey. *Alternatives: Global, Local, Political* 11 (2):185–217.

Yuchtman-Yaar, Ephraim, and Tamar Hermann. 2000. Shas: The Haredi-Dovish Image in a Changing Reality. *Israel Studies* 5 (2):78–107.

Yuchtman-Yaar, Ephraim, and Yohanan Peres. 1997. Aspects of Democracy: Tolerance, Nationalism and Trust in the Establishment. *Panim – Journal of Culture, Society and Education* 2:33–40 [Hebrew].

Yudilevitch, Merav. 2006. This Disastrous Situation Can Still be Stopped. *Ynet*, 10 August. http://www.ynet.co.il/articles/0,7340,L-3289450,00.html (accessed May 2008) [Hebrew].

Zackhem, Uri, and Yasmine Halevi. Ta'ayush – Arab-Jewish Partnership. http://taayush.tripod.com/new/2004-pn-txt.html (accessed May 2008).

Zald, Mayer N., and Roberta Ash. 1966. Social Movement Organizations: Growth, Decay, and Change. *Social Forces* 44:327–341.

Zerubavel, Yael. 2004. Battle, Sacrifice, and Martyrdom: Continuity and Change in Patriotic Sacrifice in Israeli Culture. In *Patriotism in Israel*, edited by Avner Ben-Amos and Daniel Bar-Tal, 61–100. Tel Aviv: Dyonon & Hakibbutz Hameuchad [Hebrew].

Zidon, Yoash. 1994. Peace Now or a Stable Peace. *Nativ*, April, 21–25 [Hebrew].

Ziegelman, Anat. 2002. 21 Peace Activists and Policemen Wounded. *Ha'aretz*, 4 April [Hebrew].

Zinger, Yossi. 2004. The Zionist Left and the Disengagement Plan. *The Left Bank Magazine*, 1 November. http://www.hagada.org.il/hagada/html/modules.php?name= News&file=article&sid=2858 (accessed May 2008) [Hebrew].

Zonenschein, David. 2004. I Saw What Should Be Forbidden to See. In *Refusenik!*, edited by Peretz Kidron, 138–42. Tel Aviv: Xargol [Hebrew].

Zrik-Srur, Waffa. 2003. In *Sisters in Peace: Feminist Voices of the Left*, edited by Hedva Isachar, 66–71. Tel Aviv: Resling [Hebrew].

Zukerman-Bareli, Haya, and Tova Bensky. 1989. "Parents against Silence": Conditions and Processes Leading to the Emergence of a Protest Movement. *Megamot* 32:27–42 [Hebrew].

Zur, Doron. 2006. Starting from Below: "People's Diplomacy" Model for the Resolution of the Israeli-Palestinian Conflict Based on the Experience of the People's Voice, One Voice and the Geneva Initiative Campaigns. Seminar paper for "International Negotiations and Media Strategy," Bar Ilan University, Ramat Gan [Hebrew].

Zurcher, Louis A., and Jr. Russell L. Curtis. 1973. A Comparative Analysis of Propositions Describing Social Movement Organizations. *The Sociological Quarterly* 14 (2):175–188.

Index